Insolvency and Restructuring Mar

GW01086009

Second Edition

Insolvency and Restructuring Manual

Second Edition

Simon Beale
Solicitor, Macfarlanes LLP

Bloomsbury Professional

BLOOMSBURY PROFESSIONAL LTD, MAXWELTON HOUSE, 41–43 BOLTRO ROAD, HAYWARDS HEATH, WEST SUSSEX, RH16 1BJ

© Bloomsbury Professional Ltd 2013

Bloomsbury Professional Ltd is an imprint of Bloomsbury Publishing plc

A CIP Catalogue record for this book is available from the British Library.

ISBN   978 1 78043 198 7

Typeset by Phoenix Photosetting, Chatham, Kent
Printed and bound in Great Britain by CPI Group (UK) Ltd, Croydon, CR0 4YY

Preface

It is now four years since the first edition of this book appeared. I observed then that we were seeing an unprecedented number of companies unable to continue either to comply with their ongoing obligations to their lenders or to meet their other liabilities. Despite this, we have since seen a lower number of companies entering into administration, liquidation or other formal insolvency processes than many would have predicted. There has been much lively debate as to whether we have finally developed a true rescue culture which is saving businesses without recourse to formal insolvency or whether we are simply seeing an increasing number of "zombie" companies whose lives are being prolonged but whose businesses are withering.

Whatever may be the case, the law has once again moved on during this period. The demise of various financial institutions has continued to require our judges to examine new legal issues – the administration of Lehman Brothers International (Europe) alone has now generated a significant body of case law. The restructurings of some large groups of companies has resulted in fierce battles in court between stakeholders, and from the resulting decisions we are hopefully now better able to predict how the courts will view the rights of different groups of lenders and the duties of directors. International businesses have continued to find English insolvency and restructuring tools such as pre-packaged administrations and Schemes of Arrangement more useful than those available in other jurisdictions, and we have learnt much more about when the English courts are prepared to assume jurisdiction. Even the anti-deprivation principle, which many viewed as little more than an archaic legal curiosity four years ago, has sprung back to life in a slew of decisions ranging from financial derivatives to football.

Whilst this book is a guide to the law and practice of insolvency and restructuring, it is intended to be neither an academic work nor an exhaustive guide to the relevant legislation. There are many excellent textbooks already in existence which focus in great detail on the various areas covered in this book. Instead, my aim has been to produce the manual which I wished I had had when I first started practising in this field some seventeen years ago. I hope it will serve as a useful introduction to anyone else encountering these areas for the first time. It looks to bridge the gap between a student course book and the reference works used by experienced practitioners.

I have dealt with insolvency principles and processes first, since it is necessary to know the effects of a formal insolvency in order then to consider restructuring as an alternative. Directors of an insolvent company will have concerns of their own so I have devoted a chapter to these. Some creditors will have advantageous positions – they include not only secured creditors, but also landlords, employees, pensions-related creditors and retention of title creditors – and I have examined each of their special rights and remedies. I have then sought to highlight a variety of the additional considerations involved in a restructuring. Finally, given the increasingly global nature of many groups' businesses, I have looked at some of the cross-border considerations which may apply.

Nevertheless, the law never stops moving, and some developments will occur too late for inclusion in this second edition. At the time of writing, we are still awaiting some much-needed clarification of the administration expenses regime. Legislation that assists an administrator of a trading business in dealing with key suppliers is at last expected, and I anticipate that there will be further guidance on the use of pre-packaged administrations.

In updating this book, I have been fortunate once again to have had the assistance of so many colleagues within Macfarlanes LLP. Jat Bains, Kirstie Hutchinson, Camilla Barry, Sheamal Samarasekera, Will David, Johnny Kelly, Tom Pedder, Hilary Barclay and Matthew Ramsey, amongst others, were kind enough to share specialist knowledge from their own practice areas with me. Two other members of our restructuring team, Paul Keddie and Laura Innes, devoted a considerable amount of time to reading through and picking up changes which needed to be made. Rachel Hamilton, Giles Butcher, Kyrstin Streeter and Laura Pike also deserve thanks for checking legislation and case references.

Finally, for a second time I express my love and gratitude to Clare for all of her support, despite her continuing disbelief that anyone with a busy day job would ever want to go through the process not only of writing a book but of revising it to produce a second edition.

The law in this book is that applicable to England and Wales as at the end of March 2013, although I am grateful to Bloomsbury Professional for allowing me to include two decisions on appeal (in the *Azevedo* and *Eurosail* cases) that were handed down after that date.

Simon Beale
May 2013

Contents

Contents

Table of Statutes

Table of Statutory Instruments

Table of Cases

PARA

Chapter 1

What are insolvency and restructuring?

1.1   INTRODUCTION

1.1.1   What does 'insolvency' mean?

The words 'insolvent' and 'insolvency' go to the heart of much of this book. However, neither term is defined in the insolvency legislation, and both are often used fairly loosely. Where a person refers to a company as 'insolvent', they may have one of two different scenarios in mind.

They may be thinking that the company is no longer able to meet all of its financial commitments. The legislation does not describe such a company as insolvent. Instead, it introduces the term 'unable to pay its debts', the meaning and implications of which are discussed in Section 1.3.

Alternatively, they may be referring to a company which is in a process such as administration or liquidation, where control of the company's affairs has been taken away from the directors and placed in the hands of a suitably qualified professional. Administration and liquidation are examples of formal insolvency processes, and some of the features of these processes are summarised in Section 1.4. The administrators, liquidators or other formal appointees who take over the running of a company in a formal insolvency process are often generically referred to as insolvency officeholders.

In the majority of cases, in order to take an appointment as an insolvency officeholder, an individual will need to be a suitably qualified insolvency professional who is a member of a recognised professional body and who is licensed to take such appointments. These recognised professional bodies include the Association of Certified Chartered Accountants, the Insolvency Practitioners Association, the Institute of Chartered Accountants in England and Wales and the Law Society. Such an individual will be referred to in this book as a qualified insolvency practitioner, and will in practice most often be a partner in a firm of accountants.

1.1.2   What does 'restructuring' mean?

A restructuring is a privately negotiated contractual arrangement between the company, some or all of its creditors and (possibly) some or all of its other stakeholders. Such an arrangement may allow the company to avoid a formal insolvency process altogether. Alternatively, one or more members of a group of companies may enter into a formal insolvency process as one of the steps required to achieve the restructuring. Section 1.6 gives a brief outline of the considerations involved in implementing a restructuring, although they are discussed in more detail in Chapter 10.

1.2   WHERE IS CORPORATE INSOLVENCY LAW FOUND?

1.2.1   The Insolvency Act 1986

The main piece of primary legislation codifying English insolvency law is the Insolvency Act 1986, referred to in this book as the 'IA 1986'. The IA 1986 has been amended from time to time by subsequent legislation, most significantly the Enterprise Act 2002, referred to in this book as the 'EA 2002'. As a result, the layout of the IA 1986 has grown somewhat complex – for example, the bulk of the legislation relating to the administration procedure is now found in Schedule B1 to the Act.

1.2.2   The EC Insolvency Regulation

The main piece of EC legislation in this area is Council Regulation (EC) No 1346/2000 of 29 May 2000 on Insolvency Proceedings, referred to in this book as the 'EC Insolvency Regulation'. This regulation is effective as primary legislation in the UK in its own right. The provisions of the EC Insolvency Regulation are considered further in Chapter 11. As will be seen it does not seek to create any insolvency rules in its own right, but attempts to harmonise the insolvency regimes of the different EU Member States. However, since its provisions will dictate whether many types of insolvency process can be commenced in the UK at all, it remains potentially relevant to any formal insolvency.

1.2.3   Other primary legislation

Some of the law governing the ability of a secured creditor to enforce their security are still found in the Law of Property Act 1925 although, as explained in Section 1.4.4, this is usually supplemented by the terms of any security document.

The Company Directors Disqualification Act 1986, referred to in this book as the 'CDDA 1986', contains provisions dealing with the disqualification of directors of an insolvent company by a court where it finds that they are unfit to be involved in the management of a company – these provisions are considered further in Chapter 6.

Slightly incongruously, a few provisions relating to insolvency are also found in the Companies Act 2006, referred to in this book as 'CA 2006'. These include s 754 CA 2006 (which relates to the payment of debts out of assets subject to a floating charge) and s 993 CA 2006 (which concerns fraudulent trading). The statutory provisions relating to schemes of arrangement are also found in the CA 2006 – these are considered further in Section 1.4.6.

Finally, specific legislation will sometimes supplement or amend the effect of the IA 1986 in order to introduce modified insolvency regimes for certain industries or institutions. Examples include the Buildings Societies Act 1986 and the Banking Act 2009, although discussion of these modified regimes is beyond the scope of this book.

1.2.4   The Insolvency Rules 1986

The IA 1986, and some of the other primary legislation, also gives the relevant government minister (currently the Secretary of State for Business, Innovation and Skills) the power to make additional orders and regulations, or 'secondary legislation', by statutory instrument. The most important regulations made to date are the Insolvency Rules 1986 (SI 1986/1925, as variously amended), referred to in this book as the 'IR 1986'. These heavily supplement the IA 1986 and deal, in particular, with many of the procedural aspects of the formal insolvency processes described in that Act.

1.2.5   Other secondary legislation

A large number of other pieces of secondary legislation have been made which impact upon our insolvency law, many of which implement European directives. Some, like the Insolvent Partnerships Order 1994 (SI 1994/2421), supplement corporate insolvency law, whilst others, like the Financial Collateral Arrangements (No 2) Regulations 2003 (SI 2003/3226), exclude provisions of corporate insolvency law altogether in relation to certain transactions. They are too numerous to list them all here, but will be considered where relevant.

1.2.6   Practice directions

A number of practice directions have also been issued to supplement the legislation. They aim to achieve uniformity of practice in processes where the courts are involved and indicate what the courts expect of the parties. For example, *Practice Direction: Insolvency Proceedings* [2007] BCC 842 deals with the process for putting a company into liquidation. Up-to-date versions of this, and the other practice directions discussed in this book, can be found at http://www.justice.gov.uk/courts/procedure-rules/civil/rules.

1.2.7   Court-made law

The common law also has a big part to play. The courts have been left to develop much of the law governing security and its enforcement – as a result, the bulk of the law relating to these actions will not be found in any statutory legislation, even where it concerns the interaction of secured creditors' rights with those of other stakeholders. For instance, the insolvency legislation has never completely clarified the ranking of secured creditors' claims vis-à-vis all of the other claims and expenses in a formal insolvency process. Judges have been left to decide the position, and this has at times led to some controversial and inconsistent decisions – see Chapter 2.

1.2.8   Statements of Insolvency Practice

Statements of Insolvency Practice, or 'SIPs' are guidance notes issued to qualified insolvency practitioners with a view to maintaining standards. They set out required practice and thus aim to harmonise practitioners' approaches to particular aspects of insolvency, particularly in areas where the law is thought to be silent or ambiguous.

They are prepared by the Association of Business Recovery Professionals (usually known as 'R3') for the Joint Insolvency Committee ('JIC'), an industry forum for the discussion of insolvency issues and professional ethics. If approved by the JIC, they are adopted by each of the recognised professional bodies of which qualified insolvency practitioners are members.

SIPs do not have legislative effect. However, departure from the standard(s) set out in the SIP(s) may result in disciplinary or regulatory action from the practitioner's professional body. Those SIPs which are current at any time may be found on the R3 website, http://www.r3.org.uk.

1.3 INABILITY TO PAY DEBTS

1.3.1 When is a company unable to pay its debts?

Under s 123 IA 1986, a company is deemed unable to pay its debts:

- If a creditor (by assignment or otherwise) to whom the company owes over £750 has served on the company a written demand (in the prescribed form) requiring payment of the sum due and the company has failed at any time during the following three weeks to pay that sum or to secure or compound for it to the reasonable satisfaction of the creditor (s 123(1)(a)). The written demand in question is usually known as a 'statutory demand'.

- If, in England and Wales, execution or other process issued on a judgment, decree or order of any court in favour of a creditor of the company is returned unsatisfied in whole or in part (s 123(1)(b)).

- If it is proved to the satisfaction of the court that the company is unable to pay its debts as they fall due (s 123(1)(e)). This is generally known as the 'cash-flow test'.

- If it is proved to the satisfaction of the court that the value of the company's assets is less than the amount of its liabilities, taking into account its contingent and prospective liabilities (s 123(2)). This is generally known as the 'balance sheet test'.

1.3.2 Why is there a need for a variety of tests?

The cash-flow test and the balance sheet test are the two main tests to determine whether a company is unable to pay its debts.

However, in order for a creditor to show that a company fails one of these two main tests, it has to prove to the satisfaction of the court that this is the case. This would require the creditor to produce evidence, even in cases where the company seems obviously to be in trouble. In other cases, a detailed analysis of the company's position may be required, which may be difficult, particularly if the creditor has access to little other than publicly available information (which may already be out of date). The company may well dispute the evidence put forward.

The statutory demand route and the unsatisfied judgment test therefore provide far more straightforward routes by which a creditor may establish that a company is unable to pay its debts, for example, where it intends then to present a winding-up petition (see Chapter 3).

1.3.3 The cash-flow test

Only debts need to be taken into account, and for these purposes a debt means a liquidated claim. A claim for damages, for example, is not therefore a 'debt' for these purposes.

In addition, in principle, only debts which have already fallen due but which remain unpaid need to be taken into account for the purposes of this test. Therefore, in accordance with this principle a company should not fail the cash-flow test if:

- it reaches agreement with suppliers whose debts are due for payment that the dates of payment will be extended to some new, future date;

- it has an on-demand bank overdraft, but the bank has not yet made demand for repayment; or

- it has given a guarantee of a third-party liability, but demand for repayment has not yet been made under the guarantee.

However, a company is likely to fail the cash-flow test if it fails to pay its suppliers' invoices on their due dates without agreeing otherwise with those suppliers, or if demand is made under an overdraft or a guarantee and the company cannot pay the amount demanded in full.

If a company fails to pay a debt which has fallen due and which is not disputed, this can be sufficient evidence in itself of cash-flow insolvency, even if the company can produce strong evidence that its assets exceed its liabilities. This is illustrated in the case of *Cornhill Insurance plc v Improvement Services Ltd* [1986] 1 WLR 114, where the company in question was a well-known insurance company with a substantial business, but which despite various chasing letters had failed to pay a debt of £1,154 which it had orally agreed to be due. The court was satisfied that the creditor was entitled to present a winding-up petition.

For some time, there was uncertainty as to whether the cash-flow test was a future-looking test, and if so to what extent. Those who considered that the cash-flow test looked only at whether the company could pay debts presently due could point to the fact that the balance sheet test expressly requires contingent and prospective liabilities to be taken into account – whereas the cash-flow test does not. Even so, in *Cheyne Finance plc (In Receivership)* [2008] BCC 182 the court held that a company was already being cash-flow insolvent where it was more likely than not to be unable to pay certain debts which would fall due in the near future, albeit in circumstances where the company in question was not trading and had a future cash-flow profile which was very clear.

In *BNY Corporate Trustee Services Limited v Eurosail-UK 2007-3BL plc and others* [2013] UKSC 28, the Supreme Court explained that the cash-flow test is concerned with debts falling due from time to time in the reasonably near future as well as with debts presently due. What is to be regarded as the 'reasonably near future' will depend on the circumstances at hand, but especially the nature of the company's business. However, once one moves beyond the reasonably near future, any attempt to apply the cash-flow test becomes completely speculative, and the balance sheet test becomes the only sensible test.

1.3.4 The balance sheet test

Here, it is not enough simply to look at the most recent balance sheet which the company has prepared as part of its normal accounting requirements, as this test views assets and liabilities differently to their treatment in a company's accounts.

In valuing **assets** for the purpose of this test, it is necessary to consider the likely actual realisation value of those assets, not simply their book value used in the accounts. It is also necessary to consider whether the assets should be valued on a going concern or a break-up basis. This will depend on the circumstances, but essentially the question turns on whether or not the company's business could still survive, or be sold as a going concern.

The **liabilities** to be taken into account must include any contingent and prospective liabilities – these are not found on a normal balance sheet.

A **contingent liability** is one which may arise out of an existing legal obligation or set of circumstances depending on the occurrence of some further event, which event may or may not occur. An example is the liability of a guarantor under a guarantee – a legal obligation is created when the guarantee is entered into, but the liability arises only when the principal debtor defaults.

A **prospective liability** is a liability which will certainly become due in the future, either on some date which has already been determined or on some date determinable by future events. It has been held to include not only debts which have not yet fallen due for payment, but also any undisputable claims for unliquidated damages for more than a nominal amount – even if those damages have yet to be quantified (*Re Dollar Land Holdings* [1994] 1 BCLC 404).

In the *Eurosail* case (see Section 1.3.3) it was made clear that contingent and prospective liabilities should not simply be taken at their face amount for the purposes of this test. A liability of £x which would become due in ten years' time should not be treated as a present liability of £x. This would not take account of the company's ability to find the monies to meet this liability during the intervening period. However, the Supreme Court rejected the suggestion that the test for whether a company is balance sheet insolvent is whether it has reached 'the point of no return'.

The Supreme Court preferred the view that, essentially, s 123(2) requires the court to decide whether it has been established that, looking at the company's assets and making proper allowance for its prospective and contingent liabilities, it cannot be reasonably be expected to meet those liabilities. If so, the company will be deemed insolvent even though it is currently able to pay its debts as they fall due. The more distant the liabilities, the harder this will be to establish.

In *Deiulemar Shipping SpA v Transfield ER Futures Limited* [2012] EWHC 928 (Comm), the court considered it appropriate to apply this same test to determine whether a company was 'insolvent' for the purposes of the relevant event of default in the International Swaps and Derivatives Association, Inc. ('ISDA') Master Agreement.

There is a view that an estimate of the likely expenses of any administration or liquidation should also be included as prospective liabilities when determining whether a company passes the balance sheet test. The argument is that, were the company to enter into one of these processes, the relevant expenses would need to be discharged before the company's ordinary unsecured creditors could be paid (see Chapter 2). Certainly, it seems appropriate when the balance sheet test is being applied to decide whether a company should actually be placed into administration or liquidation. It may be less relevant when the directors are simply reviewing whether to continue to trade.

1.3.5 What are the implications of a company being unable to pay its debts?

The fact that a company is unable to pay its debts does not automatically mean that it must stop trading. It is neither a criminal offence nor an actionable civil matter for a director to continue to trade a company which is unable to pay its debts. The consequences for directors occur only if a formal insolvency process subsequently ensues.

A company may fail the balance sheet test and continue to survive for some time. However, if that company enters into a formal insolvency process, it would then have insufficient resources to repay all of its creditors.

A company may still survive if it fails the cash-flow test, although the reality is that a trading company is unlikely to be able to carry on for any length of time if it runs out of cash, regardless of its net asset position. An unpaid creditor is likely sooner or later to take its own recovery action. For this reason, the cash-flow test is often regarded as the more relevant of the two tests.

The implications for a company and its directors where the company is unable to pay its debts do, however, include the following:

- an unpaid creditor can obtain an order for the company's winding-up, as described in Chapter 3;

- it is a necessary condition that a company is unable to pay its debts or is likely to become so before it can be placed into administration (unless the person seeking to put the company into administration holds a 'qualifying floating charge'), as described in Chapter 4;

- certain payments made or transactions entered into by the company will be at risk of being set aside if the company enters into liquidation or administration, as described in Chapter 5;

- the directors must consider the interests of creditors over those of shareholders, as described in Chapter 6; and

- an inability to pay debts may be an event of default in its own right under the company's finance documents and other key contracts.

In addition, the fact that the directors will be at risk of personal liability for wrongful or fraudulent trading (if the company subsequently enters into liquidation) and of disqualification (if the company subsequently enters into liquidation or administration or has an administrative receiver appointed) means that in practice directors need to be acutely aware of various factors that could mean that the company is unable to pay its debts, as described in Chapter 6.

1.4 WHAT ARE THE POSSIBLE FORMAL PROCESSES?

1.4.1 Overview

The main formal processes available for an insolvent company are set out in Table 1.1. These are also summarised briefly below. (The term 'formal process' is used here instead of 'formal insolvency process' because some of the processes covered, particularly members' voluntary liquidation and schemes of arrangement are not generally thought of as insolvency processes.)

1.4.2 Liquidation

Liquidation or 'winding-up' (the terms are broadly synonymous and used interchangeably in the legislation) is the process by which a company's operations as a going concern are terminated. The powers of its directors to manage its affairs are superseded by the powers of a qualified insolvency practitioner, the liquidator, who is appointed to implement the liquidation. The company's assets are realised (liquidated) by the liquidator and the proceeds distributed to satisfy the company's debts and liabilities, as far as possible. Chapter 2 includes a full discussion of the order in which the assets are distributed.

There are two types of liquidation. It is important to identify which type of liquidation a company is in, as different rules will apply.

Voluntary liquidation is initiated by a resolution of the company's shareholders (or 'members') that it should be wound up. There are, in turn, two types of voluntary liquidation. The distinction between the two is that:

- if the directors swear a statutory declaration that the company will be able to pay its debts (including contingent and prospective debts) and the costs of the winding-up in full within the following 12 months, the liquidation will be a **members' voluntary liquidation**;

- if the directors cannot, or do not wish to swear a declaration to that effect, the liquidation will be a **creditors' voluntary liquidation**.

There are in turn different sets of rules for these two types of voluntary liquidation. The creditors will take no part in a members' voluntary liquidation beyond receiving payment of what they are owed in full. A creditors' voluntary liquidation, however, needs to involve the creditors in the process, and the rules reflect this. Regardless of the type of voluntary liquidation, the liquidator will generally be appointed by the shareholders at the same time as they resolve to place the company in liquidation. However, in a creditors' voluntary liquidation, a creditors' meeting must be convened no later than 14 days after the date of the shareholders' resolution at which the creditors may vote to substitute their own choice of liquidator if they so wish.

Compulsory liquidation results from the court making an order, termed a '**winding-up order**', that the company be liquidated following the presentation of a petition,

Table 1.1 – Formal processes

Process (+ sub category)		Description	Insolvency officeholder	Moratorium?	Distribution mechanism to ordinary unsecured creditors?	Recognised by the EC Insolvency Regulation?
Liquidation (= winding-up)	Creditors' voluntary liquidation ('CVL')[1]	Collective insolvency procedure	Liquidator (initially chosen by shareholders)[1]	No – liquidator needs to apply for a stay	Yes	Yes
	Compulsory liquidation		Liquidator (initially Official Receiver)[1]	Yes – although will not affect secured creditors		
	Provisional liquidation	Optional precursor to a compulsory liquidation	Provisional liquidator[1]	Yes – although will not affect secured creditors	No[2]	
Administration		Collective insolvency procedure	Administrator[1]	Yes[3] – can affect secured creditors	Yes – but only if sanctioned by the court	Yes
Receivership	Administrative receivership	Secured creditors' remedy[4]	Administrative receiver[1]	No	No[2]	No
	Non-administrative receivership		Receiver			
Company voluntary arrangement ('CVA')		Statutory compromise with creditors	Supervisor[5]	Possibly[6]	Yes	Yes
Scheme of arrangement		Statutory compromise with creditors	None	Possibly[6]	Yes	No

1 Must be a qualified insolvency practitioner.
2 Although there are requirements to set aside enough monies to cover the 'prescribed part' – see Chapter 2.
3 A moratorium will commence on the date on which the application for an administration order is made, or notice of intention to appoint filed at court.
4 An administrative receiver has some additional duties, for example to pay preferential creditors.
5 Must be a qualified insolvency practitioner or otherwise be specifically authorised to act.
6 In a CVA, an 'eligible company' may obtain a moratorium for the period before the creditors vote to approve the CVA. Alternatively, in either a CVA or a Scheme of Arrangement the company might first be placed into administration to take advantage of the administration moratorium – see Chapter 7.

termed a '**winding-up petition**', requesting such an order. Normally this petition is presented by a creditor, although it may also be presented by a shareholder of the company or by the company itself (or its directors). When the court makes a winding-up order, the **Official Receiver** (who is a government official) is initially appointed as the liquidator, but the creditors have the power to appoint a replacement if they wish.

Both creditors' voluntary liquidation and compulsory liquidation are therefore 'collective' insolvency processes, carried out for the benefit of all unsecured creditors, and in which the liquidator owes duties to those creditors. In a compulsory liquidation, unsecured creditors are prevented from taking or continuing various enforcement actions without the leave of the court. A secured creditor, however, stands outside of any liquidation process and is free to enforce its security unaffected by the liquidation.

A liquidation which commences as a members' voluntary liquidation must be converted to a creditors' voluntary liquidation if it appears that the creditors will not, after all, be paid in full. In addition, a voluntary liquidation may be converted into a compulsory winding-up at any time by the court making an order to that effect.

Where a winding-up petition has been issued, the court may also appoint a **provisional liquidator** to manage the company pending the making of the winding-up order itself. The court has a wide discretion over the powers it can give to a provisional liquidator, but the intention is usually to ensure the preservation of the status quo until the liquidation proper commences.

Chapter 3 includes a fuller discussion of the liquidation process.

1.4.3   Administration

Administration is a process whereby the company is placed under the control of a qualified insolvency practitioner, the administrator, who has a statutory duty to seek one of the following objectives:

● the rescue of the company as a going concern, **failing which**

● a better result for the creditors as a whole than would be likely if the company were to go into liquidation, **failing which**

● the realisation of property to enable a distribution to be made to secured (or preferential) creditors.

To assist him in achieving one of these objectives the administrator has far wider statutory powers to manage the company's business and, if necessary, sell its business and assets than are given to a liquidator.

A company may be put into administration in one of a number of ways:

● by a court order, in response to an application by the company itself, its directors or any creditor, supported by a witness statement verifying, among other things, that the company is, or is likely to become unable to pay its debts;

● by the company itself or its directors filing a notice at court, supported by a statutory declaration verifying that the company is, or is likely to become unable to pay its debts; or

- by a creditor holding appropriate security (being a '**qualifying floating charge holder**') filing a notice at court, supported by a statutory declaration verifying that its security has become enforceable.

A key feature of administration is the moratorium, which allows the company a temporary 'breathing space' whilst the administrator seeks to achieve one of his objectives. As such, from the date on which the application for an administration order is first made or a '**notice of intention**' to appoint is first filed at court (see Chapter 4), the company is protected from enforcement action by various creditors (who might otherwise have taken steps to protect their own individual interests) unless the creditor in question first obtains the permission of the court. The moratorium continues once the company enters into administration. Unlike the liquidation moratorium, this moratorium can also prevent secured creditors from enforcing their security.

Like liquidation, administration is a collective insolvency process, but in this case the administrator owes duties to all creditors since secured creditors are largely bound by the administration process as well. Some guidance is given in the legislation as to how administrators should reconcile their potentially conflicting duties to secured and unsecured creditors.

The administrator is obliged to draw up proposals to be put to the company's creditors for approval at a meeting usually held within ten weeks of his appointment. Administration was not originally conceived to be the final process in a company's life, but merely a step on the path to some other (preferably solvent) process or result. Depending on what proposals are adopted, the company may in due course return to the control of its management (if, for example, a voluntary arrangement or Scheme of Arrangement is adopted) or go into liquidation (if, for example, its business has been sold or an attempt to adopt a voluntary arrangement or Scheme has been unsuccessful).

However, it is also possible for an administrator, with the permission of the court, to make a general distribution to unsecured as well as to secured and preferential creditors if there are sufficient realisations from which to do so before applying for the dissolution of the company. Should the administrator take this route, the administration will sometimes be termed a **distribution administration**.

Although the primary objective of administration remains the rescue of the company, in practice the process most often results in a business sale, followed by a distribution administration or a liquidation. The scope for a company to continue to trade whilst a sale is negotiated is far more flexible than in liquidation, and therefore a sale on better terms may be secured pursuant to an administration. Such a sale may take place before the creditors' meeting is held. It is also increasingly common for the administrator to enter into a pre-negotiated sale almost immediately following his appointment – this latter process is termed a **pre-packaged administration**.

Chapter 4 includes a fuller discussion of the administration process generally, including pre-packaged administrations, and includes a more detailed comparison of administration with liquidation.

1.4.4   Receivership

A creditor (typically a bank or other lender) with security in the form of a mortgage or charge over the company's assets may, if the terms of their security allow, appoint a receiver to enforce their security. Neither the receiver's appointment nor the subsequent receivership process will generally involve the court at all. A receiver will typically have the power to manage and sell the assets caught by the security to repay the creditor's debt.

A receiver appointed in respect of the whole, or substantially the whole, of a company's property by the holder of a charge comprising (at least in part) a 'floating' charge is called an **administrative receiver**. An administrative receiver is given the same wide statutory powers to manage the company's business and to sell its business and assets as are given to an administrator, and his powers may have been extended even further by the charge under which he is appointed.

However, as a result of changes introduced by the EA 2002, a secured creditor is able to appoint an administrative receiver only if:

- their security was taken **prior to 15 September 2003**; or

- one of the so-called **City Exceptions** applies.

The fact that the power to appoint an administrative receiver is not available to the holder of most charges created after 15 September 2003 means that this process is falling increasingly into disuse. Such a chargeholder may nonetheless be able to appoint an administrator (see above) or a receiver over a more limited range of assets.

A couple of terms are commonly used to describe these other types of receiver. An **LPA receiver,** or 'Law of Property Act' receiver, is, strictly speaking, appointed only to receive income from an asset and pay that income over to their appointer rather than to sell that asset. However, in practice the terms 'LPA receiver' and '**fixed charge receiver**' are now often used fairly interchangeably to describe any receiver who is not an administrative receiver. This book will refer to any such receiver simply as a '**non-administrative receiver**'.

A non-administrative receiver is given very few statutory powers, but his powers will almost always be substantially extended by the charge under which he is appointed. However, a non-administrative receiver (unlike an administrative receiver) may be ousted by the appointment of an administrator, which can mean their appointment is far less effective as a means of debt recovery.

A non-administrative receiver is concerned only with raising sufficient monies to repay the creditor who appointed him. An administrative receiver is also primarily concerned with ensuring repayment of any sums owed to his appointer, although he has in addition certain statutory duties designed to give some level of protection to other creditors, particularly in relation to the provision of information to creditors and the protection of preferential unsecured creditors. To the extent that they realise floating charge property, all receivers must set aside the 'prescribed part' of such realisations for unsecured creditors (see Chapter 2). However, no receiver has any duty to deal generally with the claims of ordinary unsecured creditors.

Accordingly, receivership remains a secured creditor's remedy, and is not recognised as a collective insolvency process by the EC Insolvency Regulation (see Chapter 11).

Chapter 8 includes a fuller discussion of receivership, and of secured creditors' remedies generally, and a more detailed comparison of this process with administration.

1.4.5 Company voluntary arrangement

A company voluntary arrangement ('CVA') is a statutory compromise of the company's debts under the supervision of a qualified insolvency practitioner or certain other approved persons (the supervisor). Typically, a CVA provides for existing creditors to accept partial repayment of their debts out of a fund set up using the existing assets of the company, topped up from the proceeds of future trading over a limited period or (possibly) a contribution from a third party. The fund is administered by the supervisor, who is also responsible for settling the amount of creditors' qualifying claims.

A CVA may be proposed by the directors of a company. Alternatively, if that company is already in administration or liquidation, it may be proposed by the administrator or liquidator. Where the directors are proposing a CVA, they and the proposed supervisor (at this stage called the **nominee**) will draw up the proposed terms. The proposal is then submitted to the court with a statement of support from the nominee and proposed dates for holding meetings of the shareholders and creditors to vote on it. Unless the court for some reason directs otherwise, the nominee will convene the meetings (for between 14 and 28 days after the court filing) and send notice to all known shareholders and creditors.

Creditors learning of the proposal may consider that their interests would be better served by taking enforcement action of their own before the proposal becomes effective. To guard against this, the directors of an 'eligible' company are entitled to file for a **moratorium**. A company is eligible if it meets at least two of the criteria for qualification as a 'small' company (as defined in s 382 CA 2006) and does not fall within a list of exceptions. The moratorium comes into force once the application has been filed and continues for an initial period of 28 days (which may be extended) to give time for the arrangement to be voted on by creditors. To obtain such a moratorium, the directors must file certain documents in court, including a statement from the nominee giving a number of confirmations. No court order is required. However, in practice it is rare for companies to seek such a moratorium – the directors will more frequently place the company into administration whilst the CVA proposal is being put together, and take advantage of the moratorium offered by that process.

To be adopted, a CVA must be:

- approved by **more than 50%** of the votes cast by the shareholders at their meeting; and

- approved by **more than 75%** of the votes cast by the creditors at their meetings; and

- **not objected to** by more than 50% of the votes of those creditors who are **not connected** with the company.

Creditors have one vote for every £1 of debt owed to them. Objecting creditors have rights to challenge the CVA within 28 days if they consider that the correct procedure was not followed or that the CVA unfairly prejudices their interests. This will result in a court hearing to decide the issue. If the creditors vote differently from the shareholders, the creditors' vote prevails unless successfully challenged by a shareholder within 28 days.

A CVA might in many ways be thought of as a contract between the company and its creditors, but by which a small minority of dissenting creditors may be bound despite their lack of consent. Therefore, it is potentially a very flexible tool, given the wide range of possible terms. It is also recognised as a collective insolvency process by the EC Insolvency Regulation. However, a CVA cannot bind any preferential or secured creditor without that creditor's consent, nor indeed is it a tool for adjusting the rights of any shareholder, and this in practice reduces its effectiveness.

Chapter 7 includes a fuller discussion of the CVA process.

1.4.6   Scheme of Arrangement

One alternative to a CVA is a Scheme of Arrangement under Part 26 CA 2006. This may apply not only as between the company and its creditors or any class of them, but also as between the company and the shareholders or any class of them. Essentially, the procedure involves three stages.

First, the company (or any creditor, shareholder, administrator or liquidator) may apply to the court for an order convening a meeting of each class of creditor or shareholder affected by the proposed scheme. At this initial hearing, any issues relating to the composition of the **class**, or classes, of creditors or shareholders who will attend these meeting(s) will be addressed. Notices of these meetings are sent to relevant creditors or shareholders. These notices must be accompanied by the Scheme document and a statement explaining the effect of the proposed arrangement in a way which will enable an ordinary lay person to exercise their judgment.

Secondly, the meeting, or meetings, are held. For the Scheme to be approved:

- a majority in number,

- representing **75% by value**

of **each of the different classes** of creditors and shareholders voting must vote in favour of the proposed scheme.

Finally, assuming the proposal has been approved at each meeting, a further application is made to court to sanction the Scheme. At this hearing, '**fairness**' issues are addressed. The court must be satisfied that the statutory procedure has been complied with. It will be concerned to ensure that each class was fairly represented by those attending the relevant meeting, and the majority in every class is acting *bona fide* and not attempting to promote an interest which is in fact adverse to the class they claim to represent. The court must also be satisfied that the arrangement is one which an intelligent and honest man who is a member of the relevant class and acting in respect of his own interest might reasonably approve. A shareholder or creditor affected by the Scheme may attend this hearing to persuade the court not to sanction the scheme on the basis that one or other of these requirements was not satisfied.

If the court sanctions the Scheme, it will become binding on all creditors and shareholders in the relevant class or classes.

Clearly, there are various similarities between this process and the CVA process. Nonetheless, a Scheme of Arrangement is not recognised as a collective insolvency process by the EC Insolvency Regulation – a Scheme does not require the company to be placed under the control or supervision of an insolvency officeholder, nor does it seek to bind all creditors of the company (as it seeks to bind only those in the class or classes voting on the Scheme).

Chapter 7 includes a fuller discussion of the Scheme of Arrangement process generally, including a more detailed comparison of this process with the CVA process.

1.5 WHAT IS THE INSOLVENT ENTITY?

1.5.1 Overview

It is always worth checking at the outset the type of entity which is insolvent.

This book generally considers the insolvency law applicable to companies registered in England and Wales under one of the Companies Acts. Chapter 11 also covers the circumstances where the English court might place a foreign company into a formal process in England. It does not consider personal insolvency law, which will apply to individuals who incur business debts in their own name. In addition, it does not consider the manner in which the formal processes described in this book might differ if the company concerned is registered in Scotland or Northern Ireland.

A number of other entities may be encountered, however, including:

- **Partnerships** or firms (the two terms are interchangeable). A partnership is 'the relation which subsists between persons carrying on business in common with a view of profit' (s 1 Partnership Act 1890). No special formalities are required to create a partnership. For administrative convenience and even for some legal purposes, it is often useful to treat a partnership as if it had an existence of its own, distinct from the individual partners. Nonetheless, a partnership has no separate legal personality in its own right. So far as an external creditor is concerned, the individual partners will each be liable without limit for the debts of the partnership.

- **Limited partnerships** or '**LPs**'. An LP is formed in accordance with and is regulated by the Limited Partnerships Act 1907. Like an ordinary partnership it has no separate legal personality in its own right. However, a distinction is drawn between different types of partner. It must have at least one **general partner**, who will be liable without limit for the debts of the partnership. The other partners will be **limited partners**, who will merely be investors. Limited partners are precluded from taking part in the management of the partnership but their liability will be limited to the amount of their investment.

- **Limited liability partnerships** or '**LLPs**'. An LLP is formed in accordance with and is regulated by the Limited Liability Partnerships Act 2000, as supplemented by the Limited Liability Partnerships Regulations 2001. An LLP does have a separate legal personality in its own right, and all of the LLP's own assets will be available to its creditors. However, the liability of the individual members will be limited. So far as an external creditor is concerned, an LLP is therefore far more similar to a limited liability company than a partnership. An LLP is required to have at least two '**designated**' **members** whose main role is to ensure that various requirements of the legislation are met.

- **Unregistered companies**. In addition to all of the above, there may be other types of association or companies which are not registered under the Companies Acts. Some, like building societies, may have their own separate legislation in place of that contained in the IA 1986 which will not be discussed further here. Others may simply be regarded as 'unregistered companies' for the purposes of the IA 1986.

The following sections give a brief overview of the insolvency processes which are applicable to partnerships, LLPs and unregistered companies.

1.5.2 Partnerships (including limited partnerships)

The main piece of legislation here is the Insolvent Partnerships Order 1994 (SI 1994/2421). It will be necessary to identify which debts are debts of the partnership and which assets are partnership property, although this does not in itself preclude a creditor from also having recourse to the individual partners (or to the general partner in the case of an LP).

The formal insolvency processes available under the Order are:

- Liquidation. The provisions of the IA 1986 which deal with the winding up of an insolvent company (see Section 1.5.4) also apply to a partnership in a slightly modified form. Partners are amongst the persons entitled to present a winding-up petition. However, the partnership can only be wound up by the court – there is no equivalent of voluntary liquidation available.

- Administration. The provisions of the IA 1986 which deal with administration will also apply to a partnership in a slightly modified form. Since a partnership cannot grant a floating charge (other than an agricultural floating charge) over its assets, there should be no qualifying floating charge holder to consider. The administrator will need to be appointed by the partners out of court or failing that by court order. A partnership cannot be placed into administration unless it is actually unable to pay its debts, which for these purposes bears the slightly modified meaning applicable to an unregistered company (see Section 1.5.4).

- Partnership voluntary arrangement ('PVA'). The provisions of the IA 1986 which deal with CVAs will also apply to a partnership in a slightly modified form. It is unnecessary that the individual partners enter into parallel individual voluntary arrangements or CVAs, although in practice they may well do so.

Certain provisions of the Company Directors Disqualification Act 1986 (CDDA 1986) apply where a partnership is wound up as an unregistered company. In general, however, the provisions of the IA 1986 described in Chapter 6 will not apply – they would have little practical relevance to a partnership, as the partners who are running the partnership business are concurrently liable anyway for partnership debts. Where a partner, including a general partner of an LP, is a company, however, it may be wise for its own directors to consider whether they might be liable as a result of these provisions through their directorships of that company.

1.5.3 Limited liability partnerships

The main piece of legislation here is the Limited Liability Partnerships Regulations 2001 (SI 2001/1090). In keeping with the fact that an LLP is much more similar to a company than to a conventional partnership, the provisions of the IA 1986 which deal with CVAs, administration, receivership and liquidation will generally also apply to an LLP in only slightly modified form.

The provisions of the IA 1986 which allow antecedent transactions to be set aside and which are described in Chapter 5 will generally apply. The provisions of the IA 1986 and CDDA 1986 which pose risks for directors and which are described in Chapter 6 will also generally apply to members of an LLP.

Furthermore, the Regulations introduce an additional s 214A IA 1986 which will apply where an LLP has gone into insolvent liquidation. This section applies to a person if:

- within the period of **two years** ending with the date of presentation of the winding-up petition or the members' resolution to place the LLP into liquidation (as the case may be) he was a member of the LLP who withdrew property of the LLP, whether in the form of a share of profits, salary, repayment of, or payment of, interest on a loan to the LLP or any other withdrawal of property; and

- the liquidator proves to the satisfaction of the court that at the time of the withdrawal that person knew or had a reasonable ground for believing that the LLP was unable to pay its debts at the time of the withdrawal **or** would become so after the assets of the LLP had been depleted by that withdrawal taken together with all other withdrawals (if any) made by any members contemporaneously with that withdrawal or in contemplation when that withdrawal was made; and

- the court is satisfied that that person knew or ought to have concluded that after each such withdrawal there was no reasonable prospect that the LLP would avoid going into insolvent liquidation.

In such a case, the court may order that person to make such contribution to the LLP's assets as it thinks proper, up to the aggregate of all withdrawals made within the two-year period in question.

The facts which a member ought to know or ascertain and the conclusions he ought to have reached are adjudged in the same way as for a wrongful trading action under s 214 IA 1986 (see Chapter 6).

1.5.4 Unregistered companies

Under s 221 IA 1986, the English courts have the jurisdiction to wind up any unregistered company if:

- the company is dissolved, or has ceased to carry on business, or is carrying on business only for the purpose of winding up its affairs; or

- the company is unable to pay its debts; or

- if the court is of the opinion that it is just and equitable that the company should be wound up.

An 'unregistered company' means any association and any company other than a company registered in any part of the United Kingdom under the Joint Stock Company Acts or under the legislation (past or present) relating to companies in Great Britain (s 220 IA 1986).

For these purposes, an unregistered company is unable to pay its debts:

- in circumstances analogous to those set out in s 123 IA 1986 (see ss 222 and 224 IA 1986); **and**

- if a debt remains unpaid after an action or other proceeding has been instituted against any member of the unregistered company for any debt or demand due from the unregistered company or from that member in his character as a member, the unregistered company has been given notice of this action in writing and it has failed to pay the debt or demand, or stay the action or indemnify the defendant to his reasonable satisfaction against the action or proceeding **within three weeks** of service of the notice (s 223 IA 1986).

There are no separate provisions which allow an unregistered company to be placed into voluntary liquidation, administration or CVA, however. (In *Re The Salvage Association* [2003] BCC 504, a creative interpretation of the EC Insolvency Regulation was used to place the association into a CVA, but the legislation was subsequently amended to prevent future use of this route.)

1.6   RESTRUCTURING AS AN ALTERNATIVE

1.6.1   Who is involved in a restructuring?

As noted previously, restructuring involves reaching an arrangement between the company, some or all of its creditors and (possibly) some or all of its other stakeholders. For these purposes, a stakeholder is anyone who has a financial interest in the outcome of the restructuring. Exactly who the stakeholders are will depend on the facts of each situation – often the first step in a restructuring negotiation will be to identify all of the stakeholders and their interests.

Where a company, or group of companies, trades it will have many creditors. It will not be practicable in any but the simplest of cases to negotiate a compromise with all of them – therefore this is rarely attempted. Instead, it is likely that only certain creditors will be involved in the negotiations, leaving the rights of other creditors unaffected.

In some cases, the largest creditors by value, for example, landlords of surplus premises occupied by the company, might be asked to compromise their claims. If the company has a defined benefit pensions scheme with a deficit, pensions aspects may play a part. In sophisticated groups of companies, however, it may well be that the only creditors involved in the negotiations are lenders and other financial creditors, on the understanding that all trade and other creditors will be unaffected by the restructuring and will continue to be paid in full.

It is likely, nonetheless, that most negotiations will involve the shareholders. As explained in Chapter 2, shareholder claims would rank behind those of the creditors on a formal insolvency. The creditors are therefore unlikely to compromise their own claims whilst leaving shareholder value intact, unless the shareholders are prepared to inject further money themselves. In addition, many restructurings will involve creditors taking shares in exchange for part of their debt in a 'debt for equity swap', which cannot be achieved outside a formal insolvency process unless the shareholders are prepared to become involved.

1.6.2 Consensual or non-consensual?

Many troubled companies are able to agree a wholly consensual restructuring with the relevant creditors and other stakeholders concerned.

However, certain of the formal processes described in Section 1.4 may still serve as mechanisms for achieving a non-consensual restructuring, where not all stakeholders are prepared to agree terms. For example:

● A CVA or Scheme of Arrangement can be used to bind, or '**cram down**', a minority of dissenting unsecured creditors.

● A pre-packaged administration or receivership can be used to circumvent the claims of dissenting shareholders or lower ranking creditors by transferring assets to a new company whose debt and capital structure reflect the desired outcome. In a sophisticated group of companies, where the primary financing arrangements are made with non-trading holding companies, this can be achieved without the formal insolvency of any trading subsidiary.

In practice, the availability of a non-consensual route will often serve as an effective negotiating tool in persuading dissenting stakeholders to adopt a consensual route.

1.6.3 Why choose restructuring?

The company and its stakeholders might prefer a restructuring for a number of reasons, including the following:

● a restructuring is likely to preserve more value for creditors and shareholders than a formal insolvency process;

● a restructuring allows the company and its stakeholders to agree almost any arrangement they wish, and is therefore necessarily more flexible than a formal process;

● a consensual restructuring will not require the involvement either of the court or an insolvency officeholder, and could therefore prove less expensive and quicker to implement;

● a restructuring is less likely to trigger defaults under the company, or group's key contracts or licences which it needs to operate its business;

● a restructuring is a private arrangement, which is less likely to attract publicity than a formal process; and

● management will usually favour a route which avoids any company of which they are a director being placed into a formal insolvency process.

1.6.4 What are the prerequisites for a restructuring?

Any successful restructuring will have certain prerequisites. Among other things:

● The company, or group, must have a **viable underlying business**. A restructuring would otherwise have no long-term benefit for the stakeholders.

● A sufficient number of **key stakeholders must support the process**. The non-consensual processes described in Section 1.6.2 are effective only to bind minority stakeholders, or those stakeholders who (as matters stand) would not receive a return on a formal insolvency.

- The company, or group, must be able to **continue to trade** until the restructuring can be implemented. This may mean, for example, putting in place interim cash-flow arrangements, injecting new money into the company or group, or agreeing a temporary rescheduling of payments to creditors at the outset.

- The other stakeholders must be able to **work with management**. It is possible that the stakeholders may be able to supplement or replace underperforming management, although if so they would probably need to do so early in the process.

If it seems clear that one or other of these prerequisites will not be satisfied, it may well be unrealistic to attempt a restructuring and a formal insolvency process may then be the most suitable option. A significant amount of preliminary work may need to be carried out to determine whether a restructuring can be achieved, as discussed further in Chapter 10.

Chapter 2

Who gets what?

2.1 INTRODUCTION

2.1.1 What happens on the liquidation of a company?

On the liquidation of a company, insolvency law prescribes how its assets, or the proceeds following the realisation of its assets, are to be distributed. As was mentioned in Chapter 1, this is not covered comprehensively in any single section of the insolvency legislation, and it is therefore necessary to read a number of different sections alongside the common law to understand the respective entitlements of the various interested parties.

The liquidation of a company is a form of collective execution by all of its creditors against all of its available assets. The resolution or winding-up order divests the company of its beneficial interests in its assets. These assets become a fund which the company then holds on trust to discharge its liabilities. The creditors have a right to have the fund administered by the liquidator in accordance with the insolvency legislation (see *Ayerst v C & K (Construction) Ltd* [1976] AC 167).

2.1.2 What if there is a secured creditor?

The court explained in *Buchler and Another v Talbot and Others* [2004] 2 AC 298 – the '*Leyland Daf*' case that the above fund applies only to the company's own property (ie its 'free assets'). It does not affect the proprietary interests of others. Assets subject to security are regarded as forming a separate fund for these purposes.

To the extent that the realisations from the secured assets prove insufficient to discharge the debt due to a secured creditor, that secured creditor might claim for any balance against the free assets, alongside all of the company's other unsecured creditors. However, the unsecured creditors have no recourse to the secured assets, save to the extent that:

● there is a balance remaining after the secured creditor has been repaid; and/or

● the legislation makes a proportion of the secured assets available to them.

In addition, the proceeds of certain actions by a liquidator will also be available to the unsecured creditors rather than to the secured creditors (see Section 2.2.2).

Where a creditor holds fixed and floating charge security over all of the company's assets, there may well be no remaining free assets. To avoid the injustice that this might create, a number of legislative provisions have been introduced to allow for some of the recoveries from the floating charge assets to be allocated towards the payment of unsecured creditors as well as towards certain insolvency-related expenses. Only the remainder of those recoveries will be available to the floating chargeholder.

Table 2.1 summarises the position on a liquidation where there is a secured creditor.

Table 2.1 – Application of realisations from secured assets when the company is in liquidation (in descending order of priority)[1]

Fixed charge holder[2]

Expenses of the winding-up (to the extent that there are insufficient 'free assets') (s 176ZA IA 1986)[3]

Preferential debts (to the extent that there are insufficient 'free assets') (s 175 IA 1986)

Prescribed part (s 176A IA 1986)

Floating charge holder

Ordinary unsecured creditors (s 107 IA 1986 and s 143 IA 1986)

Debts or other sums due from the company to its shareholders in their capacity as shareholders (s 74(2)(f) IA 1986)

Shareholders generally (s 107 IA 1986 and s 143 IA 1986)

---

1   Essentially the same order of priority will also apply in other insolvency processes.
2   The specific expenses of realising a fixed charge asset may be deducted from the sale proceeds, but not the general expenses of a liquidation (or administration) – see the *Leyland Daf* case.
3   If the company has entered into administration, administration expenses will be deducted instead of (or if the administration is a precursor to a winding up as well as) expenses of the winding-up.

2.1.3   Other formal insolvency procedures

In practice, it is possible that a company will enter into an insolvency procedure other than liquidation – indeed, a company may enter into more than one insolvency process before its life ends, with the result that the proceeds of its assets will not necessarily be realised or distributed by any single insolvency officeholder. For example:

- an administrator (who has powers that a liquidator does not have in relation to secured assets) may realise assets and pay only the secured and other higher ranking creditors, and then hand any surplus over to a liquidator to distribute amongst the ordinary unsecured creditors; or

- a receiver may be appointed over the secured assets of the company at the same time as the company is in liquidation, to allow the secured creditor (via his appointed receiver) to realise the assets subject to the security and distribute the proceeds to the secured creditor, whilst the liquidator realises any free assets for the general creditors.

Nevertheless, the underlying order of priority described in this chapter will remain the basis for determining where each creditor ranks vis-à-vis the other creditors.

When a company enters into a CVA, it is theoretically open to creditors to agree any compromise between themselves they may wish, but even so the rights of certain creditors are still recognised. The ordinary unsecured creditors cannot agree a compromise which prevents a secured creditor from enforcing its security (unless the secured creditor agrees), or obliges a preferential creditor to accept a lower level of priority than it would otherwise enjoy.

2.2 WHAT WILL BE AVAILABLE TO THE CREDITORS?

2.2.1 The company's property

The term 'property' is widely defined in s 436 IA 1986, and includes:

'money, goods, things in action, land and every description of property wherever situated and also obligations and every description of interest, whether present or future or vested or contingent arising out of, or incidental to property'.

A company's property will therefore include, for example, a claim it has against a third party, or a beneficial interest in property held on trust for it.

However, the following will not be available to a company's creditors:

- Property which the company does not own, even though it may have possession of that property, or otherwise deal with it in some way. Creditors might therefore seek to take 'commercial' security by retaining title, or obtaining title outright, to assets of the company in order to keep that property outside of any insolvency regime affecting the company, as described in Section 2.3.3.

- Property which the company holds on trust for a third party. A company might, for example, protect customer deposits paid to it at a time when it fears that it might be in financial difficulty by placing them in a specially constituted trust account, as described in more detail in Chapter 6.

2.2.2 Proceeds of insolvency officeholders' actions

A distinction is also made for distribution purposes between:

- the proceeds of claims which the company would have been entitled to bring whether it had entered into a formal insolvency process or not (eg a claim under an indemnity, or a claim for a debt owed to the company); and

- the proceeds of actions which only a liquidator or administrator can bring (eg an action seeking to set aside a transaction at an undervalue or to recover a preference, or an action against the directors for wrongful trading).

In the latter case, the proceeds of the action may not be available to the secured creditors, as discussed further in Chapter 5. In addition, whilst a liquidator, for example, may be able to sell the company's right to bring claims falling into the first category to a third party (and indeed this is often an effective way of still making money out of a claim where he has no funds to bring a legal action himself), he will not be able to sell claims falling into the second category (*Re Oasis Merchandising Services Ltd* [1998] Ch 170).

2.3 SECURED CREDITORS

2.3.1 What is a security interest?

A security interest is a right given to a party over an asset of a company to secure payment of a debt or performance of some other obligation by the company (or, in some cases, by a third party). English law recognises four main types of 'legal' security: the pledge, the lien, the mortgage and the charge. Their meanings under English law are described below, but note that these words often take different meanings in other jurisdictions. In the United States, for example, a 'lien' may be more akin to an English charge.

- A **pledge** involves the delivery of possession of an asset of the company to a creditor. Ownership of the property remains with the company. The creditor is able to sell the pledged asset if the company then defaults in payment. Because of the requirement for possession, there must be a tangible item which can be delivered to the creditor, so pledges are used only where the creditor is able to take possession of the asset itself or of a formal document of title, such as a bill of lading. In practice, except in certain specialised types of transaction, pledges are seldom used.

- A **lien** gives a person the right to retain possession of an asset of the company until money owed is paid. In practice it differs from a pledge in that the asset in question will have been initially deposited with the person in question for some purpose other than security for a debt. A lien may be created by common law, by statute or by contract. So, for example, a garage will hold a common law lien over a repaired car until the company pays money owed for those repairs. A lien does not normally confer a power to sell the asset in question, and the holder must rely upon the fact that their right to retain possession will eventually oblige the company to pay. However, a lien created by contract may expressly include an ability to sell.

- A **mortgage** involves the transfer of ownership of an asset of the company to the creditor by way of security for the company's obligations. There is an express or implied implication that ownership will be re-transferred to the company once those obligations have been discharged. The company will retain possession of the property concerned and can continue to use it. However, the mortgage will include terms to prevent the company dealing with the property in various ways whilst it is subject to the mortgage.

- A **charge** involves an agreement between the company and the creditor by which a particular asset, or category of assets, is appropriated to the satisfaction of a debt. Unlike a mortgage, a charge does not transfer ownership, or indeed any other existing interest in the asset concerned, to the creditor. Instead, it creates a new interest in the asset concerned in favour of the creditor. The creditor will be able to resort to the asset in order to realise it, and to apply those realisations towards repayment of the debt. In the meantime, the charge attaches itself as an encumbrance on the asset, and may follow the asset into the hands of a third party. It is possible for a charge to attach even to future assets (ie assets which the company does not yet own at the time the charge is entered into).

A charge may either be fixed or floating. A discussion of the different implications for a creditor in holding the other types of security described above is largely beyond this book, but for the purposes of determining where that creditor stands vis-à-vis the unsecured creditors they can be regarded as placing that creditor in essentially the same position as they would be if they held a fixed charge. It is the distinction between fixed and floating charges, and its implications, which is most important for present purposes, as explained in Section 2.3.7 below.

2.3.2 Validity of security

There are a number of issues which may affect whether or not security taken by a creditor will in fact prove as effective as the creditor originally anticipated.

- The security must **attach** to the asset concerned (ie it must be properly created over that asset). This means, amongst other things, that an agreement to take security must comply with any formalities prescribed, that the asset concerned must have been sufficiently clearly identified and that the company must owe some obligation at the time of any enforcement to the person holding the security (although this obligation need not necessarily have existed at the time the security was taken).

- The security must have been **perfected** (ie all steps which are required to be taken to ensure its validity against third parties have been taken). This might require taking possession of the assets concerned, or it might require registration of the security, or some other form of notice to be given. For example, under s 874 CA 2006, the failure to register various types of charge created by a company within 21 days of their creation will result in those charges being void against a liquidator, administrator or any creditor of the company.

- The security must have **priority** under any relevant rules. Whilst each secured creditor is still likely to have priority over the ordinary unsecured creditors, their position vis-à-vis other secured creditors will also be relevant. A discussion of the rules determining priority is beyond the scope of this book. However, where secured creditors are aware of each other's existence, they will often in practice document an order of priority amongst themselves, and sometimes also certain unsecured creditors, in an intercreditor agreement or deed of priority rather than rely on the statutory and common law rules (which are complex and can lead to uncertainty).

- The security must be able to **withstand attack** by a liquidator or administrator as a transaction at an undervalue or preference, or as an invalid floating charge. The circumstances in which security might so be attacked are discussed further in Chapter 5. In practice, of course a creditor may often still take the view that it would rather take security and run the risk of it later being set aside than not take the security at all. It may, however, also be possible to structure matters in a way which reduces this risk.

- The company must have derived **corporate benefit** from granting the security. This will be most relevant when the company has granted security in respect of the obligations of some other party. The directors of the company have a duty to act in what they consider to be the best interests of the company, and need to have properly concluded that they can justify giving security for the third party's obligations from the company's own perspective.

2.3.3 'Commercial' security

In addition to the types of legal security described above, there are various practical ways in which a creditor may improve its position. These include:

- **Retention of title,** whereby the company and a supplier agree that ownership of goods supplied will not pass to the company until the company has paid for the goods in question (and possibly other goods supplied by that same supplier as well), notwithstanding that the goods in question may already have been delivered to the company. This is discussed further in Chapter 9. (Consignment supply arrangements, where the ownership of the goods never passes to the company but the proceeds of sale are instead split by the company and the supplier, are a variation on this theme).

- **Factoring**, where instead of taking security over the debts of a company, a lender acquires outright ownership of the company's interest in those debts.

- **Set-off**, where sums are owed both by the company to another person, and by the other person to the company. A creditor of an insolvent company would normally expect only to recover a fraction of the face value of the debt owed to them by the company. However, where set-off allows that creditor to achieve a reduction in the amount they themselves owe the company, this can make the debt more valuable to them. This is discussed further in Section 2.10.

- **'Flawed asset'**, where a debt only becomes payable to a company on fulfilment of certain conditions. Thus, monies in an escrow account might be prevented from ever becoming part of the company's own assets in the event of its formal insolvency. This is discussed further in Section 2.7.3.1.

2.3.4   What is a fixed and what is a floating charge?

A fixed charge attaches, or 'fixes', immediately to the assets charged, assuming those assets are capable of being ascertained. Its key feature is that it gives the creditor who holds it control over the asset concerned. A document attempting to create a fixed charge will not do so effectively unless it contains provisions preventing the company from disposing of the asset without the secured creditor's consent. In practice, security documents will invariably also place other restrictions on the company.

A **floating charge**, in contrast, initially 'floats' above a changing pool of assets rather than attaching directly to any of those assets. It was classically described by Romer LJ in *Yorkshire Woolcombers Association Ltd* [1903] 2 Ch 284 as having three main characteristics:

- it is a charge on a class of assets of a company both present and future;

- that class of assets is one which, in the ordinary course of the company's business would be changing from time to time; and

- it is contemplated that, until some future step is taken by or on behalf of those interested in the charge, the company may carry on its business in the normal way as far as it concerns that particular class of assets.

An obvious example of an asset class which will naturally be the subject of a floating charge will be stock held by a trading company. The treatment of other asset classes is discussed at Section 2.3.8.

2.3.5   What are the advantages of a floating charge?

The practical advantage of a floating charge is that it allows the creditor to take at least some form of security over additional assets of the company without paralysing the company's ability to run its business. The consent of the secured creditor will not be required every time the company wishes to dispose of assets subject only to a floating charge.

In practice, a creditor will very often take fixed charges (or mortgages) over those assets where it is practicable to maintain the necessary level of control and a floating charge over any remaining assets. This will give the creditor 'all-asset' security, and a security document creating all-asset security in this way is often referred to as a debenture.

As discussed further in Chapters 4 and 8, only a creditor which holds security over 'all or substantially all' of a company's assets, and whose security includes a floating charge, will be able to:

- appoint an administrator to the company without the need to make an application to the court; or

- appoint an administrative receiver over the assets of the company.

2.3.6 What is 'crystallisation'?

The fact that a floating charge gives the company the ability to dispose of the assets concerned without the secured creditor's consent is a potential problem for the secured creditor. It needs a way to prevent the company disposing of the assets in question and leaving little of value in the company. The law does give some protection here. When certain events occur, a floating charge will crystallise (ie attach itself to those floating charge assets in existence at that point in time).

Crystallisation will automatically occur at common law when:

- a winding-up order is made in respect of the company;

- the company ceases to trade; or

- a secured creditor intervenes to take control of some or all the company's assets, either by taking possession directly or by appointing a receiver, administrative receiver or administrator.

The secured creditor and the company may additionally agree other events which will cause the floating charge to crystallise. The security document may provide for crystallisation to occur automatically, for example if a third party starts or attempts to start any distress or execution process against any of the charged assets. It will usually also allow the secured creditor to choose to crystallise its charge by express notice to the company in a wider range of circumstances.

Crystallisation will prevent the company from disposing of those assets without the secured creditor's consent. It may also enable the secured creditor to defeat some competing claims by a third party to those assets, for example, the charge might crystallise where the third party attempts to levy distress, etc. In this respect the practical effect is to turn the floating charge into something akin to a fixed charge.

However, crystallisation does not mean that the secured creditor will then enjoy all of the legal advantages it would have enjoyed had it taken a fixed charge over those same assets at the outset. Section 251 IA 1986 defines the term 'floating charge' as a charge which, **as created**, was a floating charge. This will be relevant for all of the purposes described in Section 2.3.7.

2.3.7 Why is the distinction between a fixed and a floating charge important?

There are a number of reasons a creditor holding a floating charge is in a less favourable position than a creditor holding a fixed charge over the same assets:

- The **remuneration and expenses** of a liquidator or an administrator (and also certain other liabilities arising in an administration) are payable out of the proceeds of the realisation of those assets in priority to a floating charge holder (see Section 2.4).

- The **preferential debts** are payable in priority to a floating charge holder (see Section 2.5).

- The '**prescribed part**' will be deducted from the property which would otherwise remain available to the floating charge holder once the deductions referred to above have been made (see Section 2.6).

- There is a risk that, if the company subsequently enters into administration or liquidation, the floating charge might be valid only to the extent that '**new value**' has been provided by the floating charge holder (see Chapter 5).

- A floating charge holder will rank behind another creditor who subsequently succeeds in taking a **fixed charge** over the same asset (although the inclusion in the security of a 'negative pledge' provision, ie an agreement by the company not to grant any further security without the existing creditor's consent, can afford some protection) and it may simply be impractical for the company to grant the second creditor an effective fixed charge over assets which it would continuously need to dispose of and replace in order to trade.

2.3.8 Over which assets can a fixed charge be taken effectively?

There are various classes of asset which would not normally be disposed of in the course of a company's business. A secured creditor can therefore maintain a fixed charge, with a requirement that the company obtain the creditor's consent before disposing of such assets, with little practical difficulty on the part of either the creditor or the company. Assets which would normally fall into this category include:

- freehold and leasehold premises;
- shares in subsidiary undertakings;
- intellectual property; and
- goodwill.

In contrast, stock has already been mentioned as an asset which will by its nature change from time to time making it impracticable to take anything other than a floating charge.

Due to the disadvantages of a floating charge, a creditor will often wish to take a fixed charge over as many assets as possible. However, in *Agnew v Commissioners of Inland Revenue* [2001] 2 AC 710 (the '*Brumark*' case), which concerned the ability of a non-clearing bank to take an effective charge over a company's book debts, the court emphasised that in deciding whether a charge is fixed or floating, it needs to consider more than just the way the parties have chosen to describe the charge in their security document. A two-stage process should be adopted:

- first, the terms of the parties' security agreement should be reviewed to ascertain the rights and obligations which the parties intended to grant to each other in respect of the charged assets; and

- second, once it has ascertained the parties' intentions, the court should categorise the charge. As a matter of law, if the parties' intentions were to grant each other rights in respect of the charged assets which are inconsistent with the nature of a fixed charge, then the charge will not be a fixed charge no matter how they have chosen to describe it.

There are therefore a number of asset classes where a secured creditor's ability to maintain a fixed charge has come under close scrutiny by the courts. Examples of these include:

- **Book debts**. The ability of a creditor to take a fixed charge over this asset class has been repeatedly considered by the courts. It is now clear that where a company is able to collect debts due to it from its customers and to use the proceeds in the ordinary course of its business without further reference to the secured creditor, the secured creditor will only hold a floating charge regardless of how that charge may be described in the security document (*Re Spectrum Plus Limited (in liquidation)* [2005] 2 AC 680). As the court in *Spectrum* made clear, however, it is possible to take a fixed charge over book debts provided the company is genuinely limited in its ability to collect the debts and to deal with the proceeds. A method often chosen to achieve this is to arrange for the proceeds of the book debts in question to be paid into a **'blocked' account**. To maintain a valid fixed charge the secured creditor must continuously review the position and give its express authorisation before any transfer can be made from this account into one of the company's general trading accounts.

- **Cash deposits**. It is certainly possible to maintain a fixed charge over a sum of money placed into an account where the secured creditor exercises the power to prohibit withdrawals from that account except in certain pre-agreed circumstances. This is often done, for example, where a landlord holds rent deposit monies. The practical difficulty is that the monies in question will not be available to the company for its general trading purposes. A charge over a current account is likely to be floating, because the secured creditor is unlikely to be regarded as having the degree of control needed to maintain a fixed charge.

- **Plant and machinery**. Again, it is possible to maintain a fixed charge over plant and machinery if the company obtains the consent of the secured creditor before dealing with such assets. Often this is achieved by reference to a pre-agreed list of the plant and machinery in question. However, if the company is able in practice to acquire, dispose of or replace its plant and machinery without specific reference to the secured creditor, then the charge may well just be a floating charge.

In practice, where it is clear that a company may be in financial difficulty, a secured creditor will often take additional security with the aim of creating a fixed charge over classes of assets which were previously subject only to a floating charge. The downside of doing so, from the company's and the creditor's perspective, will be the increased amount of time they will need to devote, respectively, to seeking and considering consents before dealing with assets. In addition, such additional security might be at risk of attack on one of the bases described in Chapter 5.

2.4   EXPENSES ASSOCIATED WITH THE FORMAL INSOLVENCY PROCESS

2.4.1   Overview

The insolvency legislation gives priority status to the costs and expenses involved in the various different types of formal insolvency process. For convenience, it is useful to consider each of liquidation, administration and receivership here, as they all enjoy a similar priority status in relation to other creditors.

2.4.2   Liquidation expenses

2.4.2.1   Where do liquidation expenses rank?

Under s 115 IA 1986, the liquidation expenses are payable out of the company's free assets in priority to all other unsecured claims, including those of preferential creditors. The liquidator must ensure that he has set aside enough monies to cover them before paying any interim dividend and must pay any outstanding liquidation expenses before paying a final dividend (see Chapter 3). However, there is no obligation to delay their payment until the end of the liquidation, and in practice the liquidator may well pay many of them on an ongoing basis if he has funds to do so.

Over the years, the courts have reached different conclusions as to where liquidation expenses rank vis-à-vis a floating charge. However, under s 176ZA IA 1986, introduced following the decision in the *Leyland Daf* case, these expenses, so far as the free assets are insufficient to meet them, now have priority over the claims of any floating chargeholder. The 'free assets' will not for these purposes include the prescribed part (s 176ZA(2)(a) IA 1986).

2.4.2.2   What expenses will be liquidation expenses?

Both s 115 and s 176ZA(4) IA 1986 make it clear that references to liquidation expenses are 'to all expenses properly incurred in the winding-up, including the remuneration of any liquidator'. Rule 4.218 IR 1986 lists these expenses in the order of priority in which they are payable. This is set out in full in Table 2.2, and as can be seen, many of these expenses rank in priority to the remuneration of the liquidator. Where the assets are insufficient to satisfy the liquidation expenses in full, the court has the power under s 156 IA 1986 to vary this order of priority. Only in exceptional circumstances, however, will it exercise its jurisdiction to give any part of the liquidator's remuneration priority over expenses which would normally rank ahead of this (see *Linda Marie Ltd (in liquidation)* (1988) 4 BCC 463).

Table 2.2 – Liquidation expenses

(a)   expenses which (i) are properly chargeable or incurred by the provisional liquidator in carrying out the functions conferred on him by the court; (ii) are properly chargeable or incurred by the official receiver or the liquidator in preserving, realising or getting in any of the assets of the company or otherwise in the preparation or conduct of any legal proceedings, arbitration or other dispute resolution procedures, which he has power to bring in his own name or bring or defend in the name of the company or in the preparation or conduct of any negotiations intended to lead or leading to a settlement or compromise of any legal action or dispute to which the proceedings or procedures relate; (iii) relate to the employment of a shorthand writer, if appointed by an order of the court made at the instance of the official receiver in connection with an examination; or (iv) are incurred in holding an examination under r 4.214 IR 1986 (examinee unfit) where the application for it was made by the official receiver;

(b)   any other expenses incurred or disbursements made by the official receiver or under his authority, including those incurred or made in carrying on the business of the company;

(c)   the fees payable under any order made under ss 414 or 415A IA 1986, including those payable to the official receiver (other than the fee referred to in (d)(i) below), and any remuneration payable to him under general regulations;

(d)   (i) the fee payable under any order made under s 414 IA 1986 for the performance by the official receiver of his general duties as official receiver; or (ii) any repayable deposit lodged under any such order as security for the fee mentioned in sub-paragraph (i);

(e)   the cost of any security provided by a provisional liquidator, liquidator or special manager in accordance with the IA or the IR;

(f)   the remuneration of the provisional liquidator (if any);

(g)   any deposit lodged on an application for the appointment of a provisional liquidator;

(h)   the costs of the petitioner, and of any person appearing on the petition which costs are allowed by the court;

(i)   the remuneration of the special manager (if any);

(j)   any amount payable to a person employed or authorised, under Chapter 6, Part 4 IR 1986, to assist in the preparation of a statement of affairs or of accounts;

(k)   any allowance made, by order of the court, towards costs on an application for release from the obligation to submit a statement of affairs, or for an extension of time for submitting such a statement;

(l)   the costs of employing a shorthand writer in any case other than one appointed by an order of the court at the instance of the official receiver in connection with an examination;

(m)   any necessary disbursements by the liquidator in the course of his administration (including any expenses incurred by members of the liquidation committee or their representatives and allowed by the liquidator under r 4.169 IR 1986, but not including any payment of corporation tax in circumstances referred to in (p) below);

(n)   the remuneration or emoluments of any person who has been employed by the liquidator to perform any services for the company, as required or authorised by or under IA 1986 or IR 1986;

(o)   the remuneration of the liquidator, up to any amount not exceeding that which is payable under Sch 6 IA 1986;

(p)   the amount of any corporation tax on chargeable gains accruing on the realisation of any asset of the company (without regard to whether the realisation is effected by the liquidator, a secured creditor, or a receiver or manager appointed to deal with a security);

(q)   the balance, after payment of any sums due under (o) above, of any remuneration due to the liquidator;

(r)   any other expenses properly chargeable by the liquidator in carrying out his functions in the liquidation.

Liabilities originally incurred before the liquidation in respect of property which the liquidator retains for the benefit of the liquidation may also be liquidation expenses, at least so far as they relate to the post-liquidation period (*Re Lundy Granite Co* (1870) 6 Ch App 462). Post-liquidation rent under a lease of premises which a liquidator continued to use falls into this category – in the *Linda Marie* case it was held to be a 'necessary disbursement'. In *Re Toshoku Finance (UK) plc* [2002] BCC 110, the court rejected an argument that there is a degree of discretion as to which expenses might fall within the scope of r 4.218 IR 1986. It held that tax on a company's post-liquidation income was a 'necessary disbursement' which must be paid as a liquidation expense.

2.4.2.3   Litigation expenses

Rules 4.218A–E IR 1986 contain special provisions in relation to **litigation expenses**. These are expenses which are properly chargeable or incurred in the preparation or conduct of proceedings which the liquidator is entitled to bring, either in the name of the company or in his own name, for the purposes of swelling the monies available to creditors, or for preserving, realising or getting in any assets of the company. Here, 'proceedings' includes not only legal actions but arbitration and dispute resolution procedures, or indeed negotiations intended to lead to a settlement or compromise of any such proceedings.

The legislature was sympathetic to floating chargeholders' concerns that a liquidator might be over eager to conduct litigation at their expense. Therefore a liquidator is generally only entitled to deduct litigation expenses from the floating charge assets if he has first obtained the consent of any preferential creditors or floating chargeholders who would receive less money were the deduction to be made. He does not, however, need consent for litigation expenses which do not exceed (or which in his opinion are not likely to exceed) £5,000. The liquidator can also apply to court for an order allowing the deduction of litigation expenses in various circumstances, for example, where the floating chargeholder concerned might be a defendant in the proceedings.

2.4.3   Administration expenses

2.4.3.1   Where do administration expenses rank?

The administrator's remuneration and expenses are dealt with in para 99, Sch B1 IA 1986. Perhaps slightly oddly, this provision considers the priority position where he has ceased to be the administrator. The former administrator's remuneration and expenses are to be:

- charged on and payable out of property of which was in the administrator's custody immediately before he ceased to be administrator; and

- payable in priority to any floating charge.

In practice, the administrator may well pay many of these expenses during the course of the administration if he has funds available. To the extent that they still remain unpaid at the end of the administration, however, they will enjoy the priority position indicated above.

2.4.3.2   What expenses will be administration expenses?

Rule 2.67 IR 1986 lists those expenses which are administration expenses in the order of priority in which they are payable. This is set out in full in Table 2.3. In a similar fashion to the liquidation expenses, many of these expenses rank in priority to the remuneration of the administrator. Where the assets are insufficient to satisfy the administration expenses in full, the court again has the power under r 2.67(3) to vary this order of priority.

Table 2.3 – Administration expenses

(a) expenses properly incurred by the administrator in performing his functions in the administration of the company;

(b) the cost of any security provided by the administrator in accordance with the IA 1986 or the IR 1986;

(c) where an administration order was made, the costs of the applicant and any person appearing on the hearing of the application and where the administrator was appointed otherwise than by order of the court, any costs and expenses of the appointor in connection with the making of the appointment and the costs and expenses incurred by any other person in giving notice of intention to appoint an administrator;

(d) any amount payable to a person employed or authorised, under Chapter 5, Part 2 IR 1986, to assist in the preparation of a statement of affairs or statement of concurrence;

(e) any allowance made, by order of the court, towards costs on an application for release from the obligation to submit a statement of affairs or statement of concurrence;

(f) any necessary disbursements by the administrator in the course of the administration (including any expenses incurred by members of the creditors' committee or their representatives and allowed for by the administrator under r 2.63 IR 1986, but not including any payment of corporation tax in circumstances referred to in (j) below);

(g) the remuneration or emoluments of any person who has been employed by the administrator to perform any services for the company, as required or authorised under the IA or the IR;

(h) the remuneration of the administrator agreed under Chapter 11, Part 2 IR 1986;

(j) the amount of any corporation tax on chargeable gains accruing on the realisation of any asset of the company (without regard to whether the realisation is effected by the administrator, a secured creditor, or a receiver or manager appointed to deal with a security).

Prior to the changes to the insolvency legislation in 2003, the rules dealing with administration expenses were less rigid than those dealing with liquidation expenses. If an administrator was inclined not to pay the sums in question, the court had a discretion as to whether or not to require them to be treated as administration expenses. However, in *Exeter City Council v Bairstow; Re Trident Fashions Ltd* [2007] BCC 236, the court made it clear that no such discretion now exists. The *Trident Fashions* case itself held that non-domestic business rates were an expense of the administration, but its impact is wider. Post-administration rent must also now be treated as an administration expense, for example, where the administrator continues to use the premises, and this is discussed further in Chapter 9.

Rule 2.67(1)(j) IR 1986 can be a major factor in some administrations, given that the capital gains on realising certain assets may be considerable. A new tax period is also deemed to start when a company enters into administration, so pre-administration trading losses will not be available to reduce these.

In *Re: Nortel GmbH (in administration)* (heard together with *Re: Lehman Brothers International (Europe) (in administration)*) [2011] EWCA Civ 1124, the Pensions Regulator had issued financial support directions against the companies concerned after the dates on which they entered into administration. The Court of Appeal held that the liability created was an administration expense on the basis that, since no provable debt had existed at the date of the administration, this liability would otherwise have fallen into a 'black hole' and could not have been recovered at all. This decision is discussed further in Section 10.8.2.4.

2.4.3.3 Liabilities ranking in priority even to administration expenses

Under para 99 Sch B1 IA 1986, sums payable in respect of debts or liabilities under contracts entered into during the course of the administration have '**super-priority**' status. They are charged on and payable out of property of which the former administrator had custody immediately before he ceased to be administrator in priority to the administration expenses. This is an important protection for parties entering into contracts with an administrator who is continuing to trade a business. Liabilities to pay post-administration wages and salary arising under contracts of employment 'adopted' by the administrator are given this same super-priority status (see Chapter 9).

2.4.4   Receivership expenses

2.4.4.1   Where do receivership expenses rank?

The position of an administrative receiver and a non-administrative receiver is dealt with in s 45(3) IA 1986 and s 37(4) IA 1986, respectively. When a receiver vacates office:

- his remuneration and any expenses incurred by him; and

- any indemnity to which he is entitled out of the assets of the company

are charged on and paid out of any property of the company which is in his custody or under his control at that time in priority to any charge or other security held by the person by or on whose behalf he was appointed. The priority status of the indemnity will be important where the receiver has become personally liable on a contract, including as a result of having adopted a contract of employment (see Chapters 8 and 9).

2.4.4.2   What expenses will be receivership expenses?

Unlike liquidation or administration, there is no prescribed list of receivership expenses. Thus, for example, neither rent on a pre-receivership lease (*Re Atlantic Computer Systems plc (No 1)* [1991] BCLC 606) nor rates (*Brown v City of London Corpn; Re Sobam BV* [1996] BCC 351) are generally receivership expenses. The creditors in question will enjoy no better status than the other ordinary unsecured creditors of the company.

2.5   PREFERENTIAL DEBTS

In a liquidation, the company's preferential debts are to be paid in priority to all other unsecured debts (s 175 IA 1986). So far as the free assets are insufficient to meet the preferential debts, they also have priority over the claims of the floating chargeholder.

Preferential debts are given this same priority status in an administration (para 65 Sch B1 IA 1986), where possession is taken of assets subject to a floating charge by or on behalf of the floating chargeholder (s 754 CA 2006), and where a receiver is appointed under a floating charge (s 40 IA 1986).

The meaning of the term 'preferential debts' is found in s 386 IA 1986. They are defined by reference to a list in Sch 6 IA 1986 and now fall into three categories:

- Any sum owed by the company to which Sch 4 to the Pension Schemes Act 1993 applies (ie unpaid company contributions to occupational pension schemes and state scheme premiums).

- Sums owed by the company to present or former employees in respect of unpaid remuneration, or unpaid amounts ordered to be paid under the Reserve Forces (Safeguard of Employment) Act 1985, subject to certain prescribed limits.

- Any sums owed by the company in respect of certain levies or surcharges for delay relating to the production of coal and steel.

The first two categories are discussed further in Chapter 9. Clearly there are likely to be few companies to which the third category now applies.

Various debts due to the Crown representing unpaid taxes were once also preferential debts, but now have no preferential status for insolvencies commencing on or after 15 September 2003. As such, preferential debts are generally now a less important consideration than they would once have been, although they can still be a factor where a company has a considerable number of unpaid employees.

Where there are insufficient assets to pay the preferential debts in full, they rank *pari passu*.

Note that where a postponement agreement simply provides for one creditor's fixed charge to rank behind another's floating charge, the result may be that the preferential debts then enjoy priority over both creditors (see *Re Portbase (Clothing) Ltd* [1993] Ch 388). However, the use of a more sophisticated postponement agreement (which, for example, prioritises realisations rather than security) can allow secured creditors to avoid this problem.

2.6 THE PRESCRIBED PART

2.6.1 What is the prescribed part?

Under s 176A IA 1986, where a company has gone into liquidation or administration, or where a receiver or provisional liquidator has been appointed, the liquidator, administrator or receiver (as the case may be) must set aside a prescribed part of the company's net property for the unsecured creditors before distributing any balance to the holder of a floating charge created on or after 15 September 2003. The company's net property means 'the amount of its property which, but for s 176A, would be available to meet the claims of the floating charge holder' (ie the floating charge property which remains once the preferential debs have been paid).

This requirement was introduced on the same date as the preferential status of various debts due to the Crown was abolished (see Section 2.5). It is generally regarded as allowing the unsecured creditors rather than the secured creditors to benefit from this latter change. However, the holder of a floating charge created before 15 September 2003 will enjoy something of a windfall (see Section 2.6.3).

2.6.2   What is the amount involved?

The amount of the prescribed part is set out in the Insolvency Act 1986 (Prescribed Part) Order 2003 (SI 2003/2097) and is:

* where the net property **does not exceed £10,000**, 50% of that property; and

* where the net property **exceeds £10,000**, 50% of the first £10,000, plus 20% of the property which exceeds £10,000, up to a maximum prescribed part of £600,000.

Where the realisations from a secured creditor's security are insufficient to satisfy their total claim, leaving them with an unsecured claim against the company for any balance, they are not entitled to claim any part of the prescribed part (see *Re Permacell Finesse Ltd* [2008] BCC 208 and *Re Airbase (UK) Ltd* [2008] BCC 213).

However, they will be able to do so if they surrender their security completely, as they will no longer then be a secured creditor (*Re PAL SC Realisations 2007 Ltd* [2010] EWHC 2850 (Ch)). Indeed, because a secured creditor is regarded as surrendering their security if they choose not to disclose that security in a proof of debt, they may conceivably then share in the prescribed part even if no deed of release has yet been provided (*Re JT Frith Ltd* [2012] EWHC 196 (Ch)).

2.6.3   When will the prescribed part not be set aside?

There is no requirement to set aside a prescribed part before distributing to the holder of a floating charge created before 15 September 2003, nor does there seem to be an obligation on any chargeholder to set aside a prescribed part where it enters into possession personally or through an agent instead of appointing a receiver.

In addition, the insolvency officeholder is not obliged to set aside the prescribed part where:

* the company's net property is less than the **prescribed minimum** (currently set by SI 2003/2097 at £10,000) and the officeholder thinks the cost of making a distribution to unsecured creditors would be disproportionate to the benefits; **or**

* Section 176A is disapplied under the terms of a CVA or scheme of arrangement; **or**

* the court orders that s 176A be disapplied on the basis that the cost of making a distribution to unsecured creditors would be disproportionate to the benefits.

In *Re Hydroserve Ltd* [2008] BCC 175, for example, the court disapplied s 176A where a prescribed part estimated at most to be £40,000 would have had to be divided amongst 126 unsecured creditors, and where all but £5,000 of this sum would have gone to four creditors within the company's own group. However, in *Re Courts Plc* [2008] BCC 917 the court held that it had no authority to make a 'qualified' disapplication order which would have allowed the officeholders to distribute only to those creditors who were owed more than £28,000. (The order had been sought on the basis that to include 260 smaller creditors in the distribution would reduce the benefit to all creditors of any distribution being made once the additional costs had been met.)

In *Re International Sections Ltd (in liquidation)* [2009] EWHC 137 (Ch), it was emphasised that courts should not be too ready to disapply s 176A just because the dividend would be too small. It should look at the benefits to the creditors as a body.

2.7 ORDINARY UNSECURED CREDITORS

2.7.1 What are the consequences of a winding-up for the ordinary unsecured creditors?

The winding-up of a company has a number of consequences for its ordinary unsecured creditors:

- They may no longer take their own action to obtain payment from the company, but must instead submit their claim in writing to the liquidator. This process is termed '**proving**' for the debt.

- They may, however, prove even for debts which are not already due and payable at the date the company enters into liquidation. Such debts therefore '**accelerate**' as a result of the liquidation.

- Their total provable debts rank *pari passu* with those of all other ordinary unsecured creditors.

As explained in Chapter 3, the term 'debt' has a wide meaning for these purposes. That chapter discusses in more detail when a debt is provable, the mechanisms by which unsecured creditors may prove in a liquidation or a distribution administration respectively, and the methods of calculating the sum provable when a debt is not already due and payable. However, the *pari passu* principle will be addressed here.

2.7.2 What is the *pari passu* principle?

The insolvency legislation makes it clear that once preferential debts have been accounted for, the provable debts of the company's ordinary unsecured creditors rank equally between themselves in a liquidation or distribution administration (see s 107 IA 1986 in relation to a voluntary liquidation, r 4.181 IR 1986 in relation to a compulsory liquidation and r 2.69 IR 1986 in relation to a distribution administration). Where there are insufficient remaining recoveries to pay each of the ordinary unsecured creditors in full, therefore, each such creditor receives a dividend representing the same percentage by value of their total provable debt as that received by the other ordinary unsecured creditors. It is common to hear references to ordinary unsecured creditors each receiving a dividend of a certain number of pence in the pound.

The *pari passu* principle is the most fundamental principle of English insolvency law. Prior to a company's liquidation, even where the company is unable to pay its debts, an unsecured creditor may well be able to obtain and enforce a judgment for the sums due to him, or can simply exert commercial pressure on the company to pay up in full. The liquidation process removes his ability to pursue his own claim ahead of those of other unsecured creditors.

As seen in Chapter 4, an administrator is given a degree of additional flexibility under para 66, Sch B1 IA 1986, entitling him to make 'duress' payments to pre-administration creditors, for example. However, this power will be used in comparatively limited circumstances, and is an exception to the normal principle.

2.7.3 What arrangements might the court set aside to protect unsecured creditors?

English insolvency law has no statutory equivalent to those provisions of US bankruptcy law which automatically invalidate contractual clauses that modify a company's interest in a contract on its insolvency.

There are various statutory provisions which give a liquidator or administrator the ability to challenge payments made to creditors and other arrangements made in the period before the start of a formal insolvency process. These are considered in Chapter 5.

Otherwise, however, it has been left to the courts to use the common law to set aside arrangements which they consider to be out of step with insolvency law. Two distinct principles have emerged here:

- the **anti-deprivation principle**; and

- the principle that parties cannot contract out of the *pari passu* basis of distribution (often referred to as '**the rule in** *British Eagle*').

2.7.3.1   The anti-deprivation principle

The anti-deprivation principle was summarised by Neuberger J in *Money Markets International Stockbrokers Ltd (in liquidation) v London Stock Exchange Ltd* [2002] 1 WLR 1150 as follows:

> 'there cannot be a valid contract that a man's property shall remain his until his bankruptcy, and on the happening of that [event] go over to someone else, and be taken away from his creditors ... [T]here is no doubt that this principle exists, and has been applied to defeat provisions which have that purported effect.'

However, he also observed that the case law was not entirely consistent, so it was not possible to discern a coherent set of rules which would enable one to assess in every case whether a provision falls foul of the principle.

The principle has been examined further in a number of recent cases, including by the Supreme Court in *Belmont Park Investments PTY Limited v BNY Corporate Trustee Services Limited and Lehman Brothers Special Financing Inc* [2011] UKSC 38.

Provisions which the courts have held to contravene this principle include:

- a clause whereby the owner of a patent was entitled to withhold a share of royalties (which would otherwise have been due to the company) upon the company's insolvency in order to repay an existing debt owed by the company (*Jeavons, ex parte Mackay* (1873) LR 8 Ch App 643);

- a clause in a building contract vesting a company's building materials in the building's owner upon the company's liquidation (*Re Harrison, ex parte Jay* (1880) LR 14 ChD 19);

- a clause which assigned the company's main asset, a patent, to a third party should the owner company become insolvent for a price which merely reflected the cost so far paid by the company of securing patent protection rather than the value of the asset (*Fraser & others v Oystertec plc and others* [2004] BCC 233); and

- a clause whereby the company's right to an indemnity from another party would automatically terminate if the company went into insolvency proceedings (*Folgate London Market Ltd v Chaucer Insurance plc* [2011] EWCA Civ 328).

Recent cases where the courts have held that the principle did not apply, however, include:

- the *Money Markets case.* Here, the company was a member firm of the London Stock Exchange. It failed to honour its obligations, and as a result ceased to be a member and went into liquidation. It was obliged to surrender its share for no consideration if it ceased to be a member. This provision was held to be valid since the share was inseparable from membership and could have no independent value to the company's creditors;

- *Lomas v JFB Firth Rixson Inc* [2012] EWCA Civ 419. A swap agreement provided that the payment obligations of the non-defaulting party were suspended, potentially indefinitely, if an insolvency event occurred in relation to the other party. These provisions were held to be valid, partly for the reasons discussed below;

- the *Belmont* case. The facts and the reasoning are set out in the box below; and

- *HM Revenue and Customs v The Football League and another* [2012] EWHC 1372 (Ch). Here, the Football League's articles of association stipulated that on a club's insolvency the league could require it to transfer its share in the Football League, which gave it the right to membership of the league, to another person for a fixed price. The club would not receive any share of the income which the league held from the sale of television broadcast rights if it ceased to be a member before the end of the season, although in practice the Football League would make interim distributions of cash to clubs during the season. These provisions were held to be valid, for the reasons discussed below.

It is possible now to identify some general themes, particularly as a result of the judgment in the *Belmont* case.

There must have been a deliberate intention to evade insolvency laws. It may be possible to infer this intention in some cases. In borderline cases, an important question is whether the parties are entering into a commercial transaction in good faith. This was an important factor in the *Belmont* case. It was also relevant in the *Football League* case, where the court was persuaded that there was a commercial basis for removing a club's membership of the Football League on its insolvency, since other clubs would otherwise be required to continue to deal with and play fixtures against that club despite the fact that it might have defaulted on its obligations to them.

The principle will not apply if the deprivation results from an event other than the company's insolvency. For example, some of the judges in the *Belmont* case took the view that, as an event of default first occurred on the bankruptcy of the company's parent, the company was not being deprived of anything as a result of its own insolvency.

The court may also be less inclined to invoke the principle where the substance of the arrangement is that, on the company's insolvency the property is assigned to a party who paid for it. In the *Belmont* case, Lord Collins was influenced by what he considered to be the real commercial substance of the arrangement between the parties.

'Flawed asset' arguments (see Section 2.3.3) might still be relevant here, on the basis that if a party only becomes entitled to property on condition that it is solvent, then it has no absolute right to that property and is not being deprived of it on its insolvency. It is on this basis, for example, that forfeiture rights in leases and licences have traditionally been treated as valid notwithstanding the anti-deprivation principle. A lease or a licence be may regarded as a limited interest in property which is qualified by various conditions, including solvency, rather than as an absolute interest.

Lord Collins was keen to stress in the *Belmont* case that it was important to view substance over form in the above regard, otherwise the anti-deprivation principle could easily be undermined. Nonetheless, in the *Football League* case, the court was unwilling to find that the Football League's practice of making interim payments to clubs meant that in practice the clubs had an immediate right to receive the monies it held. Although HMRC argued that the articles were a transparent device of drafting that purported to delay the creation of a legal liability and did not reflect the reality of the payment process, Richards J made it clear that it was not for the courts to rewrite the parties' contracts in accordance with a wider anti-avoidance principle.

A *quid pro quo* test might also be relevant. Where the insolvent party has performed its side of the bargain, the courts should be slow to deprive it of the property it received in return. Conversely however, where the insolvent party can no longer do what it contracted to do, the courts might more readily uphold a clause depriving it of property. Briggs J found this line of reasoning attractive at first instance in the *Firth Rixson* case (his decision is reported at [2010] EWHC 3372 (Ch)), and it was endorsed by Lord Mance in the *Belmont* case.

The principle does not apply to 'protective trusts'. It seems that the only real justification for this is that protective trusts have been well established by their own line of case law.

Belmont Park Investments PTY Limited v BNY Corporate Trustee Services Limited and Lehman Brothers Special Financing Inc **[2011] UKSC 38**

Lehman Brothers Special Financing Incorporated ('LBSF') set up a special purpose vehicle (the 'Issuer'). The Issuer issued a series of loan notes to a number of investors including Belmont Park Investments PTY Ltd (the 'Noteholders'). The Issuer used the monies raised to acquire Government bonds and other secure investments (the 'Collateral').

The Issuer also entered into a credit default swap agreement with LBSF under which LBSF would pay the Issuer the amounts due by the Issuer to the

Noteholders in exchange for the payment by the Issuer to LBSF of sums equal to the interest received on the Collateral.

The Collateral was charged by the Issuer in favour of the Trustee to secure both its obligations to the Noteholders under the terms of the loan notes and its obligations to LBSF under the terms of the swap agreement. It was agreed between the parties that in the absence of an event of default on the part of LBSF under the swap agreement the proceeds of sale of the Collateral would be paid to LBSF in priority to the Noteholders. However, on event of a default by LBSF, the priority for payment would be reversed and the Noteholders would be paid in priority to LBSF (the so-called 'flip').

LBSF's parent, Lehman Brothers Holdings Inc ('LBHI'), and shortly afterwards LBSF itself, subsequently filed for bankruptcy protection in the United States. This was an event of default on LBSF's part under the swap agreement, and as a result the Noteholders directed the Trustee to terminate this agreement. This in turn triggered the payment of certain 'unwind costs' due from the Issuer to LBSF.

Because LBSF had defaulted, the Noteholders considered that the flip had occurred and that they were entitled to payment of the Collateral in priority to LBSF. The present proceedings were brought against the Trustee and LBSF to require the release of the Collateral to the Noteholders. However, LBSF contended that the flip was invalid as it breached the anti-deprivation principle by depriving LBSF of its priority position as a result of its insolvency.

The High Court and the Court of Appeal ruled in favour of the Noteholders, and the matter duly reached the Supreme Court.

Lord Collins explained that when assessing if a contractual provision falls foul of the anti-deprivation principle, the court should attempt to determine whether the commercial objective of the parties was to remove property from one party, if that party became insolvent. The court should not be quick to strike down a commercially legitimate transaction, entered into by the parties in good faith.

In this case, he considered that the Collateral had in commercial reality been provided by the Noteholders to secure what was in essence their own liability, albeit subject to terms which included the provision for LBSF to have priority until the flip occurred. There was no suggestion that the flip had deliberately intended to evade insolvency law. This was obvious from the wide range of non-insolvency circumstances which were also capable of being an event of default under the swap agreement. There was also evidence that the fact the Noteholders would have priority over the Collateral in the event of LBSF's insolvency was a very material fact in obtaining the Triple A credit rating that in turn enabled the notes to be marketed by Lehman. The anti-deprivation principle did not therefore apply and the flip was valid under English law.

It was also suggested that the anti-deprivation principle only applies to contractual provisions that directly link the loss of property to the insolvency of the entity concerned. Here, the Noteholders argued, an event of default first occurred on the bankruptcy of LBHI so the flip had already taken place by the time LBSF became bankrupt and the principle could not apply. Lord Collins and Lord Walker were prepared to dismiss the appeal on this ground as well.

As a footnote to the above, it is worth noting that US bankruptcy courts considered the same question as part of LBSF's bankruptcy proceedings and concluded that the flip was invalid under US law. It was a clause that modified LBSF's interest in a contact as a result of a bankruptcy filing (an *'ipso facto'* clause) which violated the US Bankruptcy Code. These provisions of the US Bankruptcy Code have no English law equivalent.

2.7.3.2 Attempts to contract out of the *pari passu* principle

The case of *British Eagle International Air Lines v Compagnie Nationale Air France* [1975] 2 All ER 390, as outlined in more detail in the box below, provides an example of an arrangement not specifically intended to defeat insolvency laws but which has nonetheless been found to be incompatible with them. It remains possible, following the same logic as used in *British Eagle*, that, for example, clauses in contracts which try to divert sums from a sub-contractor directly to a main employer on a contractor's insolvency could be successfully attacked.

However, the *British Eagle* case remains controversial. Since the case was decided, IATA has modified its rules to make it clearer that it is contracting with airlines as principal, rather than just as agent for other airlines. In *International Air Transport Association v Ansett Australia Holdings Limited* [2008] 1 WLR 758, the Australian High Court, considering the new rules, chose not to follow *British Eagle*. The courts have also disapplied the rule where they considered that international comity so requires. In *McGrath v Riddell, In re HIH Casualty and General Insurance Ltd* [2008] 1 WLR 852, the court was prepared to allow English provisional liquidators in an ancillary winding-up to hand over assets to Australian liquidators despite the fact that the rules governing distribution were different in Australia.

The *pari passu* rule will not prevent a creditor from agreeing to **subordinate** its claim to those of other creditors (*Manning v AIG Europe Ltd, sub nom SSSL Realisations (2002) Ltd*) [2005] 1 BCLC 1).

British Eagle International Air Lines v Compagnie Nationale Air France
[1975] 2 All ER 390

Both parties, like various other airlines, were members of the International Air Transport Association (IATA). IATA operates a clearing system to provide a 'netting' mechanism for the settlement of debts and creditors where members provided services for each other. Under this mechanism, which was binding on IATA's members, a net balance due to or from each member was calculated for each month and notified to members. Contractually, the members could not claim directly from each other, but could only claim sums due to them from IATA.

When British Eagle went into liquidation, it owed money to a number of airlines. However, it did have a net claim against Air France. The liquidator pursued Air France directly. He contended that the IATA clearing system offended the *pari passu* rule because, under this system, the general body of British Eagle's creditors would not benefit from the claim against Air France; only the airlines who were members of the system would benefit.

The House of Lords (by a majority of 3:2) agreed with the liquidator that, in so far as the IATA clearing system effected a different procedure from the mandatory setting off procedure between debtors and creditors applicable to insolvent liquidation, it was contrary to public policy. The majority accepted that the IATA members had good business reasons for entering into these arrangements and had not considered how they might be affected by the insolvency of one party, but saw this as irrelevant.

The dissenting House of Lords minority did not dispute the relevant principle of law. However, their view was that, once they joined the clearing system, the members were no longer debtors or creditors of each other at all, but were merely debtors and creditors of IATA. Such an arrangement would not offend the principle, as on this analysis no creditors of British Eagle would be paid preferentially.

2.7.3.3   How do the anti-deprivation principle and the rule in *British Eagle* differ?

In many cases, it has been argued that the offending provisions fall foul of both the anti-deprivation principle and the rule in 'British Eagle'. Indeed in some of the earlier cases (such as the *ex parte Mackay* case) it is absolutely not clear which principle the court was applying. However, recent cases, particularly the *Football League* case, have emphasised some of their differences.

- The anti-deprivation principle helps determine the size of the cake to be divided amongst the unsecured creditors. The rule in *British Eagle* helps determine the manner in which that cake will be divided amongst those creditors.

- For the anti-deprivation principle to apply, there must have been an intention to remove property from a company on its insolvency. The rule in *British Eagle* will make void a contract whose effect is to contract out of the *pari passu* principle regardless of the parties' intentions – it can therefore apply even to bona fide commercial arrangements made for reasons unconnected with insolvency.

- The rule in *British Eagle* applies only to the distribution of assets belonging to the company at the start of insolvency proceedings (or coming into its ownership at a later date) whose purpose is to distribute assets to creditors. It cannot apply to assets which ceased to belong to the company before the start of those insolvency proceedings. In particular, administration will not fall into this category unless or until the administrator serves a notice that he intends to make a distribution. In contract, the anti-deprivation rule can potentially be invoked by a range of triggers for removing a company's assets, provided they are insolvency-related – in the *Oystertec* case, for example, the trigger was a clause which sought to divest the company of the relevant asset if it became unable to pay its debts within the meaning of s 123 IA 1986.

2.8   INTEREST

As will be seen in Chapter 3, outstanding interest on a debt in respect of a period prior to the date on which the company went into liquidation (or, if the liquidation was immediately preceded by an administration, from the date the company went into administration) is generally provable as part of the debt.

Section 189 IA 1986 deals with interest for the period after the date the company went into liquidation. It provides that any surplus remaining after the payment of the debts proved in the liquidation shall, before being applied for any other purpose, be applied in paying interest on those debts in respect of the period for which they have been outstanding since the company went into liquidation. Rule 2.88(7) IR 1986 makes similar provision for a company which goes into administration.

All interest payable under s 189 or r 2.88(7) ranks equally, regardless of whether or not the debts on which it is payable rank equally. Therefore, for example, no interest will be payable on preferential debts until the ordinary unsecured debts first have been paid in full.

Such interest is payable at the 'official rate', which is the greater of:

• the rate specified in s 17 Judgments Act 1838 on the day the company went into liquidation. This rate is currently 8% per annum; and

• any rate of interest which is already applicable to that debt.

Because this rate of interest is now so high compared to rates achievable elsewhere, this has led to sales of unsecured claims in the administration of Lehman Brothers International (Europe) at prices of well over 100p in the £. The buyers anticipate that not only will the debts themselves be paid in full in due course, but that they will also receive several years' interest.

2.9   DEBTS DUE TO SHAREHOLDERS IN THEIR CAPACITY AS SHAREHOLDERS

Under s 74(2)(f) IA 1986 a sum due to any shareholder of the company (in his character as a shareholder) by way of dividends, profits or otherwise is deemed not to be debt of the company where the shareholder would otherwise be in competition with other creditors, although such sum may be taken into account for the purposes of the final adjustment of the rights of the shareholders between themselves.

In *Soden v British & Commonwealth Holdings plc (in administration)* [1998] AC 298, the House of Lords reviewed the relevant authorities and made it clear that s 74(2)(f) applies only where sums to which the shareholder's right is based on a cause of action on the 'statutory contract' between the company and its shareholders or the right otherwise arises from the Companies Acts. Therefore, a debt representing dividend declared by the company but not yet paid will rank below the debts of the ordinary unsecured creditors, and will not be paid unless and until the ordinary unsecured creditors have first been paid in full. However, the following will not be subordinated:

• Outstanding loans made by the shareholder to the company. (This contrasts with certain other jurisdictions where such loans are subordinated.)

• Outstanding remuneration due to directors who are also shareholders.

• Damages awarded to a person who had bought the shares in a company from an existing shareholder in reliance on the company's misrepresentation (*Soden*).

2.10 SET-OFF

2.10.1 What is the relevance of set-off when a company is insolvent?

Set-off becomes relevant where sums are owed both by the insolvent company to another person, and by the other person to the insolvent company. Set-off will not increase the amount which that other person will receive from a formal insolvency process. However, it will increase the practical value to that person of the debt owed to him by the insolvent company. Without the operation of set-off, that other person would only receive a fraction of their debt from the insolvent company (if they receive anything at all), but he would still be liable to pay the company in full. If set-off operates, however, the amount which he owes to the company will be reduced by an amount equal to the amount of debt which the company owes to him.

In this regard, it may be possible for a person owing money to a troubled company to acquire the benefit of debt owed by that company to a third party at a fraction of its face value in order to benefit from a set-off, although certain limitations are imposed in this regard (see Section 2.10.3.3).

2.10.2 What are the types of set-off?

The following are generally regarded as the types of set-off available under English law:

- **Legal set-off**. This is just a procedural defence by one party to a claim by another, requiring the creditor making that claim to obtain judgment only for any balance of their claim. It enjoys an advantage over equitable set-off in that the claim and the counterclaim need not arise out of connected circumstances.

- **Equitable set-off**. This can apply when the claim and the counterclaim arise from the same transaction, or are otherwise so closely connected that it would be inequitable for one claim to be enforced without giving credit for the other. However, it is otherwise much wider than legal set-off, as it is not just a procedural defence.

- **Contractual set-off**. The parties involved may expressly agree the terms on which set-off will apply between them, or indeed the terms on which the forms of set-off described above will be excluded. The terms agreed between the parties are limited only to the extent that they cannot seek to exclude insolvency set-off, as described below.

- **Banker's set-off**. This is the right of a bank to set off a credit balance on one account against the debit balance on another. In practice, however, a bank will almost always extend this right by additional contractual provisions.

- **Insolvency set-off**. A mandatory insolvency set-off regime will automatically come into being once a company enters into either liquidation or a distribution administration, and this regime will override any contrary arrangements which the parties have agreed between themselves. This is discussed further in Sections 2.10.3 and 2.10.4.

45

2.10.3 Set-off in liquidation

2.10.3.1 When will set-off apply?

The special set-off rules will apply where, before the company goes into liquidation, there have been mutual credits, mutual debts or other mutual dealings between the company and any creditor of the company who is entitled to prove for a debt in the liquidation. An account is taken of what is due from each party to the other in respect of their mutual dealings, and the sums due from one party is set off against the sums due from the other (r 4.90 IR 1986).

In this respect:

- The term **mutual** means due between the same parties, acting in the same capacities. Thus, if the company owes a debt to a party acting as trustee for someone else, this cannot be set off against a debt owed to the company by that party in its individual capacity (see *Re: ILG Travel Ltd* [1996] BCC 21). For this purpose different departments of the Crown are treated as if they were the same entity acting in the same capacity. *Secretary of State for Trade and Industry v Frid* [2004] 2 All ER 1042 (the '*Frid*' case), the facts of which are set out in the box below, provides an example of '**Crown set-off**'.

- The term **dealings** should be construed in a wide sense. In the *Frid* case it was held that 'dealings' were not confined to consensual dealings, but could extend to obligations imposed by statute, or a tort. However, a claim arising in tort for conversion has been held not to be one arising from a 'dealing' (*Cosslett (Contractors) Ltd (No 2), Smith v Bridgend County Borough Council* [2002] 1 AC 336).

- The courts have made it clear that this rule is **mandatory**, and therefore it cannot be excluded by agreement between the parties (*Halesowen Presswork and Assemblies Ltd* [1972] AC 785), nor can the courts disapply it (*Re Bank of Credit and Commerce International SA (No 11)* [1997] Ch 213).

After set-off, only the balance (if any) of the amount owed to the creditor is then provable in the company's liquidation. Alternatively, if the debt due to the company exceeds the debt owed by it to the creditor, the company is entitled to recover that balance. However, as would be expected, any part of the balance which results from a contingent or prospective debt owed by the creditor need only be paid if and when it becomes due and payable.

Secretary of State for Trade and Industry v Frid **[2004] 2 All ER 1042 (the 'Frid' case)**

This case usefully illustrates several of the points on set-off discussed here.

A company went into liquidation. Its assets included a VAT credit of £7,185. Its liabilities included compensatory notice pay and redundancy payments due to employees. Under the relevant legislation, the Secretary of State for Trade and Industry ('**S of S**') was liable to pay these employees out of the National Insurance fund ('**NIF**') if the company failed to make those payments – the S of S duly paid the employees £11,574.

The legislation provided that the S of S had a subrogated claim in the liquidation for the sum paid by it. Two other Crown departments also had claims against the company.

HM Customs & Excise notified the liquidator that it proposed to allocate the VAT credit rateably between the three Crown departments and would set off £2,344 out of the £11,574 due to the S of S. The liquidator rejected this approach.

The House of Lords held that:

- the term 'mutual debts' required no more than commensurable cross obligations between the same people in the same capacity;

- that where there was a claim against HM Customs & Excise and a claim by the S of S on behalf of the NIF, the Crown was debtor and creditor in the same capacity; and

- although the debt due to the S of S only became payable once it had paid the insolvent employer's liability, it arose out of a (statutory) obligation which had existed before the date of the liquidation and therefore fell within the set-off regime.

Accordingly the set-off was allowed.

(An important consideration in this case was whether a claim which was only contingent as at the date of the liquidation was available for set-off at all, although subsequent changes to r 4.90 IR 1986 would have made it unnecessary to determine this point had the case been heard today.)

2.10.3.2   What debts are taken into account for these purposes?

A sum is regarded as being due to or from the company for these purposes regardless of whether:

- it is payable at the present or in the future;

- the obligation by virtue of which it is payable is certain or contingent; or

- its amount is fixed or liquidated, or is capable of being ascertained by fixed rules or is a matter of opinion.

Where any obligation to or from the company, by reason of its being subject to any contingency or for any reason does not bear a certain value, its value may be estimated by the liquidator in accordance with r 4.86 IR 1986 (see Chapter 3).

The debt must, however, be one which is **provable** (see the *Frid* case). Chapter 3 considers when a debt is provable. In this context a **secured creditor** is not required to set off monies owed to it by the company unless it elects to give up its security and prove for its debt (*Re Norman Holdings Co Ltd (in liquidation)* [1991] 1 WLR 10).

2.10.3.3   Excluded debts

Certain debts are excluded from this mandatory set-off regime (r 4.90(2) IR 1986). These effectively fall into two categories.

The first category comprises debts arising out of an obligation **incurred** after a certain point in time (for which see below).

The second category comprises debts **acquired** by the creditor by assignment or otherwise pursuant to an agreement between the creditor and any other party which is entered into after a certain point in time (see below) regardless of when the debt was originally incurred. This is designed to prevent people who owe money to the company buying themselves a right of set-off when they know a liquidation or administration is already afoot, or pending. It is the date of the agreement to assign which is important here, not the date on which the assignment actually takes place pursuant to that agreement.

A debt will thus be excluded if the obligation was incurred, or the agreement with the other party entered into (as the case may be):

- at a time when the creditor had notice that a meeting of creditors under s 98 IA 1986 had been summoned or that a winding-up petition was pending (see Chapter 3);

- where the liquidation was immediately preceded by an administration, at a time when the creditor had notice that an application for an administration order was pending or that a person had given notice of intention to appoint an administrator;

- during an administration which immediately preceded the liquidation; or

- after the company went into liquidation.

The word **obligation** means an obligation however arising, whether by virtue of an agreement, rule of law or otherwise.

2.10.4   Set-off in administration

A statutory set-off regime similar to that described above also applies to an administration where the administrator has given notice that he proposes to make a distribution (r 2.85 IR 1986).

Here, a debt will be excluded if the obligation was incurred, or the agreement with the other party entered into (as the case may be):

- after the company entered into administration;

- at a time when the creditor had notice that an application for an administration order was pending or that a person had given notice of intention to appoint an administrator;

- where the administration was immediately preceded by a liquidation, at a time when the creditor had notice that a meeting of creditors under s 98 IA 1986 had been summoned or that a winding-up petition was pending; or

- during a liquidation which immediately preceded the administration.

In *Kaupthing Singer & Friedlander Limited (in administration)* [2010] EWCA Civ 518 the Court of Appeal considered the treatment of **future debts** for the purposes of set-off in an administration. Various customers who had deposits with the company had also been advanced loans which had not yet matured. Future debts owed both to and by a company in either a distribution administration or a liquidation would normally be valued in accordance with the formula set out in Section 3.10.7, but it became clear that that produced a distorted result in favour of customers with long loans. The Court of Appeal held that the debts owed by and to the company should be set off against each other at their value at the time of the distribution and, to the extent that a balance remained owing by the other party following the set-off, it should remain payable on its original maturity date at its non-discounted amount.

2.10.5   Set-off in other insolvency procedures

Insolvency set-off does not apply to formal insolvency processes other than a liquidation or distribution administration (see *Isovel Contracts Ltd v ABB Building Technologies Ltd* [2002] 1 BCLC 390, a case concerning the 'old' administration regime). In particular, there are no special rules to deal with set-off in a CVA, and therefore notwithstanding that the debt due from the company to a creditor has been compromised, the company may still be able to recover any debt due to it from that creditor in full.

Chapter 3

Liquidation

3.1 INTRODUCTION

Chapter 1 gave an overview of the liquidation process and explained the distinction between voluntary liquidation and compulsory liquidation, and between the two types of voluntary liquidation, members' voluntary liquidation ('**MVL**') and creditors' voluntary liquidation ('**CVL**'). Chapter 2 considered the way in which a company's assets will be distributed between its creditors on a liquidation. Chapter 6 will consider the duties of directors, including their duties after a company has gone into liquidation.

This chapter now considers voluntary liquidation and compulsory liquidation in more detail, and in particular:

* the uses of each type of liquidation;

* the method of commencement of each type of liquidation;

* the powers and duties of a liquidator; and

* the mechanisms by which unsecured creditors prove for their debts and a distribution is made.

3.2 WHAT ARE THE USES OF EACH TYPE OF LIQUIDATION?

3.2.1 Uses of an MVL

An MVL is most likely to be used:

* where there is no perceived purpose in a company remaining in existence; and/or

* to allow shareholders to extract value from the company in circumstances where it is not possible to make distribution to them under the relevant provisions of the Companies Acts.

An MVL may well be used, for example, as part of a restructuring or rationalisation of a group of companies with many subsidiaries. It is most likely to be considered as an alternative to dissolution of the company, rather than as an alternative to other formal insolvency procedures.

3.2.2 Uses of a CVL

A CVL is most likely to be used where:

* the company is, or is likely to become, unable to pay its debts, and the **shareholders** take the view that there is unlikely to be any value in preserving the company's business; **or**

- immediately following an administration, as a distribution mechanism and/or to take advantage of a liquidator's greater powers to pursue directors and other third parties.

A CVL is most likely to be considered as an alternative to administration, or as the final remaining option where neither a restructuring of debt nor another formal insolvency process is likely to be possible.

It is possible to use a CVL as a tool for eliminating a company where there is no perceived purpose in it remaining in existence but where the directors are unable or unwilling to swear a declaration of solvency. However, there are also certain disadvantages, as set out in Table 3.1.

Table 3.1 – Disadvantages of CVL as opposed to an MVL

- In a CVL, the creditors rather than the shareholders have the ultimate say in the choice of liquidator, and are subsequently the controlling force in the process.
- The shareholders may consider that allowing the formal insolvency of their company will generate negative publicity for them. In a CVL, the creditors' meeting must be advertised and the liquidation will be recorded as an insolvent liquidation at Companies House, so the process will become public.
- Following a CVL, directors may well be required to disclose that they have been directors of a company which has entered into insolvent liquidation to the Financial Conduct Authority (where applicable) and/or when becoming involved with future business ventures.
- The insolvent liquidation of the company may cross-default finance or other agreements elsewhere within the group of companies.
- In an insolvent liquidation, the liquidator is obliged to submit a standard form report on the conduct of persons who are or have been directors of the company to the Department for Business, Innovation and Skills (BIS) who will use it to consider whether directors' disqualification proceedings are merited (see Chapter 6).
- Restrictions under s 216 IA 1986 (the **'Phoenix trading'** provisions) prevent persons who have been directors of the company during the 12 months prior to the insolvency being directors, or concerned in the management, of any other company with the same or a similar name at any time during the following five years, subject to certain exceptions (see Chapter 6). There is, amongst other things, a risk that this may inadvertently affect persons who are directors of multiple companies within groups of companies.

3.2.3   Uses of compulsory liquidation

Section 3.4 considers all of the situations where a winding-up petition can be presented, but a compulsory liquidation is most likely to occur where:

- a **creditor** takes action to recover the debt due to him; **or**

- one or more **creditors** take action to convert a CVL into a compulsory liquidation because they are concerned that the liquidator in the CVL is giving insufficient scrutiny to the company's affairs and possible actions against directors and other third parties; **or**

- the **directors** are concerned that the company is, or is likely to become, unable to pay its debts but are unable to persuade the shareholders to place the company into a CVL, or

- the shareholders wish to place the company into insolvent liquidation but are content for the Official Receiver to be appointed as liquidator.

In practice, a company is likely to allow itself to be placed into compulsory liquidation only where a restructuring of debt or other formal insolvency process cannot be achieved, or where it concludes that there is no longer any benefit in saving the company.

Table 3.2 looks at the advantages and disadvantages of a CVL compared to a compulsory liquidation.

Table 3.2 – CVL *versus* compulsory liquidation

Advantages of CVL:

Commencement of process is quicker and more convenient.

Private liquidator appointed from the outset.

Shareholders/directors have greater influence over the choice of liquidator.

Less need for involvement for the court or Official Receiver.

Disadvantages of CVL:

Creditor concerns that the liquidator will give insufficient scrutiny to the company's affairs and possible actions against directors and other third parties.

Need for a shareholders' resolution means that directors themselves cannot instigate.

Need sufficient assets in the company (or outside funding) to pay private liquidator's fees.

3.3   COMMENCING A VOLUNTARY LIQUIDATION

3.3.1   Initial steps common to either type of voluntary liquidation

Table 3.3 shows, in flowchart form, the voluntary liquidation process. There are a number of steps common to both an MVL and a CVL.

- The company would normally identify its **proposed liquidator** (although they are not obliged to do so – see below). The liquidator will be a partner or employee of a private sector firm. The proposed liquidator and their staff will usually guide the directors (and shareholders) through the pre-commencement process as well. Because of the conflict of interest which might otherwise arise, a liquidator from the firm which has acted as the company's **auditors** may not act as a liquidator in a CVL. However, the same absolute rule does not apply in the case of an MVL, and a liquidator from such a firm may prove a good choice due to the firm's existing knowledge of the company provided there is no conflict – different firms may have different internal policies in this regard.

- The directors hold a **board meeting** at which they resolve to recommend to the shareholders that the company enter into voluntary liquidation, and to convene a meeting of the shareholders if necessary. In the case of an MVL they will also resolve to make a statutory declaration of solvency.

- The company must give advance written notice of the resolution to any **qualifying floating charge holder** (or 'QFCH') (s 84(2A) IA 1986). The resolution may only be passed at the end of the period of five business days

52

Table 3.3 – The voluntary liquidation process

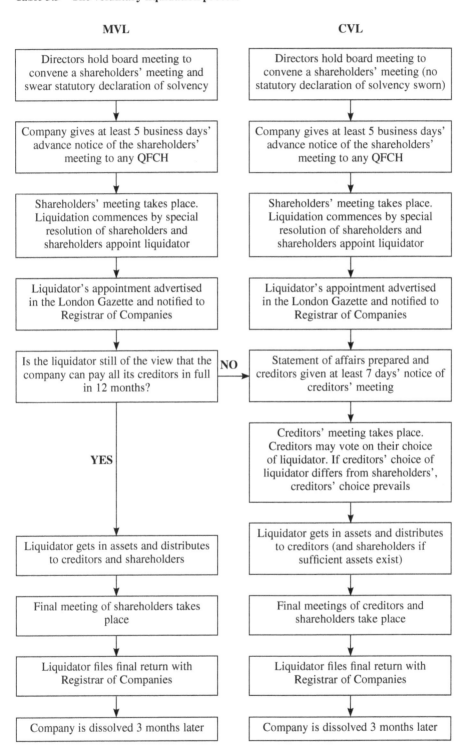

MVL

CVL

Directors hold board meeting to convene a shareholders' meeting and swear statutory declaration of solvency

Directors hold board meeting to convene a shareholders' meeting (no statutory declaration of solvency sworn)

Company gives at least 5 business days' advance notice of the shareholders' meeting to any QFCH

Company gives at least 5 business days' advance notice of the shareholders' meeting to any QFCH

Shareholders' meeting takes place. Liquidation commences by special resolution of shareholders and shareholders appoint liquidator

Shareholders' meeting takes place. Liquidation commences by special resolution of shareholders and shareholders appoint liquidator

Liquidator's appointment advertised in the London Gazette and notified to Registrar of Companies

Liquidator's appointment advertised in the London Gazette and notified to Registrar of Companies

Is the liquidator still of the view that the company can pay all its creditors in full in 12 months? NO

Statement of affairs prepared and creditors given at least 7 days' notice of creditors' meeting

YES

Creditors' meeting takes place. Creditors may vote on their choice of liquidator. If creditors' choice of liquidator differs from shareholders', creditors' choice prevails

Liquidator gets in assets and distributes to creditors and shareholders

Liquidator gets in assets and distributes to creditors (and shareholders if sufficient assets exist)

Final meeting of shareholders takes place

Final meetings of creditors and shareholders take place

Liquidator files final return with Registrar of Companies

Liquidator files final return with Registrar of Companies

Company is dissolved 3 months later

Company is dissolved 3 months later

beginning with the day the notice was given, or if the qualifying floating charge holder so consents in writing. The requirement is more likely to be relevant for a CVL than an MVL. (Chapter 4 explains the meaning of the term QFCH.)

- At the shareholders' meeting, a special resolution must be passed to wind up the company (s 84(1) IA 1986). A resolution would normally also be passed to appoint the liquidator, although it is possible for the shareholders to appoint the liquidator later or to leave the choice to the creditors in a CVL. It is normal also to include a resolution setting out the basis on which the liquidator's fees will be paid, and if there are joint liquidators, to allow each to exercise the liquidator's powers individually. Any appointed liquidator needs to provide a statement to the meeting that he is an insolvency practitioner duly qualified to act as a liquidator and that he accepts the appointment.

- The liquidator's **appointment takes effect** once the shareholders' resolution is passed appointing him (s 86 IA 1986).

- The company is required to give notice of the resolution in the **London Gazette** within 14 days after its passing (s 85 IA 1986) and to register it at **Companies House** within 15 days (s 84(3) IA 1986).

3.3.2 Additional requirements for an MVL

3.3.2.1 The statutory declaration

For a liquidation to be an MVL, the directors need also to make a **statutory declaration of solvency** before an English-qualified solicitor or their equivalent (s 90 IA 1986). The liquidation will otherwise be a CVL. The requirements for this declaration are set out in s 89 IA 1986. It must:

- be sworn by all or a majority of the directors;

- state that the directors have made a full inquiry into the company's affairs and that having done so they have formed the opinion that the company will be able to pay its debts in full (together with interest at the statutory rate) within the period stated in the declaration, which must not exceed 12 months from the commencement of the winding-up;

- be made no more than five weeks before the shareholders' resolution is passed;

- include a statement of the company's assets and liabilities as at the last practicable date before the declaration; and

- be delivered to the Registrar of Companies within 15 days.

This is **not** a declaration that the company is solvent. It is still possible for the directors to make this even where a company remains balance sheet insolvent, provided that it can still be sure of paying its debts. The route commonly adopted in practice is for the shareholder(s), or another connected entity, to provide an indemnity to the company to the effect that, if the company's assets transpire to be insufficient, they will make good the shortfall.

However, the declaration needs to be taken seriously. A director making the declaration who has **no reasonable grounds** for the opinion stated is liable to imprisonment or a fine, or both. Furthermore, if the debts, together with interest, are not paid in full within the period stated, there is a rebuttable presumption that he did not have reasonable grounds.

3.3.2.2 Conversion to a CVL

If at any time during the course of an MVL the liquidator forms the opinion that the company will not be able to pay its debts in full plus interest within the period stated in the statutory declaration, he **must** summon a creditors' meeting within the following 28 days and make out a statement of affairs to lay before that meeting (s 95 IA 1986). The creditors' meeting will then take place as if it were a Section 98 meeting (see Section 3.3.3.1) and the liquidation will become a CVL.

3.3.3 Additional requirements for a CVL

In an MVL, the creditors need have no great involvement in the process beyond proving their debts, since they can expect to be paid in full. Since they have no similar expectation in a CVL, they are given a considerably greater say in the CVL process.

3.3.3.1 Summoning a creditors' meeting

The company must summon a meeting of its creditors **within 14 days** of the date on which the winding-up resolution was passed. The creditors must be given **at least seven days' notice** of the meeting by post. In addition, the meeting must be advertised in the London Gazette (s 98(1A) IA 1986 – such a meeting is accordingly often termed the '**Section 98 meeting**'). Common practice, however, is to hold the creditors' meeting immediately after the shareholders' meeting, and therefore to deal with any notice requirements for the creditors' meeting before the shareholders place the company into liquidation.

The **notice of the meeting** needs to state **either** the name of a qualified insolvency practitioner who, prior to the date of the meeting, will furnish creditors free of charge with such information as they may reasonably require concerning the company's affairs **or** a place where, on the two business days prior to the meeting, a list of the names and addresses of the company's creditors will be available for inspection free of charge (s 98(2) IA 1986). It should also specify a place where (and a time by which) creditors may lodge proof of debt and proxies to allow them to vote at the meeting (r 4.51(2) IR 1986, and see Section 3.3.3.3).

3.3.3.2 The function of the creditors' meeting

Creditors' meetings may take various forms. Some will be lively occasions, attended by many creditors. Others may be attended only by a couple of insolvency practitioners holding proxies.

The directors must appoint one of their number to preside over the meeting as **chairman**. In practice, any existing liquidator is likely also to play a dominant role at the meeting. However, the meeting will give the creditors the opportunity to ask questions of at least one director both on the statement of affairs (see Chapter 6) and more generally.

However, perhaps the most important function of the meeting is to give the creditors the opportunity to vote to appoint their **own choice of liquidator** in place of that of the shareholders (s 100 IA 1986). Accordingly, insolvency practitioners will often agree to represent particular creditors at the meeting if they see a prospect of securing an appointment. Any shareholder, director or creditor is, in turn, entitled to appeal to the court within the seven days following the meeting for an order directing that the creditors' choice of liquidator is appointed jointly with the shareholders' choice, or appointing some person other than the creditors' choice. Accordingly, a compromise will sometimes be reached at the meeting where joint liquidators from two different firms are appointed, and the joint liquidator chosen by the creditors assumes particular responsibility for investigating the whereabouts of assets and the conduct of directors.

The creditors may also appoint a **liquidation committee** at this meeting. If such a committee is formed, it is likely to hold its first meeting immediately after the creditors' meeting. The liquidation committee is discussed further in Section 3.9.2.

3.3.3.3   Voting at the creditors' meeting

Rules 4.63 to 4.70 IR 1986 set out the procedure for voting at this, and any other, creditors' meetings and rr 8.1 to 8.8 set out further requirements in relation to proxies, but an overview is given here.

A resolution will be passed when a **majority by value** of those present and voting, in person or by proxy, have voted in favour. When the vote concerns the appointment of a liquidator, and there are multiple candidates, the liquidator selected must have a clear majority over all of the others, and successive votes may need to be held (with the candidate receiving the fewest number of votes last time dropping out of the next vote).

The **proxy** may be worded to state that the representative is only entitled to vote in one particular way. This may be the creditor's preferred approach where they wish simply to appoint the chairman of the meeting as their proxy. Where the creditor's own representative will attend, however, it may be wiser to return an 'open' proxy, which allows the representative to vote according to their discretion.

A creditor will only be **entitled to vote** if a proof of his debt and (if relevant) a proxy appointing his representative have been lodged by the time stated in the notice of the meeting, although the chairman has a discretion to allow the creditor to vote notwithstanding non-compliance with this.

A creditor is not entitled to vote on an **unliquidated debt**, or one whose value is unascertained, save to the extent that the chairman agrees to put a value on it, although in *HMRC v Maxwell* [2010] EWCA Civ 1379 (a case relating to a vote of creditors in an administration), the Court of Appeal indicated the chairman must do his best to assess the minimum value of the claim. The chairman also has a general discretion to **accept or reject proofs**, although in situations of doubt, the proper course is to mark the vote as '**objected to**' and to allow the creditor to vote. The vote may subsequently be declared invalid if the objection is sustained. There is a right to appeal to the court against a chairman's decision provided the appeal is made no later than 21 days after the date of the meeting and the court may make such order as it thinks just.

As can be seen, the decision to accept or reject a proof for voting purposes at the meeting is made on a comparatively *ad hoc* basis. It is **not conclusive for other subsequent purposes**, such as that of establishing the value of the claim for dividend purposes (*Re Assico Engineering Ltd* [2002] BCC 481).

3.3.3.4   What happens during any interlude between the shareholders' and creditors' meetings?

Under s 166 IA 1986, where a liquidator has been nominated by the company, he shall not exercise his powers (without the permission of the court) prior to the creditors' meeting except:

* to take the company's property into his custody or under their control;

* to dispose of perishable goods, or other goods whose value is likely to diminish if not immediately disposed of; and

* to do such other things as are necessary to protect the company's assets.

This section, together with s 114 IA 1986 (see Chapter 6) therefore protects the creditors until they have had the chance to vote on their own choice of liquidator.

3.3.4   Conversion to a compulsory liquidation

A voluntary liquidation does not prevent any creditor or contributory (or in certain circumstances the Official Receiver) from presenting a winding-up petition (see Section 3.4). The court may be inclined to make a winding-up order where circumstances suggest that an impartial investigation of the company's affairs is required (*Re Gordon & Breach Science Publishers Limited* [1995] BCC 261).

3.4   COMMENCING A COMPULSORY LIQUIDATION

3.4.1   When does the court have jurisdiction to wind up a company?

Table 3.4 shows, in flowchart form, the compulsory winding-up process. Under s 122(1) IA 1986, a company may be wound up by the court if, amongst other things:

* the company has by **special resolution** resolved that it be wound up by the court (s 122(1)(a)); or

* the company is **unable to pay its debts** (s 122(1)(f)); or

* at the time at which a **moratorium** for the company under s 1A IA 1986 (see Chapter 7) **comes to an end**, no voluntary arrangement approved under Part I IA 1986 has effect in relation to the company (s 122(1)(fa)); or

* the court is of the opinion that it is **just and equitable** that the company should be wound up (s 122(1)(g)).

The court has an overriding discretion as to whether to make a winding-up order and may refuse to do so if an alternative appears more appropriate (Re *Harrods (Buenos Aires) Limited* [1991] BCC 249).

Table 3.4 – The compulsory liquidation process

Petitioner presents a winding-up petition at the court and serves it on the company

↓

Petitioner advertises the petition in the London Gazette no less than 7 business days before the hearing date

↓

Hearing of the petition by the court. If a winding-up order is made, the Official Receiver becomes liquidator

↓

Official Receiver reports to the creditors and invites them to submit proofs of debt

↓

Official Receiver decides within 12 weeks whether to convene a first meeting of creditors and notifies creditors of his decision. A group of creditors comprising at least 25% by value may require him to convene such a meeting

↓

The first meeting of creditors takes place (if convened). Creditors may appoint a liquidator to replace the Official Receiver

↓

Liquidator gets in assets and distributes to creditors

↓

Final meeting of creditors takes place

↓

Liquidator files final return with the court and Registrar of Companies

↓

Company is dissolved 3 months later

3.4.2   Who can present a winding-up petition?

Under s 124 IA 1986, a petition to wind up the company may be presented to the court by:

- the **company**, or its **directors**; or

- any **creditor** or creditors (including any contingent or prospective creditor or creditors – see *Re Dollar Land Holdings* [1994] BCLC 404); or

- a **shareholder** (subject to certain provisos, outlined in s 124 IA 1986); or

- a **liquidator** or **temporary administrator** (within the meaning of the EC Insolvency Regulation); or

- the designated **officer of a magistrates' court** in the exercise of the powers conferred by s 87A Magistrates' Courts Act 1980 (enforcement of fines imposed on companies)

- or by all or any of the above parties, alone or jointly.

Other sections of the legislation also specifically allow the **supervisor of a CVA**, or an **administrator** or **administrative receiver** to present a petition in the name of the company. Finally, the **Secretary of State** can present a petition on public interest grounds (s 124A IA 1986).

3.4.3   When can a creditor present a petition?

A creditor's petition will almost always be on the grounds that the company is unable to pay its debt, although normal practice is for the petition also to contend, as a 'catch-all', that it is just and equitable that the company should be wound up.

The circumstances where a company will be treated as unable to pay its debts are set out in Chapter 1. There is an advantage to a creditor in serving a **statutory demand** (see rr 4.4 to 4.6 IR 1986) at the company's registered office and then waiting three weeks before presenting a petition. Provided the debt is then neither satisfied nor disputed during that period, the company will be deemed to be unable to pay its debts without the need for the creditor to produce any further evidence of this to the court.

There is nothing to prevent a creditor from presenting a winding-up petition on the basis of an undisputed debt due to them without first serving a statutory demand (*Taylors Industrial Flooring v M & H Plant Hire (Manchester) Ltd* [1990] BCLC 216). As noted in Chapter 1, the non-payment can in itself be treated as evidence that the company is cash-flow insolvent. The creditor need not then, in effect, extend an additional three weeks' credit to the company. However, the risk of not first serving a statutory demand is that it remains far more likely that the company will still successfully be able to contend that the debt is disputed. In addition, a creditor whose real aim is to put pressure on the company should bear in mind that once a winding-up petition is presented it will not always be possible for the company to pay the debt.

As a rule of general practice, the court will not make a winding-up order:

- when the debt is genuinely disputed on substantial grounds (*Stonegate Securities Ltd v Gregory* [1980] 1 Ch 576); or

- where the company has a genuine and serious cross-claim for an amount which exceeds the petition debt (or which, if successful, would reduce the company's net indebtedness below the 'statutory minimum' of £750) and which it has been unable to litigate (*Re Bayoil* [1998] BCC 988).

The courts have made it clear that the presentation of a petition against a solvent company in the above circumstances is an abuse of process. The company may apply to the court to seek an injunction restraining a creditor from presenting a petition, or alternatively from advertising a petition which has already been presented. Furthermore, the courts may penalise the company, and possibly even its legal adviser, in costs on an indemnity basis (see *Re A Company (No 00751 of 1993), ex parte Avocet Aviation Limited* [1992] BCLC 869).

However, the courts have been unprepared to restrain a creditor simply on the basis that the company alleges that a dispute exists (*Re a Company No 006685 of 1996* [1997] BCC 830) or where the opportunity to litigate the cross claim had not been taken (*Southern Cross Group plc v Deka Immoblien Investment* [2005] BPIR 1010). In addition, even where a dispute exists, the court may be prepared in exceptional circumstances to resolve that dispute itself (*Lacontha Foundation v GBI Investments Ltd* [2010] EWHC 37 (Ch)).

The debt must be one which the creditor could otherwise have enforced, so a petition cannot be presented on the basis of a statute-barred debt (*Re Karnos Property Co Ltd (1989)* 5 BCC 14). However, once the creditor has obtained judgment there is no further such time limitation (*Ridgeway Motors (Isleworth) Ltd v ALTS Ltd* [2005] BCC 496).

In *Ebbvale Ltd v Hosking* [2013] UKPC 1, the debt was undisputed, but the company challenged the petition on the basis of the petitioner's motives. The Privy Council held that a petition is not an abuse of process where the petitioner might also gain in some other way from the winding up provided that, objectively, at least one of its purposes behind the petition was to gain an advantage in its capacity as a creditor of the company.

3.4.4   What is the process for a winding-up petition?

The process for petitioning to wind up a company is set out in full in rr 4.7 to 4.21A IR 1986 and *Practice Direction: Insolvency Proceedings* [2007] BCC 842, but an overview is given here.

3.4.4.1   Presenting the petition

The petition will need to be accompanied by a **statement of truth**, often in practice given in the form of a witness statement from the petititioner's solicitor, verifying its content.

In addition to the court fee for presenting the petition, the petitioner must pay a **deposit**, currently £1,165. This is designed to cover the basic costs of the Official Receiver should the company have too few assets to do so. This deposit is refundable if the petition is withdrawn or dismissed.

When the petition is issued, it will be endorsed with a **hearing date**. This might typically be six weeks from the date of issue. The issued petition must be **served** at the company's registered office unless the company itself is the petitioner. The petitioner will need to prove service by a **certificate of service**, which must be filed in court as soon as reasonably practicable after service and in any event not less than five business days before the hearing.

3.4.4.2   Advertising the petition

Unless the court orders otherwise, the petition must be **advertised** in the London Gazette:

●   not less that seven clear business days after it has been served; **but**

●   not less than seven clear business days before the date when the petition is due to be heard.

The advertisement brings the petition to the attention of the outside world, and invites notices from other creditors that wish to appear to support (or oppose) the petition, so it is a critical stage. Given the effect of s 127 IA 1986, as described in Chapter 5, a petitioning creditor whose purpose is to attempt to pressurise the company into payment may well refrain from advertising until as late as possible.

At least five business days before the hearing, the petitioner or its solicitor must file a **certificate of compliance** with the court to confirm compliance with the rules relating to service and to advertisement.

3.4.4.3 Can the petition be withdrawn?

Under r 4.15 IR 1986, the petitioning creditor is entitled to apply for **permission to withdraw** the petition at any time up to five business days before the hearing, but must satisfy the court that:

- the petition has not been advertised;

- they have received no 'notice to appear' (whether of support or opposition) with reference to the petition; and

- the company consents to such an order being made.

The petition can normally otherwise only be withdrawn at the hearing. In addition, even if the petitioning creditor no longer wishes to proceed, the court can substitute any supporting creditor who would have been entitled to bring a petition themselves as petitioner.

3.4.4.4 The court hearing

Under s 125(1) IA 1986, at the hearing, the court may:

- grant the winding-up order;

- dismiss the petition;

- adjourn the hearing conditionally or unconditionally;

- make an interim order; or

- make any other order it thinks fit.

In practice, the petition will normally be listed for hearing in a busy court alongside many other petitions. If it is unopposed, the order is likely to be made swiftly provided all of the correct papers are before the court.

3.4.5 Provisional liquidation

Under s 135 IA 1986, at any time after the presentation of a winding-up petition, the court may appoint the Official Receiver or any other 'fit person' as a provisional liquidator pending the making of a winding-up order. Like a liquidator, any provisional liquidator must be a qualified insolvency practitioner.

In theory, any person entitled to present a winding-up petition is entitled also to apply for the appointment of a provisional liquidator. However, given the serious consequences of such an appointment for the company, any person seeking such an appointment must in practice first convince the court that he is likely to obtain a winding-up order when the petition is heard. Once they have crossed this first threshold, the court will then go on to consider whether to make the appointment as a matter of discretion (*HMRC v Rochdale Drinks Distributors Ltd* [2011] EWCA (Civ) 1116).

The application must make it clear that there is a need for interim control of the company pending a winding-up order, and that only an appointment will ensure that the status quo is maintained (*Re Dry Docks Corporation of London* (1888) 39 Ch D 306). In practice, the majority of applications will be made by creditors who believe that the company's assets are in jeopardy and might be dissipated before the petition is heard by the court. In *Re Namco UK Ltd* [2003] 2 BCLC 78 the court declined to make an appointment as it considered that this was not necessary to maintain the status quo.

The provisional liquidator's powers are conferred by the court order appointing them. The court has a general jurisdiction under s 135(4) IA 1986 in this regard, and may confer, for example, powers corresponding to those set out in Sch 4 IA 1986 (see Section 3.8.1). In practice, however, the court will typically give the provisional liquidators the powers they need to preserve assets, but not the power to distribute assets prior to the petition being heard.

The moratorium on proceedings found in a compulsory liquidation also applies after a provisional liquidator has been appointed (see Section 3.5.4).

3.4.6   Who will be the liquidator?

3.4.6.1   The role of the Official Receiver

When a winding-up order is made the Official Receiver becomes liquidator, and continues in office until some other person is appointed in his place (s 136(2) IA 1986). If the company was previously in voluntary liquidation, the Official Receiver will replace the existing liquidator. Different rules apply, however, when the winding-up order is made immediately after an administration or a CVA, which may allow the existing administrators or CVA supervisor to continue as liquidator (s 140 IA 1986).

The Official Receiver will advertise the fact that the company is in liquidation and notify the registrar of companies. He may require the directors to prepare a statement of affairs under s 131 IA 1986 (see Chapter 6). He has a duty to send a report to creditors and shareholders with respect to the proceedings in the winding-up and the state of the company's affairs (r 4.43 IR 1986). He will in any event contact all creditors of whose addresses he is aware to invite them to submit a proof of debt (see Section 3.10).

3.4.6.2   Can the creditors change the liquidator?

Often where a company has few or no assets no person other than the Official Receiver will be appointed. However, in other cases, creditors may wish to replace the Official Receiver with a private sector liquidator, who they may see as having a greater incentive to investigate and if necessary, to bring actions against third parties. A creditor, or group of creditors, who comprise at least **one-quarter by value** of the company's creditors may at any time require the Official Receiver to summon meetings of creditors and shareholders to choose another liquidator (s 136(5)(c) IA 1986). The creditors may choose to appoint a liquidation committee at this same meeting.

The Official Receiver also has a duty to decide within the period of 12 weeks after the order whether to summon such a meeting of his own motion. If he decides not to do so, he must give notice of his decision to the creditors and shareholders (ss 136(5) (a) and (b) IA 1986).

Finally, the Official Receiver has the ability to apply to the Secretary of State for the appointment of another liquidator in his place. Indeed, he has a duty to do so if he has summoned meetings as above, but no other liquidator is chosen (s 137 IA 1986).

3.5   WHAT ARE THE OTHER CONSEQUENCES OF LIQUIDATION?

3.5.1   What is the effect on the directors?

The role of the directors in a liquidation is discussed further in Chapter 6.

3.5.2   The company's business and status

Once a company is in voluntary liquidation, it must cease to carry on business, except as may be required for its beneficial winding-up. It is a matter for the liquidator's judgment as to when it remains beneficial to carry on the business. However, the corporate status and corporate powers of the company continue until the company is dissolved, notwithstanding anything to the contrary in its articles (s 87 IA 1986). In a compulsory liquidation, the liquidator may carry on the company's business so far as may be necessary for its beneficial winding-up, although he is likely to need the sanction of any liquidation committee (s 167(1)(a) IA 1986).

3.5.3   Transfers of shares in the company

Once the company is in a voluntary liquidation, any subsequent transfer of shares or alteration in the status of the company's shareholders is void unless sanctioned by the liquidator (s 88 IA 1986). So far as a compulsory liquidation is concerned, any transfer of shares made after the date on which the winding-up petition is presented is void unless the court orders otherwise (s 127(1) IA 1986, as discussed further in Chapter 5).

3.5.4   Effect on proceedings

In a compulsory liquidation, or where a provisional liquidator has been appointed, no proceedings or actions may be commenced or continued against the company or its property except by leave of the court and subject to such terms as are imposed by the courts (s 130(2) IA 1986). The underlying rationale for this is the *pari passu* principle, under which all claimants are expected to submit to the procedural scheme for proving claims in the winding-up. The court is likely to refuse leave if it considers that the issues in the action can be dealt with equally conveniently and less expensively in the winding-up.

In deciding whether to grant leave, the court does, however, have a complete discretion to do what is right and fair in the circumstances (*Re Aro Ltd* [1980] Ch 196). For example, leave has been given where:

- the company is insured, and the insurer will fund the company to pay any judgment; and

- the claim against the company involved issues common to a claim against third parties which is close to trial (*New Cap Reinsurance Corp Ltd v HIH Casualty & General Insurance Ltd* [2002] 2 BCLC 228).

In a voluntary liquidation there is no automatic stay of proceedings. The liquidator must make an application for a stay under his general powers to apply to the court: s 112 IA 1986. One court has suggested that the principles which should be applied are similar to those in a compulsory winding-up (*Westbury v Twigg & Co* [1892] 1 QB 77). Another has said that where it is largely just a question of determining quantum the court will normally grant such a stay, but that where the liability is being disputed the stay should normally only be granted in special circumstances (*Currie v Consolidated Kent Collieries Corp Ltd* [1906] 1 KB 134).

The normal **time limits** for commencing proceedings under the Limitation Act 1980 stop running when a winding-up order is made, so a creditor does not have to commence proceedings to simply avoid losing their rights against the company (*Re Cases of Taff's Wells Ltd* [1992] BCLC 11).

3.5.5   Effect on contracts

Liquidation does not in itself terminate the contracts of a company (*BCCI v Malik* [1996] BCC 15). Contracts of employment are a special case, however (see Chapter 9).

The terms of the contract itself may of course provide that it automatically comes to an end on liquidation or, more normally, that the other party has the opportunity to terminate. Alternatively, the company in liquidation may indicate that it is no longer able to perform its obligations under the contract, and the resulting breach will give the other party the ability to terminate and/or to prove for damages. However, the latter remedy may be of limited use against an insolvent company.

The liquidator's ability to disclaim onerous contracts will also be relevant here (see Section 3.6).

3.5.6   What is the effect on the company's documentation?

During any liquidation, every invoice, order for goods, business letter or order form (whether in physical or electronic form) sent by or on behalf of the company is required to state that the company is in liquidation. All of the company's websites must contain a similar statement. Either the liquidator or any officer of the company commits an offence if they knowingly and willingly authorise or permit a contravention of these requirements (s 188 IA 1986).

3.6   DISCLAIMER

3.6.1   When is a liquidator able to exercise a power of disclaimer?

Under s 178 IA 1986, a liquidator may disclaim any onerous property. This section defines 'onerous property' to mean 'any unprofitable contract, or any other property of the company which is unsaleable or not readily saleable or is such that it may give rise to a liability to pay money or perform any other onerous act'. This power is unique to a liquidator – administrators, for example, are not given any equivalent power.

The underlying purposes of disclaimer are:

- to allow the liquidator to complete the liquidation without being impeded by continuing obligations under contracts or continuing ownership of other property which are of no value to the company; and

- to avoid continuing liabilities in respect of onerous property which would otherwise be payable as liquidation expenses to the detriment of other creditors.

A notice of disclaimer must be sent to various parties interested in the property. A copy must also be sent to the Registrar of Companies and, where the disclaimer is of registered land, to the Chief Land Registrar, as specified in more detail in rr 4.187 to 4.190A IR 1986. (There was once a requirement that a copy of the notice of disclaimer be filed in court, and that the court be kept updated regarding the disclaimer, but as a result of changes to the legislation, this is no longer a requirement). Under s 179 IA 1986 any disclaimer of property of a **leasehold** nature does not take effect unless a copy of the disclaimer has been served on every underlessee and mortgagee.

A liquidator must disclaim an entire contract if he exercises this power – he cannot simply disclaim the unfavourable terms of the contract.

3.6.1.1   What is an 'unprofitable contract'?

In *Transmetro Corp Limited v Real Investment Limited Pty* (1999) 17 ACLC 1314, the Supreme Court of Queensland reviewed the case law and set out a summary of the principles to be extracted from prior authority to determine whether a contract was unprofitable:

- A contract is unprofitable ... if it imposes on the company continuing financial obligations which may be regarded as detrimental to the creditors, which presumably means that the contract confers no sufficient reciprocal benefit.

- Before a contract may be unprofitable [for these purposes] it must give rise to prospective liabilities.

- Contracts which will delay the winding-up of the company's affairs because they are to be performed over a substantial period of time and will involve expenditure that may not be recovered are unprofitable.

- No case has decided that a contract is unprofitable merely because it is financially disadvantageous. The cases focus on the nature and cause of the disadvantage.

- A contract is not unprofitable merely because the company could have made, or could make, a better bargain.

This summary was adopted in England in *Re SSSL Realisations (2002) Limited (In Liquidation)* [2006] Ch 610, where the court held that a deed which subordinated a debt due to the company to a debt due to one of the debtor's other creditors could not be disclaimed.

3.6.1.2   What is 'property' for these purposes?

The meaning given to the term 'property' by the insolvency legislation is considered in Chapter 2. The courts have, for example, held a waste management licence to be property which may be disclaimed (*Celtic Extraction Ltd v Bluestone Chemicals Ltd v Environment Agency* [2001] Ch 475). The court in the *SSSL Realisations* case stated that for something to qualify as property, it must involve 'some element of benefit or entitlement for the person holding it'. A deed which simply imposed a disability on the company did not fall into this category.

3.6.2   What is the effect of a disclaimer?

Section 178(4) IA 1986 provides that a disclaimer operates to determine, as from the date of the disclaimer, the rights, interests and liabilities of the company in respect of the property disclaimed. Unless a vesting order is made by the court (see Section 3.6.4), disclaimed property vests *bona vacantia* in the Crown.

However, it does not affect the rights or liabilities of any other person, except so far as is necessary for the purpose of releasing the company from any liability. As such, for example, if a lease is disclaimed, the company's rights and obligations come to an end, but the liabilities of any guarantor continue (see *Hindcastle Ltd v Barbara Attenborough Associates Ltd* [1997] AC 70).

3.6.3   When may a notice of disclaimer not be given?

Under s 178(5) IA 1986 a notice of disclaimer shall not be given if a person interested in property has applied in writing to the liquidator requiring him to decide whether he will disclaim and the liquidator fails to do so within 28 days (or such longer period as the court may allow). This tends to be seen as a useful way of pressurising a liquidator into making an early decision.

A liquidator is also specifically prohibited from disclaiming certain contracts. These include a 'market contract' or contract effected by an exchange or clearing house for the purpose of realising property provided as margin in relation to market contracts (s 164(1) CA 1989) or a transfer order or a contract for the purpose of realising security in a payment and securities settlement systems (reg 16 of the Financial Markets and Insolvency (Settlement Finality) Regulations 1999).

3.6.4   What is the remedy of a party affected by the disclaimer?

Under s 178(6) IA 1986, any person sustaining loss or damage in consequence of a disclaimer is deemed to be a creditor of the company to the extent of the loss or damage and may prove in the liquidation. In *Re Park Air Services plc* [2000] 2 AC 172, the House of Lords accordingly held that, following a disclaimer, a landlord's claim was not for further rent but for statutory compensation, calculated as if he was claiming damages under a contract which had been wrongfully terminated. They gave guidance on calculating the compensation in question.

Under s 181 IA 1986:

• 	any person claiming an interest in the disclaimed property; or

- any person under a liability in respect of the disclaimed property which has not been discharged by the disclaimer

may apply to the court for an **order vesting** the disclaimed property in them, or their trustee. It seems that the interest involved must be a proprietary, and not merely a financial interest (*Lloyds Bank SF Nominees v Aladdin Ltd (in liquidation)* [1996] 1 BCLC 720, but cf *Re Vedmay Ltd* [1994] 1 BCLC 676). The legislation also makes further provisions in relation to property of a leasehold nature (see s 182 IA 1986).

3.7   DUTIES OF THE LIQUIDATOR

3.7.1   What are the liquidator's principal functions?

The functions of the liquidator in a compulsory liquidation are to secure that the assets of the company are got in, realised and distributed to the company's creditors and, if there is a surplus, to the persons entitled to it (s 143 IA 1986). The functions of a liquidator in a voluntary liquidation are not expressed in quite the same way (s 107 IA 1986 is the closest analogous provision), although in practice his functions are similar.

3.7.2   What are the liquidator's specific duties?

A liquidator has a number of specific duties stemming from the above functions, or from other specific statutory requirements. These include:

- In a compulsory liquidation, a duty to **take under his control** all of the property and other things in action to which the company is, or appears to be entitled (s 144 IA 1986).

- A duty to **investigate the affairs** of the company (see, for example, *Re Pantmaenog Timber Co Ltd* [2004] 1 AC 158). In a compulsory liquidation the Official Receiver is under a parallel duty to investigate the causes of the company's failure and generally the promotion, formation, business, dealings and affairs of the company even if he is not the liquidator (s 132 IA 1986).

- A duty to **keep and retain accounts** (reg 15(1) of the Insolvency Regulations 1994 (SI 1994/2507)).

- In a CVL or a compulsory liquidation, a duty to **report on directors' conduct**, as discussed further in Chapter 6.

- A duty to **settle a list of contributories**, ie to determine which of the company's shareholders are liable to contribute to the company in a winding-up (s 165(4) IA 1986 for a voluntary liquidation, and s 148 IA 1986 and r 4.195 IR 1986 for a compulsory liquidation).

- A duty to **determine and discharge the liabilities** of the company (s 165(5) IA 1986 for a voluntary liquidation, and s 148 IA 1986 and r 4.179 IR 1986 for a compulsory liquidation). This is discussed further in Section 3.10.

3.7.3   What are their other general duties?

Liquidators must also observe certain more general duties when exercising their powers:

- A duty to avoid a **conflict of interests** between the liquidator's own interests and the interests of those he is expected to protect, and to act **impartially** when there is a conflict of interests between different creditors or subsidiaries or indeed between different companies where he may have been appointed liquidator (see, for example, *Re Rubber & Produce Investment Trust* [1915] 1 Ch 382). In practice, the rules of the liquidator's professional body may well also cover this area.

- A duty to **exercise skill and care** in performing his duties (*Windsor Steam Coal Company (1901) Ltd* [1929] Ch 151).

- In a compulsory liquidation, the liquidator, however appointed, is an **officer of the court** and thus under its control (s 167(3) IA 1986). As such he also has a duty, when exercising his powers to **act fairly and honourably** and not merely to rely upon his strict legal rights. This principle derives originally from the bankruptcy case of *Re Condon, Ex parte James* (1874) 9 Ch App 609 and is often referred to as the '**rule in ex parte James**'. (A liquidator in a voluntary liquidation is not an officer of the court – *In re T H Knitwear (Wholesale) Ltd* [1988] Ch 275.)

3.7.4　What is the remedy for a breach of duty?

If the liquidator fails to comply with his duties an action can be brought against him under s 212 IA 1986 (described in Chapter 6). As a general principle, however, the liquidator does not owe duties to any individual creditor (see *Hague v Nam Tai Electronics* [2008] UKPC 13). It was suggested in *A & J Fabrications Ltd v Grant Thornton* [1999] BCC 807 that a liquidator might owe a duty to individual creditors as a result of a direct contract or where those creditors had suffered some special damage.

The person aggrieved may alternatively wish to apply to court for the liquidator to be removed (s 108(2) IA 1986 for a voluntary liquidation and see, for example, *Re Keypak Homecare Ltd* (1987) 3 BCC 558).

3.8　POWERS OF THE LIQUIDATOR

3.8.1　What are the main powers of a liquidator?

The main powers which a liquidator requires in order to allow him to carry out his duties are contained in Sch 4 IA 1986. These are set out in Table 3.5. As can be seen, the liquidator will however require sanction in order to exercise certain of these powers. The necessary sanction must be obtained:

- in an MVL, by a resolution of the shareholders;

- in a CVL, from the court or the liquidation committee (or if there is no such committee, a meeting of the company's creditors); and

- in a compulsory liquidation, from the court or the liquidation committee.

(See s 165 IA 1986 for a voluntary liquidation and s 167 IA 1986 for a compulsory liquidation.)

Table 3.5 – Powers of an English liquidator

PART I – POWERS EXERCISABLE WITH SANCTION

1   Power to pay any class of creditors in full.

2   Power to make any compromise or arrangement with creditors or persons claiming to be creditors, or having or alleging themselves to have any claim (present or future, certain or contingent, ascertained or sounding only in damages) against the company, or whereby the company may be rendered liable.

3A   Power to bring legal proceedings under ss 213, 214, 238, 239, 242, 243 or 423 IA 1986.

PART II – POWERS EXERCISABLE WITHOUT SANCTION IN VOLUNTARY LIQUIDATION, WITH SANCTION IN COMPULSORY LIQUIDATION

4   Power to bring or defend any action or other legal proceeding in the name and on behalf of the company.

5   Power to carry on the business of the company so far as may be necessary for its beneficial winding-up.

PART III – POWERS EXERCISABLE WITHOUT SANCTION IN ANY LIQUIDATION

6   Power to sell any of the company's property by public auction or private contract, with power to transfer the whole of it to any person or to sell the same in parcels.

6A   Power to compromise, on such terms as may be agreed:

(a) all calls and liabilities to calls, all debts and liabilities capable of resulting in debts, and all claims (present or future, certain or contingent, ascertained or sounding only in damages) subsisting or supposed to subsist between the company and a contributory or alleged contributory or other debtor or person apprehending liability to the company; and

(b) subject to paragraph 2 above, all questions in any way relating to or affecting the assets or the winding-up of the company, and take any security for the discharge of any such call, debt, liability or claim and give a complete discharge in respect of it.

7   Power to do all acts and execute, in the name and on behalf of the company, all deeds, receipts and other documents and for that purpose to use, when necessary, the company's seal.

8   Power to prove, rank and claim in the bankruptcy, insolvency or sequestration of any contributory for any balance against his estate, and to receive dividends in the bankruptcy, insolvency or sequestration in respect of that balance, as a separate debt due from the bankrupt or insolvent, and rateably with the other separate creditors.

9   Power to draw, accept, make and indorse any bill of exchange or promissory note in the name and on behalf of the company, with the same effect with respect to the company's liability as if the bill or note had been drawn, accepted, made or indorsed by or on behalf of the company in the course of its business.

10   Power to raise on the security of the assets of the company any money requisite.

11   Power to take out in his official name letters of administration to any deceased contributory, and to do in his official name any other act necessary for obtaining payment of any money due from a contributory or his estate which cannot conveniently be done in the name of the company. In all such cases the money due is deemed, for the purpose of enabling the liquidator to take out the letters of administration or recover the money, to be due to the liquidator himself.

12   Power to appoint an agent to do any business which the liquidator is unable to do himself.

13   Power to do all such other things as may be necessary for winding-up the company's affairs and distributing its assets.

3.8.2 Specific powers of investigation

Certain specific powers are also granted to the liquidator under ss 234 and 236 IA 1986 to assist them in performing their investigative duties. Note the liquidator will also be assisted by the directors' and employees' duty to co-operate with the insolvency officeholder under s 235 IA 1986 (as discussed in Chapter 6).

These powers, coupled with the powers described in Section 3.8.3, mean that liquidation is probably the most useful formal insolvency procedure for investigating and bringing claims to swell the assets of a company.

In *Re Hellas Telecommunications (Luxembourg) II SCA (in administration)* [2011] EWHC 3176 (Ch), the court refused to allow the company to be dissolved at the end of its administration but instead ordered that it go into compulsory liquidation. When making the original administration order the court had also specifically sanctioned a pre-packaged sale to a specified buyer (see Section 4.11.5). As a term of the sale, that buyer had provided a €10 million fund to be used for certain purposes of the administration. The court noted, that despite the administrators' use of part of this sum to fund investigations, they had not managed fully to clarify why the company had suffered such large and catastrophic losses. The court took the view therefore that, rather than being returned to the buyer, the balance of this sum should be retained to fund further investigations by the liquidator. The court outlined the additional powers which a liquidator had both to carry out investigations and to bring proceedings (see Section 3.8.3).

3.8.2.1   Getting in the company's property

Under s 234 IA 1986, where any person has in his possession or control and property, books, papers or records to which the company appears to be entitled, the court may direct that person to hand them over to the liquidator. This provision is commonly used, for example, to require firms of solicitors or accountants who have advised the company to hand over the files containing their advice, on the basis that these are company property. A company in difficulty should therefore be aware that advice they are being given may later be seen by a liquidator.

3.8.2.2   Inquiry into company's dealings

Under s 236 IA 1986, the court may, on the application of the liquidator, summon to appear before it:

* any officer of the company;

* any person known or suspected to have in his possession any property of the company or supposed to be indebted to the company; or

* any person whom the court thinks capable of giving information concerning the promotion, formation, business, dealings, affairs or property of the company.

The court may also require such a person to submit a witness statement to the court containing an account of his dealings with the company or to produce any books, papers or other records in his possession or control relating to the company or its affairs. If a person summoned to appear before the court fails to do so without reasonable excuse, they may be liable to arrest or an order may be made for seizure of any books, papers, records money or goods in their possession.

There is much case law on the operation of s 236 IA 1986. The court will only make an order for examination if it is necessary in the interests of the liquidation process and not oppressive or unduly unfair to the individual concerned (*Embassy Art Products Ltd* (1987) 3 BCC 292). However, even where the respondent is a third party, an application is not unreasonable simply because it is inconvenient for them, or may cause them considerable work, or make them vulnerable to future claims (*British & Commonwealth Holdings plc (Joint Administrators) v Spicer & Oppenheim, Re British & Commonwealth Holdings plc (No 2)* [1993] AC 426).

Under s 237 IA 1986, the court is given certain enforcement powers as a result of evidence obtained under s 236 IA 1986. These overlap to a degree with s 234 IA 1986.

3.8.3   Powers to bring proceedings to swell the assets

Although most of the powers to set aside transactions described in Chapter 5 are available to both an administrator and a liquidator, the powers to bring the wrongful trading, fraudulent trading and misfeasance claims described in Chapter 6 are available only to a liquidator.

3.8.4   Joint liquidators

More than one person is entitled to act as a liquidator (or provisional liquidator). The fact that there are two or more joint liquidators does not automatically mean that each liquidator needs to sign a document or authorise any other action for it to be effective. Provided the liquidator's appointment or nomination so states, any act required or authorised to be done by the liquidator can be done by either one of more of any joint liquidators holding office (s 231(1) IA 1986). The usual practice is to have joint liquidators so that if one is unavailable another can act.

3.8.5   Consequence of agency

The liquidator is the agent of the company. As such he has the power to bind the company as its agent without personal liability (*Stead Hazel Co v Cooper* [1933] 1 KB 840). When executing documents during the liquidation, therefore, the liquidator signs in the company's name rather than his own name. However, as a matter of caution the liquidator will usually still include a provision excluding his personal liability and will therefore usually also be a separate party to the document in his own right solely to receive the benefit of this provision.

3.9   HOW IS THE LIQUIDATOR SUPERVISED?

3.9.1   MVL

In an MVL, control remains with the shareholders. The liquidator can call a meeting of the shareholders at any time in the manner required by the articles of association or the Companies Acts. He is required to do so, amongst other things:

*   to approve his **remuneration** (r 4.148A IR 1986);
*   to sanction the exercise of certain powers (see Section 3.8); and

- in the event that the liquidation continues for more than a year, at the end of that year (and each further year it may subsequently continue), to lay an account of his dealings before the shareholders (s 93 IA 1986).

3.9.2 CVL and compulsory liquidation

In a CVL or compulsory liquidation, control lies largely with the creditors. As previously described, a liquidation committee may be set up. This will consist of between three and five creditors, and usually a representative sample of different types of creditor will be chosen. The liquidator must report to the committee on all matters which he or the committee consider to be of concern, and also report in writing to the committee when the committee directs, or otherwise once every six months.

The powers and functions of the liquidation committee are set out in full in rr 4.151 to 4.172A IR 1986, but are, amongst other things:

- to approve the liquidators' remuneration; and

- to sanction the exercise of certain powers (see Section 3.8).

If there is no liquidation committee, in a CVL the liquidator will generally instead need to call a creditors' meeting to seek the relevant approvals and in a compulsory liquidation, its functions will vest in the Secretary of State.

3.9.3 The role of the court

In a compulsory liquidation, the exercise of the liquidator's powers is subject to the control of the court generally. For example:

- any creditor or contributory is entitled to apply to the court with regard to their exercise or proposed exercise of the powers described in Section 3.8.1 (s 167(3) IA 1986); and

- any person aggrieved by any act or decision of a liquidator may also apply to the court seeking an order reversing or modifying that act (s 168(5) IA 1986).

Whilst there is no directly equivalent provision for a voluntary winding-up, a creditor or contributory will be able to invoke the general supervisory powers of the court under s 112 IA 1986.

However, the court is reluctant to interfere with a liquidator's decisions. In most situations, it will tend to do so only if the decision was taken in bad faith or it was so unreasonable that no reasonable liquidator could have taken it (see, for example, *Tottenham Hotspur v Ryman, Re Edennote Ltd* [1996] BCC 718).

3.10 HOW DO UNSECURED CREDITORS RECOVER MONIES DUE TO THEM?

3.10.1 Proving in the liquidation

As discussed in Chapter 2, unsecured creditors can no longer take individual action to recover the debts due to them, but must 'prove' for these debts in the liquidation.

3.10.1.1   Compulsory liquidation

In a compulsory liquidation, a creditor who wishes to recover his debt in whole or in part must submit a claim in writing to the liquidator (unless the court orders otherwise) (r 4.73(1) IR 1986). This must be in a particular form known as a '**proof of debt**' (see r 4.75 IR 1986) and must be signed by the creditor, on his behalf. The liquidator may call for any document or further evidence to be produced to him to substantiate the claim. A liquidator must send a form to a creditor who requests one, but there is otherwise no absolute requirement upon them to do so. Nevertheless, Official Receivers will issue proof of debt forms where there is to be a creditors' meeting, where a dividend is to be paid or where it would assist investigation, and a private sector liquidator will normally do the same.

3.10.1.2   Voluntary liquidation

In a voluntary liquidation the rules are less strict. The liquidator **may** require such a creditor to submit a claim in writing (r 4.73(2) IR) IR 1986). If so, the claim, known just as a '**proof**', can be in any written form. However, the liquidator, or chairman of any meeting, may ask the creditor to provide further details of his claim.

3.10.1.3   What happens where the creditor has already proved in an administration?

Where the liquidation is immediately preceded by an administration, a creditor who has already proved in the administration is not required to submit a further proof in the liquidation (r 4.73(8) IR 1986).

3.10.2   What is a provable debt?

Rule 12.3 IR 1986 indicates that in an administration or winding-up, all claims by creditors are provable as debts against the company whether they are present or future, certain or contingent, ascertained or sounding only in damages.

Rule 13.12 IR 1986 makes it clear that when interpreting the legislation relating to a liquidation:

*   the term '**debt**' means any debt or liability to which the company was already subject at the date it entered into liquidation (or, if the liquidation was immediately preceded by an administration, the date it went into administration, termed the 'relevant date') **and** any debt or liability to which it may become subject after that date by reason of any obligation incurred before that date;

*   any **liability in tort** is a debt provable in the winding-up if either the cause of action has accrued at the relevant date, or if all of the elements necessary to establish the cause of action exist at that date except for actionable damage;

*   it is immaterial whether the debt or liability is capable of being ascertained by fixed rules or as a matter of opinion; and

*   unless the context requires otherwise, '**liability**' means (subject to the above) a liability to pay money or money's worth, including any liability under an enactment, any liability for breach of trust, any liability in contract, tort or bailment, and any liability arising out of an obligation to make restitution.

In *Haine v Day* [2008] BCC 845, the Court of Appeal rejected the liquidator's argument that a protective award in favour of an employee (see Chapter 9) was not a debt provable in the liquidation on the basis the award had only been made after the liquidator has been appointed. The circumstances giving rise to the award had existed prior to the liquidation.

This can be contrasted with *Re Nortel GmbH (in administration)* heard together with *R: Lehman Brothers International (Europe) (in administration)* [2011] EWCA Civ 1124, discussed further in Section 10.8.2.4.

3.10.3   What debts will not be provable?

There are certain debts which are nonetheless not provable. These include:

- debts which are **statute barred** (see *Re Joshua Shaw and Sons Limited* (1989) 5 BCC 188;

- **secured debts** (see Section 3.10.4); and

- claims which are otherwise not provable as a matter of public policy. **Foreign tax debts** are an example of this (see *Government of India v Taylor* [1955] AC 491, *QRS 1 Aps v Frandsen* [1999] 1 WLR 2169), although this is now the case only where the EC Insolvency Regulation does not apply.

Certain liabilities, for example for criminal compensation orders are also expressly excluded.

3.10.4   The rule against double proof

The rule against **double proof** derives from the common law rather than legislation. It states that the estate of an insolvent company can only accept one claim in respect of each debt owed by the company.

This is relevant largely where a party has guaranteed one of the company's debts. Where the guarantor has paid out under its guarantee, it is entitled to claim an indemnity from the company for the amount it has paid out. However, if part of the debt remains outstanding, the creditor still has a claim against the company for this shortfall. Since the creditor's and the guarantor's claim are for separate parts of the same debt, the rule against double proof prevents the guarantor proving for its indemnity claim until the creditor's claim has been extinguished. The rule does not in any way prevent the creditor from proving simultaneously against the company and the guarantor when both are insolvent, although the creditor's total recovery cannot exceed the amount of its original debt.

In practice, many guarantees will contain a non-competition clause which will also prevent the guarantor from taking various specified actions to pursue its indemnity claim before the creditor has been repaid in full.

Where a party is prevented from proving its claim by this rule, this means that this claim will also be unavailable to be set off against any debts which the party might in turn owe to the company. (Insolvency set off is discussed in Section 2.10.) In *Re Kaupthing Singer and Friedlander* [2011] UKSC 48, the Supreme Court confirmed that the rule against double proof also excluded the operation of the 'rule in *Cherry v Boultbee*'. This latter is an equitable rule whereby a party is not entitled to make a recovery from a fund of money without taking into account contributions it ought to have made to that fund, and which has occasionally been invoked in circumstances where two parties with claims against each other are both insolvent and for one reason or another insolvency set off does not apply.

3.10.5   Secured creditors

Under rr 4.95 to 4.99 IR 1986, where a creditor has been granted security by the company, he may:

- realise his security then prove for any balance owing;

- assess the value of his security, declare the value to the liquidator then prove for any balance;

- rely on the security for satisfaction of the debt in full and not prove at all; or

- surrender the security to the liquidator and prove for the whole debt owed.

If such a creditor proves for the whole of his debt and omits to mention his security, however, he runs the risk of inadvertently surrendering that security, unless he is able to convince a court that his omission was inadvertent or the result of an honest mistake (r 4.96 IR 1986).

The above applies only where the security was granted by the company itself. Where the security in question has been granted **by a third party**, the creditor remains free to prove for the whole of his debt.

3.10.6   The treatment of a proof

The liquidator is obliged to allow the proofs lodged with him to be inspected by any other creditor who has submitted a proof (unless this proof has been wholly rejected) or any contributory (r 4.70 IR 1986).

The liquidator may accept a proof for dividend purposes, or reject it in whole or in part, but in the latter case he must send a written statement of his reasons for rejection to the creditor. The creditor has 21 days from receipt of this statement to apply to the court to reverse or vary the liquidator's decision. Indeed, it is also open to any other creditor or contributory to make an application to court within 21 days of becoming aware of the liquidator's decision to accept or reject any proof (r 4.83 IR 1986).

The court also has the power to expunge a proof, or reduce the amount claimed on the application of the liquidator, or of any creditor if the liquidator has declined to do so (r 4.85 IR 1986).

Finally, a proof may be withdrawn or varied at any time by agreement between the creditor and the liquidator (r 4.84 IR 1986).

3.10.7   Quantification of claims

As noted in Section 3.10.2, the debts for which a creditor may prove are not limited to those which are already due and owing and/or for an ascertained amount. Where a debt is subject to a contingency, or its value is otherwise uncertain, the liquidator is obliged to estimate its value. He may also revise any estimate previously made if he thinks fit, by reference to any change of circumstances, or to information becoming available to him (r 4.86 IR 1986).

In *Re Danka Business Systems plc* [2013] EWCA Civ 92, the company concerned had been placed into an MVL. The court allowed the liquidators to use r 4.86 IR 1986 to place a value on a tax indemnity given by the company, and thus bring the company's obligations under that indemnity to an end in exchange for the payment of a specific sum to the beneficiary of the indemnity, despite objections by the beneficiary that as a result it would no longer receive the benefit of the bargain it had struck with the company.

In the case of rent of other **payments of a periodical nature**, the creditor may prove for any amount due and unpaid up to the relevant date (r 4.92 IR 1986). However, creditors are additionally entitled to prove for any **future debt**, ie rent or other payments not yet due on the date of the liquidation (r 4.94 IR 1986). In this case, their dividend is calculated according to the formula $X/(1.05)^n$, where 'X' is the value of the admitted proof, and 'n' is the period between the relevant date and the date the debt would otherwise have been due, expressed in years in a decimalised form (r 11.13 IR 1986). This reduces the dividend to reflect the early payment.

Other rules provide that:

- where the debt bears **interest**, that interest is provable as part of the debt except so far as it is payable in respect of any period after the relevant date (r 4.93 IR 1986);

- all **trade and other discounts** which would have been available to the company but for the liquidation (other than any discount for immediate, early or cash settlement) must be discounted from any claim (r 4.89 IR 1986); and

- a debt incurred in a **foreign currency** is converted into sterling at the official exchange rate on the relevant date (r 4.91 IR 1986).

In each case above, the 'relevant date' means the date on which the company went into liquidation or, if the liquidation was immediately preceded by an administration, the date it went into administration.

Finally, in quantifying a claim, the liquidator is obliged to take account of any rights of **set-off**, as discussed in Chapter 2.

3.11   THE DISTRIBUTION PROCESS

3.11.1   Dividend for creditors

The order of payment of creditors was discussed in Chapter 2. If and when the liquidator holds funds over and above those needed to cover the liquidation expenses of the winding-up and any claims of prior-ranking creditors which remain for him to deal with, he will consider a distribution of some of these excess funds to the unsecured creditors. The payment to creditors is known as a 'dividend'. In many liquidations, only a final dividend will be paid (if any dividend is paid at all), but it is possible for a liquidator holding sufficient funds also to pay one or more interim dividends to creditors.

The main steps involved in paying any dividend are as follows:

- The liquidator gives notice of his intention to declare and distribute a dividend (r 4.180 IR 1986).

- The liquidator gives notice to all creditors whose addresses he knows and who have not yet proved their debts. If the dividend in question is the first dividend in the liquidation, he must also give notice of the intended dividend by public advertisement. The above notices must specify a date, termed '**the last date for proving**', at least 21 days from the date of the notice, and state an intention to declare a dividend within four months of the last date for proving (r 11.2 IR 1986).

- Within seven days of the last date for proving, the liquidator must deal with every creditor's proof if he has not already done so. He is not obliged to deal with proofs submitted after this date, although he may do so if he thinks fit (r 11.3 IR 1986). However, if a proof, or the liquidator's decision on a proof, is contested (as per Section 3.10.5) during the four-month period, the liquidator may cancel or postpone the dividend (r 11.4 IR 1986).

- The liquidator gives a further notice declaring the dividend to all of the creditors who have proved (r 11.5 IR 1986). This can in practice be given at the same time as the dividend is paid. It will also contain various prescribed information, including the amounts realised from the sale of assets, payments made in the liquidation and the rate of the dividend.

If a creditor fails to prove before the dividend is declared, he is not entitled to disturb the distribution, although he is entitled to be paid out of monies available for any further dividend before that further dividend is paid.

3.11.2   The final dividend

When the liquidator has realised all of the company's assets, or so many of them as can in his opinion be realised without needlessly protracting the liquidation, he must give notice either:

- of his intention to declare a final dividend; or

- that no dividend (or further dividend) will be declared.

The notice will require all claims against the company to be established by a specified date, and the notice procedure is otherwise as per Section 3.11.1. After that specified date the liquidator may declare and pay any final dividend without regard to the claim of any person who has not already proved (r 4.186 IR 1986). Nonetheless, even where the liquidator has declared but not paid a final dividend, he may still cancel the dividend if new information comes to light regarding creditors' claims, since his overriding duty remains to make proper distributions between creditors (see *Lomax Leisure Ltd v Miller* [2008] BCC 686, where the liquidator cancelled cheques already posted).

3.11.3   Special provisions for an MVL

Under r 4.182A IR 1986, which applies only to an MVL, the liquidator may give notice in such newspaper as he considers most appropriate to draw creditors' attention to the fact that he intends to pay a dividend to creditors. The notice must state the last date for proving which, as above, must be at least 21 days from the date of the notice. This will allow the liquidator to make a final distribution without regard to the claim of anyone who fails to prove by the date specified.

Advertisement will not absolve the liquidator from his responsibility to contact persons who are actually known to be creditors, but have not yet proved (*Re Armstrong Whitworth Securities Co Ltd* [1947] Ch 673). Otherwise, however, it confers a useful protection on a liquidator in an MVL and enables him then to distribute a surplus to shareholders. Often a liquidator will be asked to make an earlier distribution to shareholders after providing for any known creditors, but in such cases he will be deprived of the protection of r 4.182A IR 1986 and is therefore likely to ask for an indemnity from the shareholders.

3.12   ENDING THE LIQUIDATION

3.12.1   The final meetings

Once all other steps in a liquidation have been completed, any liquidator (other than the Official Receiver) must summon a final meeting. In an MVL, this will be a meeting of shareholders (s 94 IA 1986). In a CVL, he must also summon a final meeting of shareholders, but the key meeting will be a meeting of creditors which will normally follow immediately afterwards (s 106 IA 1986 and r 4.126 IR 1986). In a compulsory liquidation, he must summon a final meeting of creditors (s 146 IA 1986).

The purposes of the final meeting are:

• to receive the liquidator's final account or report; and

• in the case of a CVL or compulsory liquidation, to vote on whether the liquidator should have his release.

The liquidator will file a return confirming that the meeting was held with the Registrar of Companies. Once he has done so, he will be deemed to vacate office and his release will become effective unless the creditors have voted against this (see ss 173 and 174 IA 1986 for a voluntary and a compulsory liquidation, respectively). Should the creditors vote against release, it becomes a matter for the Secretary of State or the court to determine (see rr 4.121 IR 1986 and 4.122 IR 1986 for a compulsory and a voluntary liquidation, respectively).

3.12.2   Dissolution

The company will automatically be dissolved three months after the liquidator files his return (see ss 201 and 205 IA 1986 for a voluntary and compulsory liquidation, respectively), although the court can order the date of dissolution to be deferred on the application of any interested person.

There is also a 'fast-track' procedure under s 202 IA 1986 where the Official Receiver, if he remains liquidator in a compulsory liquidation, may apply for an early dissolution of a company whose assets will be insufficient even to cover the expenses of the winding-up and whose affairs appear to require no further investigation.

Applications to restore a company which has been dissolved following a liquidation to the register may be made to the court within **six years** of dissolution (s 1029 CA 2006).

3.12.3   What is the release?

The effect of the release is to discharge the liquidator from all liability both in respect of acts and omissions of his in the liquidation and otherwise in relation to his conduct as liquidator. However, this does not protect the former liquidator from a later claim under s 212 IA 1986, which can be brought at any time whilst the company remains in existence. Such an action is possible even if the company has been dissolved, provided the time period for restoring the company has not yet expired.

Chapter 4

Administration

4.1   INTRODUCTION

Chapter 1 gave an overview of the administration process and Chapter 2 has already considered the order of priority which will apply to the extent that an administrator makes a distribution. Chapter 6 will consider the duties of directors, including their duties after a company has gone into administration.

This chapter considers the normal administration process in more detail, and in particular:

● the purpose of administration;

● the methods of appointing an administrator and the consequence of doing so;

● the powers and duties of an administrator;

● the methods of exiting an administration; and

● the concept of the pre-packaged administration.

Table 4.1 compares a creditors' voluntary liquidation with an administration. An administrator will, for example, have wider powers than a liquidator to run a business, but a liquidator will have wider powers to bring proceedings against third parties in order to try to swell the asset pool available to creditors. As discussed later in this chapter, an administration will often be followed by a creditors' voluntary liquidation, which may combine some of the advantage of both procedures.

In some cases, modifications to the normal administration process will apply, for example, for energy companies, railway companies, insurance companies and banks. The '**special administration**' process, which applies to 'investment banks', is a recent addition to this list. Discussion of these modified procedures is, however, beyond the scope of this book.

Table 4.1 – Creditors' voluntary liquidation *versus* **administration**

	Liquidation	*Administration*
Purpose of process	To get in and realise all of the company's property and to distribute the proceeds to the company's creditors.	Hierarchy of objectives: 1 the rescue of the company as a going concern; failing which 2 achieving a better result for the creditors as a whole than would be likely if the company were to go into liquidation; failing which 3 the realisation of property to enable a distribution to be made to secured (or preferential) creditors.

	Liquidation	*Administration*
Identity of officeholder (where administrator is appointed out of court)	Shareholders choose the initial liquidator. Creditors may replace at initial creditors' meeting, held within 14 days.	
		Subject to the views of any QFCH, director/company may choose the administrator. Creditors may replace him at a creditors' meeting, but may need to wait longer to do so.
Powers of officeholder prior to initial creditors' meeting	Very limited.	Very wide.
Powers of officeholder following initial creditors' meeting	Reasonably wide, although various powers still require the sanction of the creditors.	Very wide, although must be exercised substantially in accordance with proposals or revisions agreed with creditors
Effect on unsecured creditors	No moratorium, although liquidator may apply for a stay of proceedings and other actions by unsecured creditors.	Extensive moratorium prevents most creditor actions without either consent of the administrator or permission of the court.
Effect on secured creditors	Secured creditors free to enforce their security notwithstanding the liquidation.	Secured creditors cannot enforce their security without either the consent of the administrator or the permission of the court. Administrator has powers to sell secured assets.
Disclaimer	Ability to disclaim onerous property.	No ability to disclaim onerous property.
Proceeding against directors	Ability to bring wrongful trading, fraudulent trading or misfeasance proceedings.	No ability to bring such proceedings.
Distribution to unsecured creditors	Does not require leave of the court.	Requires the leave of the court, although some powers to make one-off payments.

4.2 WHAT IS THE PURPOSE OF ADMINISTRATION?

4.2.1 The meaning of the 'purpose of administration'

Under para 111(1) Sch B1 IA 1986, the 'purpose of administration' is defined to mean an 'objective specified in para 3 Sch B1 IA 1986'.

Paragraph 3 Sch B1 IA 1986 in turn lists three specific objectives with which an administrator must perform his functions. These are:

● rescuing the company as a going concern (the **'primary objective'**);

- achieving a better result for the company's creditors as a whole than would be likely if the company were wound up (without first being in administration) (the '**second objective**'); or

- realising property in order to make a distribution to one or more secured or preferential creditors (the '**third objective**').

These objectives are hierarchical. The administrator must perform his functions with the primary objective of rescuing the company as a going concern unless he thinks either:

- that it is not reasonably practicable to achieve that objective; **or**

- that the second objective would achieve a better result for the company's creditors as a whole.

He may perform his functions pursuant to the third objective of realising property to make a distribution to secured and/or preferential creditors only if:

- he thinks that it would not be reasonably practicable to achieve either the first or second objectives; **and**

- he does not unnecessarily harm the interests of the creditors of the company as a whole.

4.2.2   Corporate rescue or business rescue?

It is worth stressing here that the primary objective of administration is to rescue the company as a corporate entity. The second objective will not achieve this, but may well still achieve the rescue of the company's business as a going concern by selling that business to a solvent buyer. There may often be little practical difference between these two outcomes so far as the company's employees and customers are concerned. From this perspective, business rescue is a valuable aim in itself.

From the creditors' perspective, however, there will be a significant distinction as it will be the company, not the business, which remains liable to them. Following a sale of its business, the company may well be left largely as a hollow shell, although it may still hold a few assets which were not included in the sale. The creditors will share in the business sale proceeds, and any subsequent realisations, in accordance with the order of priority described in Chapter 2. An administration should nonetheless result in these sale proceeds being greater than they would have been on a liquidation, not least because an administrator is far better equipped to trade and subsequently sell the business as a going concern.

4.3   COMMENCING AN ADMINISTRATION

4.3.1   How is an administrator appointed?

Table 4.2 shows the administration process in flowchart form. A company enters into administration when the appointment of an administrator takes effect (para 1(2) Sch B1 IA 1986). An administrator may be appointed in a number of ways. One route is by application to the court for an administration order, which will involve

Table 4.2 – The administration process

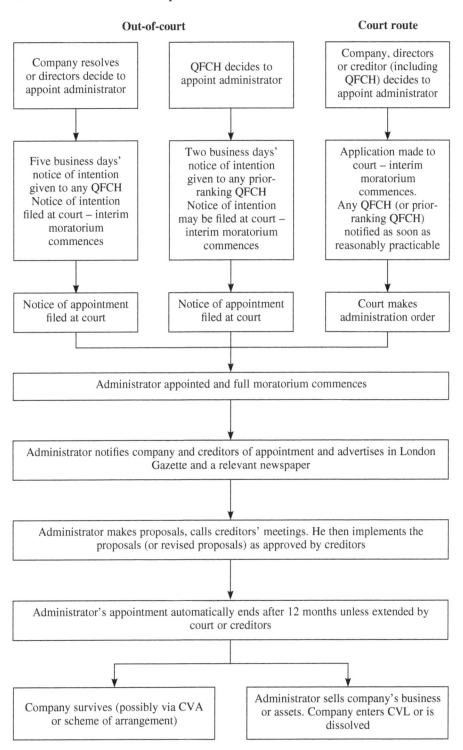

a hearing before a judge. However, there are two alternative routes available which simply involve the filing of certain papers with a court office. Because appointments by these routes do not involve a hearing before a judge, they are generally known as 'out-of-court appointments' and they are now the more commonly used. Table 4.3 compares the out-of-court and the court routes.

Unlike a liquidation, the manner is which an administrator is appointed will not affect their powers or duties once appointed.

Table 4.3 – Out-of-court vs court appointment

Advantages of an out-of-court appointment
- Quicker and cheaper than a court appointment.
- An out-of-court appointment can be made by a QFCH outside court office hours.
- No need to convince the court that the purpose of administration is reasonably likely to be achieved.

Advantages of a court appointment
- This is the only route available to a creditor (other than a QFCH – see Section 4.3.3 – whose security is enforceable).
- It may be the only route available to the company or its directors in certain circumstances, for example, where a creditor has presented a winding-up petition.
- Where there is a cross-border element, a court order may be required before the appointment will be recognised in other jurisdictions, and may also be desirable if the appointment is being made over a foreign entity to which there is no direct English equivalent (see *Re Kaupthing Capital Partners II Master LP Inc* [2010] EWHC 836 (Ch).

4.3.2   Who will the administrator be?

Only a qualified insolvency practitioner can be appointed as an administrator. In practice, any person seeking to appoint an administrator will need to identify their preferred insolvency practitioner and to discuss the process with them in advance. As explained in greater detail below, the would-be appointor must name their proposed administrator in their application or other appointment documentation, and the proposed administrator must consent to the appointment and have satisfied themselves that the purpose of administration can be fulfilled.

As discussed below, specific mechanisms exist to allow a qualifying floating charge holder (referred to here as a '**QFCH**') to substitute their own choice of administrator in place of one chosen by the company or the directors.

The unsecured creditors may also have some ability to influence the choice of administrator. In *The Oracle (North West) Ltd v Pinnacle Services (UK) Ltd* [2008] EWHC 1920 (Ch), which concerned an application to court for an administration order, the directors and the largest unsecured creditor proposed different choices of administrator. The court favoured the creditor's choice, observing that an administration was ultimately the creditors' benefit. However, it will be more difficult for unsecured creditors to intervene in the choice of administrator if there is an out-of-court appointment.

4.3.3   What is a QFCH?

The concept of a QFCH is important here. Different rules apply where a QFCH is seeking to appoint an administrator, whether by a court or an out-of-court route. In addition, any other person seeking to appoint an administrator is usually required to give advance notice to any QFCH.

There is a two-limb test to determine whether a creditor is a QFCH:

First, under para 14(1) Sch B1 IA 1986, a floating charge is a **qualifying floating charge** if it was created by an instrument which:

- states that para 14(1) applies to the floating charge; or

- purports to empower the holder to appoint an administrator; or

- purports to empower the holder to appoint a receiver who would be an administrative receiver under s 29(2) IA 1986.

Secondly, a person is a **QFCH** if he holds security over the company's assets comprising:

- a qualifying floating charge which relates to the whole or substantially the whole of the company's property; or

- a number of qualifying floating charges which together relate to the whole or substantially the whole of the company's property; or

- charges and other forms of security which together relate to the whole or substantially the whole of the company's property and at least one of which is a qualifying floating charge.

The meaning of '**the whole or substantially the whole**' is discussed in Chapter 8.

4.3.4   Out-of-court appointment by the company or its directors

Either the company or its directors (or a majority of the directors) may appoint an administrator out of court. The process for making such an application is set out in full in paras 22 to 34 Sch B1 IA 1986 and rr 2.20 to 2.26 IR 1986, but an overview is given here.

4.3.4.1   Restrictions on the power to appoint

Neither the company nor its directors may make an out-of-court appointment:

- unless the company is or is likely to become **unable to pay its debts**;

- if at any time during the **previous 12 months**, a **previous administrator** appointed by, or on the application of, the company or its directors was in office (para 23 IA Sch B1 1986);

- if at any time during the **previous 12 months**, the company was the subject of a **moratorium under Sch A1 IA 1986** without a CVA having been put into place, or was the subject of a CVA put into place following such a moratorium which ended prematurely (para 24 Sch B1 1986); or

- if a **winding-up petition** or an **administration application** has been presented and not yet disposed of, or an **administrative receiver** is in office (para 25 Sch B1 IA 1986).

If there is an existing winding-up petition, or if there was a previous administration or CVA moratorium, the company or the directors will need to make an application to court instead.

Any company or its directors seeking to make an out-of-court appointment will therefore need first to make a search for existing winding-up petitions. However, such a search will not always reveal a winding-up petition presented very shortly before the time of the search.

Where a company falls into one of the categories described in s 362(1)(a)–(c) of the Financial Services and Markets Act 2000 (FSMA 2000), the **written consent of the appropriate regulator** will be required before making the appointment (s 362A FSMA 2000). The Prudential Regulation Authority (PRA) will be the appropriate regulator where the company is a PRA-regulated person, otherwise the appropriate regulator will be the Financial Conduct Authority. In practice, an online search of the Financial Services Register will reveal whether the company falls into one of these categories and if so whether it is regulated by the PRA or the FCA. This is a check worth making prior to almost any appointment, since many companies do carry out some form of regulated activity as an ancillary function to their main business activities.

4.3.4.2   Notice of intention to appoint

The company or the directors must serve a notice of intention to appoint an administrator on any **QFCH** (para 26(1) Sch B1 IA 1986). They cannot appoint until either at least **five business days** (not counting the date on which the notice was served) have elapsed or each QFCH has consented to their doing so (para 28(1) Sch B1 IA 1986). This is designed to give a QFCH the opportunity to intervene by appointing their own choice of administrator or, if circumstances permit, an administrative receiver instead (see Section 4.3.5). In *Re OMP Leisure Limited* [2008] BCC 67, it was made clear that this notice needs to be given regardless of whether the QFCH's charge is currently enforceable. However, there was no need to give notice to a person whose security was still registered at Companies House but who had in practice been repaid and whose security should therefore have been discharged.

The notice of intention must contain a **statutory declaration** by the person making the appointment that the company is not in liquidation and that none of the restrictions referred to in Section 4.3.4.1 apply. It needs also to be **filed with the court** as soon as reasonably practicable (para 27(1) Sch B1 IA 1986) and no more than five business days after the date on which the statutory declaration was sworn (r 2.21 IR 1986). This filing must be accompanied by either a copy of the **resolution of the company** to appoint or a **record of the decision of the directors**, as the case may be.

In this respect, the court has made it clear that a decision of the directors to place the company into administration must be taken at a **validly convened board meeting** in accordance with the company's articles of association (*Minmar (929) Limited v Khalatschi* [2011] EWHC 1159 (Ch)).

The company must also **notify a range of other prescribed persons** of the proposed appointment (para 26(2) Sch B1 IA 1986). These prescribed persons are listed in r 2.20(2) IR 1986 and include any enforcement officer who is charged with an execution or other legal process against the company and any person who has distrained against the company or its property, any supervisor of a CVA and the company itself (if it is not the company making the appointment). There is no need to wait five business days after giving this notice.

A range of cases, of which *Minmar* was an early example, have recently examined whether an appointment can remain valid should the company or its directors fail to give notice to one of these prescribed persons (or to the Financial Services Authority (as the predecessor to the PRA and the FCA) under s 362A FSMA 2000). Initially, a number of conflicting decisions emerged in what became known collectively as the '*Minmar*' cases. Fortunately, however, these conflicting decisions have been rationalised by subsequent courts, and the conflict is generally considered to have ended. The approach of the courts is now to consider the consequences of the non-compliance and determine whether as a result, the entire appointment is invalid or whether the non-compliance is simply a curable defect (see *Ceart Risk Services Limited* [2012] EWHC 1178 (Ch) and *Re BXL Services* [2012] EWHC 1877 (Ch)).

Nevertheless, it is wisest still to ensure that all prescribed persons are properly given notice. On a director's appointment in particular, good practice might be to ensure that a notice of intention is delivered to the company's registered office (see r 2.8 IR 1986), and a copy also served on the company's solicitors (see rr 12A.5 and 13.4 IR 1986).

An **interim moratorium** will take effect from the point when any notice of intention is filed at court (see Section 4.4.1.3). In *Re Ramora (UK) Limited* [2011] EWHC 3959 (Ch), for example, the court duly held that a winding-up petition presented after the notice of intention was filed could not therefore invalidate the subsequent appointment of the administrators. The moratorium will end if no administrator is appointed within **ten business days**, beginning with the date of filing the notice of intention (paras 28(2) and 44(4) Sch B1 IA 1986).

It is acceptable practice for a company to secure a brief moratorium by filing such a notice even when there is no QFCH to serve it on where, for instance, the company is not quite ready to appoint an administrator and creditors are already looking to exercise 'self-help' remedies. In *Re Cornercare Limited* [2010] EWHC 893 (Ch) the court also confirmed that a company could file a second notice of intention to appoint once the ten business day period following an initial notice of intention had expired. Should an unscrupulous company attempt to engineer a continuing moratorium by filing repeated notices of intention, the court would have adequate powers to treat that as an abuse and act accordingly.

4.3.4.3   Notice of appointment

The appointment of the administrator takes effect when a notice of appointment is filed with the court, together with any accompanying documents described here and in Section 4.3.4.4. Unlike a notice of appointment filed by a QFCH, it must be filed during court hours.

- Where a notice of intention was required, therefore, two consecutive filings are needed to complete the appointment process. The notice of appointment contains a **statutory declaration** that, among other things, the statements made in the earlier statutory declaration remain accurate. It must be accompanied by the written consent of any qualifying floating charge holder unless five business days have already elapsed (r 2.23 IR 1986).

- If no notice of intention was required, a slightly different form of notice of appointment is used, containing a **statutory declaration** confirming the matters which would otherwise have been covered in the notice of intention. It must also be accompanied by the copy resolution or record of the directors' decision which would otherwise have accompanied a notice of intention (r 2.25 IR 1986).

In either case, the relevant statutory declaration must not have been made more than five business days prior to the filing (r 2.24 IR 1986).

Paragraph 28(2) IA Sch B1 IA 1986 makes it clear that, where a notice of intention was filed, the administrator must be appointed within **ten business days**, beginning with the date of filing that notice of intention. Notwithstanding this, the court has held that an appointment which was inadvertently made on the eleventh business day remained valid (see *Re Euromaster Ltd* [2012] EWHC 2356 (Ch)). However, it still seems wisest to ensure that if the appointment has not been made within the ten business day period, a new notice of intention is filed before making the appointment.

4.3.4.4   Accompanying documents

The notice of appointment must also be accompanied by:

- a statement from each proposed administrator consenting to act, giving details of any prior professional relationships he has had with the company, and stating that in his opinion the purpose of administration is reasonably likely to be achieved (para 29(3) Sch B1 IA 1986); and

- where there are joint administrators, a statement indicating which of their functions can be exercised individually and which must be exercised jointly (para 100(2) Sch B1 IA 1986).

4.3.5   Out-of-court appointment by a QFCH

Alternatively, a QFCH may appoint an administrator out of court. The process for making such an application is set out in full in paras 14 to 21 Sch B1 IA 1986 and rr 2.15 to 2.19 IR 1986, but an overview is given here.

4.3.5.1   Restrictions on the power to appoint

There are comparatively few restrictions on the ability of a QFCH to make an out-of-court appointment. However, he is not entitled to do so where:

- its floating charge has not yet become **enforceable** (para 16 Sch B1 IA 1986); or

- a **provisional liquidator** has been appointed or an **administrative receiver** is already in office (para 17 Sch B1 IA 1986). This does not prevent the QFCH applying to court for the provisional liquidation to be terminated and an administration order made instead.

4.3.5.2 Notice of intention to appoint

A QFCH must serve a notice of intention to appoint an administrator on any **prior-ranking QFCH**. For these purposes, one floating charge is prior to another if it was created first, or if it has priority pursuant to an agreement between those QFCHs. A QFCH cannot appoint until either at least **two business days** (not counting the date on which the notice was served) have then elapsed or each prior-ranking QFCH has consented to him doing so (para 15 Sch B1 IA 1986). The court has confirmed that the failure to serve a prior ranking QFCH will invalidate the appointment (*Re Eco Link Resources Ltd* Chancery Division District Registry (Birmingham), 2 July 2012).

There is no requirement to file the notice of intention with the court. However, the QFCH may choose to do so, since an **interim moratorium** will take effect when the notice of intention is filed (see Section 4.4.1.3). This will end if no administrator has been appointed within **five business days**, beginning with the date of the filing (para 44(2) Sch B1 IA 1986).

4.3.5.3 Notice of appointment

The appointment of the administrator takes effect when a notice of appointment and any accompanying documents are filed with the court (para 19 Sch B1 IA 1986).

The notice of appointment must contain a **statutory declaration** (made no more than five business days prior to the filing) that, among other things, the appointor is a QFCH and that his charge is enforceable (para 18 Sch B1 IA 1986). It must be accompanied either by evidence that the appointor has given at least two business days' notice to any prior-ranking QFCH or the written consent of any prior-ranking QFCH(s). The accompanying documents are those described in Section 4.3.4.4 (r 2.16 IR 1986).

4.3.5.4 Out of hours appointments

When the court is closed, a QFCH is entitled to fax the notice of appointment to a designated telephone number or to e-mail the notice of appointment to a designated e-mail address, each of which is published on the Insolvency Service website (http://www.insolvency.gov.uk). The appointment will take effect from the date and time of the fax transmission or the sending of the e-mail.

If faxing the notice of appointment, the QFCH will need to retain a copy of the **fax transmission report** showing the date and time of transmission and at least part of the first page of the notice of appointment. Similarly, if e-mailing the notice of appointment, the QFCH will need to retain a **hard copy of the e-mail** detailing the date and time of the e-mail and the address to which it was sent and containing a copy of the document sent as an attachment.

The QFCH must take physical copies of the notice of appointment and the other documents which would be required for an ordinary filing to the court on the **next day the court is open for business**. These must be accompanied by the fax transmission report or hard copy of the e-mail. They must also be accompanied by a statement setting out full reasons for the out-of-court filing and the reasons why it would have been damaging to the company and its creditors for the appointor to have done otherwise. If the QFCH fails to comply with these requirements, the administrator's appointment will lapse (r 2.19 IR 1986).

4.3.6 Appointment by the court

The process for making an administration application is set out in full in paras 12 and 13 Sch B1 IA 1986 and rr 2.2 to 2.14 IR 1986, but an overview is given here.

4.3.6.1 Who may apply for such an order?

Under para 12(1) Sch B1 IA 1986, an application to the court for an administration order may be made by:

- the **company**; or

- all or a majority of its **directors** (see para 105 Sch B1 IA 1986); or

- any **creditor** or creditors, including a contingent or prospective creditor (see para 12(4) Sch B1 1986); or

- the designated **officer of a magistrates' court** in the exercise of the powers conferred by s 87A Magistrates' Courts Act 1980 (enforcement of fines imposed on companies); or

- any combination of the above.

Special rules may apply where the applicant is a **QFCH**, or when a QFCH wishes to intervene in the application. These are discussed in Section 4.3.6.6.

Other sections of the legislation also specifically allow the **supervisor of a CVA**, or a **liquidator** to make an application in the name of the company. The **Financial Services Authority** is also entitled to apply (s 359 FSMA 2000). Unlike a winding-up petition, however, neither individual shareholders, nor the Official Receiver or the Secretary of State have the standing to apply.

4.3.6.2 When can a creditor make an application?

Section 3.4.3 looked at where a creditor whose debt is disputed or is subject to a counterclaim could present a winding-up petition. It appears that the court's jurisdiction to make an administration order is wider, on the basis that the consequences of administration are less drastic for the company (*Re MTI Trading Systems Ltd & others* [1998] BCC 400). The court may therefore be prepared to make an order even where a debt is disputed or where a counterclaim exists if there are good reasons to do so, although the administration process should not be used as a vehicle for resolving a dispute (*Hammonds (A Firm) v Pro-fit USA Ltd* [2008] 2 BCLC 159).

4.3.6.3 What is the application process?

The application itself will contain a statement by the applicant that it believes that the company is, or is likely to become **unable to pay its debts**.

The application must be accompanied by:

- a statement from each proposed administrator (as described in Section 4.3.4.4);

- a witness statement containing, among other things, a statement of the company's financial position and specifying (to the best of the applicant's knowledge and belief) the company's assets and liabilities, details of any insolvency proceedings which are already afoot (including any winding-up petition that has been presented) and any other matters which in the applicant's opinion will assist the court in deciding whether to make an administration order. This witness statement will in practice need to contain enough information to convince the court to make an order.

In cases of extreme urgency, the court does have the power to make an interim appointment of an administrator on the basis of an oral application, although a formal application and written evidence will need to follow (see *SB Corporate Solutions Limited v Colin Andrew Prescott* [2012] Bus LR D91). The initial application can even be made without notice to the company (see Section 4.3.6.4) if there is sufficient need for secrecy.

4.3.6.4   What are the notice requirements?

The applicant must **as soon as is reasonably practicable** notify:

- any **QFCH** (para 12(2) Sch B1 IA 1986). The QFCH may intervene by applying to the court for their own choice of administrator to be appointed in place of the applicant's choice (see Section 4.3.6.6); and

- any enforcement officer who is charged with an execution or other legal process against the company and any person who has distrained against the company or its property (r 2.7 IR 1986).

Under r 2.6 IR 1986, the application also needs to be served **at least five business days** before the hearing on the following (where relevant): the **company** (if the application is made by anyone other than the company itself); any **proposed administrator**; any administrative receiver; any petitioner who has presented a winding-up petition; any provisional liquidator; any supervisor of a CVA and any EU Member State liquidator appointed in relation to the company. This is designed to allow any such interested persons the chance to consider the application, and if necessary appear at the hearing to present their own views. However, the court may be prepared to allow expedited applications in exceptional circumstances.

An **interim moratorium** will take effect from the point when the application is made (see Section 4.4.1.3).

4.3.6.5   The court hearing

Under para 11 Sch B1 IA 1986, the court will only make an administration order if it is satisfied that:

- the company is or is likely to become **unable to pay its debts** (see Chapter 1); and

- the administration order is reasonably likely to **achieve the purpose of administration**.

In *Re AA Mutual International Insurance Company Ltd* [2005] 2 BCLC 8, the court confirmed that 'likely' meant 'more probable than not', but that 'reasonably likely' simply equated with a 'real prospect' test.

The first limb of the test was considered further in *Highberry Ltd v Colt Telecom Group plc (No 2)* [2003] BPIR 324, which related to a creditors' application made by bondholders. The court felt unable to conclude that the company was more likely than not to become cash-flow insolvent simply because there was uncertainty as to whether it would be able to repay or refinance the bonds when they matured nearly four years later.

The second limb has been considered on a number of occasions. The court was persuaded to make an order in *Auto Management Services Ltd v Oracle Fleet UK Ltd* [2008] BCC 761 on the basis, among other things, that the administration moratorium would help preserve value in a lease under which the company was a tenant and that the ability of an administrator to continue to trade would help preserve goodwill. The proposed administrator need not identify with certainty which of the three objectives of administration will be achieved (see the *Hammonds v Pro-fit* case). However, in *Doltable Ltd v Lexi Holdings Plc* [2006] BCC 918, the court considered that none of the three objectives had been established – the purpose of the application in that case appeared to be to prevent the sale of the property owned by the company by a receiver.

Under para 13(1) Sch B1 IA 1986, on hearing an administration application, the court may as an alternative (or in addition) to making an administration order:

- dismiss the application; or

- adjourn the hearing conditionally or unconditionally; or

- make an interim order; or

- treat the application as a winding-up petition and make any order which it can make under s 125 IA 1986 (see Chapter 3) – this power was used, for example, in *Re Ci4net.com Inc* [2005] BCC 277; or

- make any other order it thinks fit. This may include an order allowing pre-administration costs to be treated as administration expenses.

4.3.6.6   Special rules applicable to a QFCH

A QFCH may apply for an administration order without needing to satisfy the court that the company is or is likely to become unable to pay its debts (para 35 Sch B1 IA 1986). In addition, where the existing applicant is someone other than a QFCH, the QFCH may intervene in the application to seek the appointment of his own choice of administrator instead, and the court is required to have regard to his wishes unless the particular circumstances of the case dictate otherwise (para 36 Sch B1 1986).

In both of these cases, however, the QFCH will need to satisfy the court that he would have been entitled to make an out-of-court appointment, as described in Section 4.3.5. Among other things, he will therefore still need to provide evidence that his security is enforceable.

4.4 WHAT IS THE EFFECT OF THE ADMINISTRATION MORATORIUM?

4.4.1 How does the moratorium protect the company?

The administration moratorium is perhaps the most important feature of the administration process. It is designed to protect the company from most of the remedies that its creditors would otherwise be entitled to exercise. Unlike the liquidation moratorium, its main function is not to preserve the *pari passu* principle, but to create a temporary breathing space whilst the administrator attempts to fulfil the purpose of administration.

4.4.1.1 Moratorium on insolvency proceedings

Whilst the company is in administration:

- No resolution may be passed or order made for the winding-up of the company. (An exception applies when a petition is presented on public interest grounds or by the Financial Services Authority under s 367 Financial Services and Markets Act 2000. If an administrator becomes aware that such a petition exists, he must apply to the court for directions (para 42 Sch B1 IA 1986).)

- No administrative receiver may be appointed (para 43(6A) Sch B1 IA 1986).

4.4.1.2 Moratorium on other actions

In addition, under para 43 Sch B1 IA 1986, the following actions are prohibited whilst the company is in administration **except** with the consent of the administrator **or** with the permission of the court:

- taking any step to **enforce security** over the company's property; or

- taking any step to **repossess goods** in the company's possession under a hire-purchase agreement (which for these purposes includes a conditional sale agreement, a chattel leasing agreement and a retention of title agreement – para 111 Sch B1 IA 1986); or

- in the case of a landlord, exercising a right of forfeiture by **peaceable re-entry** in relation to premises let to the company; or

- instituting or continuing a **legal process** (including legal proceedings, execution and distress) against the company or its property.

In *Re Olympia v York Canary Wharf Ltd* [1993] BCC 154, the court took the view that the term 'legal process' did not extend to the service of a contractual notice. However, the term **'legal proceedings'** has nonetheless been held to extend a wide category of legal and quasi-legal proceedings, for example, the reference of a dispute under a building contract to a statutory adjudication procedure (*A Straume (UK) Ltd v Bradlor Developments Ltd* [2000] BCC 333) and an investigation by the Gambling Commission (*Frankice (Golders Green) Ltd* [2010] EWHC 1229 (Ch)).

In *Frankice,* the court concluded that the word 'process' suggested something with a defined beginning and an ascertainable final outcome and which in the interim was governed by a recognisable procedure. The word 'legal' indicated that the process must in some sense invoke the compulsive power of the law, and must be quasi-legal in nature. One indicator of this might be that the process envisages the possibility of an appeal although this was not determinative in itself.

The administration moratorium will not prevent a party from exercising a right of set-off against the company.

4.4.1.3   The interim moratorium

Where a person has made an application for an administration order, or has filed a notice of intention to appoint an administrator, the provisions described in Sections 4.4.1.1 and 4.4.1.2 will similarly apply pending the administrator's appointment (ignoring for these purposes any reference to the consent of the administrator). However, it will expire if no administrator is appointed within any required period of time.

4.4.2   What is the role of the administrator?

The leading authority in this area, *Re Atlantic Computer Systems plc* [1992] Ch 505, indicated that in most cases the matter can be dealt with by the administrator so that applications to the court will be the exception rather than the rule. An administrator should act reasonably when faced with such a request, since he may be criticised and possibly penalised in costs by the court should he refuse to give his consent in circumstances where he should have realised the permission of the court was likely to be granted.

4.4.3   When will the court grant permission?

In *Atlantic Computers*, the court set out a number of guidelines, although stressing that these were not intended to replace the general discretion given to the court in dealing with applications for leave. These are summarised in Table 4.4. The *Frankice* case discussed in Section 4.4.1.2 and the various cases where landlords have applied for permission to forfeit discussed in Section 9.2.3.3 are examples of the court carrying out the necessary balancing exercise.

The court is more likely to grant permission where the applicant is a secured creditor, or has some proprietary interest. In *Sinai Securities Ltd v Hooper* [2004] BCC 973, the court permitted the applicant to appoint a non-administrative receiver. It held that not only was this unlikely to impede the purpose of the administration, but might be beneficial to this purpose since the receiver would be better able to make an application for planning permission. Other cases involving landlords are discussed in Chapter 9.

Under para 43(7) Sch B1 IA 1986, the court may impose conditions when it gives permission. For example, in *Re City Logistics Ltd* [2002] 2 BCLC 103, a creditor which had supplied racking to a company on retention of title terms was only allowed to repossess its goods after a particular date to allow the administrators the time to remove other goods stored in the racking. It was held in *Atlantic Computers* that the court also has the ability to impose conditions when refusing permission. For example, it might order the administrator to pay rent to a landlord.

In *AES Barry Ltd v TXU Europe Trading Ltd* [2005] 2 BCLC 22, it was held that where the applicant has only a straight monetary claim, permission will generally only be granted in exceptional circumstances.

Table 4.4 – Summary of the *Atlantic Computers* guidelines

1	The person seeking permission must always make out a case for permission to be given.
2	If granting permission to the owner of land or goods to exercise his proprietary rights and repossess his land or goods is unlikely to impede the achievement of the purpose of the administration, permission should normally be given.
3	In other cases when a lessor seeks possession, the court has to carry out a balancing exercise, weighing the legitimate interests of the lessor against those of the other creditors.
4	In carrying out the balancing exercise, great weight should normally be given to the lessor's proprietary interests. An administration for the benefit of unsecured creditors should not be conducted at the expense of those who have proprietary rights, save where this is unavoidable.
5	It will normally be sufficient ground for the grant of permission if significant loss would be caused to the lessor by a refusal. However, if substantially greater loss would be caused to others by the grant of permission, that may outweigh any such loss to the lessor.
6	In assessing these respective losses, the court will have regard to matters such as:
	– the financial position of the company, and its ability to pay the rental arrears and the continuing rentals,
	– the administrator's proposals,
	– the period for which the company has already been in administration and the length of time for which it is expected to continue,
	– the effect on the administration if permission were given and on the applicant if permission were refused,
	– the end result sought to be achieved by the administration and the prospects of it being achieved, and
	– the history of the administration so far.
7	The court will need to take into account how probable any suggested consequences are.
8	The conduct of the parties may also be a material consideration in a particular case. A lessor should make his position clear to the administrator at the outset of the administration and, if it should become necessary, should apply to the court promptly.
9	The above considerations may be relevant not only to the decision whether permission should be granted or refused, but also to a decision to impose terms on any permission that is granted.
10	The court is also entitled to impose terms as a condition for refusing permission and in this event the above considerations will also apply.
11	A broadly similar approach will be applicable on many applications to enforce security. If the applicant is fully secured, delay in enforcement is likely to be less prejudicial than in cases where his security is insufficient.
12	On an application for permission, the court will not seek to adjudicate upon a dispute over the existence, validity or nature of the security which the applicant is seeking permission to enforce unless the issue raises a short point of law which it is convenient to determine without further ado.

4.5   WHAT ARE THE OTHER CONSEQUENCES OF ADMINISTRATION?

4.5.1   What is the effect on a winding-up petition?

Under para 40(1) Sch B1 IA 1986, a winding-up petition:

- will be **dismissed** when an administration order is made in respect of the company; and

- will be **suspended** whilst the company is in administration following an out-of-court appointment by a QFCH. In practice, the suspension means that it has no legal effect during the administration, so dispositions of the company's property will not be void under s 127 IA 1986 (discussed in Chapter 5, and see *Re J Smiths Haulage Ltd* [2007] BCC 135).

The exceptions in relation to a moratorium described in Section 4.4.1.1 also apply here (paras 40(2) and 40(3) Sch B1 1986).

4.5.2   What is the effect on a receiver?

An administration order will cause any administrative receiver to vacate office. Whilst administration will not automatically cause a non-administrative receiver to vacate office, he is obliged to do so if the administrator so requires (para 41 Sch B1 IA 1986).

4.5.3   What is the effect on the directors?

The power of the administrator to appoint and remove directors is discussed in Section 4.7. The role of the directors in an administration is discussed further in Chapter 6.

4.5.4   What is the effect on the company's business and status?

Unlike liquidation, administration does not oblige the company to cease to carry on business – this would be inconsistent with the purpose of administration. The administrator is indeed given wide powers which will allow him to continue to trade, as discussed in Section 4.7.

4.5.5   What is the effect on contracts?

Administration does not terminate the contracts of a company. The terms of a contract itself may of course provide that it terminates automatically on administration or, more normally, that the other party has the right to terminate. Alternatively, the administrator may indicate that the company is no longer able to perform its obligations under the contract, and the resulting breach will give the other party the ability to terminate and/or to pursue other remedies. The administration moratorium should not affect the other party's ability to terminate the contract (see Section 4.4.1.2), but is likely to limit that party's ability to pursue other remedies against the company.

Damages are likely to be of limited benefit against an insolvent company. However, in certain cases applicants have been able to obtain injunctive relief against administrators (see, for example, *Astor Chemicals Ltd v Synthetic Technology Ltd* [1990] BCC 97).

Unlike a liquidator, an administrator has no ability to disclaim onerous contracts.

4.5.6 What is the effect on the company's documentation?

During the administration, every invoice, order for goods or services or business letter sent by or on behalf of the company or the administrator and every website of the company is required to state the name of the administrator and the fact that the affairs of the company are now under the administrator's management. The administrator or any officer of the company will commit an offence if they authorise or permit a breach of this requirement without reasonable excuse (para 45 Sch B1 IA 1986).

4.6 HOW ARE THE CREDITORS INFORMED AND INVOLVED?

4.6.1 Overview

An administrator has quite extensive obligations to keep creditors informed. Given that in some administrations there may be a large number of creditors, many of whom will often be owed comparatively small sums, it can be a costly and time-consuming exercise in itself to write to all creditors to give notice of the appointment and of the administrators' proposals. Fortunately, rr 12A.10 to 12A.14 do now give administrators reasonable scope to communicate with creditors by electronic means. To the extent that the rules still do not assist, however, perhaps because many creditors' current e-mail addresses are not known or because it turns out that significant number of e-mails are bounced back by creditors' firewalls, the administrator may need to obtain directions from the court in order to achieve a practical solution. The case of *Re Advent Computer Training Ltd* [2010] EWHC 459 (Ch) illustrates the increasing inclination of the courts to accommodate the use of e-mail, particularly where this is the main means by which the company communicated with its creditors prior to its administration.

4.6.2 Notices

An administrator must send notice of his appointment to the company and to all creditors of the company of whose addresses he is aware (having obtained a list of creditors for this purpose) as soon as reasonably practicable. An administrator will typically aim to have complied with this latter requirement within 28 days after his appointment, although may well do so sooner. In addition, the administrator must send notice of his appointment to the Registrar of Companies within seven days and advertise his appointment in the London Gazette and an appropriate newspaper.

He will also need to give notice to any receiver who is currently in office, any person who has presented a pending winding-up petition, any enforcement officer who is already charged with execution against the company's property, anyone who has distrained against the company's property and the supervisor of any CVA (para 46 Sch B1 IA 1986 and r 2.27 IR 1986).

4.6.3 Statement of affairs

As soon as reasonably practicable after his appointment, the administrator may require one or more 'relevant persons' to provide a statement of affairs or statement of concurrence (para 47 Sch B1 IA 1986). This is discussed further in Chapter 6. The administrator is required to file copies of these with both the Registrar of Companies and the court. However, if he thinks it would prejudice the conduct of the administration or might reasonably be expected to lead to violence against any person if the whole or part of the statement of affairs were to be disclosed he may apply to court for an order for limited disclosure (r 2.30 IR 1986). Administrators have made such an application, for example, where they wish to avoid disclosing a full list of the names and addresses of the names of all creditors of the company because this list is in itself a valuable asset of the company (see the *Advent Computer Training* case).

4.6.4 Statement of proposals

In every administration, the administrator must prepare a statement setting out his proposals for achieving the purposes of the administration (para 49 Sch B1 IA 1986). He may, for example, propose a CVA or a Scheme of Arrangement, although it is still more likely in most cases that the proposals will involve a business sale. Where applicable, this statement must contain an explanation of why the administrator thinks the primary or secondary objective of the administration cannot be achieved.

As seen below, the administrator will need to consider his intended exit route even at the start of the administration, and set this out in his proposals to creditors. The various methods of ending an administration are discussed further in Section 4.10. It will sometimes be necessary to set out alternative scenarios. Should a CVA be proposed and the proposal passed, for example, the company would normally remain in administration throughout the duration of the CVA. However, the method of ending the administration is likely to depend on whether the CVA ultimately succeeds or fails.

He must send a copy of the statement of proposals to the Registrar of Companies, to every creditor whose claim and address he knows of and to every shareholder whose address he knows of as soon as reasonably practicable and in any event **within eight weeks** of the date the company entered administration (although this time period can be extended in accordance with para 107 Sch B1 IA 1986).

Further details of the required content of this statement are set out in r 2.33 IR 1986, and among other things it will include:

- an **account of the circumstances** giving rise to the administrator's appointment;

- a copy or summary of the **statement of affairs** (or appropriate explanations and information if there is no statement or if a limited disclosure order has been made);

- the proposed basis for the **administrator's remuneration**;

- except where a CVA is proposed, an estimate of the value of the **prescribed part** and of the company's net property. These estimates need not contain any information which if disclosed would seriously prejudice the company's commercial interests, but if such information is excluded this must be stated. If the administrator proposes not to distribute any prescribed part, or to seek leave of the court not to do so, this must also be stated;

- how it is envisaged that the purpose of the administration will be achieved, and the **proposed exit route**. If the proposed exit route is a voluntary liquidation, details of the proposed liquidator must be included; and

- the manner in which the affairs of the company have been (and will continue to be) **managed and financed**, including the reasons for and details of **any disposal of assets** already made.

However, the proposals may not include any action which affects the right of **secured creditors** to enforce their security, or would result in a **preferential debt** being paid otherwise than in priority to non-preferential debts or in one preferential creditor being paid a smaller proportion of his debt than another. This restriction will not apply if the creditor concerned consents, or the proposal involves the company entering into a CVA or a Scheme of Arrangement on the basis that these processes contain their own protections for these creditors (para 73 Sch B1 IA 1986).

If for any reason no statement of affairs is provided, the proposals themselves must include the names, addresses and debts of the creditors, including details of any security held. However, as would have been the case in relation to the statement of affairs, if the administrator thinks it would prejudice the conduct of the administration or might reasonably be expected to lead to violence against any person if this information were to be disclosed he may apply to court for an order for limited disclosure (r 2.33A IR 1986).

4.6.5 Initial creditors' meeting

4.6.5.1 Summoning the initial creditors' meeting

Normally, each copy of the statement of proposals must be accompanied by an invitation to an initial creditors' meeting (para 51 Sch B1 IA 1986). Such a meeting must be held as soon as reasonable practicable and in any event **within ten weeks** of the date the company entered administration (although this time period can be extended in accordance with para 107 Sch B1 IA 1986). The administrator must advertise the meeting in one or more newspapers (unless the court otherwise directs) (r 2.33 IR 1986).

Certain requirements applicable to all creditors' meetings held during the course of an administration will also apply here. As such, each creditor must be given **at least 14 days' notice** of the meeting, and the notice must specify the purpose of the meeting, explain the entitlement to vote and include a proxy form (r 2.35 IR 1986).

At the same time as he gives notice to creditors, the administrator must also give notice to any directors or officers (including past directors and officers) whose presence he thinks is required.

4.6.5.2 The function of the initial creditors' meeting

The administrator will normally preside over the meeting as chairman. The meeting will give the creditors the opportunity to ask questions of the administrator and any directors or officers present.

However, the main function of the meeting is to allow the creditors to **consider the administrators' proposals**, and they may approve them without modification, or with any modification to which the administrator consents (para 53 Sch B1 IA 1986). Approval of the proposals is likely to have implications for the remainder of the administration. As seen in Section 4.10.3, it may, for example, allow the administration ultimately to end by a CVL with no further creditors' meeting being required.

The creditors may also appoint a **creditors' committee** at this meeting (para 57 Sch B1 IA 1986). If such a committee is formed, it is likely to hold its first meeting immediately after the initial creditors' meeting. The creditors' committee is discussed further in Section 4.9.1.

4.6.5.3   Dispensing with the initial creditors' meeting

The administrator may dispense with the initial meeting of creditors if his proposals state that:

- the company has sufficient property to allow each creditor to be paid in full; **or**

- the company has insufficient property to allow any distribution to unsecured creditors other than the prescribed part; **or**

- that neither the primary nor the second objective of administration can be achieved.

The proposals must also state his reason for deciding not to call a meeting, and he must still call a meeting if this is requested by creditors whose debts amount to at least 10% of the total debts of the company (para 52 Sch B1 IA 1986).

4.6.5.4   Voting at an initial creditors' meeting

Rules 2.38 to 2.43 IR 1986 set out the procedure for voting at this, and any other, creditors' meeting and rr 8.1 to 8.8 set out further requirements in relation to proxies, but an overview is given here.

A resolution will be passed when a **majority by value** of those present and voting, in person or by proxy, have voted in favour. However, any resolution is **invalid** if those voting against it include more that half in value of the creditors to whom notice of the meeting was sent and who are not, to the best of the chairman's belief, persons connected with the company.

The proxy may be worded to state that the representative is only entitled to vote in one particular way. This may be the creditor's preferred approach where they wish simply to appoint the chairman of the meeting as their proxy. Where the creditor's own representative will attend, however, it may be wiser to return an 'open' proxy, which allows the representative to vote according to their discretion.

A creditor will only be entitled to vote if **details in writing of his debt** and (if relevant) a **proxy** appointing his representative have been lodged by noon on the business day before the meeting. However, the chairman has a discretion to allow the creditor to vote notwithstanding non-compliance with this if he is satisfied that the failure was due to circumstances beyond the creditor's control.

A creditor is not entitled to vote on an **unliquidated debt,** or one whose value is unascertained, save to the extent that the chairman agrees to put a value on it, although in *HMRC v Maxwell* [2010] EWCA Civ 1379 the Court of Appeal indicated the chairman must do his best to assess the minimum value of the claim. The chairman also has a general discretion to **accept or reject claims**, although in situations of doubt, the proper course is to mark the vote as '**objected to**' and to allow the creditor to vote. The vote may subsequently be declared invalid if the objection is sustained. There is a right to appeal to the court against a chairman's decision and the court may make such order as it thinks fit.

The decision to accept or reject a claim for voting purposes at the meeting is made on a comparatively ad hoc basis, and it is not conclusive for other subsequent purposes, such as that of establishing the value of the claim for dividend purposes.

Secured creditors are generally only able to vote in respect of the balance of their debt (if any) after deducting the value of their security. However, they will be entitled to vote in respect of the full value of their debt if the administrator has stated that the company has insufficient property to allow any distribution to unsecured creditors other than the prescribed part (see Section 4.6.5.3).

4.6.5.5   Meeting by correspondence

This, and any other, creditors' meeting can instead be conducted by correspondence (para 58 Sch B1 IA 1986). Here, 'correspondence' includes by telephone or other electronic means (para 111 Sch B1 IA 1986). In this case, the administrator must set a closing date for votes at least 14 days after he gives notice of the meeting. The administrator is still entitled to call a full meeting of creditors if a meeting by correspondence rejects his proposals. In addition, he must still call a meeting if no valid voting form has been received by noon on the closing date, or if he is requested to do so within five business days of the date he gave notice by creditors whose debts amount to at least 10% of the total debt of the company (r 2.48 IR 1986).

4.6.5.6   What happens after the meeting?

After the conclusion of the meeting, the administrator must as soon as reasonably practicable report any decision taken to the court, the Registrar of Companies, creditors who received notice of the meeting and any other person to whom the proposals were sent (para 53(2) Sch B1 IA 1986 and r 2.46 IR 1986).

The administrator is not entitled to make any **substantial amendment** to the agreed proposals without first obtaining the creditors' consent at a further creditors' meeting (para 54 Sch B1 IA 1986). If there is doubt as to whether an amendment is 'substantial', the administrator may seek directions from the court on the point under para 63 Sch B1 IA 1986 to avoid the time and expense of calling a meeting.

Under para 68(3) Sch B1 IA 1986, the court is only able to give directions in connection with the administrator's management of the company's affairs, business or property, however, if:

- no proposals have been approved;

- the directions are consistent with any approved proposals; or

- the court thinks the directions are required to reflect a change in circumstances since an earlier approval of proposals, or are desirable because of a misunderstanding about any approved proposals.

It is unclear whether the court has any residual discretion to authorise an administrator to make substantial amendments in any other circumstances.

4.6.5.7   What happens if the proposals are rejected?

If the creditors have rejected the administrator's proposals (or any revised proposals), the court may order that the administrator's appointment will cease to have effect, or adjourn the hearing, or make an interim order, or make an order on a petition for winding-up or make such other order as it considers appropriate (para 55 Sch B1 IA 1986).

Depending on the circumstances, the court may use its powers to allow the administrator time to formulate new proposals which are more likely to be accepted. The court may be reluctant to impose a set of proposals on the creditors against the will of the majority, but it may still do so, for example, where a single creditor holding a majority in value had blocked proposals supported by the majority in number (*Re Structures & Computers Ltd* [1998] BCC 348, as applied in *DKLL Solicitors v Her Majesty's Revenue & Customs* [2007] BCC 908).

4.6.6   Progress report

Under r 2.47 IR 1986, the administrator must send a progress report to the creditors, the court and the Registrar of Companies covering the first six-month period of the administration, and every subsequent six-month period. Each report should be made within one month of the end of the period covered by that report. The report must include, among other things, details of any progress made, a receipts and payments account, and details of any assets which remain to be realised. Commercially sensitive information can be excluded, but only if the administrator has first obtained an order of the court to this effect under r 7.31 IR 1986.

Rule 2.48A IR 1986 allows a secured creditor, or an unsecured creditor who has the support of at least 5% in value of the unsecured creditors (including their own claim), to make a request within 21 days of receipt of such a progress report for further information about the administrators' remuneration and expenses.

4.7   DUTIES OF THE ADMINISTRATOR

4.7.1   What are an administrator's general duties?

The administrator must:

- exercise his powers in the **interests of the company's creditors as a whole**, subject to any special considerations when pursuing the third objective only (para 3(2) Sch B1 IA 1986);

- perform his functions as **quickly and efficiently** as is reasonably practicable (para 5 Sch B1 IA 1986;

- on his appointment, **take custody and control** of all of the property to which he thinks the company is entitled (para 67 Sch B1 IA 1986); and

- manage the company's affairs, business and property **in accordance with any proposals** which have been approved by the creditors, and any directions given by the court (para 68 Sch B1 IA 1986).

Other common law duties akin to those of a liquidator described in Chapter 3 might also be regarded, broadly speaking, as applicable to an administrator. The main example in practice of an administrator's duty to exercise reasonable skill and care is his duty to obtain **the best price reasonably obtainable** on the sale of an asset. This is generally similar to the duty owed by a receiver (see Chapter 8). However, unlike a receiver, an administrator must also take reasonable care in choosing the **time** of the sale as he has no overriding duty to give priority to the interests of any appointor (see *Re Charnley Davies Ltd (No 2)* [1990] BCLC 760 and *Silven Properties Ltd v Royal Bank of Scotland plc* [2004] 4 All ER 484).

Like a liquidator in a compulsory liquidation, an administrator is an **officer of the court**.

4.7.2   How might an administrator's actions be challenged?

4.7.2.1   Challenge to conduct

A creditor or shareholder may apply to the court claiming that either:

- the administrator has acted, is acting or proposes to act in a way which **unfairly harms**, or would unfairly harm his interests (whether alone or in common with other members or creditors) (para 74(1) Sch B1 IA 1986); or

- the administrator is not performing his functions as **quickly and efficiently** as is reasonably practicable (para 74(2) Sch B1 IA 1986).

In *Re Lehman Brothers International (Europe) Limited* [2008] EWHC 2869 (Ch), it was emphasised that for a claim under para 74(1), the harm suffered must be unfair. An administrator will often be entitled to harm the interests of individual creditors if his actions are genuinely aimed at improving the position of creditors as a whole.

The court may grant relief, dismiss the application, adjourn the hearing conditionally or unconditionally, make an interim order or make any other order it thinks fit. However, an order may in particular:

- regulate the administrator's exercise of his functions;

- require the administrator to do or not do a specified thing;

- require a creditors' meeting to be held for a specified purpose; or

- provide for the appointment of the administrator to cease to have effect.

An order may be made on an 'unfair harm' claim notwithstanding that the action complained of was within the administrators' power, or was taken in reliance on a order under para 71 or 72 Sch B1 IA 1986 (see Section 4.8.3). However, no order may be made if it would prevent the implementation of a CVA or Scheme of Arrangement (where creditors enjoy their own separate protection) or of proposals or revisions approved more than 28 days before the application was made.

4.7.2.2 Misfeasance

Under para 75 Sch B1 IA 1986, the Official Receiver, a liquidator, a subsequent administrator, a creditor or a shareholder may apply to court where they allege that the administrator:

- has misapplied or retained money or other property of the company;

- has become accountable for money or other property of the company;

- has breached a fiduciary or other duty in relation to the company; or

- has been guilty of misfeasance.

The court may examine the administrator's conduct and order him to repay, restore or account for money or property, to pay interest, or to contribute a sum to the company's property by way of compensation for breach of duty or misfeasance. As a general principle, the administrator does not owe a duty to individual creditors and any recovery under this provision will be for the general benefit of all creditors (*Oldham v Kyrris* [2004] BCC 111).

4.8 POWERS OF THE ADMINISTRATOR

4.8.1 General powers

The administrator may do anything necessary and expedient for the management of the affairs, business and property of the company (para 59(1) Sch B1 IA 1986). Their powers are accordingly not restricted to the management of the business, unlike the powers of the directors. In addition, para 60 Sch B1 IA 1986 gives an administrator the wide powers contained in Sch 1 IA 1986. These powers are set out in Table 4.5.

Any person dealing with an administrator in good faith and for value need not enquire whether the administrator is acting within his powers (para 59(3) Sch B1 IA 1986).

The administrator is also given powers:

- to **remove or appoint a director** of the company (para 61 Sch B1 IA 1986);

- to **call a meeting** of shareholders or creditors of the company (para 62 Sch B1 IA 1986);

- to **apply to court for directions** in connection with the carrying out of his functions (para 63 Sch B1 IA 1986).

However, the courts have made it clear that the wide nature of the administrator's general powers should make it unnecessary in many cases for directions to be sought in respect of commercial or administrative matters, particularly where urgent action is required in the interests of the company and its creditors. Thus in appropriate circumstances, the administrator has the power to sell the company's business without the prior approval of the creditors or the permission of the court (see *Re T & D Industries Plc* [2000] 1 WLR 646 and *Re Transbus International Ltd* [2004] 1 WLR 2654). This will be particularly relevant in the case of a pre-pack (see Section 4.11).

Table 4.5 – Powers of an administrator

1	To take possession of, collect and get in the property of the company and, for that purpose, to take such proceedings as may seem to him expedient.
2	To sell or otherwise dispose of the property of the company by public auction or private auction or private contract.
3	To raise or borrow money and grant security therefor over the property of the company.
4	To appoint a solicitor or accountant or other professionally qualified person to assist him in the performance of his functions.
5	To bring or defend any action or other legal proceedings in the name of and on behalf of the company.
6	To refer to arbitration any question affecting the company.
7	To effect and maintain insurances in respect of the business and property of the company.
8	To use the company's seal.
9	To do all acts and to execute in the name and on behalf of the company any deed, receipt or other document.
10	To draw, accept, make and endorse any bill of exchange or promissory note in the name and on behalf of the company.
11	To appoint any agent to do any business which he is unable to do himself or which can more conveniently be done by an agent and to employ and dismiss employees.
12	To do all such things (including the carrying out of works) as may be necessary for the realisation of the property of the company.
13	To make any payment which is necessary or incidental to the performance of his functions.
14	To carry on the business of the company.
15	To establish subsidiaries of the company.
16	To transfer to subsidiaries of the company the whole or any part of the business and property of the company.
17	To grant or accept a surrender of a lease or tenancy of any of the property of the company, and to take a lease or tenancy of any property required or convenient for the business of the company.
18	To make any arrangement or compromise on behalf of the company.
19	To call up any uncalled capital of the company.
20	To rank and claim in the bankruptcy, insolvency, sequestration or liquidation of any person indebted to the company and to receive dividends, and to accede to trust deeds for the creditors of any such person.
21	To present or defend a petition for the winding-up of the company.
22	To change the situation of the company's registered office.
23	To do all other things incidental to the exercise of the foregoing powers.

4.8.2 Power to make distributions and payments

Under para 65 Sch B1 IA 1986, the administrator is given the power to make distributions to creditors, although he is not entitled to make a distribution to a creditor who is neither secured nor preferential without the permission of the court. This power is expressly subject to the priority status of preferential creditors (see Chapter 2).

Provided the court is willing to grant permission, however, the administrator will be able to make a general distribution to all unsecured creditors or to any class of them (a '**distribution**' administration). Rules 2.68 to 2.105 IR 1986 cover this process – these rules are substantially similar to the equivalent rules in a CVL (see Chapter 3). The unsecured creditors will receive appropriate notice that the administrator is proposing to make a distribution (r 2.68(2) IR 1986) and can then take any further action they think necessary. However, it seems that distribution administrations remain the exception rather than the norm.

In addition, under para 66 Sch B1 IA 1986, the administrator is given the power to make a payment otherwise than in accordance with para 65 Sch B1 or para 13 Sch 1 (see Table 4.5) if he thinks it likely to assist achievement of the purpose of administration. This power may be used, for example:

• to make **duress payments** to an essential supplier who stipulates the arrears must be paid off as a precondition of any future supply; and

• to make payments to employees under the national laws of EU Member States to which they would not have been entitled under English insolvency law, thus avoiding the need for secondary proceedings in other Member States (*Re MG Rover Espana* [2006] BCC 599 and *Re Collins & Aikman Europe SA* [2006] BCC 861).

The administrators will need to ensure that they will have sufficient monies to meet all administration expenses and other sums ranking in priority to these under para 99 Sch B1 IA 1986 (see Section 2.4.3) before they can make a distribution to floating charge or unsecured creditors. In *WW Realisations 1 Limited* [2010] EWHC 3604 the court was prepared to help the administrators by directing that they were not required to make provision for administration expenses unless the relevant claims had been made by a specified cut-off date.

4.8.3   Power to deal with charged or 'hire purchase' property

The administrator is entitled to dispose of property which is subject to a floating charge as if it were not subject to that security. The floating charge holder will then have the same priority in respect of the proceeds of sale as he had in the property sold (para 70 Sch B1 IA 1986).

The administrator may, however, only dispose of property which is subject to a **fixed charge** (or any other type of security other than a floating charge) without the consent of the charge holder if he obtains an **order from the court**. The court may in turn only make such an order if it thinks that disposal of the property would be likely to promote the purpose of administration. In addition, any order is subject to the condition that:

• the net proceeds of disposal of the property; and

• any additional money required to be added to the net proceeds so as to produce the amount determined by the court to be the net amount which would be realised on a sale of the property at market value,

be applied towards discharging the sums secured by the security (para 71 Sch B1 IA 1986).

Similar provisions to those which apply in relation to fixed charged property allow an administrator to dispose of goods which are in the possession of the company under a hire-purchase agreement (which for these purposes includes a conditional sale agreement, a chattel leasing agreement and a retention of title agreement), even though the company does not own that property (paras 72 and 111 Sch B1 1986).

4.8.4 Power to require continuing supply of utilities and services

Section 233 IA 1986 makes special provisions in relation to:

- a supply of gas by a gas supplier within the meaning of Part I of the Gas Act 1986;

- a supply of electricity by an electricity supplier within the meaning of Part I of the Electricity Act 1989;

- a supply of water by a water undertaker; and

- a supply of communications services by a provider of a public electronic communications service.

Should the administrator request that the providers of these utilities continue to supply the company in administration, those providers will not be entitled to insist as a condition of giving that supply, or do anything which has the effect of making it a condition of giving that supply, that any outstanding charges arising prior to the administration are paid. The providers are, however, still entitled to impose a condition that the administrator personally guarantees the payment of any ongoing charges.

The purpose of this section is to prevent providers of certain utilities from exploiting a monopoly position, for example to insist on the ransom payment of pre-administration arrears as a precondition of further supply.

At the time of writing, further legislation is begin proposed to require information technology providers and other essential suppliers to continue to supply a company in administration without varying their terms of supply or increasing charges.

4.8.5 Specific powers of investigation

The administrator has the same powers of investigation under ss 234 and 236 IA 1986 as a liquidator (see Chapter 3). The administrator will also be assisted by the directors' and employees' duty to co-operate with the insolvency officeholder under s 235 IA 1986 (see Chapter 6).

4.8.6 Joint administrators

More than one person is entitled to act as administrator. The fact that there are two or more joint administrators does not automatically mean that each administrator needs to sign a document or authorise any other action for it to be effective. Provided the administrator's appointment so states, any act required or authorised to be done by the administrator can be done by either one or more of any joint administrators holding office (para 100(2) Sch B1 IA 1986). Usual practice is to have joint administrators, so that if one is unavailable another can act.

4.8.7 Consequence of agency

The administrator is the agent of the company. As such he has the power to bind the company as its agent without personal liability (para 69 Sch B1 IA 1986). When executing documents during the administration, therefore, the administrator signs in the company's name rather than his own name. However, as a matter of caution the administrator will usually still include a provision excluding his personal liability and will therefore usually also be a separate party to the document in his own right solely to receive the benefit of this provision.

4.9 SUPERVISION OF THE ADMINISTRATOR

4.9.1 The creditors' committee

Control lies largely with the creditors. As previously described, a creditors' committee may be set up. This will consist of between three and five creditors, and usually a representative sample of different types of creditor will be chosen. The committee may require the administrator to attend upon it at any reasonable time of which he is given seven days' notice and to provide it with information about the exercise of his functions (para 57 Sch B1 IA 1986).

Various powers and functions of the creditors' committee are set out in detail in rr 2.50 to 2.65 IR 1986. It will, among other things:

● 	fix and approve the administrator's remuneration (r 2.106 IR 1986); and

● 	grant the administrator's discharge at the end of his appointment.

If there is no creditors' committee, the administrator will generally instead need to call a creditors' meeting to seek the relevant approvals.

4.9.2 The role of the court

It is possible for a creditor to apply to the court for directions as to how the administrator may perform his functions (para 68 Sch B1 IA 1986). However, in *Re Lehman Brothers International (Europe) Limited* [2008] EWHC 2869 (Ch) (already discussed in Section 4.7.2), the court indicated that, where there was no suggestion that the administrator was acting improperly, it would be disinclined to interfere in the day-to-day management of the administration.

In extreme cases creditors have also applied to court for the removal of the administrator and for another administrator to be appointed in his place (para 88 Sch B1 IA 1986). Such an application succeeded in *Clydesdale Financial Services Limited v Smailes* [2009] EWHC 1745 (Ch) where it enjoyed the support of the majority of the creditors. However, in *Finnerty v Clark* [2011] EWCA Civ 858, the court made it clear that if an administrator was unbiased and entitled on the material before him to reach a relevant decision, that decision should be respected unless the court concludes otherwise – the fact that another administrator might reach a different decision was not a reason to remove the existing administrator.

4.10   ENDING THE ADMINISTRATION

4.10.1   Overview

The legislation provides seven possible methods for ending an administration. These methods reflect the fact that administration is generally intended to be a temporary step on the way to the company's eventual survival or to some other process, although it is possible for an administration to be the last step in a company's life. In practice, some of these methods described are used more commonly than others. It is still most likely that an administration will end with the company being placed into creditors' voluntary liquidation (see Section 4.10.3).

4.10.2   Automatic end of administration

Under para 76 Sch B1 IA 1986, if no other action is taken, the administrator's appointment automatically ceases to have effect on the first anniversary of the date on which the administrator was appointed.

This one-year period may be extended:

- by **creditors' consent**, but only once, only for a period of six months, and not if the period has already previously been extended by court order (paras 76(2)(b) and 78 Sch B1 IA 1986); or

- by **court order**, for any period thought necessary (paras 76(2)(a) and 77 Sch B1 IA 1986). The court is, however, likely to require evidence that the administrator is complying with his duty to act as quickly and efficiently as possible and that the purpose of administration remains reasonably likely to be achieved.

The administrator will need to act promptly, as it is not generally possible to obtain an extension retrospectively (see *Re TT Industries Ltd* [2006] BCC 372).

4.10.3   Moving from administration to creditors' voluntary liquidation

Where the administrator thinks that the total amount which each secured creditor is likely to receive has been paid to it or set aside for it, and that a distribution will be made to unsecured creditors (if any), he may convert the administration into a creditors' voluntary liquidation (para 83 Sch B1 IA 1986). To do so, he sends a prescribed form notice to the Registrar of Companies (with copies to the court and to each creditor of whose name and address he is aware). On the date this notice is registered:

- the company is placed into creditors' voluntary liquidation as if a shareholders' resolution in this effect had been passed on that date; and

- the administrator's appointment ends.

In *Re Globespan Airways Limited* [2012] EWCA Civ 1159, the Court of Appeal noted the difficulty that could potentially emerge if administrators lodged a conversion notice prior to the date the administration was due to end, but it was not registered until after this date. The court addressed this by finding that the administrators' term of office was automatically extended by implication until the date of registration.

The **liquidator** will be either the person previously nominated as such by the creditors when the administrator's proposals were passed or, if no-one has been nominated, the administrator. This therefore provides a very streamlined approach for moving to liquidation, as it expressly avoids the need to hold a further meeting of either shareholders or creditors for the purpose.

4.10.4   Moving from administration to dissolution

Alternatively, if the administrator thinks that the company has no property which would permit a distribution to its creditors, he may instigate its dissolution. To do so, he sends a prescribed form of notice to the Registrar of Companies (with copies to the court and to each creditor of whose name and address he is aware). On the date this notice is registered the administrator's appointment ends. The company is deemed to be dissolved three months afterwards.

This method, coupled with the administrator's ability to make distributions to creditors, will enable him to bring the company's affairs to an end without the need for a separate liquidation (*Re GHE Realisations Ltd* [2006] 1 WLR 287).

4.10.5   Termination by application to court by the administrator

Under paras 79(1) and (2) Sch B1 IA 1986, the administrator may apply to court to end the administration, and indeed he must do if:

• he thinks that the purpose of the administration cannot be achieved;

• he thinks the company should not have entered into administration; or

• a resolution is passed at a creditors' meeting requiring him to do so.

The court may adjourn the hearing conditionally or unconditionally, dismiss the application, make an interim order or make any other order it thinks appropriate. In *Re TM Kingdom Ltd* [2007] BCC 480 this route allowed a company to move to a creditors' voluntary liquidation where, for various reasons, other routes were unavailable.

4.10.6   Termination where the purpose of administration is achieved

Where the administrator was originally **appointed by court order**, he must apply to the court if he thinks the purpose of administration has been sufficiently achieved (para 79(3) Sch B1 IA 1986). The court may make the same range of orders as in Section 4.10.5.

In *Re Hellas Telecommunications (Luxembourg) II SCA (in administration)* [2011] EWHC 3176 (Ch), the court refused to allow the company to serve a notice on the Registrar of Companies to instigate its dissolution but instead ordered that the company go into compulsory liquidation. This case is discussed further in Section 3.8.2.

Where an administrator **appointed out of court** thinks the purpose of administration has been sufficiently achieved, he may alternatively end the administration by filing a prescribed form of notice with the court and the Registrar of Companies (para 80

Sch B1 IA 1986). He must also comply with certain requirements to give notice to creditors (r 2.113 IR 1986).

4.10.7 Termination on application by a creditor

A creditor may apply to court for the administration to end if he considers that the applicant for a court order or the out of court appointor had an improper motive (para 81 Sch B1 IA 1986). The court may make the same range of orders as in Section 4.10.5. The court has suggested that a director who transferred all of a company's assets to another company which he owned before appointing an administrator of his own choice might be found to have an 'improper motive' (*Coyne & Hardy v DRC Distribution Ltd & Foster* [2008] BCC 612).

4.10.8 Termination following a public interest winding-up petition

Under para 82 Sch B1 IA 1986, when a winding-up order is made following a petition presented on public interest grounds, or by the Financial Services Authority under s 367 FSMA 2000, or a provisional liquidator is appointed following such a petition, the court may order that the administrator's appointment ceases to have effect. Alternatively, it may allow the administrator to remain concurrently in office with a liquidator, but modify his powers.

4.10.9 The administrator's discharge

Under para 98 Sch B1 IA 1986, the administrator will be discharged from all liability in respect of any of his actions as administrator:

- where the administrator was appointed out of court, at a time appointed by a resolution of the creditors' committee or, if there is no such committee, by resolution of the creditors. Note here that if the administrator has stated that the company has insufficient property to allow any distribution to unsecured creditors other than the prescribed part (see Section 4.6.5.3), any resolution requires the approval of each secured creditor and (to the extent that a distribution has been or may be made to preferential creditors) 50% by value of the preferential creditors; or

- in any case, at a time specified by the court.

However, this does not protect the former administrator from a later claim under para 75 Sch B1 IA 1986, which can be brought at any time whilst the company remains in existence. Such an action is possible even if the company has been dissolved, as long as the time period for restoring the company has not yet expired.

4.11 PRE-PACKAGED ADMINISTRATIONS

4.11.1 What is a pre-packaged administration?

The essential difference between a conventional (or 'trading') administration and a pre-packaged administration is that the latter is entirely pre-planned before the administrator is appointed. The purchaser is identified, and will agree the sale assets and the price in advance. The sale agreement is also drafted and negotiated. The administrator enters into the pre-agreed sale agreement almost immediately after his appointment.

A 'pre-packaged' sale of a company's business or other assets by an insolvency officeholder can involve a formal insolvency process other than administration. Indeed, historically such a sale would more likely have involved a receivership or liquidation. However, various features of the administration process, including the ability of the directors to appoint an administrator out of court and the ability of the administrator to sell the company's entire business without prior reference to the creditors mean that it is mechanistically well-suited to a pre-packaged sale. The term '**pre-pack**' therefore has become largely synonymous with a pre-packaged administration.

The uses of a pre-pack as a restructuring tool are discussed in Chapter 10. This section discusses some of the general considerations involved in a pre-pack.

4.11.2   How is the proposed administrator involved prior to appointment?

The proposed administrator will be chosen at an early stage. He will play a key role in negotiating the sale terms prior to his appointment, since ultimately it is he who will direct the company to enter into the sale.

On any sale of the business, the administrator will need to show that he has complied with his duty to obtain the best price reasonably obtainable (see Section 4.7.1). In a conventional administration, the administrator will seek to comply with this duty by advertising the business for sale on the open market, using whatever method is most appropriate.

In a pre-pack, the administrator may be able to rely on marketing carried out prior to his appointment. In many pre-packs, however, the business will not be marketed in advance, as this could draw attention to the impending insolvency and could adversely affect the business. The proposed administrator will instead need to obtain professional valuations prior to the sale and rely on these. In this case, normal practice is to obtain two such valuations as a precaution. Typically, the administrator will also wish to ensure that the price payable is comfortably in excess of the higher of these valuations to ensure that he cannot be successfully challenged for not having exposed the business to the market.

4.11.3   What are the advantages of a pre-packaged administration?

The key advantage to the business going forwards, and therefore to the purchaser, is that the speed of the sale preserves goodwill by helping to retain those employees, suppliers and customers who are crucial to the business. A conventional administration will always involve a period of uncertainty before the fate of the business is known, and this might unnerve these parties. In a pre-pack the business will have been transferred to a solvent purchaser before the majority of them ever learn of the administration. The administration and the completed sale can therefore be announced both within the business and to the outside world in a single, upbeat statement.

A sale out of administration is attractive to the directors because it will be the administrator, not the directors, who is legally responsible for ensuring that a proper price is achieved on the sale.

It is argued that creditors also benefit because a pre-packaged business sale enables the business to be sold as a going concern, which should realise more than the break-up and sale of assets. A potential administrator may regard a conventional administration as unfeasible for a number of reasons, including the difficulty of funding an ongoing administration process, the effect of TUPE, the likelihood that key suppliers will seek duress payments, the possibility that no buyer will ultimately be found and the inherent risks of continued trading generally, leaving a pre-pack as the most attractive option for selling the business.

4.11.4   What are the criticisms of pre-packs?

Pre-packs are controversial for a number of reasons, including the following:

- The existing insolvency legislation does not expressly contemplate their use (although see Sections 4.11.5 to 4.11.7), and a process which results in the immediate sale of the company's business seems to be the reverse of the primary objective of administration, ie to rescue the company as a going concern.

- The majority of creditors are only told what has happened after the event. They have no opportunity to vote on the proposed sale, leading to a sense of impotence and frustration.

- The purchaser is often a company controlled by existing management and/ or other existing stakeholders. Without testing the market, it is impossible to know with certainty that no 'outside' purchaser exists who would be prepared to pay more.

In a report commissioned by the Association of Business Recovery Professionals, Dr Sandra Frisby has considered the use of pre-packs against this background. Her conclusions are summarised in Table 4.6.

Table 4.6 – Summary of Dr Sandra Frisby's conclusions regarding pre-packs

1	Pre-packs are increasing sharply in number over time, notably in administrations.
2	A wide range of firms carry out pre-packs, ranging from the Big Four to smaller practices.
3	It may be that pre-packs are being used in predominantly 'small' cases.
4	There are grounds for calling for a more rigorous disclosure regime, particularly in relation to practitioners' statements of proposals and other reports to creditors. However, overall, pre-pack reports tend to be more informative than reports on other business sales.
5	While pre-packs give creditors no chance to vote on the sale of a business, this is also true of the majority of cases where the business is sold other than through a pre-pack.
6	Proportionally more pre-pack sales are to connected parties than are non pre-packaged business sales, and this trend is accelerating in post-EA pre-packaged administration sales.
7	There is some evidence to suggest that pre-packs result in lower overall returns for unsecured creditors.

8   There is clear evidence that pre-packs perform better than non pre-packaged business sales in preserving employment.

9   Businesses sold by pre-packs may fail slightly more often than non pre-packaged business sales, but this is inconclusively demonstrated. There is however clear evidence that where a business is sold to a connected party, it is more likely to fail afterwards.

4.11.5 What is the attitude of the courts?

As noted in Section 4.8.1, the courts had recognised for some time that even in a conventional administration assets may need to be sold urgently with the result that the approval of creditors cannot always be sought, but had still not contemplated specific sales at the time they granted an administration order. *DKLL Solicitors v Her Majesty's Revenue & Customs* [2007] BCC 908, the facts of which are summarised in the box below, is the first reported case where the court was prepared to grant an administration order where it was aware that the intention was to carry out a pre-packaged sale immediately after the administrators' appointment.

In *Kayley Vending Limited* [2009] EWHC 904 (Ch), the court reviewed some of the main criticisms of pre-packs and gave guidance as to the approach it would take when faced with such an application. The court would be alert to see, so far as it could, that the procedure was at least not obviously being abused to the disadvantage of creditors. As such, it would normally expect the evidence supporting the application to include in most cases the information identified in SIP 16 (see Section 4.11.7), insofar as this was known or ascertainable at the date of the application. Where some of this information was still commercially sensitive, appropriate arrangements could be made with the court to protect its confidentiality.

In *Hellas Telecommunications (Luxembourg) II SCA* [2009] EWHC 3199 (Ch), the court made it clear that in general the question of whether to enter into a sale remained one for the administrator, and that in the majority of cases the making of an administration order, even in the context of a pre-pack, should not be taken as the court's blessing of the pre-pack sale. Nonetheless, in the *Hellas* case itself, the court determined that the sale proposed was 'the only real way forward' and was prepared not only to make the administration order sought but also expressly to give the administrators liberty to enter into the pre-pack.

Given that the majority of administrators are appointed out of court, however, there will be relatively few occasions where creditors will have the opportunity to question the proposed sale in advance at a court hearing. Normally, creditors would need to challenge the sale after it had already occurred.

> *DKLL Solicitors v Her Majesty's Revenue & Customs* [2007] BCC 908
>
> The partners of DKLL applied to the court for an administration order. It was proposed that, once appointed, the administrators would immediately sell the partnership's business to a newly incorporated partnership for a total consideration of £400,000.
>
> The proposed administrators had concluded that based on the information available to them, the proposed sale represented a better outcome for creditors

and stakeholders than would be achieved on a liquidation. There was some evidence that a forced sale on a liquidation would realise only £105,000. In addition, a liquidation would create an extra £44,000 of preferential claims by employees.

HMRC argued that, as the majority creditor of the partnership by value, it would be in a position to defeat the administrator's proposals at a creditors' meeting. It would therefore effectively be disenfranchised if the sale were to proceed without a creditors' meeting taking place.

The court noted, however, that even a majority creditor does not have an absolute veto on the implementation of an administrator's proposals. Even if the pre-pack route were not followed here, allowing HMRC to defeat the administrators' proposals at a creditors' meeting, there was a real prospect that a court would subsequently be prepared to authorise the proposed sale.

In the light of this, the court considered fully whether the proposed administration order was reasonably likely to achieve the purpose of the administration. It took into account HMRC's opposition, but also the interests of the 'other stakeholders'. It was particularly influenced by the fact that the proposed sale appeared to be the only way of saving the jobs of the 50-odd employees of the partnership. It also noted that the proposed sale was also likely to result in the affairs of the partnership's clients being dealt with, with the minimum of disruption. It therefore made the administration order sought.

4.11.6   Pre-pack costs

When implementing a pre-packaged administration, significant costs will almost inevitably be incurred before the date when the administrator is formally appointed. Rule 2.33(2A) to (2C) IR 1986 makes specific provision for an administrator to put together a statement of fees charged and expenses incurred prior to the company entering into administration but with a view to it doing so. Under r 2.67A IR 1986, the creditors' committee may then determine whether and to what extent unpaid pre-administration costs are approved for payment as an expense of the administration.

If there is no creditors' committee, or the creditors' committee fails to give its approval, or if the administrator considers the amount approved to be insufficient, the task of approving pre-administration costs will then be passed to a full meeting of creditors. However, if the administrator has stated that the company has insufficient property to allow any distribution to unsecured creditors other than the prescribed part (see Section 4.6.5.3), approval is required from each secured creditor and (to the extent that a distribution has been or may be made to preferential creditors) 50% by value of the preferential creditors.

If this in turn still fails to produce an approval at a level the administrator considers sufficient he may apply to court for an appropriate determination. The courts have made it clear that it is a matter for their discretion as to whether to allow such costs. In exercising this discretion, the courts have looked at whether the effect of the pre-pack was to allow management to retain the business and if so, whether the advantage to them in doing so outweighed the advantage of the pre-pack to the creditors. In *Kayley Vending* the court was satisfied that there was a benefit to creditors and no question of a purchase by management, and thus approved the payment of the pre-administration costs. In *Re Johnson Machine and Tool Co Limited* [2010] EWHC 582 (Ch), however, which did involve a purchase by a company connected with the existing directors, the court declined to give its approval as these costs should more appropriately be borne by those directors.

4.11.7 What professional guidance has been given to insolvency practitioners?

4.11.7.1 Statement of Insolvency Practice 16

SIP 16 was introduced specifically to address pre-packs, and applies to sales taking place on or after 1 January 2009.

The administrator must:

- Keep a detailed record of the reasons why a pre-packaged sale has been chosen as the best course of action for creditors.

- Make it clear to the directors of the company that he has been appointed to advise the company, and not the directors on their personal positions, where that is the case.

- Encourage the directors of the company to take independent advice, in particular if any director proposes to acquire assets in the sale.

SIP 16 reminds administrators that they need to demonstrate that they have performed their functions in the interests of the company's creditors as a whole and have avoided unnecessarily harming the interests of creditors as a whole when realising property to distribute to secured or preferential creditors (see Section 4.2).

In addition, SIP 16 recognises that unsecured creditors have no opportunity to provide input on the sale before it takes place, and a number of its provisions are intended to improve transparency. Unless there are exceptional circumstances, the administrator must disclose certain specified information to creditors, including:

- the identity of the buyer of the business or assets;

- any valuations of the business or underlying assets obtained;

- any alternative courses of action considered by the administrator;

- the consideration for the sale and the terms of payment; and

- any connection between the buyer and the directors, former directors, shareholders or secured creditors of the company.

If information is withheld due to exceptional circumstances, the administrator must disclose the nature of these circumstances. SIP 16 notes that if the sale is to a connected party it is unlikely that considerations of commercial confidentiality would outweigh the need for creditors to be provided with this information.

A revised form of SIP 16 is due to be introduced in May 2013.

4.11.7.2 Statement of Insolvency Practice 13

SIP 13 might also be relevant here, as it deals with the administrator's duties upon the acquisition of assets of an insolvent company by its directors. The administrator must take steps to ensure that the transaction is carried out on an arm's-length basis, and that documents are retained to evidence this. He should not assist with conduct which might undermine confidence in the insolvency profession, and should not assist in behaviour which amounts to misfeasance.

4.11.7.3 Insolvency Service complaints hotline

The Insolvency Service has introduced a hotline for creditors wishing to complain about a pre-packaged administration or who consider that they have been unduly disadvantaged by an administration (or any other corporate insolvency process). Details of this are currently on its website at http://www.insolvency.gov.uk/howtocomplain/complainprepack.htm.

Chapter 5

Antecedent transactions

5.1 INTRODUCTION

5.1.1 Overview

As was explained in detail in Chapter 2, if a company goes into liquidation, its assets (if any) after secured and preferential creditors have been paid will be distributed among its unsecured creditors *pari passu* ie in proportion to the amount of the admitted debt owed to each creditor. This is the liquidation 'dividend'. The purpose of liquidation is to achieve equality among unsecured creditors. Similarly, if a company goes into a 'distribution' administration, its assets may be distributed in a similar manner.

The IA 1986 contains a number of provisions designed to prevent steps being taken ahead of liquidation or administration to defeat the *pari passu* principle. In particular, liquidators and administrators (and in some cases creditors) have powers to seek redress in circumstances where assets have been removed from the company at less than their proper value, or individual creditors have been given preferential treatment. These are discussed in this chapter. As discussed further in Chapter 6, directors found to have been involved in approving transactions of this kind may incur personal liability or disqualification.

In addition to the specific types of antecedent transaction described in this chapter, the courts have also been prepared to set aside arrangements which they regard as attempts to contract out of applicable insolvency law, on the basis that they are therefore void as a matter of public policy. This has already been discussed in Chapter 2.

5.1.2 Actions available

Table 5.1 illustrates the possible actions available.

Table 5.1 – Possible actions available

Section of IA 1986	Transaction avoided	Available to
Section 238	Transactions at an undervalue	Liquidator or administrator
Section 239	Preferences	Liquidator or administrator
Section 244	Extortionate credit transactions	Liquidator or administrator
Section 245	Floating charges for no new value	Liquidator or administrator
Section 423	Transactions defrauding creditors	Liquidator, administrator or a creditor
Section 127	Distributions post-presentation of winding-up petition	Liquidator
None (common law remedy)	Arrangements in contravention of the anti-deprivation principle or rule in *British Eagle* (discussed in Chapter 2)	Affected party

As will be discussed further below, many of these actions will depend on the transaction or other event in question having occurred during a particular time period. These time periods are sometimes described as the 'hardening periods' for a transaction, since once they have elapsed without the 'onset of insolvency' having occurred, the transaction can no longer be attacked under the relevant section of the legislation. For certain actions, the time period in question will also differ depending on whether a beneficiary of the transaction was connected to the company. These time periods are summarised in Table 5.2.

Table 5.2 – 'Hardening periods'

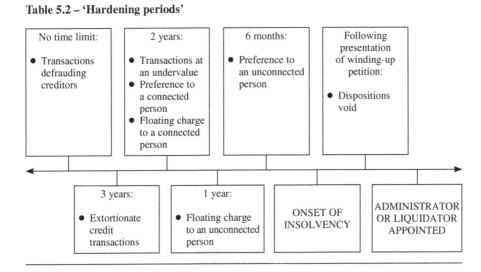

5.1.3 What is the 'onset of insolvency'?

The onset of insolvency is the end point from which the various time periods indicated above are calculated. It does not depend on when the company first becomes unable to pay its debts, but on when a specific step is taken to instigate the company's formal insolvency. It is defined in s 240(3) IA 1986 as follows:

- where a company goes into **administration** as a result of a **court order**, the date on which the administration application was made;

- where a company goes into **administration** as a result of an **out of court appointment**, the date on which the copy of the notice of intention to appoint was filed at court (or if no notice of intention is filed, the date on which the administrator's appointment takes effect);

- where a company goes into **compulsory liquidation** (except where that liquidation follows an earlier administration process), the date of presentation of the winding-up petition;

- where a company goes into **voluntary liquidation** (except where that liquidation follows an earlier administration process), the date on which the resolution was passed for the winding-up of the company;

- where a company goes into any type of **liquidation following an earlier administration process**, the date on which the onset of insolvency occurred in relation to that earlier administration process, as described above.

5.2 TRANSACTIONS AT AN UNDERVALUE

5.2.1 What is a transaction at an undervalue?

The liquidator or administrator of a company which has at a 'relevant time' entered into a transaction with any person at an undervalue may apply to the court under s 238 IA 1986 for an order restoring the position to what it would have been if the company had not entered into the transaction.

'**Transaction**' is not exhaustively defined in the IA 1986. It expressly includes a gift, agreement or arrangement, but is sufficiently wide to cover any dealing with the company whether formal or informal.

A transaction is at an **undervalue** if:

- the company makes a gift or otherwise enters into a transaction on terms that provide for the company to receive no consideration (ie payment or other benefit); or

- the company enters into a transaction for a consideration the value of which, in money or money's worth, is **significantly less**, in money or money's worth, than the consideration provided by the company.

This is considered further in Section 5.2.2.

A transaction at an undervalue is entered into at a **relevant time** if:

- the company is unable to pay its debts at that time, or becomes unable to pay its debts as a result of the transaction, and

- if the **onset of insolvency** occurs within **two years** of the company entering into the transaction, or if the transaction is entered into between the date on which an administration application is made or a notice of intention is filed and the date on which the administrator is appointed.

If the transaction is entered into with a person **connected** with the company, however, the onus is on the connected person to show that the company was able to pay its debts at the time of the transaction and remained so immediately afterwards. Section 5.8 considers when a person is connected.

Transactions at an undervalue – summary

A transaction cannot be set aside as a transaction at an undervalue under s 238 IA 1986 if:

- the company received consideration which was not significantly less in money's worth than true value of any asset transferred by (or released by) it; **or**

- the company was able to pay its debts at the date of the transaction and remained so immediately afterwards; **or**

- no administration or liquidation process is successfully instigated for at least two years after the date of the transaction; **or**

- the court can be convinced that the transaction was entered into in good faith and for the purpose of carrying on its business and that at the time there were reasonable grounds for believing that the transaction would benefit the company.

5.2.2   How is 'value' determined?

As a starting point, the value of an asset should be regarded as not less than the amount which a well-informed purchaser is prepared in arm's-length negotiations to pay for it (as per *Phillips v Brewin Dolphin Bell Lawrie Limited* [2001] 1 WLR 143).

In light of this, the safest way of determining value would be properly to expose the asset to the market (if a market exists). The alternative is to obtain an expert valuation, although as case law has shown this may not be sufficient in itself if mistakes have been made in the valuation. Indeed, any two valuers may disagree significantly as to the value of the asset. In some cases, particularly where there is not a ready market for the asset in question, the court may accept that there are a range of possible figures within which the value might lie (*Ramlort v Reid* [2005] 1 BCLC 331). Nonetheless, a buyer may consider it prudent to insist that the company obtains two valuations to guard against a single valuation falling outside the accepted range.

The value in question is the value to the company, not to the counterparty. Thus the consideration provided by a company will include any loss of value it suffers to its remaining assets. This is illustrated by *Agricultural Mortgage Corporation plc v Woodward* [1994] BCC 688 (a case which principally concerned s 423 IA 1986), where the counterparty was granted a protected tenancy. Although a market rent was payable, the counterparty's security of tenure also significantly reduced the value of the land. In contrast, if the asset has a special value to the counterparty which does not affect the company or its remaining assets, this need not be taken into account.

It may be necessary to look at the combined effects of a series of linked transactions to determine value. Among other things, consideration provided by a third party may be taken into account in determining value (*Phillips v Brewin Dolphin Bell Lawrie Limited*, the facts of which are described in the box below).

The court may apply hindsight to determine value (*Phillips v Brewin Dolphin Bell Lawrie Limited* and also *Re Thoars (Deceased)* [2003] 1 BCLC 499).

Phillips v Brewin Dolphin Bell Lawrie Limited **[2001] 1 WLR 143**

A J Bekhor & Co ('AJB') negotiated to sell its business to Brewin Dolphin & Co Limited ('B Ltd') for £1.25m. To achieve this, AJB transferred the business to its wholly-owned subsidiary, Bekhor Securities Limited ('BSL') for £1. It then sold its shares in BSL to B Ltd. In return:

- B Ltd assumed AJB's liability to its employees for certain redundancy payments, later assessed at £325,000.

- Under a separate agreement, B Ltd's parent, Private Capital Group ('PCG') agreed to pay £312,500 per annum (in arrears) to AJB over four years under a sub-lease of certain computer equipment which AJB had itself leased from third parties.

- PCG made a loan of £312,500 to AJB which was intended to be set off against the first payment of sub-rent.

AJB defaulted on their rental payment under the head leases of the computer equipment, and the third parties duly repossessed the equipment. PCG thus treated the sub-lease as terminated and made no payments to AJB.

AJB was subsequently wound up and its liquidator brought proceedings contending that the arrangement under which the BSL shares were sold was a transaction at an undervalue.

The court concluded that:

- The linked agreements together constituted a single overall transaction. It was irrelevant who provided the various elements of the total consideration. PCG's agreement to pay sub-rent formed part of the consideration received by AJB and had to be valued.

- The court was entitled to give precedence to reality over speculation, and could therefore use the benefit of hindsight to value the consideration actually given by PCG. The subsequent default by AJB and consequent termination of the sub-lease by PCG meant that the element of the consideration provided by PCG had no value.

There was therefore an undervalue of £725,000, being the difference between the value of the shares (£1,050,000) and the assumed obligation to pay the employees, which B Ltd must pay. However, credit would be given for PCG's loan provided PCG withdrew its proof for that sum in AJB's liquidation.

5.2.3   What defences exist to such an action?

Under s 238(5) IA 1986 there is one statutory defence to such an action. The court cannot make an order under s 238 in respect of a transaction at an undervalue if it is satisfied that:

- the transaction was entered into in good faith and for the purpose of carrying on the company's business; and

- at the time there were reasonable grounds for believing that the transaction would benefit the company.

Whilst potentially useful in some cases, this is generally regarded as a relatively narrow defence with limited application. The good faith involved is that of the company, not the other party. Nonetheless the onus is still on the person resisting the order, most likely to be that other party, to establish the defence (*Re Barton Manufacturing Co Limited* [1999] 1 BCLC 740). The courts have also made it clear that, whilst the first limb of the defence contains subjective elements, the second limb of the test is a purely objective one (*Lord v Sinai Securities Ltd* [2004] BCC 986).

5.2.4   Examples of a transaction at an undervalue

The following types of transaction are among those at risk of being set aside as transactions at an undervalue:

- a sale of assets, or provision of services by the company for a price which is significantly less than the actual value of those goods or services;

- a payment by the company for assets sold or services provided to the company which is significantly greater than the actual value of those goods or services;

- the making of a loan, or the sale of an asset, by the company where the other party's ability to pay is in significant doubt;

- the release of one of the company's debtors where the benefit received in return by the company (if any) is significantly less than the value of the debt.

5.2.5 The position of a secured creditor

In *MC Bacon Limited* [1990] BCC 78, the court held that the granting of a charge was not capable of being an undervalue. The security in question could not be said to have been granted for no consideration, as the bank had in return agreed not to call in its overdraft. So far as a comparison of the value obtained by and the value given by the company was concerned, the court held that there had been no depletion of the company's assets or diminution of their value. Whilst the company may have lost the ability to apply the proceeds of sale of the assets charged otherwise than in satisfaction of the secured debt, this was not capable of valuation in monetary terms.

However, in *Hill v Spread Trustee Co Ltd* [2006] BCC 646 (a case which principally concerned s 423 IA 1986), the court observed, whilst there may be no change to the assets of the company when security was taken, there seemed no reason why the value of the right to take priority to unsecured creditors which the company gives the other party by granting the security should be left out of account. Whilst it was not ultimately necessary to decide this point in *Hill*, these remarks do cast doubt on the decision in *MC Bacon*.

There is no reported case on whether the granting of a guarantee is capable of being an undervalue. However, it is certainly theoretically possible since, whilst it will not necessarily be a straightforward exercise, the value of both the consideration received by the guarantor and that provided by the guarantor can be measured in monetary terms. (This is usefully illustrated by Professor Roy Goode in sections 13–34 to 13–37 of *Principles of Corporate Insolvency Law*) (4th Edn, Sweet & Maxwell, 2011.)

5.2.6 What orders can the court make as a result?

Where it finds that there has been a transaction at an undervalue, the court may make such order as it thinks fit to restore the position. Section 241 IA 1986 lists a number of possible orders, but makes it clear that this is not an exhaustive list. Among other things, such an order may:

- require property transferred as part of the transaction, or the proceeds of its sale, to be returned to the company;

- where property has been vested in any person, apply either the proceeds of sale of the property transferred or of the money so transferred;

- release or discharge (in whole or in part) any security given by the company;

- require any person to pay such benefits to the insolvency officeholder as the court may direct;

- provide for any surety or guarantor whose obligations to any person were released or discharged (in whole or in part) under the transaction to be under such new or revived obligations as the court thinks appropriate;

- provide for security to be given for the discharge of any obligation imposed by or arising under the order, for such an obligation to be charged on any property, and for the security or charge to have the same priority as a security or charge released or discharged (in whole or in part) under the transaction; and

- provide for the extent to which any person whose property is ordered to be returned (or transferred) to the company, or on whom obligations are imposed by the order, is to be able to prove in the liquidation for debts or other liabilities which arose from, or were released or discharged (in whole or in part) under the transaction.

The position to be restored is that of the company, not that of the other party.

A person purchasing an asset from an insolvent company at a potential undervalue cannot simply assume that a court will allow them to retain their purchase by means of paying a further sum to make good any element of undervalue (*Walker v W A Personnel Ltd* [2002] BPIR 621, approved in *Ramlort Ltd v Reid* [2005] 1 BCLC 331).

As can also be seen, such an order may even apply to a person who was not a direct party to the original transaction with the company. However, a third party in this position does have a defence if the benefit acquired by them was acquired in good faith and for value. This begs the question of when the third party is acting in good faith. Where that third party, at the time it acquired or received the property in question:

- had notice of the relevant surrounding circumstances **and** of the fact that the first steps had already been taken to bring administration or liquidation proceedings against the company; or

- is connected with, or is an associate of, the company or the person who entered into the original transaction,

they are presumed **not** to have received the benefit in good faith, unless they can prove otherwise. The courts have observed however that the practical reality is that the onus is always on the third party to prove good faith (*Re Sonatacus Ltd* [2007] BCC 186).

5.2.7 Who benefits from the proceeds of the action?

Actions for undervalue and preference are vested in a liquidator, not the company, and accordingly any recoveries are held by the liquidator on trust for the general body of creditors among whom he has to distribute the company's assets (*Re MC Bacon Ltd (No 2)* [1991] Ch 127, following *In re Yagerphone* [1935] Ch 392). One key consequence of this is that they will fall outside of the scope of any floating charge over the company's assets, and thus such an action is likely to benefit a floating chargeholder only insofar as he could prove for the unsecured balance of their claim.

This is not free from debate, since this is somewhat inconsistent with the requirement on the court to make an order to restore the position to what it would otherwise have been. Comments in *Ciro Citterio Menswear Plc (in administration) v Rasik Lalij Thakrar* (unreported, but discussed by Paul Fleming in *Insolvency Intelligence* in 2003) may lend support to a view that the secured creditor should also benefit.

5.3 PREFERENCES

5.3.1 What is a preference?

Under s 239 IA 1986, the administrator or liquidator of a company which has at a 'relevant time' given a preference to any person may apply to the court for an order restoring the position to what it would have been if the preference had not been given.

A company gives a preference to a person if:

- that person is either one of the company's creditors or a surety/guarantor for any of the company's debts or other liabilities; **and**

- the company does anything or suffers anything to be done which has the effect of putting that person into a position which, in the event of the company going into insolvent liquidation, will be better than the position he would have been in if that thing had not been done; **and**

- the company, in deciding to give the preference, was 'influenced by a desire' to improve the third party's position (see Section 5.3.3 below).

A preference is given at a **relevant time** if:

- the company is unable to pay its debts at that time, or becomes unable to pay its debts as a result of the preference; and

- if the **onset of insolvency** occurs within **six months** (or, if the company and the recipient of the preference are **connected**, within **two years**) of the company giving the preference, or if the preference is given between the date on which an administration application is made or a notice of intention is filed and the date on which the administrator is appointed.

Preferences – Summary

A transaction cannot be set aside as a preference if:

- the company remained able to pay its debts at the date of, and immediately after, the transaction; **or**

- the beneficiary of the alleged preference is someone other than a creditor, surety or guarantor; **or**

- the beneficiary of the alleged preference is not in fact placed in a better position than that in which they would otherwise have been on an insolvent liquidation, eg because they hold security; **or**

- no administration or liquidation process is successfully instigated for at least six months after the date of the transaction (unless the beneficiary is connected to the company, in which case this time period is two years); **or**

- the liquidator/administrator cannot establish that the company was 'influenced by a desire' to produce the result in question (although note the presumption which applies when the beneficiary is connected to the company).

5.3.2 When is a creditor or guarantor put in a better position?

One question here is when the 'insolvent liquidation' should be regarded as having occurred. Indeed, it is open to an administrator to bring a preference action, even though the company concerned may never enter into liquidation at all. The legislation does not assist here. However, commentators have suggested that it is most appropriate to consider the creditor's or guarantor's position in a hypothetical insolvent liquidation occurring immediately after the preference was given.

Given the underlying purpose of s 239 IA 1986, logically the action in question must also deplete the assets available to the remaining body of creditors in some way before it will be a 'preference'. Therefore, for example, if the company arranges for a third party to repay one of the company's creditors in full on terms which do not create any new liability on the part of the company, this payment should not be regarded as a preference.

A further potentially relevant question is what is meant by the word '**suffers**'. In *Parkside International Limited (in administration)* [2008] EWHC 3354 (Ch), the court explained that for a company to suffer something to be done, the company must permit something to happen that it has the power to stop or to obstruct. Accepting, or simply remaining passive in reaction to, the occurrence of an event over which the company has no control does not amount to suffering that event to be done.

5.3.3 When is a company 'influenced by a desire'?

The meaning of 'influenced by a desire' was considered in *Re MC Bacon Limited* [1990] BCC 78. It was held that:

- whilst the desire to improve the other party's position must have influenced the minds of those making the decision, it need not have been the only factor (or even the decisive one); but

- desire is subjective and does not simply mean intention – a person may choose the lesser of two evils without desiring either, so there must be some basis on which to conclude that the decision makers had the requisite desire over and above the mere fact that the company's actions have placed the other party in a better position.

A later court suggested that there must be 'a positive wish' to improve the creditor's position (*Re: Fairway Magazines* [1992] BCC 924).

A consequence of this is that where the company makes a payment to a creditor, or takes some other action as a result of genuine commercial pressure, the requisite element of desire may be absent – a point specifically made in *Fairway Magazines*. Whilst the **result** of such a payment or other action might still be to improve the position of the recipient, the company may be influenced by a desire to enable its business to survive, rather than by a desire to prefer the recipient. (Indeed, if the directors can properly take the view at the time that the company's prospects of survival are likely to be improved overall as a result of the payment, they might well conclude that it is likely to be to the benefit of all creditors, although this is a point they do need properly to consider before reaching that conclusion.)

This might be used to justify payments to key suppliers who were threatening otherwise to cease to supply. Examples of other situations where there was no desire to prefer include:

- the grant of security for an existing overdraft as a condition of the bank's continued support (*Re MC Bacon Limited*, above);

- payment of arrears of fees to professional advisers whilst other creditors remained unpaid in order to secure those advisers' continued services (*Re Ledingham-Smith* [1993] BCLC 635).

The onus is normally on the liquidator/administrator to prove the various components of preference, and the need to demonstrate that the company was influenced by a desire in particular may make preference claims hard to bring. However, where the recipient is **connected** to the company (unless they are connected only by virtue of being an employee), there is a presumption that they were influenced by such a desire unless they can demonstrate to the contrary. Section 5.8 considers when a person is connected.

5.3.4   Examples of preferences

The following actions are among those most at risk of being set aside as preferences:

- grant of security to secure an existing debt (eg *Mistral Finance Limited* [2001] BCC 27);

- the repayment of a loan which is guaranteed by the directors; and

- payment to a company connected to the debtor.

5.3.5   The position of a secured creditor

As noted above, the grant of security is at risk of being set aside as a preference where the company was influenced by a desire to prefer that creditor. However, provided the original grant of the security itself cannot be set aside as a preference, or avoided on some other grounds, payments to a creditor who already holds security to reduce or discharge their debt are generally not regarded as a preference. The basis for this is that they do not place that creditor in any better position than that in which they would have otherwise been on an insolvent liquidation. Nonetheless, it is wise to consider such payments with some caution, since a payment will still improve the secured creditor's position if, for example:

- it exceeds the likely realisable value of the assets over which the security is held; or

- it erodes the moneys which would, on a liquidation or administration, need to be available to pay the prescribed part.

5.3.6   What orders can the court make as a result?

The court has the same wide powers as regards the types of order which can be made as for transactions at an undervalue, and the circumstances in which the rights of third parties can be affected are also the same. In addition, the comments in Section 5.2.7 apply equally to the proceeds from a preference action.

5.4 TRANSACTIONS DEFRAUDING CREDITORS

5.4.1 What is a 'transaction defrauding creditors'?

Under s 423 IA 1986, the liquidator or administrator of a company or, where the company is not in liquidation or administration, any person prejudiced by a transaction of the type described below, may apply to the court for an order restoring the position to what it would have been if the transaction had not been entered into, or otherwise for protecting the interests of anyone prejudiced by it.

The applicant must establish that the company:

- entered into a transaction with another person at an undervalue; and

- did so for the purpose of putting assets beyond the reach of creditors or potential future creditors, or otherwise prejudicing their interests.

Despite the statutory title of this remedy, there is therefore no need for an applicant to establish actual fraud or dishonesty on the part of the directors.

A transaction is at an **undervalue** if:

- the company makes a gift or otherwise enters into a transaction on terms that provide for the company to receive no consideration (ie no payment or other benefit); or

- the company enters into a transaction for a consideration the value of which, in money or money's worth, is significantly less, in money or money's worth, than the consideration provided by the company.

Transactions defrauding creditors – summary

A transaction cannot be set aside under s 423 IA 1986 if:

- the company received consideration which was not significantly less in money's worth than the true value of any asset transferred by or right release by it; **or**

- the substantial purpose(s) of the transaction did not include that of putting assets beyond the reach of creditors or potential future creditors, or otherwise prejudicing their interests.

5.4.2 How does this differ from s 238 IA 1986?

The 'transaction at an undervalue' component of s 423 is the same as s 238, and accordingly comments in Section 5.2.2 on 'value' also apply equally to s 423.

However, there are some important differences between the two sections. For the purposes of an action under s 423:

- the action need not be brought by a liquidator or administrator but can be brought by **any victim**;

- there is **no set period of time** prior to the onset of insolvency during which the transaction must have occurred (indeed it is not even a necessary precursor to such an action that the company has subsequently entered into administration or liquidation). Thus a transaction can never completely 'harden' for the purposes of s 423, although in practice the courts may sometimes be reluctant to open up transactions going back many years;

● it is unnecessary to prove that the company was unable to pay its debts when it entered into the transaction;

● there is **no defence** equivalent to that contained in s 238(5) IA 1986; **but**

● the company's '**purpose**' is material.

The slightly unusual use of s 423 in *Dornoch Ltd v Westminster International BV* [2009] EWHC 1782 (Admlty) illustrates various of these points. The claimant was an insurer, and no insolvency proceedings were involved.

Perhaps most importantly, however, s 423 can therefore catch transactions entered into at a time when the company was solvent, but where the directors considered there was a risk of future insolvency and wished to protect assets from creditors in that event. In *Sands v Clitheroe* [2006] B.P.I.R. 1000 (a case involving an individual), the court held that s 423 could apply to a sale of a property 15 years prior to that individual's eventual bankruptcy.

5.4.3 What does 'for the purpose of putting assets beyond the reach of creditors' mean?

If the court finds that the purpose of the transaction was to put assets beyond the reach of creditors, this is sufficient for the purposes of s 423. Note that:

● The fact that the company was not dishonest, and acted on legal advice does not preclude it from having the necessary purpose (*Arbuthnot Leasing International Limited v Havelet Leasing Limited (No 2)* [1990] BCC 636).

● It need not be the **only** purpose of the transaction, provided it was a **substantial** purpose (*Royscot Spa Leasing Ltd v Lovett* [1995] BCC 502, followed in *Kubiangha v Ekpenyong* [2002] 2 BCLC 597). (Note here, however, that some courts have favoured a 'dominant' purpose test, as used at first instance in *Chohan v Saggar* [1992] BCC 306 and the point has never been completely resolved.)

● The fact that the **result** of the transaction was to place assets outside the reach of creditors was not sufficient in itself, however, as purpose and result are different things (*Royscot Spa Leasing Ltd v Lovett*).

5.4.4 What orders can the court make as a result?

The court generally has the same wide powers as regards the types of order which can be made as for transactions at an undervalue, and the circumstances in which the rights of third parties can be affected are also the same. However, note that where an action is brought under s 423 the burden of proof is not reversed in the case of connected persons.

In *4Eng Limited v Harper* [2009] EWHC 2633 (Ch) the court also suggested that if the beneficiary of the transaction had received the benefit in good faith and without knowledge of the transferor's purpose, and had subsequently changed their position as a result of receiving that benefit, this might affect the order the court would make.

5.5 EXTORTIONATE CREDIT TRANSACTIONS

5.5.1 What is an extortionate credit transaction?

Under s 244 IA 1986, a liquidator or administrator of a company which entered into a transaction which is or was extortionate within the three-year period ending on the day on which the company entered into administration or went into liquidation may apply to the court for an appropriate order.

There is no requirement to show that the company became unable to pay its debts as a result of the transaction. It is also worth noting that, in the case of a compulsory liquidation, the three-year period is counted back from the date the company actually went into liquidation, and not the date the petition was presented.

A transaction is **extortionate** if, having regard to the risk accepted by the person providing the credit:

- its terms are or were such as to require grossly exorbitant payments to be made (whether unconditionally or in certain contingencies) in respect of the provision of the credit; or
- it otherwise grossly contravened ordinary principles of fair dealing.

Historically, this provision derives from consumer credit legislation rather than insolvency legislation. The burden of proof is placed on the other party to the transactions to show that the transaction was **not** extortionate. However, the court has a full discretion as to whether to make any order. The courts recognise that high risk can justify high interest rates, so it seems that the terms will need to be unusually unfavourable to the company before they will intervene. A comment of the court in *Wills v Wood* (1984) 81 LSG 1211 suggests also that a court should be disinclined to make an order unless it considers that the terms reflect a substantial imbalance of bargaining power between the parties.

The judgment of Floyd J in *White v Davenham Trust Ltd* [2010] EWHC 2748 (Ch) contains a useful resummary of the law here.

5.5.2 What orders can the court make?

An order made by the court may do any one or more of the following, as the court thinks fit:

- set aside the whole or part of any obligation created by the transaction;
- otherwise vary the terms of the transaction, or vary the terms on which any security for the purposes of the transaction is held;
- require any person who is or was a party to the transaction to repay to the officeholder any sums paid to that person to the company;
- require any person to surrender to the officeholder any property held by him as security for the purposes of the transaction; and/or
- direct accounts to be taken between the parties.

5.6 FLOATING CHARGES FOR NO NEW VALUE

5.6.1 When will a floating charge be invalid?

Under s 245 IA 1986, a floating charge on a company's undertaking or property which was created at a 'relevant time' will be invalid upon the company's liquidation or administration except to the extent that 'new value' was received by the company.

Note that this section applies only to floating charges. The scope for its application is still wide, given that (as discussed in Chapter 2) a floating charge means a charge which, as created, was a floating charge regardless of whether it may subsequently have crystallised. However, it will not apply to charges which were genuinely created as fixed charges.

A charge is granted at a relevant time if:

- (where the person in favour of whom the charge was created is **not connected** with the company) the company is unable to pay its debts at that time, or becomes unable to pay its debts in consequence of the transaction in which the charge is created; and

- the **onset of insolvency** occurs within **12 months** (or, if the company and the person in favour of whom the charge is created are **connected**, within **two years**) after the company creates the charge, or if the charge is created between the date on which an administration application was made or notice of intention filed and the date of the appointment of the administrator.

Where the charge is created in favour of a person **connected** with the company there is no requirement that the company must have been unable to pay its debts at the time the charge was created. Section 245 does not make it clear where the burden of proof lies in other cases, but it has been suggested that, by analogy to the earlier legislation on which this provision is based, it is for the person seeking to uphold the charge to establish solvency. Section 5.8 considers when a person is connected.

Floating charges for no new value – summary

A charge cannot be invalid under s 245 IA 1986 if:

- it is a fixed, rather than a floating charge; **or**

- where the company and the chargeholder are unconnected, the company was able to pay its debts at the date of the charge, and remained so immediately afterwards; **or**

- no administration or liquidation process is successfully instigated for at least a year after the date on which the charge was granted (unless the chargeholder is connected to the company, in which case this time period is two years).

Even if none of the above assists, the charge will not be invalid to the extent that it secures new value.

5.6.2 What is 'new value'?

For these purposes, new value means:

- the value of so much of the consideration for the creation of the charge as consists of money paid, or goods or services supplied, to the company at the same time as, or after, the creation of the charge;

- the value of so much of that consideration as consists of the discharge or reduction, at the same time as, or after, the creation of the charge, of any debt of the company; and

- the amount of such interest (if any) as is payable on the amount of the consideration referred to above in pursuance of any agreement under which the money was so paid, the goods and services were so supplied or the debt was so discharged or reduced.

The meaning of **at the same time as** was considered in *Re Shoe Lace Ltd, Power v Sharp Investments* [1993] BCC 609. The court held that, where no existing charge had been created by any agreement or company resolution prior to the execution of the formal debenture, then moneys advanced before the execution of the debenture would not constitute 'new value' unless the interval between payment and execution was so short that it could be regarded as de minimis (such as a 'coffee break'). Clearly, therefore, floating charges created with the aim of securing pre-existing indebtedness are likely to be at risk.

The court in *Shoe Lace* did identify, however, that a binding agreement to create a debenture may create an immediate equitable charge, even if formal execution of the debenture only takes place later. Nonetheless, a person seeking to argue that such a charge was created needs to bear in mind that the registration requirements for any such charge will also apply from the date of its creation.

The court will look at whether new value has genuinely been received by the company. Thus a refinancing may not create new value if the incoming payment is matched by an outgoing payment, or payments, by the company in the same amount (*Re Destone Fabrics* [1941] Ch 319). In *Re Fairway Magazines Ltd* [1992] BCC 924, payments made by a lender directly to the company's bank which reduced its overdraft were held not to be new value since the company was never able to make use of the monies as it liked, although this decision has been criticised as the payment did reduce a debt of the company.

Where a floating charge is taken to secure a pre-existing **overdraft**, subsequent payments into the overdrawn account are treated as satisfying the earlier indebtedness first, and subsequent drawings are regarded as constituting new value (*Yeovil Glove Co Limited* [1965] Ch 148, following the rule in *Clayton's case*). The turnover on the account thus progressively converts old indebtedness into new. This is another route by which the charge may 'harden'.

5.7   DISTRIBUTIONS POST-PRESENTATION OF WINDING-UP PETITION

5.7.1   In what circumstances will a disposition be avoided?

Under s 127 IA 1986, in a compulsory liquidation:

- any disposition of the company's property, and

- any transfer of shares or alteration in the status of the company's members, made after the commencement of the winding-up is void unless the court orders otherwise.

The **commencement of the winding-up** is defined in s 129 IA 1986. In most cases it will mean the date of presentation of the winding-up petition. However, if the winding-up petition is presented by a creditor after the company has already passed a resolution for voluntary winding-up it will mean the date this earlier resolution was passed. If the court elects to make a winding-up order on the hearing of an administration application, it will mean the date of the order.

5.7.2   What is a disposition of the company's property?

The term disposition is not defined. However, its meaning is wide enough to cover not only gifts, sales or payments by the company, but other transactions by which the company gives up some existing right, or creates new rights in favour of a third party, in respect of one of its assets. It makes no difference for these purposes whether or not full value is received by the company in return for the disposition in question, although this may influence the court in deciding whether to validate the transaction (see Section 5.7.3). The property in question must, however, be that of the company.

The courts have given particular consideration as to whether payments both into and out of a company's bank account constitute a disposition of its property (see Section 5.7.4). For this reason, a company's bank may well freeze its accounts if they learn of the presentation of a petition unless or until the petition is withdrawn or the court grants an appropriate validation order.

5.7.3   When will a court 'order otherwise'?

The legislation gives no guidance here, but the courts have set out various general principles. In *Denney v John Hudson* [1992] BCC 503, the Court of Appeal indicated that:

- The discretion of the court is at large.

- The basic principle is of *pari passu* distribution.

- In determining whether a validation order should be made, the court should ensure that the interests of the unsecured creditors are not prejudiced.

- The court should not, except in special circumstances where it was in the interests of creditors generally, validate a transaction which would result in one or more pre-liquidation creditors being paid in full where others would not.

- A disposition carried out by the parties in good faith at a time when they were unaware that a petition had been presented should normally be validated unless there are grounds for thinking that the transaction was an attempt to prefer the disponee.

However, whilst a powerful factor, good faith is not sufficient in itself. In *Denney*, the essential further questions to ask were:

- Were the parties acting in the ordinary course of business? and

- Were the relevant transactions likely to be for the benefit of creditors generally?

Therefore payments to suppliers which enabled a trading company in turn to obtain further supplies and thus to continue trading would normally be validated.

In practice, an application for validation will most often be made after advertisement of a winding-up petition but in advance of any winding-up order, usually on the basis that the company expects the petition to be dismissed when it is eventually heard by the court. The court can make a 'blanket' order validating payments made in the general continuance of trading and (for that purpose) the continued operation of the bank account. Before doing so, the court will wish to see suitable evidence that such an order will benefit all creditors. However, provided the court can be convinced that the company is in fact solvent, the onus would normally be on any person opposing leave to persuade the court to justify their position (*Re Burton and Deakin Ltd* [1977] 1 WLR 390).

Practice Direction – Insolvency Proceedings [2012] BCC 265 gives directions in relation to such an application. It deals among other things, with what evidence is required, urgent applications and the standard of proof required.

5.7.4 Payments passing through the company's bank account

Various cases have considered the consequences of payments passing through a company's bank account following the presentation of a petition. Here, the courts and commentators have separately considered:

- payments into and payments out of the account;
- accounts in credit and accounts which are overdrawn; and
- payments in cash and payments by cheque

so there are a number of situations to review.

5.7.4.1 Payments into an account in credit

This area has given rise to some debate. On a strict analysis, when moneys are paid into an account in credit, the moneys in question will not become (or remain) the property of the customer. The bank will instead become indebted to the customer for the sum in question. The question is therefore whether, on such an analysis, the payment in is a disposition of the company's property.

It has been held that where a company pays a cheque into its account, this is not a disposition of the company's property to the bank and is not therefore rendered void. The property disposed of is that of the drawer of the cheque, and all that happens between the company and the bank is an adjustment of entries in the statement recording the account (*Re: Barn Crown Ltd* [1995] 1 WLR 147). This analysis has been questioned by commentators on the basis that there must still be a transfer of some asset by the customer to the bank in turn for the bank's promise of repayment.

If the company holds free cash which it subsequently pays into its account, however, it seems that this must be a disposition of the company's own property and, unless the court is prepared to validate the payments, they should be recoverable by a liquidator.

5.7.4.2 Payments into an overdrawn account

The position is much clearer when monies are paid into an overdrawn account. By reducing its overdraft and therefore its debt to the bank, the company is transferring property to the bank in the amount of the cash or cheque in question (*Re Gray's Inn Construction Co Limited* [1980] 1 WLR 711). Unless the court is prepared to validate the payments, they can therefore be recovered by a liquidator.

In *Re Tain Construction Limited* [2003] 2 BCLC 374, the court declined retrospectively to validate payments into an overdrawn account even where they had been made in the ordinary course of business and at a time before the petition had been advertised. It regarded these factors as material, but not decisive. Here, the court was influenced by the fact that one of the company's directors had personally guaranteed its liability to the bank so there was a suggestion of preference. The court also rejected an argument that the validation order was justified because the bank had changed its position to its detriment. (It had released a charge in support of the guarantee in the belief that the overdraft had been discharged).

5.7.4.3 Payments out of an account in credit

A withdrawal from an account in credit is regarded as a disposition of the company's property. However, this begs the further question of whether the money is recoverable from the payee, the bank, or both. In *Hollicourt (Contracts) Ltd v Bank of Ireland* [2001] Ch 555 the Court of Appeal held that only the payee can be liable, as they are the only recipient of the disposition. The bank acts merely as an agent of the customer and in making the payment is simply carrying out the customer's instructions.

5.7.4.4 Payments out of an overdrawn account

In *Re Gray's Inn Construction Co Limited*, the court took the view that payments out of an overdrawn account could equally be dispositions of the company's property. This approach has also been followed in later cases although its logic has been criticised by commentators on the basis that, where the account is overdrawn, the money disposed of is not the customer's but the bank's. Again, following *Hollicourt (Contracts) Ltd v Bank of Ireland*, only the payee and not the bank will in practice be liable in respect of such payments.

5.7.5 Who benefits from the proceeds of the action?

Unlike recoveries under various other actions, sums recovered by a liquidator under s 127 IA 1986 are deemed to have remained the property of the company throughout. It is this fact which gives the liquidator the ability to recover them. Therefore where the company's assets are subject to a floating charge, the charge will continue to attach to the recovered property (see *Mond v Hammond Suddards* [2000] Ch 40).

5.8   WHO IS A 'CONNECTED' PERSON?

The Insolvency Act uses the term **'person'** to mean a legal person, including both a company and an individual.

Under s 249 IA 1986, a person is **connected** with a company if

- he is a director or shadow director of the company, or is an associate of such a director or shadow director; or

- he is an associate of the company.

This begs the question of what is meant by an associate, and this term is defined in s 435 IA 1986.

A **company** is an **associate of another person** if that person has control of it or if that person and persons who are his associates together have control of it.

A **company** is also specifically defined to be an **associate of another company**:

- if the same person has control of both, or a person has control of one and persons who are his associates, or he and persons who are his associates, have control of the other; or

- if a group of two or more persons has control of each company, and the groups either consist of the same persons or could be regarded as consisting of the same persons by treating (in one or more cases) a member of either group as replaced by a person of whom he is an associate.

The definitions in turn beg two further questions: the meaning of control, and the question of when a person is associated with another person.

A person is taken as having **control** of a company if:

- one or more directors of the company, or of another company which has control of it are accustomed to act in accordance with his directions or instructions; **or**

- he is entitled to exercise, or control the exercise of, **one-third or more** of the voting power at any general meeting of the company or of another company which has control of it.

(Note, in relation to the first criterion above, that there is subtle distinction between this and the criteria for being a shadow director. Here it is sufficient if only one of the directors is accustomed to act in accordance with that person's instructions.)

A **person** is an **associate of another person** if:

- he employs or is employed by that other person (and for these purposes a director or other officer of a company is treated as employed by that company);

- he is in partnership with that person, or that person is the husband or wife or civil partner or a relative of any individual with whom he is in partnership;

- he is a trustee of a trust (other than a pension scheme or an employees' share scheme), and the beneficiaries of that trust include, or the terms of that trust confer a power that may be exercised for the benefit of, that other person or an associate of that other person.

In addition, a **person** is specifically defined to be an **associate of an individual** if that person is:

- the individual's husband or wife or civil partner;

- a relative of the individual or the individual's husband or wife or civil partner; or

- the husband or wife or civil partner of a relative of the individual or the individual's husband or wife or civil partner.

A **person** is a **relative of an individual** if he is that individual's brother, sister, uncle, aunt, nephew, niece, lineal ancestor or lineal descendant. This definition is a wide one: relationships of half blood are regarded as being of full blood, stepchildren and adopted children are included as children and illegitimate children are regarded as legitimate children of their mother and reputed father.

Examples of 'connected' persons:

- A lender holds more than one-third of the voting shares in the company following a debt to equity swap. The lender will now be connected as it is has 'control'.

- A person holds more than one-third of the voting shares in an intermediate holding company which in turn holds half of the voting shares in a joint venture company with an outside party. The person will have 'control' over the joint venture company.

- An investor holding less than one-third of the voting shares appoints one of its employees as a director of a company to protect its investment. The investor is a connected person on at least one, and possibly two bases here. First, the investor will be an associate of its employee, and therefore connected to the company by virtue of being an associate of a director of the company. Secondly, if the investor gives instructions to its appointee director, it will be connected by virtue of having 'control'.

In contrast, the following are examples where the circumstances concerned do not in themselves mean that the persons are connected:

- A lender holds a large number of non-voting preference shares in the company following a debt to equity swap. Preference shares which are non-voting do not contribute towards 'control', regardless of how many may be held. (In practice the situation is often complicated by the fact that the preference shares are given voting rights in certain circumstances, for example, if a dividend is unpaid. However, practitioners tend to take the view that this fact in itself should not give the holder 'control', notwithstanding the reference in s 435(10)(b) IA 1986 to the exercise of one-third or more of the voting power at 'any' general meeting.)

- An investor holding less than one-third of the voting shares appoints one of its employees as an observer to the company's board (assuming that the observer is careful not to render himself a shadow director by giving instructions to the board).

Chapter 6

Position of directors

6.1 INTRODUCTION

As will be discussed in more detail in Chapter 10, a company, or group of companies, may face financial difficulty for a variety of reasons. Sometimes the difficulties will have been apparent for some time, for example, where they result from poor trading which eventually leads to the company's earnings no longer covering its costs of borrowing and other overheads. Alternatively, it might be a sudden catastrophic event or change of circumstances which is the cause, such as the loss of a key customer or supplier (perhaps through their own insolvency).

Directors faced with difficulties may be tempted to struggle on in the hope (or unrealistic belief) that things will turn round until, faced with a cash crunch – such as an inability to meet the month-end payroll – there is no further room for prevarication. Leaving things to the last moment is of little benefit to the company's creditors, as it may leave insufficient time to find a solution. As insolvency law has developed, it has aimed to encourage directors to seek help and advice earlier, and thus minimise losses to creditors.

In general, the adverse consequences for directors described in this chapter only occur if the company has first entered into a formal insolvency process. In some cases, it will be possible to reach an agreement with stakeholders which allows the company's (or the group's) debts to be restructured outside of any formal insolvency process, and it may well be that the earlier negotiations start, the greater the chances of achieving this. However, a restructuring may not prove possible without placing one or more companies in the group into a formal insolvency process as part of a pre-planned strategy. In other cases, a restructuring may not prove possible at all, with the result that the company enters into an unplanned formal insolvency. Therefore directors will remain mindful of these possible consequences until any restructuring has been implemented.

6.2 WHO IS A 'DIRECTOR'?

6.2.1 *De jure* directors

Anyone duly appointed as a director in accordance with the company's articles of association is clearly a director (whether or not his details have been registered at Companies House).

6.2.2 *De facto* directors

The term 'director' is defined in s 251 IA 1986 to include 'any person occupying the position of director, by whatever name called'. A *de facto* director, ie a person

138

who acts as a director and is treated as if he were a director by other members of the board notwithstanding that they may not have been formally appointed as such, will also be a director for these purposes (*Re Richborough Furniture Ltd* [1996] 1 BCLC 507).

Anyone involved in management decision making of the kind conventionally dealt with at board level might fall into this category. Persons who might fall into this category without so intending include:

- a person who formally attends board meetings as an observer, but in practice takes an active role in the directors' decision-making processes;

- a person who controls the operation of the company's bank account and decides which creditors are to be paid and in which order (*Re Tasbian Ltd (No 3)* [1992] BCC 358); and

- a person held out as a director, for example by inclusion of the word 'director' in his job title or on his business card. (This is less likely where there is a functioning board at which key management decisions are taken and the person concerned is not entitled to participate in this.)

Directors appointed by investors and other non-executive directors often sit on the board of a group's main holding company only. However, these persons may nonetheless be seen as *de facto* directors of the trading subsidiaries if in practice decisions as to how those subsidiaries run their affairs and manage their creditors are taken by the board of that holding company.

In *Holland v HMRC* [2010] UKSC 51, the Supreme Court held (by a 3:2 majority) that a person who was director of a company which in turn served as a corporate director of a second company would not automatically be considered a *de facto* director of that second company simply by virtue of the fact that he was the guiding mind of the company which was its corporate director.

6.2.3   Shadow directors

A 'shadow director' is defined in s 251 IA 1986 as 'a person in accordance with whose directions or instructions the directors of the company are accustomed to act (but so that a person is not deemed a shadow director by reason only that the directors act on advice given by him in a professional capacity)'. Many provisions of both the IA 1986 and the CDDA 1986 are stated to apply to shadow directors just as they do to 'real' directors. The purpose is to ensure that the same sanctions are available against an individual or entity who, without themselves being on the board, effectively tells the board what to do.

The Court of Appeal has made a number of statements about the statutory definition of shadow director (*Secretary of State for Trade and Industry v Deverell & Another* [2000] 2 All ER 365):

- the definition should not be strictly construed;

- the purpose of the legislation is to identify those, other than professional advisers, with real influence in the company's corporate affairs, but this influence does not have to be over the whole field of its corporate activities;

- whether a communication is classed as a 'direction or instruction' has to be objectively ascertained by the court in the light of all the evidence;

- non-professional advice might come within the statutory definition (company doctors may, for example, therefore be in an ambiguous position); and

- a person can still be a shadow director even if the board has not adopted a subservient role to him or has not surrendered its discretion.

However, in determining whether a person is a shadow director, the courts will look at the frequency with which instructions were given and whether such instructions tended to be acted on. Furthermore, in *McKillen v Misland (Cyprus) Investments Ltd* [2012] EWHC 521 (Ch) it was made clear that it was unnecessary that all of the directors of the company act in accordance with the instructions; it was enough that a majority did.

Persons who are unlikely to fall within the definition, provided they do not exceed their normal role, include:

- A shareholder appointing a single nominated member of the board who acts in accordance with his wishes. A shadow director must effectively give instructions to the majority of the directors, not merely to an individual director. However, the shareholder is at risk if the board as a whole acts as they direct.

- A bank lender. There was initial concern among banks when the legislation was first passed. In practice, however, there is no recorded case of a bank actually having been found liable as a shadow director. A bank should be less at risk if it presents its requirements as conditions for its further support rather than as outright instructions.

- A lawyer or accountant advising the company. They will fall within the 'professional capacity' exception provided they merely advise and leave the commercial decisions to the board.

As noted in Section 6.4.4, legislation creating liabilities on the part of an 'officer' of a company may conceivably extend to *de facto* directors but not to shadow directors.

6.2.4 Non-executive directors

An executive director will be a full-time employee engaged in the day-to-day management of the company. A non-executive director will devote only part of his time to the company's affairs. He is nonetheless a director, and therefore has the same general duties as does an executive director.

6.3 DIRECTORS' DUTIES

6.3.1 What are a director's general duties?

The general duties of a director are set out in ss 171 to 177 CA 2006 and comprise:

- A duty to act in accordance with the company's constitution and only to exercise powers for the purposes for which they are conferred (s 171).

- A duty to act in the way the directors consider in good faith would be most likely to promote the success of the company for the benefit of its shareholders as a whole, and in doing so having regard (among other matters) to six listed considerations. These include the interests of the company's employees and the need to foster the company's business relationships with suppliers, customers and others (s 172, but see below).

- A duty to exercise independent judgement (s 173).

- A duty to exercise reasonable care, skill and diligence (s 174).

- A duty to avoid a situation in which he has, or can have, direct or indirect interests that conflict, or possibly may conflict, with the interests of the company (s 175).

- A duty not to accept benefits from third parties conferred by reason of his being a director or his doing (or not doing) anything as a director (s 176).

- A duty to declare to the other directors the nature and extent of any direct or indirect interest he has in any proposed transaction or arrangement with the company (s 177).

6.3.2   To whom are the duties owed?

The directors' general duties are owed to the company. When a company is solvent, the directors must have regard predominantly to the interests of the shareholders in discharging their duties.

However, when the company is unable to pay its debts, its directors must instead have regard predominantly to the interests of the creditors (*West Mercia Safetywear Ltd v Dodd* [1988] BCLC 250), because it is they who will now stand to gain or lose most according to the actions the directors take. This is expressly recognised by s 172(3) CA 2006, which provides that the duty set out in that section (as described in Section 6.3.1) has effect subject to any rule of law requiring directors, in certain circumstances, to consider or act in the interest of creditors of the company.

In this context, the directors of a company which is unable to pay its debts might be regarded as having certain additional duties, such as a duty to avoid entering into transactions at an undervalue and a duty to avoid giving preferences, since a breach of these duties will impact on the creditors (see Section 6.4.4).

6.3.3   Ratification

In a solvent company, the acts of the directors may still be ratified by the shareholders. Where a company is insolvent, however, because of the shift towards the interests of creditors, this remedy cannot be relied upon.

6.3.4   Groups of companies

Groups of companies present a particular issue here. The distinction between companies within a group is often blurred where the group is solvent and managed effectively as a single unit. Elaborate structures may be set up for administrative or tax-planning reasons and transactions between group members may take place on terms which would not be offered to external third parties. Specific group members may employ the group workforce, or own its buildings, and make these available on cost cover terms only to other members of the group. Payment between group members may well not be settled regularly in cash, but give rise to intercompany debts and credits.

However, arrangements which are legally unobjectionable within a solvent group may cease to be so when companies within the group become unable to pay their debts. The directors of each company must act in relation to each company without regard to their duties as directors of other group companies. This may of course give rise to particular difficulties where duties owed to different companies within a group conflict, and in those circumstances it may become necessary for directors to relinquish multiple directorships.

In practice, the success of one company in a group may depend on the success of another, either because the assets of the first substantially comprise shares in or debts owed by the second, or the first has guaranteed the debts of the second (as is commonly the case where group borrowing arrangements are in place). In these circumstances the strategic interests of all companies within the group may well be the same. Nonetheless, the directors of each company must have primary regard to the effect which actions taken, or permitted, by that individual company may have on the creditors of that company, rather than the creditors of other companies within the group or the overall solvency of the group as a whole.

6.4   RISKS TO DIRECTORS

6.4.1   Overview

The risks to directors who continue to trade an insolvent company fall into three main categories:

- a risk of civil liability to pay financial compensation out of that director's own personal resources;
- a risk of disqualification from acting as a director; and
- a risk of criminal liability.

In many cases these categories will overlap. For example, a court which finds a director liable for wrongful trading may also disqualify him from acting as a director, and a director found liable for fraudulent trading may subsequently also be prosecuted.

6.4.2   Wrongful trading

6.4.2.1   What are the risks here?

A director may be held personally liable to contribute to a company's assets if he allows the company to continue trading at any time when **he knows or ought to conclude** that there is **no reasonable prospect** that the company will avoid insolvent liquidation (s 214 IA 1986). The point where the director reaches, or ought to reach this conclusion is often termed the '**critical date**'.

An action for wrongful trading can only be brought by the liquidator of a company which has subsequently gone into insolvent liquidation (whether voluntary or compulsory). For this purpose insolvent liquidation means that it goes into liquidation at a time when its assets are insufficient for the payment of its debts and other liabilities and the liquidation expenses (s 214(6) IA 1986).

The liquidator bringing an action will need to identify some date as the critical date (*Re Sherborne Associates Ltd* [1995] BCC 40). For example, this may be the date on which the directors knew, or ought to have concluded that there was no longer any reasonable prospect that funding required by the company in order to continue to trade would be available (see for example, *Roberts v Frohlich* [2011] EWHC 257 (Ch)).

The concept of a critical date, however, means that a director is not liable for wrongful trading simply because the company has been trading whilst insolvent. This important distinction is discussed further in Section 6.5.1.

6.4.2.2   What standards are expected of the director?

Under s 214(4) IA 1986, the standard to be applied by the court in deciding whether a director has been guilty of wrongful trading is that of a 'reasonably diligent person' having:

- the general knowledge, skill and experience which may reasonably be expected of a person entrusted with carrying out the same functions as are carried out by that director in relation to the company; and

- the general knowledge, skill and experience which that director actually has.

A director will therefore be judged both objectively (he must show the abilities which the reasonable director holding his position would be expected to have, regardless of his own ability) and subjectively (the more experienced director must show a higher standard of competence). In *Singla v Hedman* [2010] EWHC 902 (Ch), the court refused to accept an argument that the standard of responsibility expected of a director was lower in an inherently risky industry, such as the film industry. Further, a director will be judged in relation to the functions which have been entrusted to him even if, in fact, he failed to carry them out.

Each director will be judged individually according to these tests. Higher standards may apply to some than to others on the same board. The sales director might not be expected to be as familiar with the details of the company's day-to-day cash movements as the finance director. However, every director shares a responsibility for ensuring that the company is capable of surviving financially, and this responsibility cannot simply be left to one or two individuals on the basis that it is their job, not the job of others. At the very least, there is an obligation to ensure that proper financial management is being exercised by someone with appropriate expertise.

6.4.2.3   What defences are available?

There is a specific statutory defence to a wrongful trading action. The court will not find a director liable if it is satisfied that, once he knew or ought to have concluded that there was no reasonable prospect of the company avoiding insolvent liquidation, he took every step which he ought to have taken to minimise the potential loss to the company's creditors (s 214(3) IA 1986).

The steps to be taken are those which a director with the objective (ie reasonably expected) and subjective (ie actual) levels of knowledge, skill and experience which that director has, or is expected to have, ought to take if he knew that there was no reasonable prospect of avoiding insolvent liquidation (see Section 6.4.2.2). A director will **not**, however, be able to obtain relief from a wrongful trading action under s 1157 CA 2006 on the basis that he acted honestly and reasonably (*Re Produce Marketing Consortium Ltd* [1989] BCLC 513).

6.4.2.4 What will be the extent of the director's liability?

Section 214 does not specify a means by which the director's contribution is to be calculated, so this is left to the court's discretion. In *Re Produce Marketing Consortium Ltd (No 2)* [1989] BCLC 520, however, it was made clear that the court's jurisdiction here was primarily compensatory rather than penal. Without seeking to limit the court's discretion, the appropriate amount that a director was to be declared liable to contribute was the amount by which the company's assets could be seen to have been depleted by the director's conduct.

In practice the amount the director may be obliged by the court to pay is likely to be based on the amount by which the losses to the company's creditors have increased after the critical date.

There is an unresolved debate as to whether a director may still be liable to contribute personally to a company's assets if some creditors' positions have worsened but others have improved by an equivalent amount. In *Re Marini* [2004] BCC 172, the court thought that no liability could arise unless the liquidator could demonstrate that the company was in a worse position overall than it had been on the critical date. However this decision has been criticised, as it ignores the fact that it is the directors' continued trading which has caused further losses to those creditors who are in a worse position. Many advisers still therefore take the more cautious view that another court could still calculate a director's liability by reference only to the extent to which continued trading has worsened individual creditors' positions, without giving credit for any improvement in other creditors' positions.

There is a distinction, however, between creditors whose positions would have worsened anyway, regardless of the director's actions, and creditors who might have been protected had the director ceased trading earlier. The first category might include lenders who have advanced term loans to the company, where the principal sum has not increased after the critical date, and where interest would have continued to accrue at the same rate (until payment), even had the directors placed the company into a formal insolvency process earlier. This second category, however, might include persons who have delivered further goods or provided further services after the critical date but who remain unpaid. This category might include not only trade suppliers but also, for example, providers of utilities and the company's employees. It is this second category which will be most relevant here.

Regardless of the method by which a director's liability is calculated, any compensation paid by the directors will go to the liquidation funds for the benefit of creditors generally. It will not be payable only, for example, to those creditors directly prejudiced by the wrongful trading. As in the cases of awards made where a court sets aside an antecedent transaction (see Chapter 5), the award will also not be caught by a secured creditor's floating charge.

At the same time as making an order imposing personal liability, the court may disqualify a director from acting as a director.

6.4.3 Fraudulent trading

If, in the course of a company's liquidation, it is established that the business has been carried on with intent to defraud creditors, any persons who were knowingly party to carrying on the business in this way (which could include some or all of the directors) may be found liable for fraudulent trading (s 213 IA 1986). As with wrongful trading, the court may order any such directors personally to make a payment to the liquidation fund, and may also disqualify them from acting as directors.

Fraudulent trading requires the liquidator to prove some element of dishonesty on the part of the directors. For this reason, it was once thought that this provision would be of limited relevance once the wrongful trading provisions, which include no such requirement, were introduced. However, more recent case law has made it clear that this section still has a role to play. Dishonesty may be inferred where, for example, it should have been clear that the company was incurring debts which would never be repaid, or where the directors make deliberately misleading statements about their intentions or take active steps to avoid paying particular debts. It is sufficient that only one creditor has been defrauded in this way. (For an example of a case which illustrates a number of these points, see *Morphitis v Bernasconi* [2003] BCC 540.)

Creditors of insolvent companies whose directors have made promises to pay may have direct rights of action against those directors in deceit. These rights operate separately from, but in addition to, the provisions of s 213 IA 1986 (see, for example, *Contex Drouzhba Limited v Wiseman and another* [2008] BCC 301 and *Lindsay v O'Loughnane* [2010] EWHC 529 (QB)).

Fraudulent trading may also result in criminal proceedings for which directors found guilty may be fined or even sent to prison (s 993 CA 2006).

6.4.4 Misfeasance or breach of duty

If a company has gone into liquidation, the liquidator (or a creditor or shareholder) may apply to the court for an order compelling anyone who is or has been an officer of the company (or any other person who has taken part in the promotion, formation or management of the company) to account for any money or assets which they may have 'misapplied', or to pay compensation in respect of any misfeasance or breach of any fiduciary or other duty (s 212 IA 1986).

A liquidator could use this provision, for example, to pursue directors who have caused the company to enter into transactions at an undervalue, or to give preferences or to pay unlawful dividends (in addition to pursuing the beneficiaries of those transactions or other payments). It may also be used to pursue a straightforward negligence claim. Note that the reference to 'officers' of the company will extend to *de facto* directors but not to shadow directors (*Holland v HMRC* [2010] UKSC 51).

Section 212 IA 1986 creates no new duties on the part of the directors. Its purpose is to provide a simpler procedure for pursuing directors who have breached duties they already have to the company. One consequence of this is that a director will still be able to obtain relief under s 1157 CA 2006 on the basis that he acted honestly and reasonably (see *Re D'Jan of London Ltd* [1993] BCC 646). Nonetheless, this defence may not allow the directors to retain payments they have received themselves at the expense of the company's creditors (*Re Marini Ltd* [2004] BCC 172).

6.4.5 Re-use of company names

6.4.5.1 What are the risks here?

If a company goes into insolvent liquidation (whether voluntary or compulsory), it is an **offence** for a person who was a director of that company at any time during the **12-month period** prior to the commencement of the liquidation:

- to be a director of another company known by a **prohibited name** (see Section 6.4.5.2); or

- in any way, whether directly or indirectly, to be concerned or take part in the promotion, formation or management of another company known by a prohibited name; or

- in any way, whether directly or indirectly, to be concerned or take part in the carrying on of a business carried on (other than by another company) under a prohibited name

at any time in the **five-year period** beginning with the day the insolvent company went into liquidation, unless one of a number of exceptions applies (s 216 IA 1986). The exceptions are discussed in Section 6.4.5.3.

Furthermore, a person who is involved in the management of another company:

- in contravention of s 216 IA 1986; **or**

- who acts or is willing to act on instructions given by another person who he knows to be in contravention of s 216 IA 1986 in relation to that company

will also be **personally responsible** for all debts and liabilities of that company incurred at a time when they were involved in the company's management, or acted or were willing to act on the other person's instructions (as the case may be) (s 217 IA 1986). In practice, this will become relevant only if the other company is unable to discharge these debts and liabilities itself.

6.4.5.2 What is a 'prohibited name'?

A name is prohibited if it is a name by which the insolvent company was known at any time within the **12-month period** before the liquidation, or if it is a name **so similar** as to suggest an association with the insolvent company (s 216(2) IA 1986). Furthermore, references to a name by which a company is known include not only the company's name, but any trading name under which it **carries on business** (s 216(6) IA 1986).

For example, in *Ricketts v Ad Valorem Factors Ltd* [2004] BCC 164, the insolvent company was named 'The Air Component Co Limited' and the other company 'Air Equipment Co Limited'. The court held the latter to be a prohibited name. (The court made it clear, however, that it was necessary to make a comparison of the names in the context of all of the circumstances in which they were actually used or likely to be used: the type of product dealt in, the locations of the businesses, the type of customers dealing with the companies and those involved in the operation of the two companies.) The case of *ESS Production Ltd v Sully* [2005] BCC 435 shows that these risks may occur where both the insolvent and the new company allow themselves to be known by a common acronym, in this case 'ESS'.

Sections 216 and 217 IA 1986 were introduced to address the '**Phoenix trading**' phenomenon, where an insolvent company's business is sold to a new company controlled by the same individuals, and continues to trade free of its previous debts, whilst benefiting from the goodwill of the insolvent company. They protect creditors of the new company, who might well be unaware of the individuals' past history, and might otherwise suffer in due course as a result of a second failure. Nonetheless, should a person breach these provisions, his degree of culpability will be irrelevant – the court has no discretion to absolve him, or limit his liability. In the *Ricketts* case, there was no evidence that anyone had been misled by the similarity of the names. The court recognised that its decision to impose liability was therefore potentially a harsh one, but emphasised that the director concerned could have protected himself by obtaining the prior permission of the court (see Section 6.4.5.3).

Directors who carry out a restructuring using a planned formal insolvency therefore need to take care in choosing the name of the purchasing company. However, they may also inadvertently fall foul of these provisions if they are directors of other companies within the same group which have a similar name to the insolvent company (which will not be unusual in a group), unless they can take advantage of an exception.

6.4.5.3   What exceptions will apply?

A person will avoid liabilities under ss 216 and 217 IA 1986, however:

• Where the insolvent company's business is acquired from its liquidator, administrative receiver, administrator or supervisor of its CVA **and** that person has **given notice** to every creditor of the insolvent company whose name and address he knows, or is ascertainable on making reasonable enquiries, and also published that notice in the London Gazette. This notice must state his intention to act, or continue to act, in the management of the other company, and must also state the prohibited name. He will be protected provided the notice is given **within 28 days** of completion of the acquisition (r 4.228 IR 1986).

• Where he obtains the **permission of the court** to act, or continue to act, as director of the other company (s 216(3) IA 1986). A director cannot obtain permission retrospectively. However, if he has been acting in breach he can at least seek permission to protect himself in respect of the company's future dealings. The legislation also recognises that the court might take time to dispose of such applications. Therefore, provided a director applies for permission within seven days of the date of liquidation he is protected until the application is determined or until six weeks have elapsed since the date of liquidation (whichever occurs sooner), even if the application for permission is unsuccessful (r 4.229 IR 1986).

• Where the other company has already been known by the prohibited name for the **whole of the 12-month period** before the insolvent company went into liquidation and has not been dormant within that 12-month period (r 4.230 IR 1986).

6.4.6   Disqualification of directors

6.4.6.1   What are the risks here?

Under s 6 CDDA 1986, the Secretary of State for Business, Innovation and Skills may apply to the court for a disqualification order to be made against:

*   any director of a company which has gone into insolvent liquidation, administration or administrative receivership (whether while he was still a director or subsequently); and

*   whose conduct (either taken alone or together with his conduct as a director of any other company or companies) makes him 'unfit to be concerned in the management of a company'.

The court also has the jurisdiction to entertain disqualification proceedings where the company has been dissolved without having first been in a formal insolvency process (*Secretary of State for Trade and Industry v Arnold and another* [2008] BCC 119).

The courts have interpreted the '**unfitness**' test in a number of slightly different ways. However, the general strand of thinking seems to be that to qualify for disqualification, the conduct in question must ordinarily be either dishonest or lacking in commercial probity, or display incompetence to a marked degree. (See, for example *Re Uno plc and another: Secretary of State for Trade and Industry v Gill and others* [2006] BCC 725.)

It is a criminal offence to act in breach of such an order. A person doing so is also automatically **personally liable** for the debts of the company involved (s 15 CDDA 1986).

6.4.6.2   Scope of a disqualification order

A disqualification order is wide in its scope. It will prohibit a person from:

*   being a director of a company;

*   acting as a receiver of a company's property; or

*   in any way, directly or indirectly, being concerned or taking part in the promotion, formation or management of a company

for as long as the order remains in force (s 1(1) CDDA 1986). A management consultant who acted as advisor to the board of a company has therefore, for example, been held to have been 'concerned in' and 'taken part in' that company's management (*R v Campbell* [1984] BCLC 83).

A disqualified individual may still work as a company employee, provided they no longer hold themselves out as a director or seek to exercise continuing control behind the scenes. However, disqualification may still have severe repercussions for a person who has previously made their living as a professional director.

6.4.6.3   What is the role of the insolvency officeholder?

The official receiver in a compulsory liquidation, any liquidator in a voluntary liquidation, any administrator, or any administrative receiver has a duty to report a director to the Secretary of State if they consider that grounds exist for applying for a disqualification order (s 7(3) CDDA 1986). However, additional rules have in practice made it a requirement for any liquidator in a voluntary liquidation, any administrator or any administrative receiver to report within six months of their appointment on the conduct of **every person** who was a director of the company at any time during the **three-year** period prior to it entering into formal insolvency (the Insolvent Companies (Reports on Conduct of Directors) Rules 1996 (SI 1996/1909)). The report is made on a Form D1 where the insolvency officeholder considers that grounds exist for disqualification, or a Form D2 in other cases – these are known colloquially as '**D Forms**'.

Statement of Insolvency Practice 4 ('**SIP 4**') and the BIS's own guidance notes (http://www.bis.gov.uk/insolvency/Publications) provide further guidance to insolvency officeholders here, and are useful reading generally.

6.4.6.4   What factors will the court consider?

Under s 9 CDDA 1986, the court is required to have particular regard to a list of matters set out in Sch 1 CDDA 1986 when deciding whether to disqualify a director. However, this list is not intended to be exhaustive. The matters which might be applicable to a director of an insolvent company can be summarised as follows:

- misfeasance or breach of any fiduciary or other duty by the director in relation to the company (eg acting in his personal interest at the expense of the company);

- misapplication of property of the company by the director;

- the extent of the director's responsibility for any failure to maintain and retain accounting records and statutory books or to prepare annual accounts;

- the extent of the director's responsibility for the causes of the insolvency;

- the extent of the director's responsibility for the company's failure to supply any goods or services which have been paid for (in whole or in part);

- the extent of the director's responsibility for the company for giving preferences or entering into other transactions which are liable to be avoided or set aside on an insolvency under s 127, 238, 239 or 423 IA 1986 (see Chapter 5), and

- any failure to comply with the various duties placed on him once the company is in formal insolvency (as described in Section 6.7).

SIP 4 also lists a set of particular matters to which the Secretary of State will have regard when deciding whether to bring disqualification proceedings against a director, and one or more of these matters have tended to be relevant in many cases where disqualification orders have been made. These are set out in Table 6.1. It is worth noting in particular the frequency with which disqualification proceedings are brought and orders made against directors who have funded continued trading by failing to pay PAYE, national insurance contributions and other Crown debts when due (see, for example, *Secretary of State for Business Innovation and Skills v Cathie* [2012] EWCA Civ 739).

The court will take into account the extent of the directors' own responsibility for the matters in question. However, any director has a duty to keep himself informed, and a director who has played no active part in the running of the company is unlikely to escape liability for disqualification where he has delegated inappropriately or simply relied on occasional verbal assurances from others as to the company's financial position (see, for example, *Secretary of State for Trade and Industry v Thornbury* [2008] 1 BCLC 139).

As noted above, the court may make a disqualification order against a director whom it has found liable for wrongful (or fraudulent) trading, even if no application has been made by the Secretary of State.

Table 6.1 – Particular matters to which the Secretary of State will have regard when deciding whether to bring disqualification proceedings

- Attempted concealment of assets or cases where assets have disappeared or a deficiency is unexplained;
- Appropriation of assets to other companies for no consideration, at an undervalue, or on the basis of unreasonable charges for services;
- Preferences;
- Personal benefits obtained by directors;
- Overvaluing assets in accounts for the purpose of obtaining loans, or other financial accommodation, or to mislead creditors;
- Loans to directors in making share purchases;
- Dishonoured cheques;
- Use of delaying tactics;
- Non-payment of Crown debts to finance trading;
- 'Phoenix' operations;
- Misconduct in relation to operation of a factoring account;
- Taking of deposits for goods or services ultimately not supplied; and
- Cases where criminal convictions have resulted.

6.4.6.5   Undertakings

The Secretary of State may, as an alternative to seeking a disqualification order, ask directors to enter into binding undertakings imposing restrictions similar to those available under an order (s 1A CDDA 1986). This is regarded as a quicker, cheaper (and perhaps less public) alternative to court proceedings, but the restriction upon an individual's ability to make a living through the medium of a limited liability company is the same. In recent years, approximately 80% of all disqualifications of directors of failed companies have been achieved by way of an undertaking.

6.4.6.6   Permission to act in certain circumstances

It is possible for a director against whom a disqualification order has been made (or who has given an undertaking) to apply to the court for permission to act as a director in particular circumstances notwithstanding his disqualification (s 17 CDDA 1986). Typically, consent will only be given where the court is satisfied both that the director's involvement in the management of a specific company is desirable, and that safeguards are in place to protect creditors (eg that he will not have sole discretion in relation to financial matters and the company's management will include other suitably qualified directors capable of exercising financial control).

6.4.7   Criminal liability

As noted in Sections 6.4.3 and 6.4.5 respectively, fraudulent trading and reuse of company names may result in criminal, as well as civil, liability.

The IA 1986 also includes a number of other provisions under which past or present officers (including directors) may be prosecuted and, if found guilty, fined or sent to prison. Examples of conduct which may result in criminal prosecution are:

- concealing or fraudulently 'removing' property belonging to the company worth £500 or more;

- concealing, destroying, mutilating or falsifying books or records relating to the company (or being privy to anything of the kind being carried out by a third party);

- pawning, pledging or disposing of property obtained by the company on credit (except in the ordinary course of the company's business); and

- failing to disclose, or hand over, to the liquidator property or records belonging to the company.

6.5   PRACTICAL CONSEQUENCES FOR DIRECTORS

6.5.1   Overview

The courts have made it clear that the legislation does not impose a statutory duty on directors to ensure that their company does not trade whilst it has negative net assets or an obligation to ensure that the company does not trade at a loss. The directors may properly take the view in appropriate circumstances that it is in the interests of the company and its creditors that the company should continue to trade out of its difficulties.

Even if the company has negative net assets, if it can expect to pay creditors as they arise from its cash flow or from new capital, it may conceivably continue to trade for some time with the aim eventually of becoming profitable. Indeed, many start-up companies are in exactly this position, and new commerce might be stultified if the legislation required the directors to stop trading at the first sign of trouble (see the court's comments in *Re Hawkes Hill Publishing Co Ltd* [2007] BCC 937).

Indeed, the courts have accepted that even where a company had been cash flow insolvent for most of its history, the directors might still reach a *bona fide* conclusion on the facts available that it would return to profit over time (see *Langreen Limited* (unreported, 21 October 2011, Registrar Derrett). The judgment in this case contains a useful review of the previous case law.

However, the directors of a company which continues to trade whilst 'insolvent' will inevitably be at greater risk of personal liability should the company not survive. Additionally, there is in practice a significant overlap between the wrongful trading test and the criteria for disqualification – if it is established in disqualification proceedings that a director continued to trade beyond the 'critical date' he may well be held unfit to be concerned in the management of a company (see the court's comments in *Secretary of State for Trade and Industry v Gash* [1997] 1 BCLC 341).

A particular concern for the board must therefore be to satisfy itself that, if the company continues to trade, there is at least a reasonable prospect of it avoiding insolvent liquidation. If at any stage the point is reached when the board cannot reasonably conclude, after a careful analysis of the facts and after proper advice, that there is a 'reasonable prospect' of this, the board must ensure that they take every step with a view to minimising the potential loss to creditors. This is discussed further in Section 6.5.5.

The courts in the above cases made it clear that directors' decisions need to be reviewed in the context of what the directors knew or ought to have known at this time, not with the benefit of hindsight. However, it will be harder for directors to demonstrate their thinking without contemporaneous records. This is discussed further in Section 6.5.5.

6.5.2 What should the directors do?

Unless or until the financial difficulties are resolved, the directors will need to:

- Ensure that they have accurate, comprehensive and regularly updated financial and trading **information and forecasts** to enable them properly to monitor the company's position and to form the basis for their decision making.

- Take **advice** from a professional. If the company's own systems cannot reliably provide the information and forecasts the directors need, urgent external support from an accountancy firm will be required. In addition, the directors should seek independent external professional advice from corporate recovery specialists if they are concerned that formal insolvency is a significant risk.

- Hold **regular board meetings** to consider the above, to discuss the progress of any steps already being taken to improve the company's position and to agree appropriate actions. The board will need, among other things, continuously to consider whether continuing trading or other significant actions will be in the best interests of creditors. It must review and if necessary revise any earlier decisions as further developments occur.

The directors and their advisers should also therefore keep written minutes of each meeting and copies of the information and advice before the meeting since this will be evidence, if needed later, that the board considered the correct issues, was properly advised and acted appropriately. The minutes of each meeting of the directors will therefore need to be reasonably detailed, describing the reasons behind any decision, and the facts upon which they are based.

The courts have been supportive of directors who have properly followed these steps – see for example *Singer and another v Beckett and others* [2007] 2 BCLC 287 (the '**Continental Assurance**' case), the facts of which are set out in the box below.

Singer and another v Beckett and others **[2007] 2 BCLC 287**

Continental was a small insurance company. It had a full-time managing director and a part-time finance director. It also had six non-executive directors, some of whom represented major investors and others who had been invited to join the board due to their general expertise.

In June 1991, the 1990 accounts were put before the board. Instead of the expected profit, the executive directors reported a considerable loss, reflecting

---

unexpectedly high claims. The board instructed the finance director to prepare a solvency statement and forecast, to be verified by the auditors.

At a board meeting on 19 July, the board carefully considered the information then before it and concluded Continental was still solvent and met its DTI solvency margin. The board also considered that, even if it could not attract the further capital it would need to secure its medium- to long-term future, an outside purchaser could still be found. In the shorter term, the forecasts showed that on current trading, Continental ought to make a small profit, and it was felt that it had now withdrawn from particularly unsatisfactory lines of business.

For the rest of the year, the directors met frequently. They attempted to secure fresh capital from existing investors and to find a purchaser. In November, Continental reported to the DTI that its net asset position had fallen below its solvency margin, but the DTI allowed it to continue to trade whilst it produced a plan to rectify this. Finally, however, it was resolved that the company was no longer solvent, and it was placed into liquidation in March 1992.

The directors had taken care to minute all of their meetings and other discussions. The liquidator brought a wrongful trading action against Continental's directors. He chose 19 July 1991 as the critical date, arguing that the accounts that were before that meeting were wrong, as inappropriate accounting policies had been followed. The finance director settled, but other directors contested the action.

The key issues were: (1) whether correct accounts would have shown Continental to be insolvent at the critical date; (2) whether the directors should have known that the accounting policies were inappropriate; and (3) whether the directors should have concluded, if appropriate policies had been applied, that Continental was insolvent.

The court found in favour of the directors. It held that it would have imposed an unrealistically high burden on them to expect them all to have had a full understanding of the accounting policies behind the management accounts. Once they discovered that the company was in difficulty, they had instructed the finance director and auditors to investigate and report. When advised that Continental was solvent, they had still considered that advice with care, and had questioned the auditors and finance director at length before making their decision to trade on. It was reasonable for the other directors to rely on the advice given to them by the finance director in these circumstances.

One of the directors' reasons for continuing to trade was that they believed the business could be sold. On the evidence the directors were not at fault for assuming that there was a reasonable prospect of this.

6.5.3   Can a director resign?

Resigning will not exempt a director from liability for wrongful trading up to the time of resignation. It might even exacerbate the risk of a finding of wrongful trading, since it is unlikely to fulfil the obligation to take 'every step with a view to minimising the potential loss to the company's creditors'. There are circumstances where it might be the only option, for example, for a director on a divided board who, having done his best to put forward his case for action, is overruled by the majority. It is also possible that conflicts of interest, such as in the context of a proposed refinancing, might make it difficult for an individual director representing particular interests to remain on the board.

6.5.4 Customer deposits

Where the company's business involves taking deposit monies from customers, the directors should ideally ensure that these monies are separated from the company's own monies. It is possible to achieve this by taking steps to ensure that monies so received will be held on trust for the customers concerned until the goods or services in respect of which the deposits had been paid had actually been supplied (*Re Kayford Ltd* [1975] 1 WLR 279). In this case, it is prudent:

- to prepare a written trust deed, expressly declaring the trust and providing as to how the trust monies are to be administered;

- to place the trust monies concerned into a separate bank account; and

- to obtain the consent of any lender who holds security over the company's assets.

In reality, this method may not be practicable for many companies which use customer deposits as part of their day-to-day working capital. Directors would, of course, be ill-advised to continue to accept and use deposits if they considered that the company may already have reached the critical date. However, they might be justified in doing so where they properly believed that this was in the best interests of all creditors and the company retained a reasonable prospect of avoiding insolvent liquidation. In *Re Uno plc and another: Secretary of State for Trade and Industry v Gill and others* [2006] BCC 725 the Secretary of State argued (in disqualification proceedings) that a director's conduct still showed a serious lack of probity if the company had continued to accept deposits or advance payments in circumstances where there was no certainty that it could meet the customer's order, notwithstanding that the company had **not** yet reached the critical date. However, this argument was rejected by the court in that case.

6.5.5 Continued trading beyond the critical date

6.5.5.1 General considerations

In many cases, where the directors consider that the critical date may have occurred, they will need to place the company into a formal insolvency process to avoid further losses to creditors. However, in some cases, continued trading might still be in creditors' best interests. The directors might believe that keeping the company going for a short time longer will enable them to sell the business as a going concern and at a higher price than an insolvency officeholder would achieve.

The directors will, however, need to take every step to minimise potential losses to creditors during any period of continued trading (see Section 6.4.2.3). At the most cautious level, this would mean that they need to ensure that no new creditors are created, that the net liabilities to existing creditors are not increased and that assets (including cash) which would otherwise be available on a liquidation are retained. This may make continued trading more or less impossible, at least without the support of other interested parties. The directors might be able to do little more than selling existing stock for at least the price (net of costs) which a liquidator would achieve.

In appropriate circumstances, however, it might be possible to continue trading on a 'ring fenced' basis. Assets and liabilities which exist at the critical date would, in effect, be left untouched. The further trading must be funded from some source other than the existing assets. This might consist of income from the further trading itself, but this could be difficult to achieve in practice. Alternatively, a third party might provide the necessary funds, although these funds cannot be provided on terms which create an obligation for the company to repay that third party in competition with existing creditors. Where the beneficiary of the continued trading is a secured creditor, they may be prepared to agree in advance that an appropriate portion of their enhanced recoveries will be made available to unsecured creditors who suffer loss as a result of the continued trading.

6.5.5.2 Pre-packs

Where they are preparing for a pre-packaged sale, the directors will know in advance that a formal insolvency process is inevitable. Theoretically it might still be possible for a company to enter into administration and then to be dissolved without ever having entered into insolvent liquidation, with the result that the wrongful trading provisions (and those other provisions described in Section 6.4 which only apply on an insolvent liquidation) will never apply. However, it is difficult for the directors to predict the outcome of the administration with any certainty. In addition, the directors will still be at risk of disqualification whether or not insolvent liquidation occurs. Directors would be wise therefore to treat the company as having passed the critical date once it is clear that the pre-pack will go ahead.

The parties who will benefit from the pre-pack, who may include a number of the company's lenders or other stakeholders, will almost certainly wish any trading company to continue to trade during the lead up to a pre-pack. The directors may therefore wish them to agree to put in place one of the measures discussed in Section 6.5.5.1 to protect creditors.

6.5.6 Insurance and indemnities

In practice, directors of many companies will have the benefit of directors and officers ('D&O') insurance. This may well cover the cost of defending some of the proceedings listed in Section 6.4, and may indeed also cover the cost of a compensatory award. Nonetheless, it should not be relied upon to do so. Insurance will also generally be subject to an aggregate limit of liability for all claims (including the legal cost of defending such claims).

D&O insurance also commonly operates on a 'claims made' basis, ie it will be necessary to have cover in place at the time any claim is made against the director, not just at the time the events which gave rise to the claim occurred. The directors also therefore need to consider buying 'run off' cover prior to any formal insolvency, so that they will still have the necessary cover in place.

Sometimes a director, for example, where he has been appointed by a particular shareholder, will be able to obtain an indemnity from a third party for all claims which he may face as a result. The terms of this will be a matter for negotiation.

Regardless of other factors, insurance and indemnities can provide financial cover only. They cannot benefit a director should an order for disqualification or criminal conviction result, or compensate harm to his reputation.

6.6   ADDITIONAL ISSUES FOR PUBLIC COMPANIES

6.6.1   Serious loss of capital

Where the net assets of a 'public company' fall to half, or less, of the amount of the company's called-up share capital, the directors of the company must, within four weeks of learning of that fact, call a general meeting of the company (to be held within eight weeks) at which to consider whether any, and if so what, measures should be taken to deal with the situation (s 656 CA 2006). This applies to any company whose name ends in 'plc' or 'public limited company' – not merely to publicly quoted companies. If a meeting is not held within the time limits, the directors responsible for failing to call a meeting may be fined.

'**Net assets**' for these purposes are the aggregate of a company's assets less the aggregate of its liabilities (including provisions for contingent and future liabilities and losses). A company's 'called-up share capital' is the amount paid up on its issued share capital, or called but not yet paid, and any further amount payable on a specified future date (whether under the articles, the terms of allotment or any other arrangements for payment for the shares). It is not clear whether a premium paid (or payable) to the company should be included. It would be safer to assume that it should not.

6.6.2   Stock exchange announcements

Where a company is listed, there is an obligation under the Listing Rules of the Financial Conduct Authority to notify the Company Announcements Office of the London Stock Exchange without delay of 'all relevant information' not in the public domain concerning a change:

- in the company's financial condition;

- in the performance of its business; or

- in its expectation as to its performance which (in any case) if made public would be likely to lead to substantial movement in the price of its listed securities.

A change in the company's financial condition leading it to consider any form of insolvency procedure, or requiring it to enter into negotiations with its lenders, or to call a meeting under s 656 CA 2006 is likely, once news reaches the outside world, to lead to substantial movements in its share price.

The company need not make an announcement in respect of impending developments, or matters in the course of negotiation, and it may give information on a confidential basis to certain categories of people, including its advisers and those with whom it is negotiating. But if at any time confidentiality is, or is likely to be breached, a warning announcement must be made. Once negotiations extend beyond a relatively limited group of creditors, it is unlikely that confidentiality will be maintained. The UK Listing Authority is likely, in that event, to suspend listing of the company's shares.

A fuller discussion of these issues is beyond the scope of this book.

6.7   THE DIRECTORS' ROLE IN A FORMAL INSOLVENCY PROCESS

6.7.1   What is the effect on the directors' powers?

6.7.1.1   Liquidation

In a voluntary liquidation, the powers of the directors cease once the liquidator is appointed, except in so far as the liquidator or the company in general meeting (in the case of an MVL), or the liquidation committee (in the case of a CVL) sanctions their continuance (ss 91(2) and 103 IA 1986, respectively).

The liquidator would normally be appointed at the same time as the shareholders' resolution is passed. However, if they are not, s 114 IA 1986 provides that the directors' powers can only be exercised with the sanction of the court during the intervening period, except:

● as far as may be necessary (in the case of a CVL) to call the Section 98 meeting and prepare a statement of affairs; and

● to dispose of perishable goods, or other goods whose value is likely to diminish if not immediately disposed of, and to do such other things as are necessary to protect the company's assets.

The legislation does not specifically address the powers of directors following a winding-up order, but it has been generally accepted that their powers come to an end (see, for example, *Union Accident Insurance Co Ltd* [1972] 1 WLR 640 at 642). The liquidator will again take control of the company's affairs, and exercise his own powers to progress the liquidation.

6.7.1.2   Administration

When the company is in administration, the directors remain in place unless or until they are removed. However, neither the company nor its directors are entitled to exercise any management powers without the consent of the administrator. Here, a 'management power' means a power which could be exercised so as to interfere with the exercise of the administrator's powers (para 64 Sch B1 IA 1986). In practice, administrators will generally lay down guidelines for any continuing involvement of the directors in managing the company's business. An administrator has the power to remove and appoint directors, if necessary (see Chapter 4).

6.7.1.3   Receivership

When an administrative receiver is appointed, he assumes the power, in place of the board, to carry on the business and to realise the company's assets. The directors are left with little to manage, but their statutory obligations as directors continue, and they remain entitled to exercise the company's powers to the extent that the administrative receiver does not wish to, and to the extent that such exercise will not interfere with his dealing with the assets under his control. The directors, for example, may take steps to put the company into liquidation where they think this is advisable.

The directors also retain authority to institute, on behalf of the company, proceedings against the administrative receiver and his appointor, if appropriate (eg to challenge the validity of the appointment).

In other types of receivership, the receiver will assume the power to manage and realise the assets of which he has been appointed, but the directors will otherwise retain their normal powers.

6.7.1.4 CVA

The directors remain in office and retain their powers both whilst the arrangement is being proposed, and after it is adopted. They will, however, be subject to the supervision of the nominee/supervisor to ensure that the arrangement is properly implemented.

6.7.2 What duties will the directors have?

In a liquidation, administration or administrative receivership, the directors will have a number of specific duties. Some of these duties extend not just to individuals who are directors of the company as at the date the company enters into the insolvency process, but to individuals who have been directors and to other 'relevant persons'. For these purposes, a relevant person will include:

- a person who is or has been an officer of the company; and

- a person who, during the period of one year ending with the date of the formal insolvency process, took part in the formation of the company, or was employed by the company, or was an officer or employee of a company which is or has been an officer of the company.

These specific duties are as follows:

- A relevant person must provide a **statement of affairs** where required by the insolvency officeholder. This is discussed further in Section 6.7.3.

- A relevant person must **co-operate with the officeholder** by providing such information concerning the company and its promotion, formation, business, dealings, affairs or property as the officeholder may reasonably require. They must also attend on the officeholder at such times as he may reasonably require (s 235 IA 1986). This duty applies notwithstanding that the information provided may be used against the person concerned in subsequent disqualification proceedings. Indeed, an insolvency officeholder's normal practice will be to require individuals on whose conduct he will be required to report to the Secretary of State (see Section 6.4.6.3) to complete a **director's questionnaire** shortly after his appointment.

- A director must also **attend an initial creditors' meeting** when required to do so by a liquidator or administrator.

In addition, even where the directors' management powers have effectively ceased, their statutory duties under the Companies Acts to prepare annual accounts and lay them before a general meeting and to make filings with the Registrar of Companies remain. Strictly speaking, the directors could still be fined for non-compliance, although in practice, the Registrar does not require the further filing of accounts once he becomes aware of a liquidation or administration. Best practice is probably for the insolvency officeholder still to make sufficient information available to the directors to allow them to compile statutory accounts, although the officeholder may be unprepared to do this where the insolvency process in question is likely soon to lead to the end of the company's life.

6.7.3 Statement of affairs

Shortly after (or possibly just before) the company enters into formal insolvency, the directors are likely to be required to prepare a statement of affairs. This requirement may extend not only to individuals who remain directors as at the date of the formal insolvency but also to past directors. The prescribed form and content of the statement of affairs will differ according to the insolvency process involved, but essentially it will need to give details of:

- the company's assets, debts and liabilities;

- the names and addresses of the company's creditors; and

- the security held by each creditor and the date on which that security was granted.

A statement of affairs (and any statement of concurrence) will need to be verified by affidavit statement of truth.

6.7.3.1 Liquidation

In a creditors' voluntary liquidation, the directors are required to prepare a statement of affairs, verified by some or all of the directors, **to be laid before the creditors' meeting** (s 99 IA 1986). In practice therefore where the creditors' meeting is held immediately after the shareholders' meeting the statement of affairs will be prepared just before the liquidation.

In a compulsory liquidation, the Official Receiver may require the directors to submit a statement of affairs **within 21 days** of the date on which he gives them notice, although this time limit may be extended by the Official Receiver or, failing that, the court (s 131 IA 1986).

6.7.3.2 Administration

Here, the legislation is fairly comprehensive as to what is required. As soon as is reasonably practicable after his appointment, the administrator may require one or more relevant persons (see Section 6.7.2) to provide a statement of affairs (para 47 Sch B1 IA 1986). Under para 48 Sch B1 IA 1986, a person required to submit a statement of affairs must do so **within 11 days** beginning with the day on which they receive notice to do so. However, the administrator may (and frequently does) agree to extend this period. Indeed they can even revoke the requirement to supply a statement of affairs completely.

The administrator may also require any other relevant person to submit a **statement of concurrence**, stating that he concurs with the statement of affairs. However, the statement of concurrence may be qualified if the maker does not agree with the person making the statement of affairs, considers the statement of affairs to be erroneous, or does not have the direct knowledge necessary to concur. The statement of concurrence must be submitted within five business days beginning with the day on which the maker receives the statement of affairs, although again the administrator can agree to extend this (r 2.29 IR 1986).

6.7.3.3 Administrative receivership

The legislation here is similar in substance to that described in Section 6.7.3.2. When an administrative receiver is appointed, he must forthwith require one or more relevant persons (see Section 6.7.2) to submit a statement of affairs **within 21 days** beginning with the day on which they receive notice to do so. Again, this period can be extended or the requirement revoked (s 47 IA 1986). The receiver can require a statement of concurrence from another relevant person (r 3.4 IR 1986).

Chapter 7

CVAs and Schemes of Arrangement

7.1   INTRODUCTION

Chapter 1 gave an overview of the CVA and Scheme of Arrangement processes. This chapter considers both processes in more detail. They are similar to each other in that, among other things:

- they are both statutory procedures used to reach arrangements with creditors, and each may allow a specified majority of creditors voting in favour to impose the arrangement on a minority of dissenting creditors;

- compared to liquidation and administration, neither process has detailed rules, and in particular both allow for a degree of flexibility as to how creditors will be treated – the flexibility is limited largely only by an inability to bind secured or preferential creditors without their consent (in the case of a CVA) and by creditors' rights to object if they are being unfairly treated;

- the directors largely or wholly retain their management powers and neither process gives rise in itself to the various potential sanctions against directors associated with liquidation and administration; and

- there is no specific requirement that the company need be unable to pay its debts in order to enter into either process.

Table 7.1 shows some of the main differences between these two processes. In many cases, only one or the other of them (if either) will be a viable alternative. The CVA process was originally designed to be a low-cost option for companies in difficulty, although the inability to bind secured creditors without their consent does reduce its usefulness to some extent. The Scheme of Arrangement process is not a low cost option, given the need for significant court involvement (although the cost may still be comparable with those of other alternatives for larger companies). However, there will still be eventualities where both processes are worth considering.

The CVA has become a valuable tool to compromise the claims of landlords for companies with surplus rented premises. The CVA is also regularly used in football club insolvencies. In both of these cases, its usefulness derives from the fact that, although all creditors are entitled to vote on the proposal, it is possible for a CVA to treat some of those creditors differently from others. This is discussed in more detail in Section 7.2.4.2.

Schemes of Arrangement have frequently been used as a tool to compromise the claims of financial creditors in high value corporate restructurings. They have also been used to compromise multiple claims against companies, for example under contracts of insurance and for asbestosis. This is discussed in more detail in Section 7.3.2.

Table 7.1 – The CVA process versus the Scheme of Arrangement process

	CVA	*Scheme of Arrangement*
Is it a 'formal insolvency process'?	Yes – recognised as such by the EC Insolvency Regulation	No – although a Scheme can still be used for a foreign company which could be wound up as an unregistered company under the IA 1986 and which has sufficient connection with this jurisdiction
Does a qualified insolvency practitioner need formally to be involved?	Yes – as a nominee prior to implementation and as a supervisor during implementation	No
How is the court involved?	Certain filings must be made with the court office but no court hearings are required	At least two court hearings are required as part of the process
How do creditors vote?	All creditors vote at a single meeting	Creditors are divided into classes, and each meeting of each class vote separately. Not all classes of creditors need hold meetings, although classes that do not will not be bound by the Scheme
What are the voting thresholds for approval?	More than 75% by value of creditors must vote in favour **but** approval will not be effective if more than 50% by value of unconnected creditors vote against	At least 75% by value **and** a majority in number of **each class** must vote in favour
What is the effect on secured creditors?	Secured (and preferential) creditors cannot be bound without their consent	Can be used to bind secured creditors falling into the class, or classes, voting on the Scheme
What is the effect on shareholders?	Although creditors can approve a CVA notwithstanding shareholder opposition, cannot be used to alter shareholder rights	Can be used to alter shareholder as well as creditor rights
How are 'fairness' issues and procedural defects addressed?	A creditor who considers that he has been unfairly prejudiced or that there was a material irregularity must initiate their own challenge following approval	The company must convince the court at a sanction hearing that the Scheme is fair and that the procedure was correctly carried out

7.2   COMPANY VOLUNTARY ARRANGEMENTS

7.2.1   Overview

A CVA is defined in s 1(1) IA 1986 as:

● a **composition** in satisfaction of a company's debts; or

- a **scheme of arrangement** of the company's affairs (which term should not be confused with the separate Scheme of Arrangement procedure described later in this chapter).

The terms are not synonymous. A composition is an agreement with creditors that they will receive the payment of a sum of money in place of some existing debt or obligation. The courts have made it clear that a scheme of arrangement differs from a composition in that it need not offer any compromise or release of creditors' debts (*March Estates plc v Gunmark* [1996] 2 BCLC 1). In *IRC v Adam & Partners Ltd* [2001] BCLC 222 it was held that a proposal where no payment at all was envisaged to unsecured creditors could still give rise to a valid CVA. Normally, however, a CVA proposal will offer some payment to the creditors concerned.

7.2.2 Commencing a CVA

Table 7.2 shows the CVA process in flowchart form.

7.2.2.1 Who may propose a CVA?

A CVA may be proposed by:

- the directors of the company (provided it is not in administration or liquidation); or

- an administrator or liquidator.

7.2.2.2 Proposal by the directors

Where the directors plan to propose a CVA, their first step will be to identify an appropriately qualified insolvency professional and to discuss the process with them in advance. The insolvency professional will then have various roles. They will need to advise the directors as to whether a CVA is appropriate and to act as nominee prior to approval of the CVA, as chairman of the meetings and as supervisor in the event that the proposal is approved. A nominee or supervisor must either be a qualified insolvency practitioner **or** a person otherwise qualified so to act. Statement of Insolvency Practice 3 ('**SIP 3**') addresses their various roles and responsibilities.

The directors' formal role is:

- To prepare a **proposal** for the intended nominee. This will include a short explanation of why, in their opinion, a CVA would be desirable, and will give reasons why the creditors might be expected to concur. The contents of a proposal generally are discussed in Section 7.2.4. In practice, the insolvency professional is likely to have provided the directors with considerable assistance in formulating this.

- To prepare a **statement of affairs**. Rule 1.5(2) IR 1986 sets out the matters to be covered here, but essentially it will need to give details of the company's assets and their estimated values, details of any security over those assets and of the claim of the security holder, the names and addresses of the company's unsecured creditors and the amounts of their respective claims, details of any debts owed by or to the company to or by a person connected with it and the names and addresses of the company's shareholders and details of their shareholdings.

Table 7.2 – The CVA process

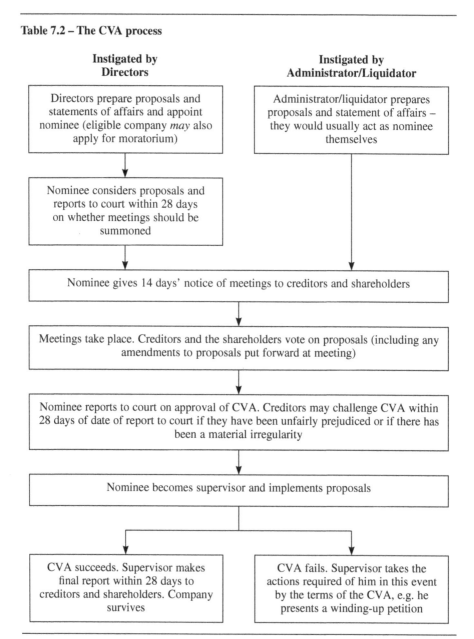

Instigated by Directors	Instigated by Administrator/Liquidator
Directors prepare proposals and statements of affairs and appoint nominee (eligible company *may* also apply for moratorium)	Administrator/liquidator prepares proposals and statement of affairs – they would usually act as nominee themselves

Nominee considers proposals and reports to court within 28 days on whether meetings should be summoned

Nominee gives 14 days' notice of meetings to creditors and shareholders

Meetings take place. Creditors and the shareholders vote on proposals (including any amendments to proposals put forward at meeting)

Nominee reports to court on approval of CVA. Creditors may challenge CVA within 28 days of date of report to court if they have been unfairly prejudiced or if there has been a material irregularity

Nominee becomes supervisor and implements proposals

CVA succeeds. Supervisor makes final report within 28 days to creditors and shareholders. Company survives	CVA fails. Supervisor takes the actions required of him in this event by the terms of the CVA, e.g. he presents a winding-up petition

The insolvency practitioner's formal role as nominee is to submit a **report to the court** within 28 days of receiving the proposal stating whether, in his opinion, the proposed CVA has a reasonable prospect of being approved and implemented and whether therefore meetings of the shareholders and creditors should be summoned to consider the proposal (s 2 IA 1986). Given that there is no formal requirement for the directors to take advice when putting together their proposal, this provision is designed to ensure that a proposal is still reviewed in advance by an appropriately skilled and qualified person.

The case of *Re a Debtor (No 140 IO of 1995), Greystoke Hamilton-Smith and Others* [1996] 2 BCLC 429 (which concerned an individual voluntary arrangement) suggested that the nominee needs to satisfy himself on three counts:

- that the company's true position as to assets and liabilities is not materially different from that which it is represented to creditors to be;

- that the proposal has a real prospect of being implemented in the way which it is represented to be; and

- that there is no already manifest but unavoidable prospective unfairness.

The second count is effectively the same as that now required by s 2 IA 1986. If the nominee cannot satisfy himself that the other two conditions are met, but still recommends that the meetings should be held he needs to make the circumstances clear in his report. The case also makes it clear that, whilst the nominee does not have a statutory duty to investigate the company's affairs, he should still review the financial information provided by the directors and, if he has doubts, make further enquiries.

7.2.2.3 Proposal by an administrator or liquidator

An administrator or liquidator's proposal needs to specify the same matters as would a directors' proposal, and such other matters as they consider appropriate for ensuring that the shareholders and creditors of the company are able to reach an informed decision, together with information regarding the prescribed part and the nature and amount of the company's preferential creditors (r 1.10 IR 1986). It is likely that any administrator or liquidator making a proposal will themselves perform the role of nominee. There is no need for a report to the court.

7.2.2.4 Summoning the meetings

The nominee will fix a time and a venue for meetings of the creditors and the shareholders (s 3 IA 1986). The meetings must be held within five business days of each other. In practice, however, they will normally be scheduled for the same place on the same day, with the creditors' meeting being held first, then the shareholders' meeting (r 1.13 IR 1986).

The nominee must give at least **14 days' notice** of the meetings to all creditors of whose claim and address he is aware (which will include all of those creditors specified in the statement of affairs) and to all persons who are, to the best of his belief, shareholders (r 1.9 IR 1986). This notice must be accompanied by:

- a copy of the proposal;

- a copy of the statement of affairs or, if the nominee thinks fit, a summary of it which includes a list of creditors and the amount of their debts;

- in the case of a directors' proposal, the nominee's comments on the proposal; and

- a form of proxy.

In practice it will also generally include a form for the creditor to complete in order to give formal written notice of their claim, termed for these purposes a 'statement of claim'.

The nominee must also give at least 14 days' notice to attend to the directors, and to any other officers or persons who have been directors or officers during the last two years whose presence he thinks is required. However, he also has the power to exclude any present or former director from the meeting (r 1.16 IR 1986).

7.2.3   Is a moratorium available?

7.2.3.1   Overview

If creditors become aware that a CVA is proposed which might affect their ability to recover their debts in full, there is a risk that they will take enforcement actions in the period prior to the meetings. There is therefore a procedure which allows certain companies to file for a moratorium during this period. Whilst this procedure will be described briefly here, in practice, it is rarely used due, among other things, to the eligibility requirements and the obligations which it places on the nominee. In most circumstances, an applicant considering this type of moratorium will tend instead to place the company into administration to take advantage of the administration moratorium.

7.2.3.2   Will the company be eligible?

Paragraph 3 Sch A1 IA 1986 sets out the qualifying requirements for this procedure. During the financial year ending with the date of filing, or which ended most recently before that date, the company must have satisfied at least two of the requirements for being a '**small company**' under s 382(3) CA 2006, which at the time of writing are:

- a turnover of no more than £6.5 million;

- a balance sheet total of not more than £3.26 million; and

- no more than 50 employees.

A holding company which satisfies these requirements will not qualify for this procedure if it and its subsidiaries would together exceed the necessary limits.

Under para 4 Sch A1 1986 the company will be ineligible if:

- the company concerned is presently in administration or liquidation or the subject of a CVA, or an administrative receiver or provisional liquidator has been appointed; or

- at any time **during the previous 12 months** the company was the subject of a similar moratorium without a CVA having been put in place or was the subject of a CVA put in place following such a moratorium which ended prematurely, **or** an administrator appointed by the company or its directors out of court was in office, **or** the company was the subject of a CVA as a result of a proposal by a liquidator or administrator and the liquidation or administration proceedings were stayed by the court.

Paragraphs 4A to 4K Sch A1 1986 introduce a number of further, more specialised exceptions. Broadly, a company will also be ineligible if it is a party to a capital markets arrangement which fulfils certain criteria, it is a project company of a public–private partnership project which includes step-in rights, or it has incurred a liability under an agreement of £10 million or more. In other words these exceptions reflect the City Exceptions discussed in chapter 8.

7.2.3.3   How is the moratorium obtained?

The directors submit their proposal and statement of affairs to the nominee as described in Section 7.2.2. The nominee then prepares a **statement** indicating, among other things, whether or not in his opinion the proposed CVA has a reasonable prospect of being approved and implemented and whether the company is likely to have sufficient funds during the proposed moratorium to allow it to carry on in business. In this regard, the nominee is entitled to rely upon the information provided by the directors unless he has reason to doubt its accuracy (para 6 Sch A1 IA 1986).

Assuming the nominee supports the proposal, the directors then file various documents with the court. These are: the proposal and statement of affairs, a statement that the company is eligible for the moratorium, a statement from the nominee that he has consented to act and the nominee's statement as described above (para 7 Sch A1 IA 1986).

The moratorium becomes effective once these filings have been made. It comes to an end if the meetings have not been held **within 28 days** beginning with the date of the filing, although the creditors and shareholders may vote to extend this period (para 8 Sch A1 IA 1986). (Should they choose to extend the moratorium, they may also resolve to create a moratorium committee.)

The nominee must continue to monitor the company's affairs during the moratorium period to ensure that he remains of the opinion that the CVA has a reasonable prospect of being approved and implemented and that the company will have sufficient funds. Should his opinion change, he must withdraw his consent to act and the moratorium will end (paras 24 and 25 Sch A1 IA 1986).

7.2.3.4   What is the effect of the moratorium on third parties?

The effect of the moratorium is broadly similar to that of the administration moratorium (see Chapter 4). Under para 12 Sch A1 IA 1986:

- No winding-up petition may be presented, nor may an order be made or resolution passed to place the company into liquidation (although the same exceptions apply here as apply under the administration moratorium).

- No administration application may be made, no administrator may be appointed out of court, nor may an administrative receiver be appointed.

- No landlord may forfeit by peaceable re-entry, no steps may be taken to enforce security or to repossess goods in the company's possession under a 'hire-purchase agreement' (which has an extended meaning) nor may any other proceedings, execution or other legal process be taken without the leave of the court and subject to such terms as it may impose.

The rights of a floating charge holder are, however, more restricted than under the interim moratorium which applies prior to an administration. In particular, they are unable to appoint an administrator or administrative receiver. In addition, any provision which would allow the chargeholder to crystallise their floating charge, which would otherwise cause the floating charge to crystallise or which would cause any restriction to be imposed on the disposal of the company's property, will be ineffective during the moratorium (para 13 Sch A1 IA 1986).

7.2.3.5   What obligations are placed on the company?

Various obligations and restrictions are placed on the company during the moratorium period. Among other things:

- every invoice, order or business letter issued by or on behalf of the company (whether in hard copy, electronic or any other form) and all of the company's websites must contain the nominee's name and indicate that a moratorium is in force (para 16 Sch A1 IA 1986);

- the company must disclose the existence of the moratorium when obtaining credit of £250 or more (para 17 Sch A1 IA 1986); and

- the company may only dispose of property other than in the ordinary course of its business or pay a pre-moratorium debt if there are reasonable grounds for believing that the disposal or payment will benefit the company and the disposal or payment is approved by any moratorium committee, or in the absence of such a committee, the nominee (paras 18 and 19 Sch A1 IA 1986).

7.2.3.6   Other consequences of the moratorium

When there is a moratorium, the rules which apply to some of the other processes described in the chapter are replaced by slightly different rules to accommodate the moratorium (see rr 1.35 to 1.54 IR 1986). However, the principles involved remain substantially similar and an analysis of any differences is beyond the scope of this book.

7.2.4   The content of a proposal

7.2.4.1   General provisions

Rule 1.3 IR 1986 sets out a list of matters required to be dealt with in the proposal. SIP 3 suggests that in drafting the proposal, it is helpful to follow the order set out in the above rule and indicates a number of other matters which the proposal and statement of affairs should include:

- The nature of the arrangement, ie whether it is a composition in full and final settlement of debts or a scheme of arrangement.

- The background to the proposal, including details of the circumstances in which the company has become insolvent (if relevant).

- A comparison of the estimated outcomes of the CVA and of liquidation, including their comparative costs.

- The actual financial proposal which is being put to the creditors. This will include details of assets being realised for the benefit of creditors and details (with reasons) of any assets of the company which are being excluded. It will often also include proposals for payments to the supervisor out of any future income received over the CVA period. In order to persuade creditors to accept a CVA proposal, a third party may also be offering to inject funds which would not be available on a liquidation, and if so details of these will also be provided.

- The intentions regarding the company's business. Given that the directors will remain responsible for managing the company and its business during the CVA period, the proposal will need to clarify the extent to which the supervisor will exercise control over their activities.

- The powers, duties and responsibilities of the supervisor. This will include the manner in which the supervisor will distribute funds to creditors, the action which he is required to take if the company fails to comply with the terms of the CVA and the basis on which he will report.

- Such other matters (if any) as the directors consider appropriate for ensuring that shareholders and creditors are enabled to reach an informed decision on the proposal.

If the CVA does not have the benefit of a continuing administration moratorium, it is wise to make it expressly clear that creditors' rights are limited to the receipt of their entitlements under the CVA and that they no longer therefore have the right to take independent action against the company. The proposal will generally also state what will happen to the CVA assets, should the CVA fail. In *Re NT Gallagher & Sons Ltd* [2002] BCC 867, the court held that a provision stipulating that the CVA assets were to be held on trust for the CVA creditors remained effective following the failure of the CVA and the company's consequent liquidation, but that the company's other assets would be available for distribution in the liquidation.

A set of standard proposal terms has been issued by the Association of Business Recovery Professionals and these will assist in many cases.

7.2.4.2   Can the proposal treat some classes of creditor differently from others?

The legislation contains special provisions to protect secured and preferential creditors (see Section 7.2.5.3). However, there are no special rules regarding the treatment of unsecured creditors, and the *pari passu* principle has no application to a CVA. This gives a useful degree of flexibility where, for example, the company only needs to reach a compromise with one type of creditor or where it is necessary to agree to pay particular creditors in full to ensure that the company can continue to trade.

All unsecured creditors are entitled to vote on the CVA proposal regardless of how they are treated by the proposal (see Section 7.2.5), so it is entirely possible for a proposal to be approved despite the creditors who are being treated less well voting against it. Differential treatment does nonetheless raise the prospect that creditors who are being treated less well will subsequently challenge the CVA on the basis that they are being unfairly prejudiced (see Section 7.2.7.2). However, the courts have made it clear that differential treatment is not conclusive in itself of unfair prejudice.

The CVA has therefore become a useful restructuring tool for **companies with surplus rented premises** (or premises where the rent is otherwise regarded as too high) which are unable to reach consensual arrangements with the landlords concerned. CVA proposals of this kind have been approved by the creditors of, amongst others, JJB Sports, Focus DIY, Blacks Leisure and Travelodge. These proposals have typically divided landlords into separate categories, depending on whether or not the company wished to retain the premises concerned. Typically, most classes of creditors other than landlords have continued to be paid in full. Notwithstanding the approval of their CVA proposals, however, not all of the above companies have survived in the longer term.

Similarly, the CVA has also frequently been used as an exit in football club administrations. The Premier League and the Football League are each entitled to expel from the league a club which enters administration. However, they will not do so where they are satisfied that a CVA or scheme of arrangement has been approved and that debts due to **football creditors** have been paid in full. These football creditors include other football clubs (for unpaid transfer fees) and players (for unpaid wages) and the leagues themselves. This can lead to a substantial disparity of treatment. In the case of Plymouth Argyle FC, for example, the football creditors were paid in full and the other unsecured creditors received only 0.77p in the pound, albeit from funds provided by a third party purchaser – these other unsecured creditors would have received nothing on a liquidation.

HMRC, in its capacity as one of these other unsecured creditors, has frequently but unsuccessfully challenged CVAs of this kind – see, for example, *IRC v Wimbledon FC* [2004] BCC 638 and *HMRC v Portsmouth City Football Club Limited* [2010] EWHC 2013 (Ch). (It has also separately but unsuccessfully challenged the Football League's rules as a breach of the anti-deprivation principle and/or the *pari passu* basis of distribution – see Section 2.7.3.1).

7.2.5 The shareholders' and creditors' meetings

7.2.5.1 What is the function of the meetings?

The convenor of the shareholders' and creditors' meetings summoned under s 3 IA 1986 will normally preside over those meetings as chairman, although if for any reason he is unable to attend provisions are made for him to nominate another suitably experienced insolvency professional in his place (r 1.14 IR 1986).

The main function of the meetings is to decide whether to approve the proposed CVA. If those voting are unwilling to support the proposal as it stands, it is possible to make modifications to the original proposal at a meeting. These may include the replacement of the existing nominee with some other appropriately qualified person. Modifications must not, however, result in the proposal ceasing to be a proposal for a composition or scheme of arrangement (ss 4(1) and 4(2) IA 1986).

7.2.5.2 Voting at the meetings

Rules 1.17 to 1.21 IR 1986 set out the normal procedure for voting at the meetings and rr 8.1 to 8.8 set out further requirements in relation to proxies, but an overview is given here.

Shareholders vote in accordance with their normal rights under the articles of the company. Unless the articles provide otherwise, any resolution will be passed if **more than 50%** of the votes cast by shareholders present in person or by proxy are in favour.

Creditors' votes are calculated according to the amount of the creditors' debt as at the date of the meeting or, where the company is in liquidation or administration, as at the date on which the liquidation or administration commenced. At the creditors' meeting there is effectively a two-stage test to determine whether any resolution is passed:

- **more than 75%** of the votes cast by creditors present in person or by proxy must be in favour of any resolution **approving any proposal or modification**, or (as the case may be);

- more than 50% of votes cast by those creditors must be in favour of any other resolution which may be put to the creditors; **but**

- any resolution will be invalid if, when the votes of creditors who are **connected** with the company are disregarded, **more than 50%** of the votes cast by the remaining creditors present in person or by proxy are against it.

The proxy may be worded to state that the representative is only entitled to vote in one particular way. This may be the creditor's preferred approach where they wish simply to appoint the chairman of the meeting as their proxy. (The rules prevent the chairman using a proxy to increase or reduce the remuneration or expenses of any nominee or supervisor unless the proxy expressly allows him to do so.) Where the creditor's own representative will attend, however, it may be wiser to return an 'open' proxy, which allows the representative to vote according to their discretion.

A creditor's vote will be disregarded if written notice of their claim was not given to the chairman or convenor of the meeting either prior to or at the meeting. Nonetheless, the fact that, as SIP 3 also notes, proxies or statements of claim to be used at the meeting may be lodged during the course of the meeting as well as at any time beforehand is helpful.

A nominal value of £1 will be placed on an **unliquidated** debt, or one whose value is **unascertained**, save to the extent that the chairman agrees to put a higher value on it. The chairman should only do so where a specific figure for that higher value can safely be ascertained without the need for speculation (*Chittenden v Pepper* [2007] BCC 195). The court considered the meaning of 'unliquidated' and 'unascertained' in *HMRC v Portsmouth City Football Club Limited* [2010] EWHC 2013 and concluded in that case that it was appropriate to put a value of £1 on the claims which HMRC would have if payments to players for 'image rights' were established to be a sham.

The chairman also has a general discretion to **accept or reject claims**, although in situations of doubt, the proper course is to mark the vote as '**objected to**' and to allow the creditor to vote. The vote may subsequently be declared invalid if the objection is sustained.

There is a right to appeal to the court against a chairman's decision, although such an appeal must be made **within 28 days** of the date on which the chairman's report on the outcome of the meeting is submitted to the court (see Section 7.2.5.5). If the chairman's decision is reversed or a vote declared invalid, the court may order another meeting to be summoned or make such order as it thinks fit.

Secured creditors are generally only able to vote in respect of the balance of their debt (if any) after deducting the value of their security.

7.2.5.3   Secured and preferential creditors

No proposal or modification may be approved:

- which affects the right of a **secured creditor** to enforce his security, except with the concurrence of the secured creditor concerned (s 4(3) IA 1986); or

- under which any **preferential creditor** is to lose their priority status vis-à-vis the other creditors, or is to be paid a smaller proportion of its debt than another preferential creditor, except with the concurrence of the preferential creditor concerned (s 4(4) IA 1986). In the *IRC v Wimbledon* case described above, however, the court held that this applied only to the treatment of the company's own assets. Where **third-party monies** were used to pay certain creditors in full even where preferential creditors suffered a shortfall these strictly speaking fell outside the CVA.

7.2.5.4 What happens if the shareholders and creditors reach different decisions?

Should the shareholders reach a different decision from the creditors, the decision of the creditors' meeting prevails over that of the shareholders. However, a dissatisfied shareholder may apply to court **within 28 days** beginning with the date of that creditors' meeting (or, if later, the date of the shareholders' meeting). The court may order that the shareholders' decision has effect instead, or make any other order it thinks fit (s 4A IA 1986).

7.2.5.5 Reporting the outcome

Within four business days of the conclusion of the meetings, the chairman must report their result to the court, and immediately after this must send notice of the result of the meeting to anyone who was originally sent notice of the meeting. Assuming that the CVA was approved, the newly appointed supervisor also needs to send a copy of the chairman's report to the Registrar of Companies (s 4(6) IA 1986 and r 1.24 IR 1986).

7.2.6 The effect of approval

7.2.6.1 Who is bound?

Once approved, the CVA takes effect as if made by the company at the creditors' meeting and binds every person who:

- had notice of and was entitled to vote at that meeting (whether or not he was in practice present or represented at it); **or**

- would have been entitled to vote had he had notice of it

as if he were a party to the CVA (s 5(2) IA 1986).

A creditor falling into the second category above might conceivably still challenge the CVA on the basis that there has been a material irregularity (see Section 7.2.7.3). He will otherwise remain bound, but will gain an entitlement under the CVA. If he has not been paid his entitlement when the CVA comes to an end, then the company must then pay him his entitlement at that point (unless the CVA has ended prematurely) (s 5(2A) IA 1986). This raises a potential problem if the company has not factored in the possibility of this additional creditor emerging when calculating the amounts due to each creditor under the CVA. In cases where the company considers there is a good chance that there will be creditors who do not receive notice of the meeting, it may be wise for the CVA to contain provisions allowing adjustments should such creditors later emerge.

Where a creditor would not have been entitled to vote at the meeting, whether or not they received notice of it, they will not be bound by the CVA and can continue to pursue their existing rights. However, if the company was in administration prior to approval of the CVA and this is not brought to an end, the administration moratorium will remain in place and the usual considerations apply (see Chapter 4).

7.2.6.2   What is the effect on an existing formal insolvency process?

Under s 5(3), if the company is already in liquidation or administration, the court may:

- stay the liquidation proceedings, or provide for the administrator's appointment to cease to have effect; **and/or**

- give such directions with respect of the conduct of the liquidation or administration as it thinks appropriate for facilitating the implementation of the CVA.

However, it will not make any order until **either** 28 days have elapsed, beginning with the date on which the chairman's report has been filed without an application by an aggrieved party having been made, **or** at any time whilst such an application or an appeal in respect of such an application remains pending, or during a period within which such an appeal might be brought.

7.2.6.3   What is the effect on a co-debtor or guarantor?

If a creditor enters into a consensual compromise with a principal debtor, then a third party co-debtor or guarantor may well be released as a result of the variation of the terms of the debt, unless they have specifically consented to it. Historically, the courts have taken the view that these parties will not be released when the debtor enters into a CVA because this is a statutory, not a consensual, compromise (*March Estates Plc v Gunmark* [1996] 2 BCLC 1). However in *Johnson v Davies* [1998] 2 BCLC 252, the court held that in principle such a party might still be released as a result of a CVA, because he is effectively deemed to have consented to the arrangement. Often this will not be an issue – a well-drafted guarantee or other agreement will expressly provide that third parties will not be released as a result of a compromise between the creditor and the debtor (*Lombard Natwest Factors v Koutrouzas* [2003] BPIR 444). Nonetheless, because of *Johnson v Davies*, the position is not absolutely clear where there is no such provision.

It is also legally possible for the CVA itself expressly to provide that a creditor cannot enforce an obligation against a third party who would then in turn have a right of recourse against the company, such as a co-debtor or guarantor (*Prudential Assurance Co Ltd v PRG Powerhouse Ltd* [2007] BCC 500, para 60). The facts of the *Powerhouse* case are set out in the box in Section 7.2.7.

A CVA subsequently proposed by Sixty UK Ltd also attempted to compromise claims against guarantors, but like that of Powerhouse, failed to survive an unfair prejudice challenge (*Mourant & Co Trustees Ltd v Sixty UK Ltd* [2010] EWHC 1890 (Ch)).

7.2.7   Can a party challenge the CVA?

7.2.7.1   The mechanism for a challenge

Under s 6 IA 1986, any person entitled to vote at either meeting (or who would have been entitled to vote had he had notice) may challenge the decisions arrived at by the meetings on the grounds that:

- the arrangement **unfairly prejudices** the interests of a creditor or shareholder; or

- that there has been some **material irregularity** at or in relation to either of the meetings.

The nominee or (if the company is in liquidation or administration) the administrator or liquidator may also challenge on the same bases.

Any challenge must be made:

- **within 28 days** beginning with the date on which the chairman's report is filed with the court (see Section 7.2.5.5); or

- in the case of a person who was not given notice of the meeting, within 28 days of the date on which he became aware that the meeting had taken place. However, such a person may not challenge a decision where the CVA has already come to an end, unless it ended prematurely.

The courts have made it clear that this 28-day time limit is fixed and **cannot be extended** (*Re Bournemouth and Boscombe AFC Co Ltd* [1998] BPIR 183). (In *Gold Fields Mining LLC v Tucker* [2009] EWCA Civ 173, the court drew a distinction between this rule and the construction of a provision within the CVA itself dealing with the submissions of claims by creditors who had not originally had notice of the meeting.)

The court has the power to revoke or suspend any decision approving the CVA, and/or to give a direction that further meetings should be summoned either to reconsider the original proposal or to consider any revised proposal. It can also give supplemental directions, in particular to deal with things done since the CVA took effect. The court's role is not, however, to impose terms of its own which might be more advantageous than those accepted by the creditors (*Sisu Capital Fund Ltd v Tucker* [2006] BCC 463).

7.2.7.2   Unfair prejudice

It is insufficient for these purposes that the applicant has been prejudiced – the applicant must demonstrate that the prejudice in question was unfair. The courts have made it clear that there is no universal test for unfairness, but that it is necessary to consider all of the circumstances and alternatives available and practical consequences of a decision to confirm or reject the CVA. In the *Powerhouse* case, the facts of which are set out in the box below, it was suggested that this exercise might include:

- a 'vertical' comparison with the position under a liquidation. If the CVA is likely to result in creditors receiving less than they would on a liquidation which is concluded within a reasonable timeframe, then it is hard to see a case where the courts will not intervene (see comments made in *Re T&N Ltd* [2005] 2 BCLC 488). The court should not normally speculate here as to what other proposals might have been accepted and been capable of implementation. Unless it is satisfied that better terms or some other compromise would have been on offer, the comparison is between the proposed compromise and no compromise at all (see the *Sisu Capital Fund* case);

- a 'horizontal' comparison with the treatment of other creditors or classes of creditors under the CVA. As noted in Section 7.2.4.2, the courts have rejected arguments that differential treatment is in itself unfair prejudice, and have noted indeed that in some circumstances differential treatment may be necessary to ensure fairness; and/or

- a comparison with the position under a Scheme of Arrangement. The tests for when a Scheme is fair are discussed in Section 7.3.4, and the courts have suggested that it is equally appropriate to consider whether a reasonable and honest man in the applicant's position might have approved the CVA. The fact that the applicant could have blocked a Scheme because it would have constituted a separate class of creditor is also relevant and potentially important, although the courts have emphasised that this is not determinative in itself.

It is also clear that the prejudice must have been caused by the terms of the CVA itself and affect the applicant in the capacity in which they are bound by the Scheme, not in some other capacity (see the list of principles outlined in the *Sisu Capital Fund* case).

Prudential Assurance Co Ltd v PRG Powerhouse Ltd [2007] BCC 500

The company, an electrical goods retailer, wished to close 35 underperforming stores but to retain its other stores. It proposed a CVA, whereby the rights of creditors in respect of the closing stores would be compromised, but the rights of other creditors would be unaffected. The company's parent, PRG, agreed to provide funds to pay a dividend of up to 28p in the £ to the creditors of the closing stores. These creditors included landlords who had claims for future rent, and the CVA provided a mechanism for valuing such claims. However, the CVA also included terms designed to release any guarantees or indemnities which PRG had given to these landlords.

All creditors, including those creditors who were being paid in full, were able to vote on the CVA proposal, and it was duly approved. However, it was challenged by the landlords holding guarantees, both on the basis that the provisions which purported to affect their rights were ineffective and that it was unfairly prejudicial to them.

The court held that, although it was legally possible for a CVA directly to provide that a creditor cannot enforce a guarantor's obligations, the clauses in the present CVA which were intended to achieve that result did not succeed in

---

doing so. Nonetheless, another clause in the CVA which provided for the release of every guarantee given by PRG for a debt of the company to a landlord of a closing store could be enforced by the company on PRG's behalf.

However, the court held that the CVA was unfairly prejudicial to the landlords holding guarantees on the following bases:

- if the company had entered into liquidation, these landlords' position would be substantially better than under the CVA. Although they may have received no dividend from the company on a liquidation, they would still have been able to rely upon their guarantees;

- if the company had proposed a Scheme of Arrangement, these landlords would have been treated as a separate class from other creditors, and the creditors who were being paid in full would have been prevented from voting altogether;

- although it is possible for a CVA to treat different groups of unsecured creditors differently, this CVA discriminated against these landlords by giving more weight to the other creditors and forcibly compromising the landlords' claims at a fraction of their proper value.

The court was unpersuaded by the company's argument that earlier possession of the closing stores would be valuable to the landlords as it would give them the chance to re-let, since this was simply a matter of chance. It was also unpersuaded by the argument that PRG's guarantee might be of little real value, since at the very least the CVA prevented the landlords from negotiating with PRG and obtaining some form of compensation for the loss of the guarantees.

7.2.7.3   Material irregularity

A claim of material irregularity might be based on either a breach of the rules or on some other problem with the conduct of the meeting. This might include:

- a failure to give notice of the meeting to a creditor (*Re a Debtor (No 259 of 1990)* [1992] 1 All ER 641);

- a failure to provide full information to the meeting (*Somji v Cadbury's Schweppes plc* [2001] 1 WLR 615, a case concerning an individual voluntary arrangement);

- a failure by the chairman properly to include a creditor's vote; or

- the inclusion of sham claims for voting purposes at the meeting (*Gatnom Capital & Finance Limited* [2010] EWHC 3353 (Ch)).

In *Kapoor v National Westminster Bank plc* [2011] EWCA Civ 1083 (another case concerning an individual voluntary arrangement), a connected creditor had assigned a debt to a friend in order to circumvent the provisions concerning the votes of connected creditors. The court made it clear that, notwithstanding that no attempt had been made to conceal this arrangement from the meeting, this was still a material irregularity.

An irregularity will, however, not be regarded as 'material' unless it affected the outcome of the meeting (*Re a Debtor (No 259 of 1990)* above).

7.2.8 Implementation of the CVA

Once the CVA is approved, the nominee will become the supervisor of the CVA. The supervisor's main role is then to ensure that the CVA proceeds in accordance with the terms approved by the meetings. The exact scope of this role will depend on those terms, but will almost certainly include receiving assets or payments and then distributing monies to the creditors in accordance with the terms of the CVA. In this respect, the directors, or the liquidator or administrator (as appropriate) must do all that is required to put them into possession of the assets included within the CVA (r 1.23 IR 1986). The supervisor is able to apply to the court for directions on any matter arising under the CVA or to seek a winding-up or administration order should the CVA fail. Any creditor or any other person dissatisfied with an act, omission or decision of the supervisor may apply to the court to seek relief (s 7 IA 1986).

In the absence of a moratorium, there is no need to disclose the existence of the CVA to the outside world other than through the relevant Companies House and court filings.

7.3 SCHEMES OF ARRANGEMENT

7.3.1 Overview

7.3.1.1 What is a 'Scheme of Arrangement'?

Part 26 CA 2006 sets out a statutory procedure whereby a company may make a compromise or arrangement with its members or creditors, or any 'class' of them. For the purposes of this book this process is referred to as a '**Scheme of Arrangement**', or 'Scheme'.

The terms 'compromise' and 'arrangement' are not defined. The courts have made it clear that an arrangement is to be interpreted broadly, and is not limited to something analogous to a compromise (*Re Guardian Assurance Co* [1917] 1 Ch 431). The crucial requirement, however, is that the proposal involves an element of accommodation on each side. The court has held that if the rights of the shareholders are merely being expropriated without any compensating advantage, there is no compromise or arrangement with the company (*Re NFU Development Trust Ltd* [1973] 1 All ER 135). The same principle is generally thought to apply to a compromise or arrangement with creditors.

The term 'creditor' is not limited to persons who have already a claim against the company, but may extend to persons with contingent claims for damages (*Re T&N Ltd* [2005] EWHC 2870).

A Scheme may, however, bind creditors only in their capacity as creditors. The administrators of Lehman Brothers International (Europe) sought to use a Scheme to compromise the potential claims of account holders for the return of trust property to them, but the Court of Appeal held that proprietary interests in assets cannot be made subject to a Scheme (*Lehman Brothers (International) Europe (in administration)* [2009] EWCA Civ 1161), notwithstanding that the account holders may also have had monetary claims which made them creditors of the company.

7.3.1.2   What is the procedure for adopting a Scheme of Arrangement?

Table 7.3 shows the Scheme of Arrangement process in flowchart form. The proposer would normally be the company itself or, where applicable, its administrator or liquidator. However, it is possible for any creditor or member to propose a Scheme. For example, in *Re Countrywide PLC and others* [2009] EWHC 1347, the Scheme was proposed by a group of loan note holders who were keen to eliminate any risk that the company would become cash flow insolvent.

Table 7.3 – The Scheme of Arrangement process

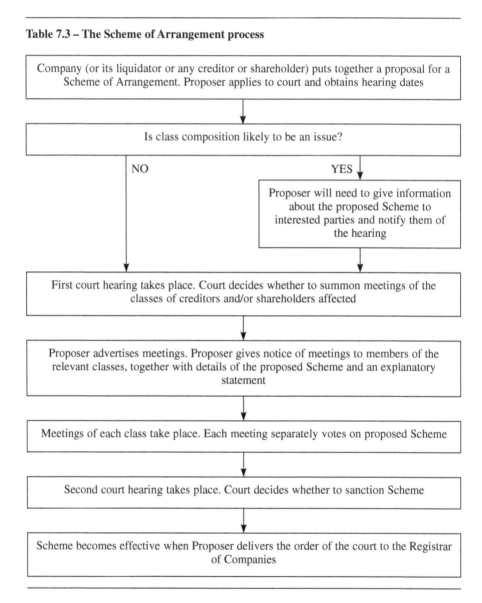

Company (or its liquidator or any creditor or shareholder) puts together a proposal for a Scheme of Arrangement. Proposer applies to court and obtains hearing dates

Is class composition likely to be an issue?

NO   YES

Proposer will need to give information about the proposed Scheme to interested parties and notify them of the hearing

First court hearing takes place. Court decides whether to summon meetings of the classes of creditors and/or shareholders affected

Proposer advertises meetings. Proposer gives notice of meetings to members of the relevant classes, together with details of the proposed Scheme and an explanatory statement

Meetings of each class take place. Each meeting separately votes on proposed Scheme

Second court hearing takes place. Court decides whether to sanction Scheme

Scheme becomes effective when Proposer delivers the order of the court to the Registrar of Companies

The procedure for adopting a Scheme is, broadly speaking, a three-stage process, involving two court hearings:

- The proposer draws up the terms of the proposed Scheme and applies to the court. At this first hearing the court makes an order requiring the proposer to convene meetings of the relevant classes, and gives directions on matters such as how the proposer should give notice of the meetings (s 896 CA 2006).

- The proposer gives notice of the meetings to all members of relevant classes in accordance with the court order. This notice must be accompanied by a copy of the terms of the Scheme, a proxy form and an **explanatory statement** on the effect of the Scheme. Section 897 CA 2006 sets out the requirements for the explanatory statement in more detail. At each meeting, the Scheme is proposed, considered and voted on.

- Provided each of the meetings approves the Scheme by the required majority, the proposer then re-applies to the court for final approval, or '**sanction**'. The Scheme becomes effective when the company makes a filing following the hearing (s 899 CA 2006).

As a result of these various requirements, a Scheme will typically take at least two and a half months to implement. The proposer will also need to obtain court dates for the hearings in advance.

7.3.2 Composition of the classes

7.3.2.1 Who determines the compositions of the classes?

The courts have issued a practice direction, *Practice Statement (Schemes of Arrangement with Creditors)* [2002] 1 WLR 1345, the aim of which is to enable issues concerning the composition of classes of creditor and the summoning of meetings to be identified and if appropriate resolved early in the proceedings. This is designed, so far as possible, to avoid class issues being raised only at the sanction hearing.

It is the applicant's responsibility to determine the compositions of the classes. However, where class composition is likely to be an issue, the applicant is expected to bring this to the court's attention as soon as possible. Any class composition issues are therefore likely to be considered at the first hearing. For this purpose, unless there is a good reason for not doing so, the applicant will be expected to send the affected creditors a preliminary circular, setting out details of the Scheme and the proposed composition of the meetings, to give them an opportunity to appear at the first hearing and make representations. The court may then give directions for the resolution of any class composition issue, which will include, if necessary, postponing the meetings until the issue has been resolved. Creditors will still be entitled to raise class issues at the sanction hearing, but will need to show good reason why they did not do so earlier.

7.3.2.2 When will a group of persons fall within the same class?

The proper identification of the classes is fundamental to the successful adoption of a Scheme. In order for persons to fall within the same class, their rights must 'not be so dissimilar for it to be impossible for them to consult together with a view to their common interest' (*Sovereign Life Assurance Co v Dodd* [1892] 2 QB 573).

It is necessary to consider both a person's existing rights which are to be released or varied and the new rights and benefits which they are to receive under the Scheme (*Re Hawk Insurance Company Ltd* [2001] 2 BCLC 480). It is their **legal rights**, as opposed to commercial or other interests, which are relevant here, although these latter interests might be relevant to the 'fairness' test at the sanction stage. Therefore creditors whose legal rights will be affected in the same way may be placed within a single class, even if some of them have other interests in relation to the company which might be affected by the adoption (or rejection) of the Scheme.

Where a Scheme is being proposed as an alternative to liquidation or administration, it is appropriate to consider how creditors would have been treated in a liquidation or administration when determining classes (*Marconi Corporation plc and Marconi Plc* [2003] EWHC 663 (Ch).)

As such, secured and unsecured creditors will almost inevitably comprise different classes. However, it may be necessary to create different classes, or further different classes to deal, for example, with secured creditors with differing priority rankings, subordinated creditors or contingent creditors.

Creditors may nonetheless form a single class, even if their legal rights are not identical. Various cases illustrate the courts' approach here.

In the *Hawk* case, an insurance company in run off was seeking to compromise claims under re-insurance contracts. The scheme offered these creditors payments at three different rates according to whether, for example, those creditors had yet paid out to the parties which they in turn had insured. The Court of Appeal held that all of these creditors could nonetheless fall within the same class. It made it clear that, when considering the composition of the classes, it was also necessary to ensure those whose rights were sufficiently similar to the rights of others could properly consult together should they be required to do so, lest by ordering separate meetings the court gave a veto to a minority group over a Scheme which otherwise had widespread support.

In *Re Cape plc* [2006] EWHC 1316 (Ch), where the court declined to divide creditors with existing but unresolved asbestosis claims into a separate class from those who had not yet made a claim but may potentially do so in the future.

In *Re Telewest Communications plc (No 1)* [2005] BCC 29, bondholders holding bonds denominated in sterling were held to form a single class with those holding bonds denominated in US dollars, despite the fact that the exchange rate mechanism chosen as part of the proposed Scheme was likely adversely to affect the former, due to currency fluctuations. The court observed that the sterling bondholders would still be able to address any questions of fairness at the sanction hearing.

Finally, in *Cortefiel SA v MEP 11 Sarl* [2012] EWHC 2998 (Ch), which concerned a group of senior lenders under a facility agreement, the court indicated that, rather than considering or comparing single rights, it should look at the various rights of each lender as a bundle and to consider and compare them in that context.

7.3.2.3   Who needs to meet to vote on the Scheme?

The company need only call meetings of those shareholders or creditors who will be affected by the Scheme. If a company is to continue to trade, its trade creditors may be excluded from the Scheme if they are to continue to be paid in full. A Scheme may indeed relate only to one class of unsecured creditor, with the other unsecured creditors being dealt with outside of the Scheme, provided the division of creditors shows a commercially rational approach (*PT Garuda Indonesia* [2001] All ER (D) 53).

The court is able to sanction a Scheme, despite the opposition of shareholders or creditors who have no real interest in the company's assets (*Re Tea Corporation* [1904] 1 Ch 12). In *MyTravel Group plc* [2005] 2 BCLC 123, the court made it clear at first instance that a finding that a creditor had no economic interest was a serious one which needed to be considered carefully. However, the court was nonetheless entitled to look at the reality, rather than speculate as to what value might theoretically be returned to the creditors concerned following a successful restructuring. In the *MyTravel* case, the court was satisfied that it was appropriate to view insolvent liquidation as the realistic alternative to the proposed Scheme and that on the evidence it was clear that the creditors concerned would receive nothing in that liquidation. (The decision was appealed, but the Court of Appeal concluded that it had no need to reconsider the economic interest point.)

Similar reasoning has since been applied in, for example, *Re McCarthy and Stone plc* [2009] EWHC 1116 (Ch) and in *Re Bluebrook Ltd* [2009] EWHC 2114 (Ch) (the '*IMO Car Wash*' case). The latter case is discussed further in Section 10.6.2.2.

This has important consequences for the restructuring of an insolvent company. Lower-ranking classes of creditors who have no real economic interest may, for example, be excluded entirely from a Scheme which contemplates the subsequent transfer of the company's assets to a new company. This will not affect their rights as creditors, but will leave them as creditors only of the empty shell of the old company, so their rights are likely to have little remaining value.

7.3.3 What is the function of the meetings?

At each meeting, the persons present formally consider the Scheme and vote whether to approve it. In order to be adopted, the Scheme must be approved by:

- a majority in number;
- representing 75% in value;
- of those persons present and voting at each meeting.

The requirement for a majority in number as well as by value helps to ensure that a low number of large shareholders or creditors holding the majority of the value cannot oppress the smaller shareholders or creditors.

If a class consists of only one person, they can still hold a 'meeting'. However, problems can emerge if only one person from a larger class attends, as there is doubt as to whether a 'meeting' will validly have been held (*Re Altitude Scaffolding Ltd* [2006] BCC 904).

7.3.4 What is the function of the sanction hearing?

Whilst approval of the Scheme at each of the relevant meetings is a necessary precursor to the sanction hearing, this approval does not mean that the court will then automatically sanction the Scheme. The court needs to consider three further 'fairness' issues:

- Were the meetings properly convened and held? The court may consider the Scheme to be unfair if some of the procedural requirements, such as those relating to the circulation of information have not been complied with. It will consider among other things whether the explanatory statement was fair and provided the recipients with all of the information they reasonably required to decide how to vote.

- Were the classes fairly represented? The court will be concerned to ensure that each class was fairly represented by those attending the relevant meeting, and the majority in every class is acting *bona fide* and not attempting to promote an interest which is in fact adverse to the class they claim to represent. If the turnout at the meeting was low, the court may wish to ensure that those attending and voting nonetheless represented a significant proportion of their class by value.

- Is the proposal itself 'fair'? This requires the court to be satisfied that 'the proposal is such that an intelligent and honest man, a member of the class concerned, acting in respect of his interests might reasonably approve' (*Re Dorman Long & Co Ltd* [1934] Ch 635). The court may still reject the Scheme at this stage if, for example, it considers that it **unfairly prejudices** one or more of the minority creditors who opposed it. The above test does not, however, require the court to superimpose its own view of whether the proposal is beneficial to the creditors – the courts recognise that a creditor acting on sufficient information and given sufficient time to consider it will normally be the best judge of his own commercial interests (*Re English, Scottish and Australian Chartered Bank* [1893] 3 Ch 385).

7.3.5   What happens once sanction is given?

7.3.5.1   When does the Scheme of Arrangement become effective?

If court sanction is given, the company may file a copy of the court order with the Registrar of Companies. It comes into effect when this filing is made. The company may choose to make this filing at a particular time in order to synchronise the Scheme with other events which have to be completed at the same time. However, the court will not typically approve a Scheme whose effectiveness is conditional on events outside the company's own control.

7.3.5.2   Who is bound?

Once it becomes effective, the Scheme binds the company and all persons within the classes participating in the Scheme, including those who failed to vote, or who voted against it. It does not, however, bind members of classes who were not included within the Scheme.

7.3.5.3   What is the effect on a co-debtor or guarantor?

The release of rights against one company jointly liable with a second does not of itself release the second company. The same applies where the second company is merely a guarantor of the first, and not directly jointly liable with it. However, the court held in *Re La Seda de Barcelona SA* [2010] EWHC 1364 (Ch) that a Scheme might validly include a specific provision releasing a third party from debts owed to the scheme creditors where there was a genuine compromise between those creditors and the third party and the creditors' rights against the third party were closely connected to their rights against the scheme company. In the *La Seda* case, a release of a third party guarantor satisfied the requirement for a 'geniune compromise' because the guarantor was in turn releasing substantial claims of its own against the group.

7.3.6　Powers of the court to facilitate reconstruction

Section 900 CA 2006 allows a court in sanctioning a Scheme to make certain provisions where:

- the compromise or arrangement in question has been proposed for the purposes of, or in connection with, the reconstruction of the company (or group of companies); and

- under the Scheme the whole or any part of the undertaking or any property of any company concerned in the Scheme is to be transferred to another company.

The court is empowered, among other things to make provision for the transfer itself, and for the allotting by the transferee company of any shares or like interests in the company to any person under the compromise or arrangement. However, the usefulness of s 900 CA 2006 is likely to be limited for restructuring an insolvent company. It was held in the *MyTravel* case that a Scheme can only be regarded as a 'reconstruction' where the shareholders are substantially the same in both the transferor and transferee companies, and this probably precludes the use of this section for achieving a debt to equity swap (see Chapter 10).

Chapter 8

Secured creditors

8.1 INTRODUCTION

Chapter 2 considered the circumstances in which a creditor will hold security and the priority status which such a secured creditor will enjoy on a liquidation or administration. This chapter considers the ability of a secured creditor to enforce its security in more detail. For the purposes of this chapter, a secured creditor will be taken to mean a creditor holding either a mortgage or a charge.

This chapter will focus to a large extent on receivership, and will expand on the overview of this process given in Chapter 1. In addition it discusses briefly the ways in which the Financial Collateral Arrangements (No 2) Regulations 2003 (SI 2003/3226) might improve a secured creditor's position in certain circumstances.

8.2 HOW MIGHT A SECURED CREDITOR ENFORCE ITS SECURITY?

8.2.1 What are the remedies available?

8.2.1.1 Overview

A security document granted by the company by way of a deed will typically give the secured creditor four main remedies. These are:

- a power to take possession of the secured property;
- a power of sale;
- a right of foreclosure, subject to an order of the court; or
- a power to appoint a receiver to manage and/or sell the secured property.

8.2.1.2 Power to take possession

If a secured creditor takes possession, it becomes accountable to the company for what he might have received, but for his own negligence or wilful default (*White v City of London Brewery Co* (1889) 42 ChD 237). A mortgagee in possession of land may also now risk liability for environmental damage and clean-up costs. A mortgagee might well therefore choose to take possession directly only as a precursor to the exercise of a power of sale.

8.2.1.3 Power of sale

A secured creditor has no obligation to exercise its power of sale. However, should it choose to do so, it is obliged to exercise this power in good faith for the sole purpose of recovering its debt. Perhaps more significantly, he will also have a duty to obtain the best price reasonably obtainable on the sale.

The court reviewed the duties of a secured creditor exercising its power of sale directly in *Silven Properties Ltd v Royal Bank of Scotland plc* [2004] 4 All ER 484 and noted the similarity to the duties of a receiver selling property. (These are discussed more fully in Section 8.7.2.2 and apply equally here).

In *Michael v Miller* [2004] EWCA Civ 282, the Court of Appeal also noted that, just as a valuer will not breach his duty if his valuation falls within an acceptable margin of error, a secured creditor would not breach its duty if it exercised its judgment reasonably. To the extent that that judgment involves assessing the market value of the property, it would have acted reasonably if its assessment falls within an acceptable margin of error. It will only therefore be liable if its conduct is plainly on the wrong side of the line.

8.2.1.4   Right to foreclosure

Foreclosure is a process whereby the secured creditor takes outright ownership of the secured property in satisfaction of the debt. However, it requires an order of the court. The court is only likely to make such an order if the debt exceeds the value of the secured property. In addition, before the court makes a final order it will usually give the company six months to repay the debt and redeem the security. Once the final order has been made, the creditor will no longer be able to sue either the company or any guarantor in respect of any unpaid balance of the debt.

8.2.1.5   Power to appoint a receiver (or administrator)

Given the duties of, and other disadvantages to, the secured creditor in exercising the powers described above, a secured creditor is in practice most likely to appoint a receiver (or conceivably an administrator if they are entitled to do so) rather than to exercise any of his other remedies. This is because, as discussed further in Section 8.5, a receiver will normally remain independent of the secured creditor and the secured creditor will not therefore be liable for the receiver's defaults.

8.2.2   Can the secured creditor buy the secured property itself?

As discussed in Section 8.2.1.4, the secured creditor is entitled to acquire outright ownership of the secured property by foreclosure, but this process is generally unattractive. A secured creditor is not entitled to sell the secured asset to itself, or to another person which is simply its trustee or nominee. Similarly, it cannot appoint a receiver or administrator to achieve the same result. However, this is easily surmountable, since the law does not prevent the secured creditor from selling to another legal entity of which it is a shareholder (*Farrar v Farrars Ltd* (1888) 40 ChD 395).

As a result, it is not unusual for a secured creditor to form a new subsidiary to act as buyer. Where some of the secured property consists of floating charge assets, the buyer may still need to pay sufficient cash to the company to cover preferential debts and any prescribed part. However, the bulk of the consideration for the sale is likely to be the release of the company from the secured debt (this is often termed a '**credit bid**').

The secured creditor, or any receiver (or administrator) must of course still comply with their other duties on any such sale. Where the secured creditor holds a large beneficial interest in the buyer, the onus may shift onto it to show that it has done so (*Tse Kwong Lam v Wong Chit Sen* [1971] Ch 949). However, from the secured creditor's perspective, the independence of a receiver is a particular advantage here. If a receiver is found to have failed to obtain the best price reasonably obtainable, he may well be ordered to compensate the company out of his own resources. However, it is highly unlikely, in the absence of bad faith, that the sale will be set aside or, provided the secured creditor has allowed the receiver to retain his independence, that the secured creditor will be required to contribute to any shortfall in the purchase price.

These duties were usefully re-examined in *Saltri III Ltd v MD Mezzanine SA SICAR* [2012] EWHC 3025 (Comm) in the context of a security trustee selling shares as part of a restructuring, although at the time of writing this decision is being appealed.

8.3 APPOINTING A RECEIVER OR ADMINISTRATOR

8.3.1 What are the secured creditor's options?

The secured creditor will need to decide whether it wishes to appoint an administrative receiver, a non-administrative receiver or an administrator. Table 8.1 compares the main advantages of receivership with those of administration from the secured creditor's perspective.

Table 8.1 – Receivership vs administration

Advantages of receivership

- A receiver owes his primary duty to his appointor. An administrator owes duties to the creditors generally, and the creditors are able to exercise greater control over the process.
- A non-administrative receiver need not be a qualified insolvency practitioner (a secured creditor could, for example, appoint a surveyor as a receiver of a freehold property).
- The administration expense regime is less favourable. In particular, both capital gains tax (on the realisation of an asset) and rent and non-domestic business rates (where the company occupies the property) will be expenses of an administration.
- The costs of receivership generally are likely to be lower, particularly if enforcement only requires a receiver to be appointed over a single secured asset.
- Administration will not be available unless the company's COMI is in the UK (see Chapter 11).

Advantages of administration

- Administration offers a moratorium.
- The appointment of an administrator is likely to be required to run and/or sell any business (unless the secured creditor is able to appoint an administrative receiver).
- Administration is likely to be the better-recognised process internationally if the company has assets in other jurisdictions, provided the company's COMI is in the UK (see Chapter 11).
- An administrator has the power to force management co-operation, to deal with employees and/or to require that records are delivered up.
- An administrator has full control over the company's VAT affairs, so is able to recover VAT without requiring the co-operation of other persons.

8.3.1.1 Administrative receivers

Under s 29 IA 1986, an administrative receiver is defined as a receiver or manager:

- of the whole (or substantially the whole) of the company's property;

- appointed by or on behalf of the holders of any debentures of the company secured by a charge which, as created, was a floating charge, or by such a charge and one or more other securities.

(It also includes a person who would be such a receiver or manager but for the appointment of some other person as non-administrative receiver of part of a company's property.) An administrative receiver must be a **qualified insolvency practitioner** (s 230 IA 1986).

The exact meaning of 'substantially the whole' has never been clarified by the English courts, and secured creditors therefore need to form their own view in this regard. However, it is clear that the security must contain a floating charge. If it does, a receiver appointed under this security can still be an administrative receiver notwithstanding that the vast majority of the company's assets are in practice fixed charge assets (see *Re Croftbell* [1990] BCC 781). Conversely, however, a receiver appointed under a **fixed charge only** will not be an administrative receiver, even if the asset over which he is appointed is the sole asset of the company (*Meadrealm Ltd v Transcontinental Golf Construction* (1991) unreported, but noted by Marks in (1993) 6 Insolvency Intelligence 41).

In many cases a secured creditor will be unable to appoint an administrative receiver, for the reasons explained in Section 8.3.2.

8.3.1.2 Non-administrative receivers

The restrictions which prevent the secured creditor appointing an administrative receiver do not prevent him appointing a receiver over fixed charge assets only, or possibly over a more limited range of fixed and floating charge assets. Such a receiver might be appointed to manage and/or sell a freehold property or the company's shareholding in a subsidiary, for example. Unlike an administrative receiver, they need not be a qualified insolvency practitioner. In addition, they will have fewer other duties than will an administrative receiver or an administrator. However, it is unlikely that they could be appointed over sufficient assets to allow them to sell the company's entire business.

8.3.1.3 Administrators

Alternatively, a secured creditor who is a qualifying floating charge holder (or '**QFCH**') may appoint an administrator if it wishes to enforce over all of the assets of the company, for example to promote a sale of the company's business. The proposed administrator will need to be satisfied that he will be able to fulfil the purpose of administration which is a concern a receiver does not have, although in practice this should seldom pose a difficulty. The meaning of the term 'QFCH' and the route by which a QFCH may appoint an administrator are discussed in Chapter 4. This chapter will therefore discuss considerations involved in appointing an administrator only where they parallel those involved in appointing a receiver.

8.3.1.4 Court-appointed receivers

The court also has the power to appoint a receiver of a company's assets. It seems unlikely, however, that a secured creditor would wish to apply to the court where it already has the power to appoint a receiver out of court under the terms of its security. A secured creditor is likely only to seek the assistance of the court where its security is in some way inadequate. Historically secured creditors have sought such an appointment where, for example, they were concerned that their security was in jeopardy but the right to appoint had not yet arisen. Further discussion of court-appointed receivers is beyond the scope of this book.

8.3.2 Can the secured creditor appoint an administrative receiver?

8.3.2.1 What limitations apply to the ability to appoint an administrative receiver?

Under 72A IA 1986, a secured creditor will only be able to appoint an administrative receiver if:

- its security was taken **prior to 15 September 2003**; or

- one of the exceptions set out in ss 72B–72GA IA 1986 (usually referred to as the '**City Exceptions**') applies.

8.3.2.2 What are the City Exceptions?

Table 8.2 lists the existing City Exceptions. They apply to specific financing structures or borrowers where the continued availability of administrative receivership as a remedy is thought to be necessary to ensure that that lending will continue to be available on the favourable terms associated with those particular structures.

The exceptions contained in ss 72C to 72E are worth discussing further here, as they may be capable of more general application. They allow the secured creditor to appoint an administrative receiver in respect of a project company for certain specified types of project where the project includes step-in rights. For these purposes:

- a company is a '**project company**' if it holds property for the purpose of the project **or** has sole or principal responsibility under an agreement for carrying out all or part of the project or is one of a number of companies which together carry out the project **or** provides finance to enable the project to be carried out. A holding company of such a company will also fall within the definition. However, a company will not be a project company if it also performs other functions not related to the project (para 7 Sch 2A IA 1986); and

- a project has '**step-in rights**' if a person who provides finance to a project has a conditional entitlement under an agreement to assume sole or principal responsibility for carrying out all or part of the project or to make arrangements for the carrying out of all or part of the project (para 6 Sch 2A IA 1986).

The project finance exception in s 72E IA 1986 was considered in *Cabvision Ltd v Feetum* [2006] BCC 340, where the court gave its views on the meaning of a 'project' and the question of when a company might be 'expected to incur' a debt of at least £50 million. The court also made it clear in this case that a contractual right to appoint an administrative receiver was not itself a step-in right.

Table 8.2 – The 'City Exceptions'

A secured creditor remains entitled to appoint an administrative receiver in the following circumstances:

1. Capital market arrangements (s 72B IA 1986)

Pursuant to an agreement which is, or forms part of, a 'capital market arrangement' (as defined in para 1 Sch 2A IA 1986) where a party incurs (or is expected to incur) a debt of at least £50 million and the arrangement which involves the issue of a capital market investment (as defined in para 2 Sch 2A IA 1986).

2. Public-private partnerships, utilities or urban regeneration (ss 72C, 72D, 72DA IA 1986)

In respect of a project company of one of the following types of project where the project includes step-in rights:

●   a '**public-private partnership project**', ie a project where resources are provided partly by one or more public bodies and partly by one or more private persons or which is designed wholly or mainly for the purpose of assisting a public body in discharging a function;

●   a '**utility project**', ie a project designed wholly or mainly for the purpose of a regulated business. Regulated businesses are providers of public services, and include gas, electricity and water suppliers, sewerage undertakers, railway operators and postal businesses;

●   an '**urban regeneration project**', ie a project designed wholly or mainly to develop land which, at the commencement of the project, is wholly or partly in a 'designated disadvantaged area' (outside Northern Ireland) (see the Stamp Duty (Disadvantaged Areas) Regulations 2001).

3. Project finance (s 72E IA 1986)

In respect of a project company that incurs (or is expected to incur) a debt of at least £50 million for the purposes of carrying out the project where the project includes step-in rights.

4. Financial market contracts (s 72F IA 1986)

In respect of a company that has granted:

●   a market charge as per s 173 CA 1989; **or**

●   a system charge as per the Financial Markets and Insolvency Regulations 1996 (SI 1996/1469); **or**

●   a collateral security charge as per the Financial Markets and Insolvency (Settlement Finality) Regulations 1999 (SI 1999/2979).

5. Registered social landlord (s 72G IA 1986)

In respect of a company registered as a social landlord for the purposes of Part I Housing Act 1996 (generally speaking, a housing association).

6. Protected railway and other companies (s 72GA IA 1986)

In respect of:

●   a water or sewerage company holding an appointment under Chapter I Part II Water Industry Act 1991; **or**

●   a protected railway company as per s 59 of the Railways Act 1993 (as extended by the Channel Tunnel Rail Link Act 1996); **or**

●   a company licensed to provide air traffic services as per s 26 Transport Act 2000.

8.3.3 What is the appointment process?

8.3.3.1 When can the secured creditor appoint a receiver?

Before a secured creditor can appoint a receiver, this right must have arisen under its security. (A secured creditor seeking to appoint an administrator by the out-of-court route must similarly be able to state that its security has become enforceable – see Chapter 4). There must therefore be some breach of the terms of a loan or security document by the company.

Once the right to appoint has arisen, however, the secured creditor is entitled to have regard first and foremost to its own interests in determining when or whether to appoint. In *Shamji v Johnson Matthey Bankers Ltd* [1991] BCLC 36, the court made it clear that, if the power to appoint a receiver were granted to the mortgagee by the security documents in completely unqualified terms, a decision by the mortgagee to exercise the power could not be challenged except perhaps on the grounds of bad faith.

8.3.3.2 Making demand on the company

Sometimes a security document will state that it is enforceable if specific defaults have occurred without the need for the secured creditor to take any further action. However, normal practice is nonetheless to make demand, even if this is not expressly required as a precursor to enforcement. The courts may regard an enforcement without any form of advance notice to the company as oppressive, as this gives the company no prior opportunity to repay the debt and redeem the security.

Once it has made demand, the secured creditor needs only to give the company the time it would reasonably require to move funds 'from some convenient place' to make payment. There is no need to give the company time to negotiate a deal to produce the money if the company does not already have the funds available. This is sometimes known as the **mechanics of payment** test. The time required may be no longer than one hour provided the demand is made during banking hours (*Cripps (Pharmaceutical) Ltd v Wickenden* [1973] 1 WLR 944). If the company has already made it clear that it does not have the funds available there is no need to give the company any further time at all (*Sheppard & Cooper Ltd v TSB Bank plc (No 2)* [1996] BCC 965).

If the company clearly has insufficient funds available, a mistake in the amount demanded (even if this means that the sum demanded is too large) or a failure to specify an exact sum which the company must pay will not normally invalidate the demand (*Bank of Baroda v Panessar* [1987] Ch 335). If there is any doubt as to the correct amount when putting together the demand, however, the secured creditor would probably still be wise to omit any items likely to be disputed. The real function of the demand is to enable the secured creditor to enforce. Excluding disputed items from the sum demanded will not prevent the secured creditor recovering them during the enforcement process, particularly if it expressly reserves its rights in this regard.

In practice, many lenders wish to avoid a 'hostile' appointment if possible and prefer the company to invite them to appoint a receiver (or for the company or its directors themselves to appoint an administrator of the lender's choice out of court). Even if the directors are reluctant to make such an invitation, they may well be advised that they have little option but to do so if they have received a demand which the company cannot meet. In these circumstances the company will clearly be cash-flow insolvent, and were the directors to ignore the demand and attempt to trade on they are likely to be at increasing risk personally (as outlined in Chapter 6).

8.3.3.3   Making the appointment

Assuming the company has not made payment, or otherwise remedied the stated breach, the secured creditor can appoint. To do so, it sends a written notice of appointment to the person, or persons, whom it intends to appoint as receiver(s). The appointment:

- Need not be by deed (unless the security document so requires). However, it is common practice for it to take this form (*Phoenix Properties Ltd v Wimpole Street Nominees Ltd* [1992] BCLC 737).

- Should state the property over which the receiver(s) are to be appointed and should indicate the powers which they are entitled to exercise. Often it will simply provide that they are entitled to exercise all of the powers conferred upon receivers by the security document and otherwise by law.

- Should state, if more than one person is to be appointed as receiver, which of their powers can be exercised by any one of them individually (see s 231(2) IA 1986 in the case of administrative receivers).

- Should comply with any other requirements stipulated in the security document regarding the appointment of receivers.

In order to be effective, the appointment must be **accepted** by each receiver (or on his behalf by a person authorised by him) before the end of the **next business day** after that on which he receives the appointment. It may be orally accepted, but an oral acceptance must be confirmed in writing within seven days. The acceptance or confirmation must state the date and time of receipt of the instrument of appointment and the date and time of acceptance. Provided these requirements are complied with, the appointment takes effect from the time when the instrument of appointment was received (s 33(1) IA 1986 and r 3.1 IR 1986).

8.3.4   What are the consequences of an invalid appointment?

The directors of the company retain the power to challenge the appointment of a receiver (see Chapter 6). A challenge is, however, most likely to come from a liquidator because if the security can successfully be attacked on one of the grounds set out in Chapter 5 there will be more assets available for the unsecured creditors.

If the security under which the receiver was appointed is invalid or there was a defect in his appointment, or indeed if he otherwise acts outside of the powers vested in him, the receiver may be personally liable to the company in trespass or conversion. His liability in this respect could potentially be serious. However, the courts have held that an invalidly-appointed receiver can commit the tort of conversion only in respect of chattels and not choses in action, and that he will not have committed the tort of wrongful interference with the performance of the company's contracts (*OBG Ltd v Allan* [2008] 1 AC 1).

Under s 232 IA 1986, an administrative receiver's appointment is valid notwithstanding any defect in his appointment, nomination or qualifications. Where s 232 applies it will protect the administrative receiver as well as any party dealing with him. However, there is a distinction between an appointment in which there is some defect and a case where there is no appointment at all, for example because the security document was invalid. In the second case s 232 will not apply (*OBG Ltd v Allan*).

The receiver will therefore need to check the validity of the security prior to his appointment. A newly-appointed receiver will therefore normally seek **formal advice** on the validity of his appointment. A receiver may also seek an **indemnity** from his appointor to cover any losses he may suffer, whether as a result of a defect in his appointment or otherwise. This is a matter for negotiation. It is unlikely that a major bank will give such an indemnity, but it is more common in other cases. Under s 34 IA 1986, the court may also order the appointor to indemnify the receiver against any liability which arises solely as a result of the invalidity of his appointment.

8.4   WHAT IS THE STATUS OF A RECEIVER?

8.4.1   The receiver's status as agent

An administrative receiver is deemed to be the agent of the company unless and until the company goes into liquidation (s 44(1)(a) IA 1986). A non-administrative receiver is also deemed to be the company's agent (s 109(2) LPA 1925). However, the security document will in any case almost always expressly state that the receiver is the company's agent.

This is an unusual type of agency in that the receiver still owes his primary duty to the secured creditor who appointed him rather than to the company (see Section 8.7). The company is unable to give the receiver instructions or to dismiss him. However, because the receiver is the agent of the company, it is the company (rather than the appointor) who is liable for the receiver's acts. Furthermore, it is the receiver himself rather than his appointor who will be responsible for any breach of duty by the receiver.

The receiver's special status will be lost if his appointor behaves in a way which constitutes the receiver its own agent (*American Express International Banking Corp v Hurley* [1985] 3 All ER 564). The appointor would then be liable for the receiver's actions. A well-advised secured creditor will therefore allow the receiver to retain his independence by avoiding giving him direct instructions or liaising with him so closely that his independence might be called into question.

8.4.2   Entry into contracts

A receiver will be personally liable on any new contract entered into by him in the performance of his functions, except in so far as the contract provides otherwise. Should he incur personal liability, the receiver will be entitled to an indemnity out of the assets of the company (s 37 and s 44 IA 1986 in the case of non-administrative and administrative receivers, respectively). However, in practice, any receiver will aim to make it expressly clear that he is contracting as the company's agent without personal liability.

8.4.3   The effect of liquidation

A company will frequently be placed into liquidation at some point after a receiver has been appointed. Liquidation will not bring the receiver's appointment to an end – the two processes operate in parallel, as the receiver is appointed over particular property of the company, rather than to the company itself (see Chapter 2). However, the receiver's status as the company's agent will terminate when a liquidator is appointed.

This will not prevent the receiver continuing to exercise all of his powers in relation to the property over which he is appointed. He may still, among other things, begin or continue proceedings in the company's name to recover property which is subject to his appointor's security (see *Gough's Garages Ltd v Pugsley* [1930] 1 KB 615). It does mean, however, that he will no longer be able to commit the company to any new liabilities (see *Gosling v Gaskell* [1897] AC 575). So as to continue to preserve his appointor's independence, the receiver would normally enter into any further contracts as principal in his own right rather than as agent of the appointor. He will remain entitled to an indemnity out of the assets over which he has been appointed under ss 37 and 44 IA 1986.

In practice, however, a receiver will be concerned that the company's assets might conceivably be insufficient to satisfy any such indemnity. He may therefore ask for an additional indemnity from his appointor where the company enters into liquidation even where he did not obtain an indemnity at the start of the receivership.

8.5   WHAT ARE THE OTHER CONSEQUENCES OF RECEIVERSHIP?

8.5.1   What is the effect on other insolvency proceedings?

The appointment of an administrative receiver will prevent any person appointing an administrator out of court (paras 17 and 25 Sch B1 IA 1986). The court will also have no jurisdiction to make an administration order without the consent of the administrative receiver's appointor and in the absence of circumstances which might render the security suspect (para 39 Sch B1 IA 1986, and see *Chesterton International Group plc v Deka Immobilien Inv GmbH* [2005] BPIR 1103).

Otherwise, however, receivership should not prevent an administration or a liquidation being commenced or continued. The fact that a non-administrative receiver has already been appointed over some of the company's assets will not prevent the appointment of an administrator, and indeed the administrator can require such a receiver to vacate office. Similarly, as already noted the appointment of a receiver (of any kind) will not prevent the company from being placed into liquidation.

8.5.2   What is the effect on the directors?

The role of the directors once a receiver has been appointed is discussed in Chapter 6. If a non-administrative receiver is appointed only over certain assets of the company, the directors will need to continue to manage its remaining assets.

8.5.3 What is the effect on existing contracts?

The appointment of a receiver does not terminate the contracts of a company. The terms of the contract itself may of course provide that the contract automatically comes to an end on the appointment of a receiver or, more normally, that the other party has the opportunity to terminate. Alternatively, the receiver may indicate that the company is no longer able to perform its obligations under the contract, and the resulting breach will give the other party the ability to terminate and/or to pursue other remedies. Should a receiver decide to continue an existing contract, this does not mean that he will become personally liable for pre- or even post-receivership liabilities under that contract, or that such liabilities will be receivership expenses – they will simply be unsecured liabilities of the company. In practice, a receiver will always make this expressly clear to the other party. The position is usefully analysed by the court in *Powdrill v Watson* [1995] 2 AC 394. Special rules apply to employment contracts (see Chapter 9).

Damages are likely to be of limited use against an insolvent company. The other party may alternatively seek injunctive relief against the receiver. The courts have been disinclined to grant such relief in general (see, for example, *Airlines Airspares v Handley Page* [1970] Ch 193). The other party may, however, still obtain specific performance of a contract under which it has already acquired an equitable interest in land (*Freevale Ltd v Metrostore Holdings Ltd* [1984] Ch 199). The court has also required a receiver to honour the terms of an existing contract rather than obtain an additional 'ransom' payment for continuing to supply goods (*Land Rover Group Ltd v UPF (UK) Ltd* [2003] 2 BCLC 222).

8.5.4 What is the effect on the company's documentation?

Where a receiver or manager has been appointed, every invoice, order for goods or services, business letter or order form (whether in hard copy, electronic or any other form) issued and all of the company's websites must contain a statement to this effect. The receiver or manager or any officer of the company commits an offence if they knowingly and willingly authorise or permit a breach of this requirement (s 39 IA 1986).

8.6 HOW ARE THE CREDITORS INFORMED AND INVOLVED?

8.6.1 Overview

A non-administrative receiver has few obligations to keep creditors informed. He need do little more than to ensure that the secured creditor files notice of his appointment (see Section 8.6.2) and then send periodic receipts and payments accounts to the Registrar of Companies (see Section 8.6.6). An administrative receiver has more extensive obligations in this regard, and the majority of this section will therefore relate just to administrative receivers.

8.6.2 Notices

A secured creditor appointing any type of receiver must give notice of the appointment to the Registrar of Companies within seven days (s 871 CA 2006), although in practice the receiver will often carry out this task on its behalf.

An administrative receiver must send notice of his appointment to the company immediately and to all creditors of the company of whose addresses he is aware **within 28 days** after his appointment (unless the court directs otherwise). He must also advertise his appointment in the London Gazette and an appropriate newspaper (s 46(1) IA 1986 and r 3.2 IR 1986).

8.6.3   Statement of affairs

Immediately following his appointment, an administrative receiver must require one or more 'relevant persons' to provide a statement of affairs (s 47 IA 1986). This is discussed further in Chapter 6. If he thinks it would prejudice the course of the receivership for the whole or part of the statement of affairs to be disclosed he may apply to court for an order for limited disclosure.

8.6.4   Administrative receiver's report

The administrative receiver must then prepare a report giving details of the events leading up to his appointment, how property has been (or is proposed to be) disposed of and how the business has been carried on. It must stipulate the amounts payable to the secured creditors who appointed him and to preferential creditors and the amount (if any) likely to be available for the payment of other creditors. It must also include a summary of the directors' statement of affairs and the administrative receiver's comments on this. It need not, however, include any information the disclosure of which would seriously prejudice the carrying out of the administrative receiver's functions.

The administrative receiver must send the report to the Registrar of Companies, the trustees for the secured creditors and the individual secured creditors (so far as he is aware of their addresses) within **three months** after his appointment (or such longer period as the court allows). Within the same time period, he must also either send a copy of the report to the unsecured creditors (so far as he is aware of their addresses) or publish an address to which unsecured creditors can apply for copies of the report (s 48 IA 1986 and r 3.8 IR 1986).

8.6.5   Meeting of creditors

The administrative receiver must (unless the court directs otherwise) call a meeting of the unsecured creditors on not less than 14 days' notice to consider the report (s 48(2) IA 1986). In practice, the main function of any meeting will simply be to supply information to the unsecured creditors. Among other things, the unsecured creditors may decide at this meeting to establish a creditors' committee. Any such committee will consist of three to five creditors and has a statutory duty to help the administrative receiver. This committee may require the administrative receiver to attend on it and furnish details to it as requested on seven days' notice (s 49 IA 1986 and rr 3.16 and 3.18 IR 1986).

8.6.6   Receivership accounts

A non-administrative receiver must send receipts and payments accounts to the Registrar of Companies covering the 12-month period commencing on the date he was appointed and every subsequent period of six months. When he ceases to act he must also send accounts covering the remaining period of the receivership, together with a cumulative account. Each set of accounts must be submitted within one month of the end of the period covered, unless the registrar agrees otherwise (s 38 IA 1986).

An administrative receiver has similar obligations, save that he is only obliged to provide accounts for every 12-month period and when he ceases to act he has two months to submit the final accounts. He must also send copies of the accounts to each member of any creditors' committee (r 3.32 IR 1986).

8.7 DUTIES OF THE RECEIVER

8.7.1 To whom are the receiver's duties owed?

A receiver's primary duty is owed to his appointor, and is to bring about a situation where the debt due to his appointor can be repaid. However, the receiver will also owe a secondary duty to any other parties who have an interest in the secured property or its equity of redemption. Such other parties might include the company itself, a lower ranking secured creditor or a guarantor of the secured debt. The receiver will not owe a separate duty to individual unsecured creditors or shareholders, as they have no direct interest in the secured property (*Medforth v Blake* [1999] BCC 771).

8.7.2 What are the receiver's secondary duties?

In many respects, a receiver's secondary duties will parallel those owed by the secured creditor itself to these same parties (see *Silven Properties Ltd v Royal Bank of Scotland plc* [2004] 4 All ER 484). One key difference, however, is that whereas the secured creditor has no duty to take possession of the secured property or to exercise any of its other powers, once a receiver is appointed he must take possession and take certain other actions in order to fulfil his functions. His secondary duties will therefore be wider in some respects than the duties of the secured creditor itself.

8.7.2.1 Duty to act in good faith

The receiver has a duty towards other interested parties to exercise his powers in good faith, regardless of any competing interests of the secured creditor. A breach of this duty requires some dishonesty, improper motive or other actual element of bad faith. Mere negligence will not suffice here. However, complete indifference to the interests of the other parties or deliberately shutting his eyes to the consequences of his actions may constitute bad faith (*Medforth v Blake*).

It was also emphasised in *Medforth v Blake* that the receiver's duties to the other interested parties were not necessarily confined to the duty of good faith. The extent and scope of any additional duty will depend on the facts of each case, but a number of clear principles do exist, as set out below.

8.7.2.2 Duties in relation to a sale

Provided he acts in good faith, the receiver can give priority to his appointor's interests in determining when to sell. As was made clear in the *Silven Properties* case, he has no obligation to wait for the market to improve, or to incur time and expense in trying to enhance the value of the property prior to a sale (such as by seeking planning permission).

If the receiver does decide to sell however, he will have a duty to seek the **best price reasonably obtainable** at the time of the sale. This normally means that, unless there is a need for an urgent sale (eg because goods over which he is appointed are perishable), he must fairly and properly expose the property to the market or sell at a price based on previous exposure to the market. He should not omit to mention key information to interested parties which could affect price, and should respond to enquiries from interested parties appropriately.

The other points made in Section 8.2.1.3 in relation to a secured creditor exercising a power of sale are also likely to be relevant to a receiver.

8.7.2.3   Duties in relation to a business

The receiver also owes a duty to manage the property over which he is appointed with due diligence. In *Medforth v Blake* it was made clear that whilst due diligence does not oblige the receiver to continue to carry on a business of the company, if the receiver does carry on the business due diligence requires him to take reasonable steps to try to do so profitably. In *Medforth* itself, the receivers failed in this duty by not taking advantage of substantial discounts which were available.

8.7.2.4   Duties in managing property generally

Although he may not be obliged to sell the secured property immediately or to trade any business, the duty to manage with due diligence means that the receiver cannot simply remain passive. He must exercise his powers to preserve and protect the property over which he has been appointed. For example, a receiver who failed to trigger a rent review clause in a lease was in breach of this duty (*Knight v Lawrence* [1991] BCC 411).

8.7.3   Additional duties of an administrative receiver

Like a liquidator in a compulsory liquidation, an administrative receiver is an officer of the court. He also has a specific duty to pay preferential creditors (s 40 IA 1986), as discussed further in Chapter 2.

8.8   POWERS OF A RECEIVER

8.8.1   Where are a receiver's powers found?

Assuming that his powers are not limited by the terms of his appointment, the receiver will have:

● the powers conferred upon him by law; and

● any additional powers conferred upon him under the terms of the security document under which he is appointed.

Under s 42 IA 1986, an administrative receiver is already given the very wide powers set out in Sch 1 IA 1986 (see Table 4.4 in Chapter 4). A non-administrative receiver is only given very limited powers by the Law of Property Act 1925. However, these limited powers will not be discussed further in this book, since normal practice now is for the security document expressly to confer powers equivalent to those in Sch 1 IA 1986 on all receivers.

Any receiver is given the power to apply to court for directions (s 35 IA 1986).

8.8.2   What is the receiver's status when selling property?

Normally, the receiver sells property as agent in the name of the company. As such he cannot transfer any better right that the company itself has. In order for the buyer to acquire the property free of the security under which the receiver was appointed, his appointor will need to enter into a deed of release. Similarly, a deed of release will also be required from any other person holding security over the property (*Re Real Meat Co* [1996] BCC 254).

If the holder of a **prior or equal-ranking** security refuses to give a release, an administrative receiver has the power to apply to court (see Section 8.8.3.1). Additionally, a secured creditor is able to overreach **lower-ranking** security by exercising its own power of sale and will appoint the receiver as its own agent just for the purposes of the sale, the lower-ranking security holder's rights then attach to any surplus sale proceeds.

If the buyer is connected to one or more of the directors of the company, s 190 CA 2006, which seeks to limit a director's ability to sell a company's property to himself, will continue to apply. (Section 193 CA 2006 disapplies s 190 CA 2006 where an administrator or liquidator has been appointed, but makes no reference to a receiver – see *Demite Ltd v Protec Health Ltd* [1998] BCC 638.) The sale may therefore still require the approval of the company's shareholders if the value of the property being sold exceeds 10% of the company's net assets value and is more than £5,000 or if its value exceeds £100,000. Where shareholder approval is not forthcoming, however, directors will typically seek to circumvent the operation of this section by resigning from the company's board prior to the sale.

8.8.3   What additional powers does an administrative receiver have?

8.8.3.1   Power to dispose of charged property

An administrative receiver may apply to the court for an order to dispose of a property free of any security which is **prior or equal-ranking** to that of their appointor. The court may make such an order if it thinks that disposal of the property in question (with or without other property) would be likely to promote a more advantageous realisation of the company's assets than would otherwise be affected. In addition, any order is subject to the condition that:

- the net proceeds of the disposal; and
- where those proceeds are less than such amount as may be determined by the court to be the net amount which would be realised on the sale of the property

in the open market by a willing vendor, such sums as may be required to make good the deficiency

be applied towards discharging the sums secured by the security (s 43 IA 1986).

8.8.3.2   Specific powers of investigation

The administrative receiver has the same powers of investigation under ss 234 and 236 IA 1986 as a liquidator (see Chapter 3). He will also be assisted by the directors' and employees' duty to co-operate with an insolvency officeholder under s 235 IA 1986 (see Chapter 6).

8.9   ENDING THE RECEIVERSHIP

The receivership is complete when the receiver's appointor has been paid in full or when the receiver has sold all the property over which he was appointed and distributed all the proceeds to his own appointor and to any other persons to whom he is required to pay monies in priority to his appointor (see Chapter 2). He will have no responsibility to make any distribution to ordinary unsecured creditors. He will hand any surplus proceeds to a lower-ranking secured creditor if there is one. In the absence of any lower-ranking secured creditor, he will hand them over to any liquidator, or if the company remains outside of liquidation, to the company itself. Once he has done so, his appointment comes to an end.

Besides filing his final accounts (see Section 8.6.6), the only further formality required will be to notify the Registrar of Companies that he has ceased to act (s 871 CA 2006). Administrative receivers are required to give this notice to the Registrar **within 14 days** (s 45(4) IA 1986).

8.9.1   Financial Collateral Arrangements (No 2) Regulations 2003

8.9.1.1   To what do these Regulations apply?

The Financial Collateral Arrangements (No 2) Regulations 2003 (SI 2003/3226) were introduced to implement an EC Directive whose goals were to simplify the process of taking financial collateral throughout the EU by, among other things, setting out minimum criteria for the creation, perfection and enforcement of security in 'financial collateral'.

Many of the transactions falling within the ambit of these Regulations are specialised and beyond the scope to this book. However, the Regulations are drafted more widely than the Directive itself and so may improve a secured creditor's position even where he holds more commonplace types of security over cash or shares. In *R (on the application of Cukurova Finance International Ltd) v HM Treasury* [2008] EWHC 2567 (Admin), the claimant argued that HM Treasury's decision to extend the Regulations beyond the scope of the Directive was inappropriate, but the court was not sufficiently impressed by this argument to grant the claimant the extension of time it needed to bring judicial review proceedings to challenge the Regulations.

The Regulations apply to **financial collateral arrangements** between non-natural persons (including companies) which were entered into **on or after 26 December 2003**. These include an arrangement where a security interest is taken over financial collateral which is **in the possession or under the control** of the collateral-taker.

The regulations define:

- **financial collateral** as cash or financial instruments, including shares in companies and equivalent securities. (HM Treasury has stated that the Regulations do not apply to non-financial collateral such as commercial property, plant and machinery or book debts); and

- a **security interest** to include a mortgage, fixed charge, pledge, lien or floating charge, although in the latter case the collateral must still be delivered, transferred, held, or registered in a manner to be in the control or possession of the collateral-taker.

In *Gray and others v G-T-P Group Limited: Re F2G Realisations Limited (in liquidation)* [2010] EWHC 1772 (Ch), the court made it clear that, for the Regulations to apply, it was necessary that 'legal control' as opposed to 'administrative control' of the underlying collateral must be transferred to the chargee. Therefore despite the fact that floating charges are included within the definition of security interest, it is unlikely that a typical English law floating charge, ie a charge over a fluctuating class of assets with which the company is free to deal until a future time, will in practice ever fall within the scope of the Regulations.

8.9.2 What advantages do the Regulations confer?

8.9.2.1 Enforcement

Where a financial collateral arrangement creates a security interest, certain provisions of the IA 1986 will not apply to the enforcement of that security (reg 8 of the Regulations). As a result where the company is in administration:

- the secured creditor is able to enforce its security without requiring the consent of an administrator or the permission of the court;

- the administrator has no ability to deal with the collateral under paras 70 and 71 Sch B1 IA 1986 (which would normally allow him to deal with charged property); and

- the administrator cannot require a receiver appointed over the collateral to vacate office.

The secured creditor will not be able to appropriate collateral unless the documents contain wording allowing him to do so, but most security documents should now contain such wording. Furthermore, where the financial collateral arrangement creates a legal or equitable mortgage on terms which give the secured creditor the right to appropriate the financial collateral, it may exercise this power in accordance with the terms of the arrangement without first seeking a foreclosure order (reg 17 of the Regulations). There is a useful analysis in *Cukurova Finance International Ltd v Alfa Telecom Turkey Ltd* [2009] UKPC 19 as to whether an appropriation had validly occurred on the facts of that case.

8.9.2.2 Avoidance provisions

In addition, certain other provisions of the legislation are disapplied in relation to financial collateral arrangements (reg 10 of the Regulations). As a result, among other things:

- the prescribed part will not apply to any charge created or arising under a financial collateral arrangement;

- a floating charge created or otherwise arising under a financial collateral arrangement cannot be avoided under s 245 IA 1986.

8.9.2.3 Creation and perfection of security

Finally, certain requirements for the creation and perfection of security are disapplied (reg 4 of the Regulations). As such:

- a financial collateral arrangement need only be in writing, and there is no signature requirement; and

- a failure to register the security interest under s 860 CA 2006 will not invalidate it.

In practice, creditors are usually advised to continue to create, register and otherwise perfect that security as if the Regulations had not been introduced. However, they may provide a useful fallback if one of the normal requirements, such a registration, is overlooked.

Chapter 9

Other special types of creditor

9.1 INTRODUCTION

Chapter 8 considered the position of secured creditors. This chapter considers the positions of certain other types of creditor who, whilst they do not hold security over the assets of the company, are for various other reasons in a different position from other unsecured creditors. These are:

- landlords;

- employees;

- pension scheme trustees; and

- retention of title creditors.

9.2 LANDLORDS

9.2.1 Overview

Table 9.1 summarises the effect of various different formal insolvency processes on a landlord's rights. These rights, and therefore the landlord's potential options will differ significantly, depending on the insolvency process which his tenant has entered into. However, his concerns are likely to revolve around his ability:

- to recover any arrears of rent, whether from the tenant, or from any other source;

- to recover rent falling due during (and after) the formal insolvency process, whether from the tenant or from any other source; and

- to forfeit the lease.

A landlord will receive a CVA proposal in advance of any CVA being implemented and will have the chance to consider it. In contrast, the first a landlord may learn of a receivership, administration or liquidation may well be when he is contacted on behalf of the newly-appointed insolvency officeholder. In each case, however, the landlord would be wise to consider his overall strategy as early as possible to avoid losing out on possible options. For example:

- He may need to retain the threat of forfeiture as a means of exerting leverage, and if so he will need to ensure he does not inadvertently waive any breach of the lease by continuing to demand or accept rent. In this regard, any managing agents should be given clear instructions to ensure that rent demands are no longer sent out automatically shortly before each payment date.

- A surrender may be less attractive than other options, and he will need to be cautious not to accept a surrender by operation of law by retaining keys which the insolvency officeholder returns or attempts to return to him.

Table 9.1 – Remedies available to landlord for tenant's breach of covenants where tenant is insolvent

Remedies	Receivership	Administration	Compulsory liquidation	Voluntary liquidation	CVA proposed	CVA approved
			Types of Insolvency			
Distress for arrears of rent	Yes	No, unless consent of the administrator or permission of the court obtained	No, unless leave of the court obtained (cannot be commenced after date petition is presented)	Yes, but liquidator may apply to the court for a stay	Yes, unless moratorium in place (in which case leave of the Court required)	Yes, for rent due under the terms of the CVA, but only if CVA terms breached
Court proceedings for recovery of arrears of rent/damages	Yes	No, unless consent of the administrator or permission of the court obtained	No, unless leave of the court obtained	Yes, but liquidator may apply to the court for a stay	Yes, *unless* moratorium in place (in which case leave of the Court required)	Yes, for rent due under the terms of the CVA, but only if CVA terms breached
Forfeiture by court proceedings	Yes	No, unless consent of the administrator or permission of the court obtained	No, unless leave of the court obtained	Yes, but liquidator may apply to the court for a stay	Yes, *unless* moratorium in place (in which case leave of the Court required)	Yes, but only if CVA terms breached
Forfeiture by peaceable re-entry	Yes	No, unless consent of the administrator or permission of the court obtained	No, unless leave of the court obtained (although some argue that not an 'action or proceeding')	Yes, but liquidator may obtain temporary relief from the court	Yes, unless moratorium in place (in which case leave of the Court required)	Yes, but only if CVA terms breached
Notice to sub-tenants under s 6 Law of Distress Amendment Act 1908 to recover sub-rent direct	Yes	Yes	Yes	Yes	Yes	Yes, subject to the terms of the CVA, and on whether terms breached
Notice to officeholder requiring him to elect whether to disclaim	N/A	N/A	Yes	Yes	N/A	N/A
Drawdown on rent deposit[1]	Yes	Yes	Yes	Yes	Yes	Yes, subject to the terms of the CVA
Pursue guarantor or former tenant	Yes	Yes	Yes	Yes	Yes	Yes, subject to the terms of the CVA

1 This assumes that the rent deposit is secured by a registered charge and allows drawdown in these circumstances.

9.2.2 Tenant in receivership

Neither an administrative nor a non-administrative receiver has any special protection against a landlord's rights. As such, the onus will be on the receiver to come to an appropriate arrangement with the landlord, and he may well offer to pay ongoing rent. (For the same reason, however, it is unlikely that a tenant and its secured creditor(s) will choose administrative receivership as an option, even when this is still available, if it is important to the business that it retains its premises.)

There is no requirement on a receiver to deal with unsecured creditors' claims generally, however. Therefore to the extent that the receiver fails to pay the rent and the landlord is unable to recover it through its other remedies, he is likely to need to prove as an unsecured creditor in a subsequent liquidation of the company.

9.2.3 Tenant in administration

9.2.3.1 Arrears of rent

The landlord again will only be an unsecured creditor in respect of any arrears of rent relating to the period prior to the start of the administration. Due to the administration moratorium, the landlord will need the consent of the administrator or the permission of the court to take any enforcement action to recover this rent and it is unlikely that such leave will be given, since this is purely a financial loss (see Chapter 4). The landlord is likely to have to prove alongside any other unsecured creditors in the administration itself (if it becomes a 'distribution' administration), or more likely in a subsequent liquidation.

However, many administrations will result in the sale of the company's business to a buyer who wishes to remain in the premises. If, as in most cases, the lease requires the landlord's consent to any assignment, the landlord may be able to negotiate for the buyer to pay all or part of these arrears as a condition of granting its consent. This assumes, of course, that the landlord is happy in other respects for the lease to be assigned to the buyer. Even if this is the case, the landlord may also need to maintain the threat of forfeiture in the short term as leverage, although see Section 9.2.3.3 in this respect.

9.2.3.2 Ongoing rent

In *Goldacre (Offices) Limited v Nortel Networks UK Limited (in administration)* [2009] EWHC 3389 (Ch), it was held that rent payable in advance and falling due during a period when the administrator is using the premises for the purpose of the administration was automatically payable as an administration expense in accordance with the terms of the lease. The court had no discretion to order that administrators pay part only of the rent falling due under the lease on the basis that they were using part only of the demised premises for the purposes of the administration.

In *Cheshire West and Chester Borough Council v Springfield Retail Limited (in administration)* [2010] CSOH 115, the administrators sold the company's business on terms whereby the buyer would be allowed into the premises on a licence to occupy. The buyer failed to make any of the payments due under the licence. The Scottish court held that, since the administrators had allowed the buyer into occupation under the sale agreement, the buyer's occupation was for the purpose of the administration and in accordance with *Goldacre*, rent falling due during the contractual period of the buyer's licence was payable to the landlord as an administration expense. (Scottish decisions are not binding on the English courts but are of highly persuasive value).

In *Re MK Airlines Ltd (In Liquidation)* [2012] All ER (D) 142 (May), a case relating to a provisional liquidation, the court held that the provisional liquidators who were merely retaining and securing property situated on the leased premises were not using the premises for the purposes of the provisional liquidation.

The main impact of *Goldacre*, however, has related to the timing of rent payments. It was made clear in *Leisure (Norwich) II Limited v Luminar Lava Ignite Limited & others* [2012] EWHC 951 (Ch), that:

- where rent is payable in advance and a rent payment falls due on a date before the start of the administration but remains unpaid, it is not payable as an administration expense – even if an administrator is later appointed and uses the premises for the purpose of administration for part of the period in respect of which the unpaid rent was due. The landlord will simply have an ordinary unsecured claim for that period; but

- where rent is payable in advance and a rent payment falls due on a date during which the premises are being used for the purposes of the administration, the whole of that rent payment is payable as an administration expense, even if in practice the administrator ceases to use the premises long before the end of the period covered by that rent payment.

Should the company cease using the premises, rent payments falling due after the date of vacation will no longer be an administration expense, and the landlord will again simply have an unsecured claim.

Commercial leases normally provide that the annual rent is payable in advance in equal quarterly instalments, falling due on the four 'quarter' days: 25 March, 24 June, 29 September and 25 December. If the company fails to pay the rent on the quarter day and an administrator is appointed a day or two afterwards, he may then be able use the premises for an initial period of almost three months for which the landlord will only be able to recover the unpaid rent as an ordinary unsecured debt. Whilst *Goldacre* was initially seen as a landlord-friendly decision, it is therefore now viewed far less favourably by many landlords.

Note, however, that under some leases, especially those where the rent payment dates have recently been varied to assist a tenant in financial difficulties, the rent may be payable monthly rather than quarterly in advance. In this case *Goldacre* may have less impact for the landlord.

The fact that rent is payable as an administration expense does not mean the landlord will be actually able to recover the rent on the days when it falls due under the lease, since an administrator is only required to discharge the administration expenses at the end of the administration. Although the landlord will gain priority status, treatment as an administration expense also does not automatically mean that he can be certain of being paid in full, as there may be too few floating charge recoveries at the end of the administration from which to discharge all of the administration expenses.

However, if the rent is not paid when due, the landlord may be able to exercise its right to forfeit the lease (see Section 9.2.3.3). It is possible therefore that a landlord may be able to use the threat of forfeiture to persuade the administrator to pay rent on an ongoing basis.

9.2.3.3 Forfeiture

Any non-payment of rent and indeed the tenant's entry into administration are both likely to trigger the landlord's right to forfeit (unless the landlord waives this right). Again, however, due to the administration moratorium, a landlord will not be able to exercise this right without the consent of the administrator or the permission of the court. The court will apply the principles set out in the *Atlantic Computers* case in deciding whether to grant permission. The fact that the administrators are not paying ongoing rent will not be determinative here, but it should be a powerful factor in favour of granting permission. The administrator may choose therefore to come to an arrangement to pay all, or at least part, of the rent on an ongoing basis whilst the premises are being used for the purposes of the administration.

The landlord will sometimes find that a sale of the business has already taken place, and the administrator has allowed the buyer into occupation on a licence arrangement either on a short-term basis or pending the grant of landlord's consent to a formal lease assignment. This will generally not be permitted under the terms of the lease, and so would be a further breach.

The landlord may not wish to consent to an assignment even if the licensee's sub-rent is funding the continuing rent under the lease. He may consider its financial standing to be of dubious strength, he may wish to avoid losing a guarantee from a previous tenant of better financial standing arising under a current 'authorised guarantee agreement' or he may simply have a stronger alternative tenant available to whom he might re-let. In this case he will wish to remove the unlawful licensee.

In *Metro Nominees (Wandsworth) (No 1) v Rayment* [2008] BCC 40, the administrator had agreed to assign the lease to the buyer and had allowed the buyer into occupation, but had agreed no provision for compensation in the event that the landlord refused consent to assign. The court granted the landlord permission to commence forfeiture proceedings on the basis that this would not impede the purpose of administration, as the retention of the lease would not have resulted in any further benefit to the company in administration. *Lazari GP Ltd v Jervis* [2012] EWHC 1466 (Ch) is another example of a case where the court granted permission to forfeit on substantially similar grounds.

In the case of *Innovate Logistics Ltd v Sunberry Properties Ltd* [2009] BCC 164, however, the facts of which are set out in the box below, the Court of Appeal refused the landlord's application for an injunction to terminate an illegal licence. The landlord had been positioning itself to remove the buyer in order to preserve bargaining power to oblige the buyer to accept a full assignment of the lease.

As the above cases illustrate, each case will be determined on its own facts, but among other things the question of whether the buyer's occupation of the premises is genuinely continuing to benefit the company in administration and the conduct of the parties will remain relevant.

Innovate Logistics Ltd v Sunberry Properties Ltd [2009] BCC 164

The company was placed into administration. On the same day, its business and assets were sold to a buyer, YHL. The company's book debts of approximately £9 million were excluded from the sale, although YHL was obliged to assist in their collection. The administrators were concerned that if the goods stored at the company's premises were not delivered in accordance with customer contracts, this would impede YHL's ability to collect the book debts. Therefore the terms of the sale also obliged YHL to take on the company's obligations under these outstanding customer contracts. To facilitate this, YHL was granted an occupational licence to the premises for six months, in breach of the terms of the lease.

The landlord wished YHL to take an assignment of the lease. When YHL refused to do so, the landlord sought permission of the court to commence proceedings for an injunction to terminate the licence.

At first instance, the judge took the view that the purpose of the administration had been achieved on the first day by the pre-pack sale to YHL and that the granting of permission to bring proceedings would not therefore impede the purpose of the administration. He also considered that, because the licence had been granted in breach of the lease, there was no 'legitimate' interest on the part of the company and its other creditors to balance against that of the landlord. He held that he did not therefore need to carry out the balancing exercise outlined in *Atlantic Computers*, and granted permission.

The Court of Appeal held, however, that the judge's reasons for not carrying out the balancing exercise were inadequate. The injunction, if granted, would remove YHL's ability to carry out the contracts and to assist in getting in the book debts. The landlord's main loss if it were refused permission would be its bargaining position in attempting to require YHL to take on a new lease (in which respect the court inferred that the passing rent must therefore be greater than the market rent). After carrying out the balancing exercise on this basis, the Court of Appeal held that the result was very much in favour of refusing permission.

9.2.3.4   Does the landlord want the premises back?

Unlike a liquidator, an administrator has no ability to disclaim the lease. He will therefore need the landlord's co-operation to bring the lease to an end prematurely. Unless the landlord has another proposed tenant or use for the premises, there may be a disadvantage to the landlord in forfeiting or accepting a surrender. So long as the company is the tenant, it remains the 'occupier' for the purpose of non-domestic business rates, whether or not it has vacated the premises. (If the company is continuing to use the premises these rates will be administration expenses although if it has vacated the premises it will be granted relief against the requirement to pay further rates under the Non-Domestic Rating (Unoccupied Property) (England) Regulations 2008 (SI 2008/386)). If the lease is determined, however, the landlord as owner will become liable for the rates, subject to a limited period of relief.

9.2.4 Tenant in liquidation

9.2.4.1 Arrears of rent

The landlord will only be an unsecured creditor in respect of any arrears of rent relating to the period prior to the start of the liquidation. He will have to prove alongside the other unsecured creditors in the liquidation to the extent he is not able to recover this rent by the exercise of other remedies. A voluntary liquidation will not prevent the landlord from bringing proceedings for unpaid rent (although there is likely to be little benefit in doing so) or from distraining, although the liquidator may apply for a stay. The moratorium in a compulsory liquidation will prevent the landlord taking these actions without the leave of the court – whilst there is some debate, commentators believe that the moratorium will apply to a distress which has not been completed before the winding-up order is made (see *Memco Engineering Ltd* [1986] Ch 86). The court's approach to applications for a stay or for leave is discussed generally in Chapter 3.

9.2.4.2 Ongoing rent

For the reasons discussed in Chapter 2, any rent relating to a period when the liquidator is using the premises for the purposes of the liquidation should be a liquidation expense, and will thus be given priority status. The case of *Re MK Airlines Ltd (In Liquidation)* (see Section 9.2.3.2), which also confirmed that the liquidation expenses principle applies equally to a provisional liquidation, is helpful in determining when a liquidator is using the premises for these purposes. If he needs to use the premises more extensively, however, it may be that a liquidator will still need to come to an arrangement to pay rent to the landlord on an ongoing basis.

9.2.4.3 Forfeiture

A voluntary liquidation will not prevent the landlord from exercising rights of forfeiture, and whilst the liquidator may be able to obtain a stay, he would have to move quickly to prevent forfeiture by peaceable re-entry. The moratorium in a compulsory liquidation will prevent the landlord forfeiting without the leave of the court. However, it is unlikely that a court would grant a stay (or relief from forfeiture) in a voluntary liquidation, or refuse a landlord leave to forfeit in a compulsory liquidation, if rent were not being paid.

As an alternative to forfeiture proceedings, a landlord may give 28 days' notice to a liquidator to require him to decide whether to disclaim. This may encourage the liquidator to vacate the premises during this period if he does not require them in the longer term (see Chapter 3 and Section 9.2.4.4 below).

9.2.4.4 Disclaimer versus surrender?

Given that a liquidator is unlikely to trade a company's business, it is unlikely that the liquidator will wish to retain premises in the longer term. If he is using the premises at all, it is more likely to be for short-term storage of assets which he will dispose of in the liquidation, in which case he should be content to vacate fairly early. It is rare therefore for a landlord to need to forfeit, and he is more likely to need to decide whether he wishes the liquidator to disclaim or to agree a surrender of the lease.

The advantages to the landlord of a disclaimer over surrender (or forfeiture) are:

- whilst the tenant company's obligations under the lease come to an end, the landlord has a claim for compensation against the tenant which he can prove in the liquidation (see *Re Park Air Services plc* [2000] AC 172 regarding the calculation of this). This may be relevant if there is likely to be a significant dividend to unsecured creditors; and

- because the disclaimer does not affect the obligations of other parties, it will be the landlord's route of choice if he is seeking to recover arrears/ongoing rent from a previous tenant or guarantor.

However, a landlord may still prefer a surrender:

- where he will be seeking to recover ongoing rent direct from a sub-tenant. As also discussed in Section 9.2.6.2, a disclaimer of a lease will also determine a sub-lease, enabling the sub-tenant to walk away if he wishes (although the sub-tenant may also choose to remain in occupation by continuing to pay the rent and observing the covenants in the headlease – *Re A E Realisations (1985) Ltd* [1988] 1 WLR 200); or

- where there will be no significant dividend in the liquidation, in which case the surrender may simply be a cleaner way of bringing the lease to an end.

9.2.5 CVA

9.2.5.1 Before the CVA is approved

In the absence of a 'small companies' moratorium, the CVA process imposes no restriction on a landlord's ability to exercise his rights prior to approval of the CVA. However, if it is important to the company's business that it retains its leasehold premises, the company may well either seek such a moratorium, or (more likely) obtain a moratorium by entering into administration pending approval of the CVA.

The landlord will, however, wish to examine the terms of the CVA carefully to see how he will be affected if it is approved. In this respect, landlords suffer a disadvantage when voting against a CVA in that the chairman of the meeting is entitled to put a nominal value of £1 only on any claim he may have for future rent (*Chittenden v Pepper* [2007] BCC 195). He should perhaps therefore also consider whether he is likely to wish to challenge the CVA, if approved, on the basis that he is unfairly prejudiced given the fairly short period of time allowed for such a challenge (see Chapter 7).

9.2.5.2 After the CVA is approved

The range of possible terms for a CVA is wide, so it is difficult to state with certainty how a CVA, once approved, will affect a landlord. However, it may well reschedule the date for payment of any arrears of rent and/or reduce the amount of such arrears which can be recovered. Additionally or alternatively, it may seek to reduce the ongoing rent which the landlord will receive during the period of the CVA. The landlord will be unable to forfeit for non-payment of sums due under the lease unless this is a breach of the terms of the CVA. His ability to forfeit for any other breach which may occur ought to be unaffected, however, and indeed he may still separately be able to forfeit on the basis of the tenant's insolvency if the lease so provides, provided he has not waived this right (*Thomas v Ken Thomas Ltd* [2007] BPIR 959).

9.2.6   Repayment from other sources

As a general rule, the fact that the tenant is in a formal insolvency process should not prevent the landlord from drawing down on a rent deposit or from pursuing any third party who might be liable, such as a guarantor, an original tenant (where the lease pre-dates 1 January 1996), a previous tenant who has entered into an authorised guarantee agreement and a sub-tenant. However, it is worth commenting further in a couple of these cases.

9.2.6.1   Rent deposits

The landlord will need to check the terms of the rent deposit agreement to ensure that they permit him to draw down. Normally a rent deposit will also be secured by a fixed charge over the cash deposited in a bank account. The landlord will also need to check that the charge has been properly registered, although there is an argument that the Financial Collateral Arrangements (No 2) Regulations 2003 can overcome defects in registration in this situation – see Chapter 8. Drawing down on the deposit would therefore normally constitute an enforcement of security, and it is considered in this context:

- If the tenant is in receivership, this should not prevent drawdown even if another secured creditor holds all-asset security, since the landlord is still likely to hold the prior-ranking fixed charge over the deposit monies.

- If the tenant is in administration, an enforcement of security would normally require the consent of the administrator or the permission of the court. However, if the security was set up after 26 December 2003, the landlord can argue that, under the Financial Collateral Arrangements (No 2) Regulations 2003, the administration moratorium does not apply to the charged deposit of cash (see Chapter 8). Regardless of this, it is suggested that an administrator ought normally to give this consent provided that he is satisfied that the charge has been properly registered, since the rent deposit monies, as fixed charge assets, are never likely to become available to anyone other than the landlord, at least to the extent that the landlord is still owed sums secured by the deposit.

- If the tenant is in liquidation, this will not prevent drawdown, since not even the moratorium in a compulsory liquidation prevents the enforcement of security.

- If a CVA is passed, a similar argument to the above ought to apply to a CVA moratorium. Even if the CVA is passed, it is arguable that the landlord should still be able to draw down, given that a CVA cannot bind a secured creditor without their consent. However, the situation may be more complicated if the landlord has not highlighted the fact of its security to the nominee prior to the CVA meetings, particularly if he has subsequently voted in favour of the CVA or done anything else to suggest his consent. A landlord should therefore act early to protect its position in each case.

9.2.6.2 Sub-tenants

The fact that the tenant is in formal insolvency should not prevent the landlord serving notice on any sub-tenant pursuant to s 6 Law of Distress Amendment Act 1908 to allow him to collect rent from the sub-tenant direct. Even the administration moratorium should not restrict use of this remedy. Case law has made it clear that a s 6 notice is not the equivalent of levying distress (*Wallrock v Equity and Law* [1942] 2 KB 82) and to the extent that service of the notice might be viewed as a 'legal process' at all, it is logically a process against the sub-tenant, not the company.

As seen in Chapter 3, a disclaimer of a headlease by a liquidator will also determine a sub-lease, subject to the sub-tenant's right to apply to court for an order vesting the disclaimed property (ie the headlease) in the sub-tenant, or to remain in the premises anyway on continuing to pay the headlease rent and performing the headlease covenants. This will mean that the landlord is no longer then able to recover rent from the sub-tenant who no longer wishes to remain in occupation.

9.2.6.3 Effect of a CVA on guarantors or former tenants

In *Prudential Assurance Co Ltd v PRG Powerhouse Ltd* [2007] BCC 500, the court confirmed that it is legally possible for a CVA to prevent a creditor enforcing rights against a guarantor (see Chapter 7). Although on the facts of the case the landlords concerned were able to establish that they were unfairly prejudiced, it remains possible that a similar CVA will be proposed in the future on terms which will survive such a challenge.

9.3 EMPLOYEES

9.3.1 Overview

An employee's rights will also depend to an extent on the insolvency process which his employer has entered into. His concerns are likely to include the following:

- Will his employment be terminated, and if so what claims will he have?

- To what extent will he be able to recover any sums which are already due to him, or which may become due as a result of the termination of his employment?

- If his employment continues during the formal insolvency process, will any ongoing salary due to him be paid?

- If the company's business is sold, will he be able to recover anything due to him from the buyer?

This section summarises the relevant considerations where the employee is employed in England by an English company. Note that where an employee is employed overseas by an English company, additional considerations may apply which are beyond the scope of this book.

9.3.2 Termination of employment

9.3.2.1 When will an employee's contract be terminated?

On a compulsory liquidation (technically, on the publication of the winding-up order), the employees are dismissed with immediate effect (*Re General Rolling Stock Co, Chapman's case* (1866) 1 Eq 346). Thus even the directors' contracts of employment are terminated (*Fowler v Commercial Timber Co Ltd* [1930] 2 KB 1), although the directors' other duties continue. Should the liquidator decide to carry on the business, the liquidator and the employee may agree that the latter's employment continues (*Re English Joint Stock Bank, ex parte Harding* (1867) 3 Eq 341).

In contrast, the employees are not automatically dismissed on a voluntary liquidation (*Midland Counties District Bank Ltd v Attwood* [1905] 1 Ch 357). In practice, however, if the liquidator ceases to carry on the business, their employment will also cease (*Reigate v Union Manufacturing Co (Ramsbottom) Ltd* [1918] 1 KB 592 at 606).

Neither administration (see *Powdrill v Watson* [1995] 2 AC 394 at 448F), nor a CVA will automatically terminate the employment of the company's employees. This would be inconsistent with the functions of these processes as 'rescue' procedures.

Receivership will not normally terminate employment, except in certain special circumstances (*Griffiths v Secretary of State for Social Services* [1974] QB 468).

However, even where employees are not automatically dismissed, the insolvency officeholder may well need to dismiss some, and possibly all of the employees. The considerations which will apply if a sale subsequently occurs are discussed in Section 9.3.5.

9.3.2.2 What claims may an employee have as a result?

The claims which an employee may have on termination of his employment contract may include the following:

- **Statutory redundancy pay**. To qualify the employee must have had two years' continuous service, and the amount of the payment will depend on the numbers of years' employment, the employee's age, and his weekly wage prior to dismissal.

- **Wrongful dismissal**. An employee may bring a wrongful dismissal claim if the employer terminates the contract in breach of its terms, for example, by failing to give the required contractual period of notice. The most common wrongful dismissal claim is for unpaid notice pay.

- **Unfair dismissal**. An employee who has had sufficient continuous service has a statutory right not to be unfairly dismissed (s 94 ERA 1996). What is sufficient depends on the employee's start date – those who started on or after 6 April 2012 need two years' service, while those whose employment began before that date only require one year's service (s 108 ERA 1996). An employee may bring a claim of unfair dismissal (in addition to any wrongful dismissal claim) if the employer has breached this right, for example, by failing to carry out a proper individual redundancy consultation of employees prior to their dismissal. An unfair dismissal award is comprised of a basic award, currently capped at £13,500, and a compensatory award, currently capped at £74,200. The compensatory award is based on the employee's losses.

An employee cannot recover both a statutory redundancy payment and a basic award for unfair dismissal in respect of the same dismissal.

In addition, the employer has a statutory obligation to consult collectively with employee representatives where it proposes to dismiss 20 or more employees at one establishment in a period of 90 days or less (s 188 TULRCA 1992). If the employer fails to do so, then the employee representative may complain to an employment tribunal, which may make an award, termed a '**protective award**' of up to 90 days' pay per employee (s 189 TULRCA 1992).

The case of *USDAW v WW Realisation 1 Ltd (in Liquidation)* (Case No 3201156/2010) illustrates the operation of s 188 TULRCA 1992. Woolworths Plc went into administration at the end of November 2008 and traded for about a month whilst the administrators tried unsuccessfully to find a buyer. At the end of this period all 814 shops were closed and all 28,000 or so employees made redundant. The administrators provided relatively little information to union and employee representatives, but did hold a meeting in mid-December at which they explained what would occur if no buyer could be found. The Employment Tribunal regarded this consultation as inadequate to comply fully with the legislation: the fact that the employer considered fuller consultation to be futile did not excuse the failure to consult. However, the Tribunal was willing to regard the stores as separate establishments and made no protective award in respect of stores with fewer than 20 employees.

Note, however, that at the time of writing the above decision is being appealed. It is arguably inconsistent with certain ECJ decisions which suggest that the concept of establishment should be interpreted broadly to minimise the number of redundancy exercises that are not covered by the collective obligations (see *Rockfon A/S v Specialarbejderforbundet I Danmark* [1996] IRLR 168 and *Athinaiki Chartopoiia AE v Panagiotidis* [2007] IRLR 284).

9.3.2.3   The effect of the administration moratorium

The employee will need to establish his entitlement to any wrongful dismissal, unfair dismissal or protective award, and potentially also to a redundancy payment, which would normally require his claim to be heard by an employment tribunal. Applications to an employment tribunal will be subject to the administration moratorium (see Chapter 4). However, proceedings started without consent are not a nullity – they are simply stayed pending the court granting its permission (*Carr v British International Helicopters* [1993] BCC 855).

In *Unite The Union, McCartney and others v Nortel Networks UK Ltd (in administration)* [2010] EWHC 826 (Ch), a number of employees sought the permission of the court to continue claims for protective awards, unfair dismissal, breach of contract, unpaid expenses claims and discrimination claims. The administrators subsequently gave consent for the employees to continue the protective award claims on the basis that, if the claims (which were being contested) were successful, the employees would be able to apply to the Government for the statutory element of such award and thus receive money quickly (see Section 9.3.3.2). However, they continued to withhold consent to their continuing the other claims. Amongst other things, the employees raised arguments that the claims needed to continue to be litigated since, until a judgment was obtained, they were not provable debts. The court refused permission to continue the claims, as it was satisfied that they were provable (and could be resolved by the insolvency officeholder).

9.3.2.4   Other considerations

The termination may, however, also release the employee from any restrictive covenants contained in the contact.

9.3.3   Unpaid remuneration and sums due following termination of employment

9.3.3.1   When will these be a preferential debt?

The **first £800** of an employee's claim for **unpaid remuneration** in respect of any part of the period of up to four months prior to the date of the insolvency will be a preferential debt. The status of a preferential debt is explained in Chapter 2. For these purposes, the term 'remuneration' includes:

*   wages or salary;

*   guarantee payments under Part III of the Employment Rights Act 1996 (the '**ERA 1996**') (employee without work to do);

*   any payments for time off for ante-natal care or to look for work or arrange training (under ss 53 and 56 ERA 1996, respectively) or to carry on trade union duties (under s 169 of the Trade Union and Labour Relations (Consolidation) Act 1992 (the '**TULRCA 1992**'));

*   remuneration on suspension on medical grounds or on maternity grounds under Part VII ERA 1996; and

*   remuneration under a **protective award** under s 189 TULRCA 1992.

A claim for **unpaid holiday remuneration** relating to any period prior to the insolvency is also a preferential debt, and this is not subject to any cap.

So far as the balance of any unpaid remuneration is concerned, however, the employees will only be ordinary unsecured creditors. They will also be ordinary unsecured creditors in respect of any debts which do not have preferential status, such as redundancy, unfair dismissal awards, and damages for wrongful dismissal.

9.3.3.2   What can the employee claim from the government?

The government recognises that, if he were to need to wait to be paid out of an insolvency, an unpaid employee may receive little or nothing, and even if there were enough assets to allow him to recover at least something, he would still have a considerable time to wait.

There is therefore a scheme whereby an employee of an insolvent company whose employment has been terminated may apply directly to the Redundancy Payments Office (the '**RPO**') to recover certain sums from the National Insurance Fund (the '**NIF**') (s 182 ERA 1996). For these purposes, a company is insolvent if it is in liquidation, administration, receivership or a CVA, or if possession has been taken of any of its property by a secured creditor holding a floating charge over that property (s 183 ERA 1996). The sums recoverable under this scheme include:

- up to eight weeks' arrears of pay, subject to a limit (currently £450 per week), which includes the same items that were described as 'remuneration' in Section 9.3.3.1 (s 184(1)(a) ERA 1996);

- up to eight weeks' unpaid notice pay, subject to a limit (currently £450 per week) (s 184(1)(b) ERA 1996);

- up to six weeks' unpaid holiday pay accrued during the 12-month period prior to the insolvency, subject to a limit (currently £450 per week) (s 184(1)(c) ERA 1996); and

- the basic award of compensation for unfair dismissal (currently £5,500) (s 184(1)(d) ERA 1996).

Statutory redundancy payments are also recoverable from the NIF under s 166 ERA 1996.

Finally, certain unpaid contributions to an occupational or personal pension scheme are recoverable from the NIF.

Besides the limits described above, tax and national insurance will still be deducted from payments to the employees where appropriate. So far as any claim for pay in lieu of notice is concerned, the employee will still need to mitigate his loss by claiming benefits and attempting to seek new employment.

However, subject to all of these considerations, the employee should at least receive his payments within about four to six weeks of making his claim. A copy of an easy-to-follow booklet setting out more details of this scheme can be found on the Insolvency Service website (www.insolvency.gov.uk).

9.3.3.3   What is the interaction between the above two claims?

If it makes a payment, the NIF will then be able to claim a like sum back in the insolvency in place of the employee. So far as the employee is also making a claim for any balance he has still not received, the two will rank on a pro rata basis in respect of any payment received.

For example, say an employee is normally paid £700 per week, and is owed one week's wages at the date of the insolvency. He will receive £450 from the NIF. He will claim the remaining £250 in the insolvency, and the NIF will claim £450. Because the combined sum of £700 which they are both owed is less than £800 in total, both claims will fully rank as preferential. If then, for example, there are sufficient assets to repay preferential creditors at 50p in the £1, the employee will then receive £125 from the insolvency (in addition to the £450 he received from the NIF) and the NIF will receive £225 (as a partial recovery of the £450 it paid out).

9.3.3.4   What happens when the employee is also a director or controlling shareholder?

It was once thought that the controlling shareholder of a company could not make a claim as an employee on the NIF. However, it appears now that he is not precluded from making such a claim if he still has a written contract of employment with the company and that contract actually gave rise to a genuine employer–employee relationship (*Secretary of State for Trade and Industry v Bottrill* [1999] ICR 592 and *Clark v Clark Construction Initiatives Ltd* [2008] ICR 635). The same principle should apply to a director.

Table 9.2 – Status of employee claims on formal insolvency

Employment claim	Preferential debt?	Payable out of NIF?
Arrears of pay	Yes – for up to four months before date of formal insolvency,[1] up to a maximum of £800. Includes: • guarantee payments; • remuneration on suspension on medical or maternity grounds; • payments for time off on certain grounds; • remuneration under a protective award	Yes – for up to eight weeks at up to £450 per week. Includes: • guarantee payments; • remuneration on suspension on medical or maternity grounds; • payments for time off on certain grounds; • remuneration under a protective award
Holiday pay	Yes – for accrued holiday remuneration relating to any period of employment before date of formal insolvency	Yes – for up to six weeks at up to £450 per week for holiday taken but not paid in 12 months before date of formal insolvency
Notice pay	No	Yes – for up to eight weeks' unpaid notice pay at up to £450 per week
Statutory redundancy pay	No	Yes – for statutory entitlement
Unfair dismissal	No	Yes – for basic award
Employer pension contributions	12 months (limited to contracted-out percentage) to occupational pension scheme (only).	12 months (limited to 10% of payroll) to occupational or personal pension scheme.
Employee pension contributions (if deducted from pay)	4 months to occupational pension scheme only.	12 months to occupational or personal pension scheme.

1   Except in the case of a protective award.

9.3.3.5   Other considerations

In practice, the directors of a company may be advised that there could be wrongful trading issues should the remuneration of employees falling due between the critical date and the date the company eventually enters into the formal insolvency remain unpaid. The fact that employees may recover some or all of the sums due to them from the NIF does not in itself reduce the overall figure for the loss, given that the Crown steps into the employees' shoes. The directors may therefore make special arrangements to ensure that the employees' remuneration for any such period can be paid.

9.3.4   Ongoing wages or salary

9.3.4.1   Administration

Wages or salary payable under a contact of employment **adopted** by the administrator enjoy a 'super-priority' status. They are payable in priority even to the administrator's remuneration and general expenses. An administrator is deemed to have adopted a contract of employment if he retains the employee in question for more than 14 days. The legislation makes it clear, however, that this super-priority status does not apply to wages or salary relating to the period prior to the administrator's appointment. In addition, if the administrator decides to terminate an employee's contract within the first 14 days they will gain no super-priority status (para 99(5) Sch B1 IA 1986).

Under 99(6) Sch B1 IA 1986, wages or salary includes:

- a sum payable in respect of a period of holiday, in lieu of holiday, or in respect of a period of absence or other good cause;

- in respect of any period, a sum which would be treated as earnings for that period for the purposes of any enactment about social security; and

- a contribution to an occupational pension scheme.

In practice, an administrator is likely to pay employees who are needed during the administration on an ongoing basis in any case, if funds permit.

The courts have made it clear that the following do **not** amount to wages and salary for these purposes and therefore do not enjoy super priority status:

- redundancy payments and unfair dismissal awards (*Re Allders Department Stores Ltd* [2005] BCC 289);

- protective awards made under s 188 TULRCA 1992 (*Re Huddersfield Fine Worsteds Ltd, Re Ferrotech Ltd and Re Granville Technology Group Ltd* [2005] BCC 905); and

- wrongful dismissal awards (*Re Leeds United Football Club Ltd* [2008] BCC 11).

9.3.4.2   Administrative receivership

Similar provisions to the above apply in relation to an administrative receiver. Unlike an administrator, however, a receiver is deemed to be personally liable on a contract of employment adopted by him. In this respect, he is entitled to an indemnity out of the assets of the company (s 44 IA 1986).

9.3.5   Recovery from a buyer

9.3.5.1   What are the normal rules?

The Transfer of Undertaking (Protection of Employment) Regulations 2006 ('**TUPE**') apply when there is:

- a transfer to another person of an undertaking, business or part of an undertaking or business;
- which was situated immediately before the transfer in the UK; and
- which involves a transfer of an economic entity that retains its identity.

The term 'economic entity' here is defined to mean an organised grouping of resources which has the effect of pursuing an economic activity, whether or not that activity is central or ancillary. In practice, therefore, TUPE applies to a sale of a UK-based business as a going concern.

Under reg 4 TUPE, on such a sale the contracts of employment of the employees of the business, and all of the rights, powers, duties and liabilities under or in connection with such contracts transfer to the buyer. Their contracts of employment are treated as if they had originally been made between the employee and the buyer and accordingly the employees will have no further claim against the seller.

In addition:

- any **variation** of the contract of the employment will be void (reg 4(4) TUPE), and
- any employee **dismissed** (whether before or after the transfer) will be automatically treated as having been unfairly dismissed (reg 7 TUPE), resulting in a liability to the buyer

unless the sole or principal reason for the variation or dismissal was:

- a reason **unconnected** with the transfer; or
- an **economic, technical or organisational** ('ETO') reason entailing changes in the workforce.

The situation can be complicated where an insolvency officeholder has dismissed employees shortly before an eventual sale. In practice, in determining whether a dismissal was for an ETO reason, employment tribunals have taken into account factors such as:

- whether the reason was connected with the future conduct of the business as a going concern (although the fact that streamlining the business may make it more attractive generally to a buyer will not automatically mean that TUPE applies);
- whether there was any collusion between the insolvency officeholder and the buyer; and
- whether the insolvency officeholder had funds to carry on trading at the time of the decision to dismiss.

(See, for example, *Thompson v SCS Consulting Ltd* [2001] IRLR 801, EAT.)

In *Spaceright Europe Limited v Baillavoine* [2011] EWCA Civ 1565, the Court of Appeal was satisfied that the dismissal of a company's chief executive officer on the date of the administrators' appointment was connected with a sale of the business a month later, even though no buyer has been identified at the time of the dismissal, and was not justified by an ETO reason. The CEO occupied a unique role which would be surplus to the requirements of any likely buyer, and his high salary might also have caused a buyer difficulties.

9.3.5.2 Specific exceptions applying to insolvency sales

Certain special provisions have been introduced in relation to insolvency sales, as it was perceived that potential buyers might otherwise be deterred by the level of obligations to employees they would need to take on.

- If the company is under bankruptcy proceedings or any analogous insolvency proceedings instituted with a view to the liquidation of its assets under the supervision of an insolvency practitioner (described here as '**liquidation proceedings**'), the transfer and dismissal provisions in regs 4 and 7 of TUPE, respectively, will not apply (reg 8(7) TUPE).

- If the company is under insolvency proceedings under the supervision of an insolvency practitioner which were not instituted with a view to the liquidation of its assets (described here as '**non-liquidation proceedings**'), regs 4 and 7 of TUPE will apply generally. However, the obligation to pay those pre-existing debts which would have been recoverable under the NIF guarantee scheme under ERA 1996 had there been no transfer remain with the seller and are still recoverable from the NIF as if the employment had been terminated on the date of the transfer. The buyer will only be liable for the balance of any pre-existing debts (regs 8(2) to 8(6) TUPE).

- In addition, if the company is in non-liquidation proceedings, the buyer may impose new employment terms on a transferred employee provided that, among other things, the variation has been agreed with an employee representative and is made with the intention of safeguarding employment (reg 9 TUPE).

The wording of TUPE was taken from the relevant EC Directive, and does not attempt to classify the various formal insolvency processes discussed in this book as either liquidation proceedings or non-liquidation proceedings. BIS has issued its own guidance ('Redundancy and Insolvency Payments', URN 06/1368), which is summarised in Table 9.3. Although this guidance is not authoritative, in *Key2Law (Surrey) LLP v De'Antiquis* [2011] EWCA Civ 1567 the Court of Appeal held that any administration will be a non-liquidation proceeding, thus resolving a conflict between two earlier Employment Appeal Tribunal decisions.

Table 9.3 – Summary of BIS's guidance ('Redundancy and Insolvency Payments', URN 06/1368)

Proceeding	Category
Compulsory liquidation	Liquidation proceedings
Creditors' voluntary liquidation	Liquidation proceedings
Members' voluntary liquidation	Not insolvency proceedings at all, so TUPE applies normally
Administration	Non-liquidation proceedings
CVA	Non-liquidation proceedings
Administrative receivership	Non-liquidation proceedings
Other types of receivership	Not insolvency proceedings at all, so TUPE applies normally
Proceedings in other jurisdictions where a relevant transfer occurs in Great Britain	Necessary to consider whether they are analogous to liquidation proceedings – if so, they are treated as such

9.4 PENSION SCHEMES

9.4.1 Overview

If the principal employer under a defined benefit pension scheme enters into formal insolvency, this is likely to crystallise a debt from the company to the trustees of the scheme equal to the amount by which the liabilities of the scheme exceeds the value of the scheme assets. This is sometimes termed the 'section 75 debt'.

The section 75 debt is deemed to crystallise immediately before a 'relevant event' occurs (s 75(4) Pensions Act 1995). The insolvency events listed in Table 9.4 are relevant events. As Table 9.4 shows, however, a number of other processes are excluded from this definition. The section 75 debt may also crystallise if a process occurs which is not an insolvency event as defined, but is nonetheless an event which triggers the wind up of the scheme under the scheme's rules.

Given that the amount of the scheme's liabilities is calculated on a full buy-out basis, ie by reference to the amount which an insurance company would charge to provide a policy securing the benefits payable under the pension scheme, the section 75 debt may be large. It is, however, normally an **unsecured** debt of the company (and indeed s 75 specifically states that it will not be preferential), although, in some cases, security may have been provided by the employer. Also, parent company guarantees and letters of credit are sometimes provided in respect of an employer's section 75 debt which may be called upon.

The insolvency event may also trigger the start of an assessment period which may lead to the pension scheme being transferred to the Pension Protection Fund (the '**PPF**'), as discussed in Section 9.4.2. In addition, the pensions regulator ('**TPR**') has the power to impose liabilities on others. Since this power is likely to be most relevant in a restructuring context, it is discussed in Chapter 10.

9.4.2 The role of the PPF

9.4.2.1 When will a pension scheme enter into the PPF?

The scheme must be eligible for the PPF (and must not have commenced winding-up before 6 April 2005 (the date the Pensions Act 2004 came into force)). Whilst most defined benefit schemes will be eligible there are certain exceptions, although discussion of these is beyond the scope of this book.

If a qualifying insolvency event occurs in relation to the employer of an eligible scheme then an assessment period will automatically begin. For these purposes, any of the insolvency events listed in Table 9.4 will be 'qualifying' insolvency events.

During the assessment period, the PPF seeks to ascertain:

* whether the scheme can be rescued (eg if the company is able to continue as a going concern); or

* whether the scheme can afford to secure benefits which are at least equal to the compensation that the PPF would pay if it assumed responsibility.

If either of the above is possible, the PPF will cease to be involved with the scheme. It will otherwise assume responsibility for the scheme from the end of the assessment period.

Table 9.4 – Insolvency events under s 121 Pensions Act 2004

Insolvency events:

- a nominee submitting a report for a CVA;
- the directors of a company filing or lodging with the court documents and statements under para 7(1) Sch A1 IA 1986 dealing with a pre-CVA moratorium;
- an administrative receiver being appointed;
- the company entering administration;
- a resolution being passed for voluntary liquidation without a declaration of solvency under s 89 IA 1986 (ie for a CVL);
- a creditors' meeting being held under s 95 IA 1986 to convert an MVL into a CVL;
- a winding-up order being made by the court;
- an administration order being made by the court in respect of the company by virtue of any enactment which applies Pt 2 IA 1986 (administration orders) (with or without modification);
- a notice from an administrator under para 83(3) Sch B1 IA 1986 Act (moving from administration to CVL) being registered by the Registrar of Companies;
- the company moving from administration to liquidation pursuant to an order of the court under r 2.132 IR 1986; or
- an administrator or liquidator of the company, being the nominee in relation to a proposal for a CVA, summoning meetings of the company and of its creditors to consider the proposal, in accordance with s 3(2) IA 1986.

Events which are not insolvency events:

- a resolution being passed for a voluntary liquidation with a declaration of solvency (ie for an MVL);
- the appointment of a provisional liquidator;
- the appointment of a non-administrative receiver;
- entry by the company into a non-UK insolvency process.

The assessment period is likely to last for at least a year, and during this period the trustees of the scheme retain responsibility for the administration of the scheme and for communicating with and making pension payments to scheme members. However, the PPF will have a monitoring role, and can give directions to the trustees. The PPF will also liaise with any insolvency officeholder. Pensions will be restricted to PPF compensation levels during any assessment period. The scheme's recoveries in respect of the section 75 debt, either in the insolvency or pursuant to any third-party guarantees, will often be critical here.

9.4.2.2 What level of compensation does the PPF provide?

Broadly speaking, the PPF provides two levels of compensation, based largely on a member's age at the time of the assessment date:

- members who had already reached the scheme's retirement age (or had not reached the scheme's retirement age but were already receiving a survivor's pension or a pension on the grounds of ill-health) receive a starting level of compensation equal to 100% of the pension already in payment; and
- other members who had not already reached the scheme's retirement age receive a 90% level of compensation. This is also subject to an overall cap,

adjusted according to the age the compensation comes into payment. This cap is revised every year, and is currently £34,049.84 at an age of 65.

Once compensation is in payment to a member, any part of the compensation which derives from pensionable service on or after 6 April 1997 will be increased each year in line with the retail prices index subject to a cap of 2.5% in any year. This is a lower rate of increase than the scheme itself would have provided.

9.5   RETENTION OF TITLE CREDITORS

9.5.1   Overview

Under s 19 Sale of Goods Act 1979, title passes when the parties intend it to pass. It is therefore open to a supplier to agree with the company that, notwithstanding that he may have delivered goods to the company, he remains the owner of the goods until the company has paid for them. A clause to this effect is generally termed a retention of title, or 'RoT', clause. This can not only give a supplier the ability to recover from the company any goods to which he has retained title, but also a possible action for damages for conversion against an insolvency officeholder personally if he sells such goods without the supplier's authority.

The supplier will need to:

- establish that his RoT claim is valid; and

- remove the company's other rights in respect of the goods.

In many cases, the supplier may well not wish to have his goods back and would prefer instead to negotiate payment of at least some of what he is owed, but the above issues will still be relevant so that he can maintain his bargaining position.

9.5.2   Establishing valid RoT

9.5.2.1   Are the RoT provisions effective?

Generally, a clause which provides that title to the goods remains with the seller until a payment is likely to prove effective. Examples of ineffective clauses, however, have included:

- a clause which attempted to retain title both to the goods supplied and to the end product from a manufacturing process in which the goods themselves have lost their identity (eg *Borden (UK) Limited v Scottish Timber Products Ltd* [1981] Ch 25); and

- a clause which attempted to retain title to the goods and their proceeds of sale (eg *Re Andrabell Ltd* [1984] 3 All ER 407).

The above examples illustrate the danger of going too far in drafting an RoT provision.

In both of the above examples, the clauses were held to be void in their entirety as they amounted to unregistered charges. In some cases, however, the courts have been willing to sever the possible void part of the provision and hold that the remainder of the clause is effective (eg *Clough Mill v Martin* [1985] 1 WLR 111).

It is not absolutely necessary that the contract contain a clause expressly reserving title provided that it is clear from the contract, construed overall, that the parties did not intend title to pass until payment. However, the supplier may have a harder task establishing this in the absence of an express RoT provision.

9.5.2.2 Has the RoT provision been incorporated into the contract?

Normal principles of contract law apply in determining whether an RoT clause has been incorporated. This will not be an issue where the company has signed a written contract on the supplier's terms before placing its order. However, the provision may not have been incorporated where:

- the company has its own set of terms and conditions and there is doubt as to which party's terms and conditions apply (a so-called 'battle of the forms'); or

- the supplier's terms and conditions only came to the company's attention after the event, for example, because they appear only on the reverse of the supplier's delivery notes or invoices (although this is less likely to be an issue if there has been a course of dealings between the parties for some time).

In *Ghsp Inc v Ab Electronic Ltd* [2010] EWHC 1828 (Comm), the court found that on the facts the parties had not contracted on either side's terms and so the terms of the contract were those implied by the Sale of Goods Act 1979.

9.5.2.3 Can the supplier still identify his goods?

The RoT may remain effective even if the goods have been incorporated into some other product provided they have not lost their identity. In *Hendy Lennox (Industrial Engines) Ltd v Grahame Puttick Ltd* [1984] 1 WLR 485 an engine, supplied on RoT terms, had been incorporated into a generator. However, it could be unbolted and removed, so the RoT still applied.

The supplier may have difficulty, however, if the goods which he has delivered have been mixed in the company's warehouse with similar goods supplied by other suppliers, making it difficult to recognise his own goods (eg *Re London Wine Company (Shippers) Ltd* [1986] PCC 121). Nonetheless, in *Re CKE Engineering Ltd* [2007] BCC 975, a supplier was effectively able to retain title to zinc supplied by it, notwithstanding the fact that this has been mixed in a tank with zinc supplied by other parties – it was held that that supplier owned an appropriate fraction of the total zinc in the tank.

9.5.2.4 Is it a simple or all-monies clause?

A **simple** RoT clause provides that title to the goods is retained by the creditor until it has received full payment for those specific goods. An **all-monies** clause provides that title is retained until the company has paid not only for those specific goods, but also for any other goods supplied by the creditor to the company, and has paid or repaid any other moneys it owes to the creditor, regardless of how such indebtedness arose. A creditor with only a simple clause will need to relate specific goods at the buyer's warehouse to specific unpaid invoices. An all-monies clause avoids this need.

9.5.3 Removing the company's other rights

Although the company may not yet have title to the goods, it will have possession of them and in the normal course of its business it can pass title on to a buyer in good faith who has no knowledge of the creditor's RoT clause (s 25 Sale of Goods Act 1979). The creditor is therefore unlikely to be able to retain title to any goods once the company sells them on. In *Sandhu (t/a Isher Fashions UK) v Jet Star Retail Ltd (In Administration)* [2011] EWCA Civ 459, for example, the contract allowed the supplier to require the company not to re-sell or part with possession of the goods until the company had paid the supplier all monies due to it. However, the supplier had in practice taken no steps to withdraw the company's authority to do so. The supplier accordingly had no claim in conversion in respect of goods which had been sold by administrators following their appointment.

The supplier will also wish to ensure that he retains the right to bring conversion proceedings against an insolvency officeholder who sells his goods, or indeed allows any other party to take possession of them. To succeed in a conversion claim, the supplier would need to demonstrate not only that he remains the owner, but that he has an immediate right to possession and that the insolvency officeholder committed a deliberate act of conversion, interfering with his rights to possession.

Under ss 234(3) and (4) IA 1986 a liquidator, administrator or administrative receiver who seizes or disposes of any property which is not property of the company is not liable in respect of any loss or damage resulting if:

- he believed and had reasonable grounds for believing that he was entitled to seize or dispose of that property, and

- the loss was not caused by his own negligence.

A well-drafted set of terms and conditions will therefore remove the company's right to possession of the goods and allow the creditor access to the company's premises to identify and recover his goods once any one of a list of insolvency-related events occurs (although the supplier will need to check this). However, the supplier should also contact the newly-appointed insolvency officeholder as soon as possible to make the position clear.

In **administration**:

- the moratorium will still prevent the creditor from repossessing his goods without the consent of the administrator or the permission of the court (see Chapter 4). (The moratorium does not, however, preclude the supplier having an 'immediate right to possession' for the purposes of a conversion claim – *Barclays Mercantile Business Finance Ltd v Sibec Developments Ltd* [1992] 1 WLR 1253.)

- the administrator has the power to apply to the court for an order allowing him to sell the goods, but only on terms whereby he pays the proceeds of the sale, and any shortfall required to make up the market price, to the creditor (see Chapter 4).

Otherwise, however, the insolvency officeholder (including any administrator who does not wish to apply to the court) will need to agree terms with the creditor if he wishes to continue to sell the goods, or indeed to hand possession of them to a third party as part of a business sale.

Chapter 10

Restructuring

10.1 INTRODUCTION

Chapter 1 gave a brief overview of the considerations involved in a restructuring. This chapter considers the thinking involved in a restructuring more generally, and looks in particular at the following stages which might typically be involved in a successful restructuring process:

- identifying the problem and the relevant stakeholders;

- creating a stable environment;

- information gathering;

- assessing the restructuring options and implementing a solution.

For simplicity, this chapter takes as its model a restructuring of a group of English-registered companies with a structure which might typically exist after an acquisition financed with a mixture of debt and investment from a single major shareholder. A simple example of such a structure is shown in Table 10.1.

In practice, the group structure may differ from this. It may also be that, for business, tax or other reasons, some of the companies in the group are overseas entities. Where one or more of the companies in the group is listed, or the debt itself is listed (eg following a securitisation), then this will create additional issues which are largely beyond the scope of this book. Nonetheless, much of the content of this chapter will still be generally applicable.

10.2 IDENTIFYING THE PROBLEM

10.2.1 What is the problem?

For a successful restructuring to be achieved, the company, or group, must have a viable underlying business. In many cases it may not become clear whether this is the case until further work has been carried out. However, once the fundamental problem, or problems, the group is facing have been identified, the relevant stakeholders will be able to make a commercial judgement as to whether it is even worth carrying out further work.

Groups encounter financial difficulties for a variety of reasons:

- the state of the economy generally;

- problems exist in the group's industry sector generally; and/or

- problems exist which are specific to the group.

Table 10.1 – Typical post-acquisition group structure

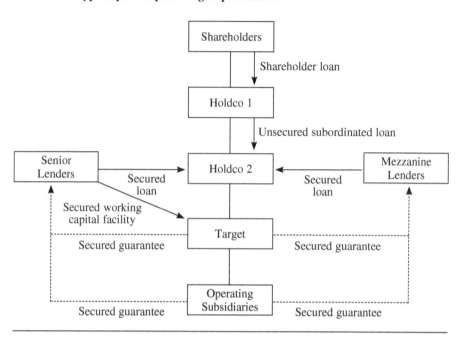

Clearly, if one or both of the first factors are also present, these may exacerbate any problems the group already has. However, groups with viable underlying businesses may still encounter difficulties even in a benign economy where their competitors are thriving.

Sources of difficulty which may not adversely affect the long-term viability of the business may include:

- an over-ambitious acquisition strategy;

- flaws in the business model;

- an underperforming non-core business draining the core business;

- loss of a major customer or supplier; and/or

- increased cost of a defined benefit pension scheme, labour, utilities, or other key purchases.

It may be clear that a simple solution which does not require a fuller restructuring of debt or equity is available – see Section 10.2.3. However, more significant action is likely to be needed if the underlying problem means that in the medium to long term the group can no longer afford the cost of servicing its existing interest payments and/or principal repayments to its financial creditors.

10.2.2   What is the 'trigger point'?

There will usually be some clear point in time before which action needs to be taken. Such 'trigger points' might typically include:

- the testing date for a financial covenant in the group's banking facilities;

- the date on which the group's annual accounts needed to be signed off by the auditors;

- the date on which the group's banking facilities are due to be repaid;

- the date by which a regulatory authority, such as the Prudential Regulation Authority (PRA) or the Financial Conduct Authority (FCA) in the financial sector or the Civil Aviation Authority (CAA) in the travel sector, is threatening to withdraw a licence or consent which the group needs to continue to trade unless action has been taken;

- the date on which the operating subsidiaries in the group are forecast no longer to have sufficient cash to operate.

The existence of such a trigger point can be a virtue in one sense, in that it may concentrate stakeholders' minds on the need to complete the whole restructuring by the date in question. However, if this cannot be achieved, interim solutions may need to be found.

10.2.3 Is a simple solution available?

If it is immediately clear that the underlying problem derives from a one-off event or is otherwise not a serious one, it may not be necessary to carry out a more fundamental restructuring of the group's debt or equity structure. Examples of simple solutions include:

- replacing underperforming senior management. Alternatively, where senior management have the skills to run a performing business but not to run a business in financial difficulties, another option is to add an experienced turnaround professional to the existing management team as a 'Chief Restructuring Officer' (or 'CRO');

- resetting of financial covenants (or waiving of a breach deriving from a one-off problem);

- a minor change in the dates for the payment of debt and/or interest by the existing lenders under a banking facility;

- an equity injection (ie a cash subscription for further shares) by a sole, or majority, shareholder, or a rescue rights issue to a larger group of existing shareholders, to provide the group with the cash it needs to cure a financial covenant breach or cash-flow problem; and/or

- raising cash by other means, for example by a sale of non-core assets or parts of the business or a sale and leaseback of freehold premises.

Groups and their stakeholders will tend to consider such options prior to deciding that more significant action is needed. However, in some cases, it may transpire that what was thought to have been a simple but permanent solution was only an interim solution.

In practice, there will also be companies or groups of companies where a series of interim solutions are found to allow them to continue to meet ongoing payments on their existing debts, but where no more serious trigger point has yet emerged to force a more extensive restructuring. (These more serious trigger points are sometimes known as 'burning platforms'.) Companies which are able to meet ongoing debt payments, but which are regarded as then having little surplus cash to develop their business without a fuller restructuring are sometimes referred to as 'zombie companies'.

10.3   WHO ARE THE KEY STAKEHOLDERS?

For a successful restructuring to be achieved, a sufficient number of the key stakeholders whose interests will be affected by the restructuring must support the process. These key stakeholders might include:

10.3.1   Shareholders

Investor shareholders are likely to have considerably more day-to-day involvement with the business itself than the financial creditors. Their appointees may well sit as non-executive directors on the board of one or more of the group companies and provide considerable expertise. The shareholders are likely also to have strong links with the rest of the management, although it is also they who have the power to remove underperforming directors.

If the group is already insolvent on a balance sheet basis, its shares will retain no present value. Where creditors are asked to compromise their claims, they are likely therefore to expect shareholders also to make some new investment in any restructuring, or otherwise relinquish their existing shareholder rights.

10.3.2   Financial creditors

Some groups may have only a single lender. However, larger, more sophisticated groups are likely to have several tiers of debt consisting, in descending order of priority, of some or all of senior, second lien (although this is not seen on 'new money' deals nowadays), mezzanine and subordinated debt.

If senior or mezzanine loans have been syndicated, there may be a number of different lenders from a range of financial institutions in each tier. Some of the tiers of debt may in turn be subdivided into more than one sub-tier.

If the group has issued bonds, these will form another tier of debt. Historically high yield bonds are likely to have been unsecured and this debt will therefore have formed part of the subordinated debt ranking behind that of senior and mezzanine lenders. However, other structures are now becoming more commonplace, particularly where some of a group's original debt has already been refinanced through the bond markets. Bonds may well now enjoy security rights too.

The subordinated debt may also include debt due to shareholders, outstanding consideration due to the seller of the business from the existing owners and/or debt due to past or present management and will typically be recorded in the form of loan notes.

The group of financial creditors who are likely to prove most active in any restructuring are those who would expect only to be partially repaid on a formal insolvency of the group. Colloquially, the value '**breaks**' in their tier of debt. Financial creditors whose debt still sits above the value break can expect to be repaid in full, whereas financial creditors sitting below the value break would be repaid nothing and might therefore be less engaged; but their agreement may still be needed to achieve a consensual restructuring. Financial creditors whose debt sits just below the value break, are also likely to be fairly active, and are likely to scrutinise any valuations carefully. In addition, financial creditors who hold debt below the value break may also hold debt at a higher level, and try to use this as leverage.

The picture will be complicated further if, since the debt was originally lent, all or part or it has been sold to other parties. Debt which is sold on in this way is known as '**secondary debt**'. Players in the secondary debt market may have bought debt, or acquired sub-participations in the debt, at a substantial discount – debt which is trading at a discount is known as '**distressed debt**'. These players may well have a very different agenda from the original financial creditors. They could still stand to make a positive return on the investment if the business is quickly broken up or sold. Alternatively, their primary objective may always have been a restructuring which converts that debt to voting shares, giving them control of the group – a so-called '**loan to own**' strategy.

The first stage of a restructuring will often therefore require the group to identify which financial creditors now hold all of its debt. Where the group has issued bonds this may be a particularly difficult exercise.

The rights of the financial creditors vis-à-vis each other will be important and will be set out in various documents, which the relevant stakeholders will also need to review. For example:

● A deed or priority, or intercreditor agreement, to which all financial creditors will be a party, will set out the priority ranking of the various creditors, limit the rights of lower ranking creditors to receive payments and/or to take their own enforcement actions, and stipulate what further actions the higher ranking creditors can take without the consent of the lower ranking creditors. It may also give lower ranking creditors the right to buy out higher ranking creditors at par.

● Individual facility agreements will stipulate how decisions are taken among the various lenders under that facility. Many lender decisions, for example to waive breaches of covenants, can be taken if a stipulated majority, normally more than 66⅔%, of those lenders by value of their commitments are in favour, but a decision to reduce the total debt due or to extend a repayment date is likely to require the unanimous consent of all of those lenders.

● Where bonds have been issued, the relationship between the individual bondholders will be governed by their own agreement. In this case, however, it would be normal to allow for many bondholder decisions to be taken if more than 50% of bondholders by value are in favour, with even fundamental decisions requiring only super-majority, eg 75%, rather than unanimous consent.

The courts have occasionally needed to consider whether there are any restrictions on the ability of a majority of finance creditors to use these provisions to make decisions against the wishes of a dissenting minority.

Some older cases such as *British American Nickel Corpn Ltd v O'Brien* [1927] AC 369 suggested that the majority must exercise such decision-making powers for the purpose of benefitting the whole. The more recent case of *Redwood Master Fund Ltd v TD Bank Europe* [2002] EWHC 2703 (Ch), which held that a relative disadvantage for the minority will not automatically mean that a majority power has been improperly exercised if it was exercised in good faith for the purpose for which it was conferred, probably better reflects modern commercial realities.

Nonetheless, the courts may still look unfavourably on arrangements which, as an inducement to support a proposal, seek either to confer an additional benefit on financial creditors voting in favour of that proposal, or a disbenefit on those abstaining or voting against it. In *Assénagon Asset Management SA v Irish Bank Resolution Corp Ltd* [2012] EWHC 2090 (Ch) the English court was unprepared to allow the use of an 'exit consent' technique, where bondholders who failed to support a resolution risked an expropriation of their bonds for a nominal consideration although at the time of writing this decision is being appealed.

10.3.3   Other major creditors

If one of the difficulties of the group is that it has an underfunded defined benefits pension scheme, it may be necessary to restructure this either as an exercise in itself or as part of a wider restructuring. Whilst the debt due to the pension scheme may be unsecured in the event of a formal insolvency (see Chapter 9), the trustees will be in a far better negotiating position than other unsecured creditors due to the special powers of the Pensions Regulator ('TPR'). Pensions issues are discussed further in Section 10.8.

The group may also be paying excessive rents on business premises, particularly where the underlying problem was an over-ambitious acquisition or expansion strategy, in which case the debts due to some of its landlords may need to be addressed.

However, it is unlikely that most consensual restructurings will be carried out in a way which affects the trade creditors, employees or most of the other operational creditors of the group, for a number of reasons:

- the process creates uncertainty and risks the ability of the business continuing as a going concern;

- key suppliers are likely to adopt ransom positions and refuse to trade further with the business, or supply it on less favourable terms going forwards as the cost of their consent;

- a far larger number of parties might need to be involved in the restructuring process, many with very small claims, which they might be reluctant to compromise consensually; and

- it would be virtually impossible to conduct such wide negotiations confidentially.

Indeed, even if a formal insolvency process is used as a restructuring tool this will frequently still provide for trade creditors or employees to be paid in full.

10.3.4   Management

The other stakeholders are likely to wish to ensure that existing management are retained and incentivised as part of the restructuring process. This is because:

- although in some case the problems of the business lie with existing management, management will often be key to the value of the business going forward; and

- the information-gathering exercise required as a precursor to the restructuring will be far more difficult without their help.

Management are likely to prefer a restructuring to an unplanned formal insolvency for a number of reasons. In the latter case executive directors could lose their jobs and all directors who hold equity or share options would lose these. Formal insolvency may lead to disqualification proceedings against the directors, and on a liquidation personal liability is a possibility. However, management will still remain wary of the risk that, by continuing to trade, they may increase their exposure to disqualification or personal liability should the restructuring fail and formal insolvency still result.

Stakeholders who are trying to resist a restructuring may well see the directors as a potential weak point, and try to put pressure on them by suggesting various ways in which the directors might be in breach of their duties. However, decisions such as that in the IMO Car Wash case should give the directors comfort here (see Section 10.6.2.2).

Non-executive directors may also have different motivations from executive directors. The group will not be their only source of income, and they are also likely to have less emotional commitment to the survival of the group. They may be more concerned that if they remain a director of a group which fails, this could adversely affect their own reputations.

In addition to creating stability generally in the other ways described in this chapter, the stakeholders may therefore need to address management's concerns:

- by addressing management's own incentivisation packages early. This may involve restoring value to management's existing shares or promising them fresh shares in a newly-solvent restructured group. However, where the proposed restructuring may not restore any value to the shareholders, management may instead need to be offered their incentive in the form of debt. This would need to be ranked at or around the point where the value breaks and therefore may need to be ranked ahead of some of the debt owed to finance creditors;

- by creating a stable financial environment, as outlined in Section 10.4; and

- by giving comfort to the existing directors that they are not being left to take the risk alone. In this respect, the stakeholders may be inclined anyway to supplement the existing board by appointing one or more further directors with specialist turnaround expertise.

10.4   CREATING A STABLE FINANCIAL ENVIRONMENT

10.4.1   What principles have historically applied here?

In the 1970s, the Bank of England developed a set of general principles to govern how a group's financial creditors should respond when they become aware that the group is facing serious financial difficulties. These principles became known as the London Approach.

The aim was to give the troubled group a breathing space whilst information was gathered to determine whether it could survive, and for proposals then to be put together. During this time, the group is likely to need continued access to its lending facilities and possibly new money. However, in return for not withdrawing facilities or enforcing, creditors need to know that their own positions will not deteriorate absolutely or relative to each other. The basic premise was that by acting collectively, the financial creditors ought to ensure a higher return for all of them than they would receive on a formal insolvency.

In 2000, INSOL International (the International Federation of Insolvency Professionals) published the INSOL Global Principles for Multi-Creditor Workouts (the 'INSOL Principles'). These were intended to be a statement of best practice to be followed in multi-creditor restructurings. Broadly speaking, the principles involved reflect the London Approach, but they were designed to be equally applicable in a variety of different jurisdictions. The INSOL Principles are set out in Table 10.2.

10.4.2 What principles would apply now?

Neither the London Approach nor the INSOL Principles has ever had any statutory force, but have always relied upon co-operation. They are no longer applied in the way that they once were and are unlikely now even to be directly referred to by name. This is largely due to the fact that it has become commonplace for a group's finance debt to be held by an increasing number of entities, often with a variety of agendas. Aggressive distressed debt investors in particular may well have very different aims to those envisaged in these principles. Even when just trying to create stability therefore, there is likely to be a far greater need to look at ways in which decisions can be taken without the need for the unanimous consent of all of the stakeholders.

However, the general principles involved might still provide a useful starting point for moving towards a restructuring which is designed to enable the survival of the group and where a majority of those stakeholders with a real economic interest in the group are inclined to co-operate to achieve this.

Table 10.2 – The INSOL principles

First Principle: Where a debtor is found to be in financial difficulties, all relevant creditors should be prepared to co-operate with each other to give sufficient (though limited) time (a standstill period) to the debtor for information about the debtor to be obtained and evaluated and for proposals for resolving the debtor's financial difficulties to be formulated and assessed, unless such a course is inappropriate in a particular case.

Second Principle: During the standstill period, all relevant creditors should agree to refrain from taking any steps to enforce their claims against or (otherwise than by disposal of their debt to a third party) to reduce their exposure to the debtor but they are entitled to expect that during the standstill period their position relative to other creditors and each other will not be prejudiced.

Third Principle: During the standstill period, the debtor should not take any action which might adversely affect the prospective return to the relevant creditors (either collectively or individually) as compared with the position at the standstill commencement date.

Fourth Principle: The interests of relevant creditors are best served by co-ordinating their responses to a debtor in financial difficulty. Such co-ordination will be facilitated by the selection of one or more representative co-ordination committees and by the appointment of professional advisers to advise and assist such committees and, where appropriate, the relevant creditors participating in the process as a whole.

Fifth Principle: During the standstill period, the debtor should provide, and allow relevant creditors and/or their professional advisers reasonable and timely access to, all relevant information relating to its assets, liabilities, business and prospects, in order to enable proper evaluation to be made of its financial position and any proposals to be made to relevant creditors.

Sixth Principle: Proposals for resolving the financial difficulties of the debtor and, so far as practicable, arrangements between relevant creditors relating to any standstill should reflect applicable law and the relative positions of relevant creditors at the standstill commencement date.

Seventh Principle: Information obtained for the purposes of the process concerning the assets, liabilities and business of the debtor and any proposals for resolving its difficulties should be made available to all relevant creditors and should, unless already publicly available, be treated as confidential.

Eighth Principle: If additional funding is provided during the standstill period or under any rescue or restructuring proposals, the repayment of such additional funding should, so far as practicable, be accorded priority status as compared to other indebtedness or claims of relevant creditors.

10.4.3 The co-ordinator

The co-ordinator is appointed by the group's lenders and the group itself, and will normally be the bank with the largest exposure. They will play the role of 'lead bank' in the restructuring. The scope of the co-ordinator's role is often set out in a specific co-ordination agreement. This role is likely to include:

- collating and disseminating the financial and other information provided by the group, and by the investigating accountants (see Section 10.5);

- providing feedback to the group on any information provided by it, and on any presentations given by the group to its lenders;

- liaising between the group and any facility agents, or possibly the individual lenders, with regard to any standstill arrangement and any requests for new money by the group; and

- liaising between the group and the other lenders in relation to any restructuring proposals put forward.

Although it may be responsible for obtaining legal and financial advice, the co-ordinator's own role is therefore administrative, not advisory, and it will ensure that the co-ordination agreement places clear limits on its responsibilities. A co-ordinator may nonetheless in practice provide much of the driving force needed to achieve the restructuring.

Any co-ordination agreement will also deal with the co-ordinator's fees and other expenses. Since these are likely to be borne by the group itself, it will usually take a particular interest in the extent of the co-ordinator's role and its ability to engage advisers. A key issue here for the co-ordinator tends to be an indemnity from the lenders for any liability they might suffer, for example as a result of being sued by a third party, or at least an exclusion of liability from fund lenders whose constitutions do not permit them to give indemnities.

It is possible that a co-ordination committee, or 'co-com', may be formed containing a number of the larger lenders and/or representatives of different lender groups. Such a committee will either play the role of co-ordinator, or form an intermediate point of liaison between the co-ordinator and the lenders generally.

Often the co-ordinator will itself already have another role as agent or as security trustee under the finance documents. It will also, of course, be a lender in its own right. These other roles will carry different responsibilities from, and be separate from its role as co-ordinator. The bank concerned may need to clarify on occasions in which role it is acting, particularly when it receives information.

10.4.4   The need for advisers

The group is likely to need the following advisers during a restructuring process:

- **Accountancy advisers**. The group's auditors will already know the group and will play an important part in helping to provide the financial information the stakeholders will need.

- **Legal advisers**. Whilst the group will already have existing legal advisers, the directors will need advice as to their responsibilities and duties as directors. If the existing legal advisers also act for a major shareholder, they and the directors will need to consider whether this creates, or may in future create, a conflict of interest requiring that a different legal adviser now needs to be retained to advise the board.

- **Financial advisers**. These will generally be bankers or accountants by training, and are likely to play a lead role in liaising with the other stakeholders and developing the restructuring proposal. A financial adviser will often also have worked in the past with many of the key individuals within the lenders' and advisers' organisations on similar restructurings. Their appointment should therefore assist in making these stakeholders feel more comfortable, and in making initial discussions more productive.

- **PR advisers**. Public relations issues will grow increasingly important in maintaining stability, as rumours will almost inevitably spread in the outside world that the group is in difficulty. (These rumours may indeed sometimes originate from minority stakeholders who have their own agendas to pursue.)

The group is likely to be actively encouraged by its various stakeholders to ensure it has the right advisers in place at an early stage in the process. The stakeholders will also wish to appoint other advisers. These may include legal advisers to the co-ordinator, and investigating accountants and valuers (see Section 10.5). The facility agreement may already provide that the cost of some of these advisers is to be borne by the group itself. Even where it does not, the lenders may consider that they are in a position to negotiate a requirement to this effect.

It is common for a group initially to resist appointing additional advisers itself, and particularly to question the need for the lenders to appoint further advisers, given the cost involved. The lenders will see this differently. If there is currently doubt as to whether they will be paid in full, they will consider that the group is spending their money, rather than its own or its shareholders' money on the costs of the advice.

10.4.5   Standstill agreement

10.4.5.1   Is a standstill agreement necessary?

Even if a group of lenders who would be entitled to enforce have already concluded that it is not presently in their interests to do so, both the group and individual stakeholders may press for a formal agreement. A standstill agreement not only governs the company's relationship with its lenders, but also those lenders' relationships with each other. The standstill gives a feeling of stability both internally and externally. Indeed, the group may specially need to be able to show an external regulator such as the FCA (or indeed TPR) that a standstill is in place.

10.4.5.2   What are the typical terms of a standstill agreement?

The standstill will typically contain provisions dealing with the following:

- suspension of the lenders' rights to accelerate facilities or enforce guarantees or security, notwithstanding a stipulated list of events of default which have occurred (or may occur);

- agreement by the lenders to allow the group to continue to use its existing facilities, notwithstanding a stipulated list of defaults;

- agreement by the lenders not to improve their positions vis-à-vis each other, for example, by setting off cash balances;

- agreement by the lenders to share any losses in an agreed manner. Such provisions may be needed if, for example, some lenders are continuing to make revolving or ancillary facilities available to the group. They are likely to provide for balancing payments at the end of the standstill by better-off lenders to worse-off lenders;

- agreement by the lenders not to trade their debt. The restructuring may be set back if new stakeholders with different agendas became involved part-way through;

- agreement by the group to provide more detailed and/or more frequent financial information (which will be relevant to the information-gathering process discussed in Section 10.5);

- agreement by the group not to take various actions which might affect the prospective returns to lenders. For example, tighter controls may be imposed on the group's ability to make disposals or to pay out any money to lower ranking stakeholders in the ordinary course. If cash flow permits, the lenders might also seek to reduce their exposure by requiring surplus cash to be used to pay down their existing facilities or placed in a blocked account for lenders to decide whether to release back if needed for cash flow or apply in prepayment; and

- terms permitting any new funding to be on a super-priority basis. If this cannot be dealt with by amendment to the existing intercreditor agreement due to the resistance of other stakeholders, it may need to be dealt with by a more limited priority agreement.

Commonly the standstill will terminate at the end of a specified period, or on earlier notice (the period of which needs to be agreed) if a stipulated majority of the creditors so require, although if the company needs the standstill to give comfort to some third party this may not be appropriate. It is likely also to terminate if an event of default other than one of those on the stipulated list occurs.

10.4.5.3   Who needs to be a party?

The group will wish any group of lenders who would immediately be entitled to enforce to be parties to the standstill agreement.

Mezzanine lenders are likely to be prevented from taking immediate enforcement action for stipulated periods of time by standstill provisions in an existing intercreditor agreement. They will nonetheless often still sign up to the formal standstill arrangements, and may need to do so, for example, if there would otherwise be a 'notifiable event' (see Section 10.8). They will wish to be clear as to whether the standstill under the standstill agreement runs concurrently or consecutively with those in the intercreditor agreement.

Other financial creditors, such as bondholders, will usually not have the ability to enforce unless there is a payment or insolvency default. They will typically not therefore join as a party to the standstill agreement.

10.4.6   Cash-flow issues

For any restructuring to succeed, the group must continue to have enough working capital to satisfy its day-to-day needs. Clearly these needs are likely to increase as a result of the costs of the restructuring itself.

10.4.6.1   Drawdown on existing facilities

Tactically, a group which has not yet breached the financial covenants under its banking facilities but which anticipates a breach, may try to place itself in a stronger position by drawing down any unused part of its banking facilities immediately to stockpile cash. It is possible that an agent or lender may still try to oppose this, if it considers that some other breach has already occurred. Possible additional events of default which will apply here are:

- Material adverse change ('**MAC**'). Whether this is applicable may depend on the exact wording of the clause, particularly the degree of discretion given to the agent or lender as to what constitutes a MAC.

- Insolvency. However, it is likely to be insufficient that the group is balance sheet or even cash-flow insolvent on paper, so long as it has not been deemed unable to pay its debts (see Chapter 1).

- Insolvency proceedings. If the group has already approached the lenders to discuss a restructuring at this stage, it may be in breach here through having taken a step in relation to a compromise or arrangement with its creditors.

Otherwise, the group's ability to continue to drawdown on facilities will be a negotiating point in any standstill agreement.

10.4.6.2   New money

In England, there is no legislative framework to provide for new money to be injected into a group which is being restructured. If new money is needed, the various stakeholders therefore need to reach agreement in each case as to who will provide any new money and where it will sit within an existing security structure. This contrasts with other jurisdictions such as the USA where the bankruptcy legislation specifically deals with this.

The senior lenders, or some of them, have historically been the natural source of new money required by the group to tide it over during the restructuring. However, new money may often also come from other lenders whose existing debts are lower ranking, or possibly from shareholders. Outside investors who have no existing interest in a group may also be willing to provide new money. Regardless of the status of any existing money owed to the new money provider, however, any new money would normally be given priority status. (Despite this, the return on any new money is often set at a higher level than that on the highest ranking of the existing facilities).

A new money request can prove a contentious issue. Whilst they recognise that the aim is to buy further time to find a solution which will protect their existing investment, lenders will still wish to assess at the point of the request how likely it is that both the new money and their existing exposures are to be repaid. Stakeholders will generally ask the company to consider other cash-flow management techniques to reduce the new money needs (see Section 10.4.6.3).

The group needs to assess the amount of new money it requests carefully. Lenders are unlikely to look favourably on a group which makes repeated requests for new money because its first request was for too low an amount. The lenders will start to lose faith in the systems used by the group in analysing its requirements, and may question the viability of any restructuring proposal put together using the same systems.

10.4.6.3   Cash-flow management

In addition to, or instead of, asking for new money the group may also ask existing lenders temporarily to postpone payments of principal and/or interest under a banking facility. Again, lenders will generally ask the company to consider other cash-flow management techniques before, or as a condition of, acceding to such a request. Table 10.3 lists some of the cash-flow management techniques commonly used. Whether any of these techniques are likely to be practicable – and if so which – will depend on the time which is likely to elapse before the restructuring is finalised.

10.5   INFORMATION GATHERING

10.5.1   What information is needed?

From a financial perspective, there are three main elements to the information-gathering process:

- The **business plan**. This will indicate the level of debt which the group can continue to service going forward and enable financial creditors to understand the projected return on any equity instruments that they may receive in connection with the restructuring.

Table 10.3 – Methods employed in managing cash (in addition to speaking to existing/new lenders)

Action	Relevant considerations
Identify and dispose of surplus premises or business assets.	Secured lenders will regard these assets as part of their security, and may wish to see these payments used to reduce overall debt instead.
Ensure that older/surplus stock is realised, and/or that unbilled work-in-progress is invoiced, promptly.	It may be desirable to sell older/surplus stock at a significant discount if cash needs are paramount.
Recover outstanding debts efficiently, for example: • improve collection procedures for 'good' debts; and • reach compromises with debtors who are disputing their liability to pay.	Where the company has an invoice-discounting facility, however, there may be limited scope for it to benefit from these steps. It may be desirable to compromise disputes over large sums swiftly, even if this is on worse terms than the company could obtain given more time.
Reduce surplus expenditure, for example: • put a hold on any non-essential capital expenditure; • reduce employment costs, eg by limiting discretionary bonuses and other non-essential benefits, stopping planned salary increases or promotions, and reducing over-staffing; • reduce costs by renegotiating with suppliers or changing supplier; • eliminate surplus overheads such as subscriptions, entertainment, advertising, training, travel, etc. Ensure that strict internal controls are placed on purchasing generally.	Obtain employment law advice before reducing over-staffing costs, since if handled badly, this approach could lead to additional employee claims against the company. Consider also the effect on workforce morale. A redundancy programme will still result in a significant one-off upfront cost. Reducing overheads will need to be part of a strategy – a prolonged decrease in some capital or other expenditure will eventually damage the business.
Extend creditor payment dates (and/or reduce sums due), for example: • agree with HMRC to defer tax payments; • agree with landlords to pay rent monthly rather than quarterly or to reduce the rent temporarily; or • agree with suppliers to extend payment dates.	It is better to reach agreements with creditors rather than just withhold payment. Directors who delay payments to HMRC in particular risk disqualification. It is also important not to misrepresent or withhold information in reaching agreements with creditors. HMRC have a dedicated Business Payments Support Service to deal with such requests (see http://www.hmrc.gov.uk/payinghmrc/problems/bpps. htm). They are supportive where appropriate but must be convinced that the company will meet rescheduled payments.

- Financial **due diligence**. Further investigation into the group's financial affairs will enable the business plan to be tested, and if necessary, amended.

- **Valuations**. These will indicate the total amount likely to be achieved on a sale of the group's business (or, if relevant, its assets).

The information revealed will determine the strength of the respective stakeholders' positions in the course of any further restructuring negotiations. Conversely, it may lead stakeholders to conclude that a restructuring would not be achievable.

10.5.2 Independent reporting accountants

The group itself will normally provide regular information to its lenders. However, the lenders will generally wish to engage independent reporting accountants of their own. The role of the reporting accountants may include the following:

- to review and verify the cash flow projections and other financial information provided by the group;

- to assess the adequacy of the business plan and systems used by management;

- to assess the performance of the group by comparison within other companies operating with a similar industry sector;

- to review the restructuring proposals put forward by the group; and

- to identify and review any alternatives which exist, including formal insolvency, and calculate the likely returns to the senior lenders in such scenarios. Sometimes this will include a fuller **contingency planning** exercise to prepare for the eventuality that one of these alternatives does ultimately occur.

The identity and scope of work of the independent reporting accountants often proves contentious. This will be partly on the costs grounds already identified in Section 10.4.3. Management may feel they are in practice assessing the adequacy of the management team themselves. Sometimes management are also nervous that the independent reporting accountants might be inclined to recommend formal insolvency if this could lead to a greater fee income for their own firm, and if so this concern needs to be identified and addressed.

As groups gain experience of restructuring – and many groups will now have been through some form of restructuring process already in recent years – they may be inclined to appoint accounting advisers themselves at an early stage. Usually, however, lenders will nonetheless continue to engage additional advisers to provide the lenders with their own analysis and support.

10.6 LOOKING AT THE RESTRUCTURING OPTIONS AND IMPLEMENTING A SOLUTION

10.6.1 What are the possible consensual options?

There are a number of possible consensual options, ie options which will require the consent of all affected stakeholders. Examples of these include the following.

10.6.1.1 Amendment and restatement

This will involve a change in the terms of the lending facilities and/or bonds. It may involve, for example a rescheduling of payments of principal or interest to give the group longer to pay and/or an increase in the facility limits (or an adaptation of the facilities to incorporate some additional source of finance such as an asset-based facility using the group's receivables).

The lenders concerned will, however, wish to see their positions improved in some other way in return for their agreement. Possibilities include:

●   a further injection of equity;

●   tighter financial and/or operational covenants;

●   more onerous continuing financial information obligations;

●   a higher interest rate;

●   guarantees from additional subsidiaries and/or new security (although s 245 IA 1986 and possibly s 239 IA 1986 will be a factor here if the group is receiving no new monies – see Chapter 5);

●   an asset disposal programme and/or a cash sweep mechanism, where proceeds or other surplus monies are used to pay down the debt;

●   greater freedom to trade their debt, for example, by removing any group consent rights; and/or

●   increased fees.

10.6.1.2 Refinancing

This will involve the advance of fresh monies to repay existing debt. A refinancing will typically involve an incoming lender or group of lenders replacing the existing lenders. It has become increasingly common in recent years for existing debt to be refinanced by the issue of bonds. Provided the refinancier is satisfied that sufficient security is available, for example because it evaluates the assets of the group in a different way from the existing lenders, it may be possible for the group to increase its overall facilities on a refinancing. However, the terms of the refinanced debt may well be less favourable to the group. The possibilities set out in Section 10.6.1.1 will also be relevant here.

10.6.1.3 Reduction of debt

An outright release of debt is generally an unattractive restructuring tool from a tax perspective, as the debt released can be credited to the debtor as an income receipt with the result that charge to tax could arise (in the absence of any losses or other reliefs to shelter the charge). However, under ss 322, 358 and 359 Corporation Tax Act 2009 ('CTA 2009') there are certain circumstances where a tax charge will not arise, for example:

●   Where the debt is released in consideration of the issue of ordinary shares in the debtor. 'Ordinary shares' may include preference shares provided they carry a right to dividends which are not at a fixed rate. This can make a **debt to**

equity swap the more attractive option for reducing debt, and this is discussed further in Section 10.7.

- Where the debt is released as part of a statutory insolvency arrangement. Such an arrangement may include a CVA or Scheme of Arrangement.

- Where the debtor meets one of a number of 'insolvency conditions'. The insolvency conditions include situations where the debtor is in insolvent liquidation, administration or administrative receivership, where a provisional liquidator has been appointed in relation to the debtor under s 135 IA 1986 or where the debtor is in an equivalent situation outside the UK.

- Subject to a number of exceptions, where the debtor and creditor are 'connected' within the meaning of s 348 CTA 2009. This requires that one has control of the other or that both are under common control at some point during the accounting period in question. This seems comparatively unlikely so far as most lenders are concerned unless they have taken shares in an earlier restructuring.

10.6.2   What is the alternative?

The stakeholders are unlikely to agree upon a consensual solution unless each of the stakeholders involved perceives that it would be placed in a worse position under any likely alternative. The group, and any stakeholders who actively wish to pursue the restructuring are therefore likely to need to convince the remaining stakeholders that a less attractive alternative exists and will be implemented should all stakeholders not achieve a consensual restructuring.

10.6.2.1   Alternatives to a restructuring

Possible alternative scenarios are:

- An **'unplanned' formal insolvency**. This is a formal insolvency process into which the group is effectively forced because a trigger point occurs, and either a creditor takes enforcement action or the boards of directors of the various group companies conclude the group has no reasonable prospect of avoiding insolvent liquidation and initiate the process themselves. The term 'unplanned' here is used to distinguish such a process from a 'planned' formal insolvency used as a restructuring tool (see below). Crucially, an unplanned process may well involve the formal insolvency of operating subsidiaries as well as holding companies within the group, and will almost certainly have a negative impact on realisations.

- A **solvent sale** of the business or assets. This is likely to generate a higher price than a sale out of formal insolvency. However, it is still likely to be perceived by potential buyers as a forced sale to some extent, which will adversely affect the level of any offers. The directors may also find it unattractive because it exposes them rather than an insolvency officeholder to any claims that the sale was at an undervalue, although if the group has exposed the business and assets properly to the market prior to any sales the risks should not be great.

- **Maintaining the status quo**. So long as an interim solution can be found every time a trigger point occurs, then there will be no need to carry out any wider restructuring. In many cases, interim solutions are found and the only real driver for a restructuring is ultimately that the group is about to run out of cash. However, maintaining the status quo will be unattractive to financial creditors who have bought debt at a discount with a view to making a return. Where interest payments to mezzanine lenders or dividend payments to shareholders are blocked as a result of a default, they may also wish to see a speedier resolution. It is also likely to be unattractive to management, who will want the group's difficulties resolved so that they can focus once again on running and growing the business. (They may also want to ensure that any shares they hold retain value or are replaced with an incentive package which gives them an equivalent return.)

10.6.2.2   Non-consensual restructuring

Section 10.3.2 has already looked at when the majority voting provisions of documents may be used to make changes to financial creditors' rights.

However, whilst these provisions may often be used to achieve a temporary fix, it will generally not be possible to use this route alone to achieve a fuller restructuring where not all stakeholders are prepared to agree terms. Various of the formal processes described in this book may then be needed as mechanisms for achieving such a 'non-consensual restructuring'. They may be required because stakeholders are actively opposed to the restructuring. However, they may also be useful tools to circumvent stakeholders who for their own internal reasons are unable to support the restructuring voluntarily, eg a collateralised loan obligation (or 'CLO') fund lender whose investment period has expired. They may also be needed to circumvent stakeholders who now see their interest in the group as valueless and therefore choose not to engage at all.

For example:

- A **pre-packaged** administration or receivership can be used to circumvent the claims of dissenting shareholders or lower ranking creditors by transferring assets to a new company buyer whose debt and equity structure reflect the desired outcome. Pre-packs have already been discussed generally in Chapter 4, but the use of a pre-pack as a restructuring tool is discussed further in Section 10.7.

- A **Scheme of Arrangement** can be used to bind, or '**cram down**', a minority of dissenting creditors and/or shareholders within a class. The use of Schemes was discussed generally in Chapter 7.

- A **CVA** can similarly be used to cram down a minority of dissenting unsecured creditors. Unlike a Scheme of Arrangement, there is no need to divide creditors into separate classes. However, its usefulness is limited by the fact that it can neither bind a secured creditor (without their consent), nor affect a shareholder's rights. The use of CVAs was discussed generally in Chapter 7.

A summary of the advantages and disadvantages of these respective processes as restructuring tools is set out in Table 10.4. Normally the costs and other disadvantages will be such that a consensual restructuring is more attractive if it can be achieved. Clearly these non-consensual routes also still require a sufficient number of the stakeholders affected to support the process – they can only be used to overcome the resistance of minority stakeholders or stakeholders who would otherwise expect to receive nothing on a formal insolvency, or to by-pass stakeholders who cannot or do not engage at all.

The case of *Re Bluebrook* [2009] EWHC 2114, often referred to as the IMO Car Wash case, is a good illustration of a restructuring where a Scheme, a pre-packaged administration and the power of release contained within the intercreditor agreement were all required in order to achieve the desired result. Fuller details of this case are set in the box below.

Re Bluebrook [2009] EWHC 2114 (the *'IMO Car Wash'* case)

The IMO group, which operated the largest car wash business in the world, owed its senior lenders £313 million and its mezzanine lenders £119 million, secured by a comprehensive guarantee and security package across the group. An intercreditor agreement expressly subordinated the mezzanine debt to the senior debt. It also gave the security agent the authority to release security and liabilities upon an enforcement action provided that the proceeds were applied in accordance with the intercreditor agreement.

A new structure was set up whereby £185 million of senior debt would be novated to a new holding company, £12 million would remain behind and the remainder would be exchanged for shares in a new holding company. All of the mezzanine debt would remain behind.

Schemes were required for Bluebrook and two other holding companies because a small minority of senior lenders would not consent voluntarily to this proposed restructuring. However, the Schemes themselves did not transfer any assets. Following sanction, various holding companies would be placed into administration, and the administrator would transfer their assets to the new holding companies. The security and guarantees held by the mezzanine lenders would then be released pursuant to the intercreditor agreement.

The Scheme did not affect the mezzanine lenders' legal rights and they were given no opportunity to vote. However, they could still object at the sanction hearing on the grounds of fairness, and raised two main arguments:

- Valuation. If there was a realistic possibility that the scheme companies' values exceeded the senior debt, it would be unfair to the mezzanine lenders if the Schemes allowed all of their assets to be stripped out for the benefit of the senior lenders.

- Directors' duties. The directors of the scheme companies had only taken account of the interests of the senior lenders, so had failed properly to exploit companies' negotiating positions in breach of their duties to the creditors as a whole.

The senior lenders relied upon a number of valuations. PricewaterhouseCoopers LLP had looked at: (a) the cashflow the group's business could be expected to generate; (b) comparable publicly traded companies and other transactions; and (c) the debt capacity of the group's business. Rothschilds had investigated whether a purchaser could be found. Finally, King Sturge LLP had valued a number of the group companies plus their sites.

The mezzanine lenders relied upon a valuation using a 'Monte Carlo simulation'. This was cashflow-based but involved repeated calculations, using random sampling of input assumptions then aggregating them to produce a distribution of probabilities.

The judge viewed the mezzanine lenders' valuation as essentially theoretical in its approach. He preferred the senior lenders' valuations, which he felt gave a better indication of what a real purchaser would pay for the group at that point in time. Whilst it may be possible to show unfairness if there was evidence that value would increase when economic conditions improved, there was insufficient evidence of this here. He also noted that the intercreditor agreement gave the mezzanine lenders the right, if they were dissatisfied with certain enforcement actions, to purchase the outstanding senior debt at par.

The judge also found no breach of directors' duties. On the basis of the senior lenders' valuations, there was no evidence that the mezzanine lenders had any economic interest. Furthermore, the mezzanine lenders were undertaking direct negotiations with the senior lenders, and had not requested that the board negotiate on their behalf.

10.6.3   The restructuring agreement

In a complex restructuring it is common to use a restructuring agreement signed by the key stakeholders to create a framework for the entire restructuring. This will typically stipulate when the various other documentation required to implement the restructuring becomes effective, and may itself implement various of the steps once other conditions precedent have been satisfied.

10.7   PARTICULAR TYPES OF RESTRUCTURING

10.7.1   The debt to equity swap

A debt to equity swap will involve shares being issued to creditors in return for the release of all or part of their debt. The main issues are likely to be:

- The amount of debt which should be converted. This will depend significantly on the amount of debt which the group will be able to continue to service going forward. The lender in whose tranche of debt the value breaks would normally expect to receive the largest share of any equity. Clearly, however, this lender is unlikely to agree to convert its own debt into equity unless most or all of the debt which ranks behind it is also converted.

- Into what the debt will be converted. As an alternative to shares, the lenders may be issued warrants or granted share options.

- The class of shares into which the debt should be converted. The lenders may be content to take non-voting preference shares which give them priority rights to a dividend. It is possible to provide for returns to the shareholders to increase as the group's fortunes improve. However, the shareholders are still likely to want the shares to carry certain blocking rights and other rights

Table 10.4 – Non-consensual restructuring processes

	Advantages	Disadvantages
Pre-packaged administration	<ul><li>Can circumvent creditors and shareholders who would receive nothing on a formal insolvency</li><li>A share transfer at holding company level avoids any disruption at an operating company level. Process can be completed before it becomes public</li><li>Relatively quick, certain outcome driven by creditors that have a real economic interest in the group</li><li>It is the administrator who bears the risk of challenge by any disenfranchised creditors</li></ul>	<ul><li>The additional fees of the administrator, the valuers and the administrator's other advisers can be substantial</li><li>Prior valuations are critical, and the most time-consuming step. The administrator might also require a marketing exercise</li><li>If guarantees and security cannot be released on a share sale, may also need an administration of operating subsidiaries as well, which is considerably more disruptive</li><li>Disenfranchised stakeholders recognise that pre-packaged administrations carry a degree of stigma, so may fight a retrospective PR campaign</li></ul>
Scheme of Arrangement	<ul><li>Binds all stakeholders in those classes which approve the Scheme, apathetic as well as recalcitrant minority stakeholders</li><li>Can be used in association with an asset transfer to circumvent classes of creditors and shareholders who would receive nothing on a formal insolvency (although those stakeholders could later challenge on value)</li><li>Needs only to involve those stakeholders whose rights are affected</li><li>Can bind secured as well as unsecured creditors</li><li>Outcome is certain once the final hearing has occurred</li></ul>	<ul><li>Multiple classes are likely to be involved and determining their composition can be complicated</li><li>Requires support of both 75% in value *and* a majority in number of *each class affected*</li><li>Court hearings and meetings make this a public process</li><li>Court hearings and meetings take time and lead to less certainty of outcome until the final court hearing has occurred</li><li>A Scheme may still be needed for every company which has given a guarantee to the creditors concerned</li></ul>
CVA	<ul><li>Can bind all unsecured creditors – no need to divide into separate classes</li><li>Likely to be cheaper than either a Scheme or a pre-pack</li><li>Onus is on creditors who have been unfairly prejudiced to bring a challenge</li></ul>	<ul><li>Cannot be used to bind secured (or preferential) creditors without their consent</li><li>Shareholders are also involved in the process</li><li>Meetings make this a public process, and need to involve all creditors even where their rights are not being affected</li></ul>

such as the right to appoint a board observer or director. The terms of any non-voting shares may also provide for their conversion to voting shares in the event that the group fails to perform as projected. In addition, lenders who have acquired distressed debt as part of a wider strategy may specifically be seeking voting shares.

- Which stakeholders should control the group following the debt to equity swap and how the equity is allocated between lenders which hold debt sitting in different tranches. The original controlling shareholders will wish to retain control if they still see long-term value in the group, but if the lenders are interested in taking voting shares, they are likely to resist this unless the shareholders are prepared to invest more capital of their own into the group.

Table 10.5 shows the debt to equity swap which might emerge where a group originally has £110m of bank debt, but the business plan has shown that the group can only continue to support £60m of bank debt.

Mechanistically, the debt will need to be owed by the company which is to issue the shares before it can be converted. In the example shown in Table 10.5, the debt is initially owed by Holdco 2. If Holdco 1 has given a guarantee, it may be possible for Holdco 1 to become the debtor by the relevant lenders calling on the guarantee, otherwise the debt will need to be novated to Holdco 1.

In practice, tax considerations may result in a more complicated swap.

10.7.2   Pre-packaged administration or receivership

10.7.2.1   Pre-packaged sale of shares

Where the only creditors to be affected by the restructuring are financial creditors of a holding company, as in the structure illustrated in Table 10.1, it is possible to achieve the restructuring by appointing an administrator or receiver to sell the shares in, rather than the assets of, the operating subsidiaries. This avoids the disadvantages described in Section 10.7.2.3. Indeed, the trade and other creditors of the operating subsidiaries need not be affected at all.

Table 10.6 shows how a pre-pack could be used to reduce a group's debt burden in a similar manner to that achieved by the debt to equity swap illustrated in Table 10.5, where a consensus has not been reached with the lower ranking stakeholders. Administration is the process used in this example. This route was used to complete the restructuring in the IMO Car Wash case discussed in Section 10.6.2.

Holdco 2 is placed into administration, and the administrator sells the shares of Target and its operational subsidiaries to a new company, 'Newco'. By way of consideration, Newco takes on the obligations to pay the senior debt in place of Holdco 2. The mezzanine lenders and any lower ranking creditors of Holdco 1 or Holdco 2 are left as creditors of assetless companies. Provided the amount of debt assumed by Newco comfortably exceeds the value of Target it will be difficult for this arrangement to be challenged – had a third party buyer paid Holdco 2 a cash sum equal to the value of the shares, this would have been paid to the senior lenders in any event as the holder of the first ranking fixed charge over the shares. The excess part of the debt assumed by Newco will then be converted into shares held by the senior lenders.

Table 10.5 – Debt to equity swap

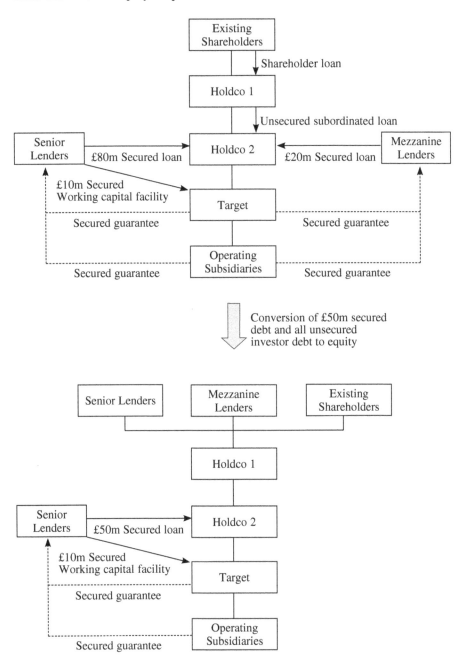

Table 10.6 – Pre-packaged administration sale

1. Newco purchases the shares of Target by assuming the £80m senior secured loan
2. £30m of the assumed debt is converted to equity in Newco

If the mezzanine lenders hold security over the shares of Target, and guarantees and security from Target and its operating subsidiaries, however, the pre-pack can only be implemented if there is a way of releasing these on the sale. As seen in Chapter 4, an administrator is able to sell assets free of any floating charge security, but not of fixed charge security without a court order. Moreover, he will have no statutory power to release the guarantees and security given by Target and its subsidiaries.

Nowadays, a well-drafted intercreditor agreement will often give the senior security holder or any administrator or receiver they appoint, the power to grant all of the necessary releases of security. It needs to allow the release of any debt owed (either as a principal borrower or as a guarantor) by any companies whose shares are being sold provided the proceeds of sale are applied in accordance with the intercreditor agreement. This was the case in the IMO Car Wash case, for example. However, the intercreditor agreement will need to be checked in each case. as older agreements may provide less assistance and drafting ambiguities may still exist. An example of this occurred in *HHY Luxembourg Sarl v Barclays Bank Plc* [2010] EWCA Civ 1248 (the 'European Directories case') where a literal reading of the document suggested that it did not allow some liabilities to the mezzanine lender to be released, although the Court of Appeal were eventually persuaded that the agreement should be read purposively.

10.7.2.2   Other considerations on a share sale

In practice, a pre-pack is still likely to require more than just a share sale, as the holding companies are likely to hold other assets and to perform groupwide functions. For example:

- Target and/or the operating companies may well owe intragroup debts to the holding companies. Unless the benefit of these debts is sold to Newco, or they are otherwise dealt with, they would remain assets of the holding companies which the administrator, or any subsequent liquidator of these holding companies would have to seek to recover from the debtor concerned. For this reason, an analysis, and possibly a rationalisation, of the group's internal debts is always an important part of the planning process;

- the holding companies may have given guarantees in respect of the operating companies' liabilities, for example to landlords of the operating companies' trading premises;

- groupwide insurance policies, for example directors' and officers' (or 'D&O') insurance, are often in the name of the holding companies; and

- whilst most group employees are likely to be employed by the operating subsidiaries, the senior employees will most likely be employed by the holding companies.

In addition, it will be necessary, for example, to review the group's key contacts to see whether a change of control of the group and/or the formal insolvency of one or more of the holding companies will allow the other party to the contract to terminate it.

10.7.2.3   Pre-packaged sale of a business

It may be necessary to place one of more of the operating subsidiaries into administration, and for the administrator to sell their businesses to Newco if:

- the intercreditor agreement fails to give the administrator the ability to release the guarantees or security given by the operating subsidiaries on a share sale; or

- the aim is to restructure some of the debts of the operating subsidiaries themselves, for example, their obligation to their landlords.

However, this route is less attractive than a share sale for a number of reasons:

- A prepack involving the formal insolvency of an operating subsidiary will require a more extensive public relations exercise, and this may be particularly difficult where the companies concerned operate in the financial, or another regulated, sector.

- The business sale will require various third parties, such as lessors, landlords and the counterparties to those companies' other contracts to agree to the transfer of those subsidiaries' rights and obligations to the buyer.

- The directors of the operating subsidiaries may regard a pre-pack of a trading company as less appealing, since they will need to be more conscious of protecting creditors' positions in the period prior to the formal insolvency.

10.8   PENSIONS ISSUES

10.8.1   Why are pensions a particular issue?

The position of a pension scheme on a formal insolvency was discussed in Chapter 9.

TPR is likely to play a role in any restructuring where there is a defined benefit pension scheme which has a deficit when calculated on the full buy-out basis. The aims of TPR include protecting the benefits of pension scheme members and reducing the risk of situations arising that may lead to compensation being payable from the Pension Protection Fund ('**PPF**').

To help TPR achieve its aims, it has been given the power to make third parties liable for the pensions deficit in certain circumstances through financial support directions ('**FSDs**') and contribution notices. These are intended to prevent stakeholders abusing the PPF by structuring a group, or carrying out a transaction, in a way which leaves the pensions liability with an underfunded company whilst funds exist elsewhere. They are therefore often referred to as the 'moral hazard' provisions and are described further in Section 10.8.2.

Employers and trustees are also required to inform TPR of any 'notifiable event' in relation to a pension scheme. This is designed to give TPR advance warning of difficulties which exist to allow it to assist or intervene before a claim for compensation from the PPF becomes necessary. Table 10.7 sets out those events which are notifiable if they occur in relation to the employer (as amended with effect from 6 April 2009).

Table 10.7 – Notifiable events in relation to an employer

(a)   any decision by the employer to take action which will, or is intended to, result in a debt which is or may become due to the scheme not being paid in full;

(b)   a decision by the employer to cease to carry on business in the UK;

(c) receipt by the employer of advice that it is trading wrongfully within the meaning of s 214 IA 1986, or circumstances being reached in which a director or former director of the company knows that there is no reasonable prospect that the company will avoid going into insolvent liquidation;

(d) any breach by the employer of a covenant in an agreement between the employer and a bank or other institution providing banking services, other than where the bank or other institution agrees with the employer not to enforce the covenant;

(e) where the employer is a company, a decision by a controlling company to relinquish control of the employer company;

(f) the conviction of an individual for an offence involving dishonesty if the offence was committed while the individual was a director or partner of the employer.

10.8.2 The moral hazard provisions

10.8.2.1 What is a financial support direction?

Under s 43 Pensions Act 2004, TPR may, if it considers it **reasonable** to do so, direct a person who is associated with or connected to an 'employer' to put financial support in place to meet the employer's pension liabilities.

This can apply where the employer is, or was in the 24-month period prior to TPR first issuing a 'warning notice' that it proposed to issue a financial support direction (or 'FSD'):

- a **service company** (ie its turnover is solely or principally derived from amounts charged for providing employees to other members of the group); or

- **insufficiently resourced** (ie the value of its resources is less than 50% of the estimated scheme deficit, calculated on the full buy-out basis and other members of the group have together sufficient resources to make up the shortfall).

The terms 'associated' or 'connected' bear the meaning given to them by IA 1986, as discussed in Chapter 5. References to 'group' here are references to entities that are associated or connected with the employer.

10.8.2.2 What is a contribution notice?

Under s 38 Pensions Act 2004, TPR may also, if it considers it **reasonable** to do so, require an associated or connected person to contribute all or part of the pension scheme deficit.

This can apply if the person in question was a party to **an act or deliberate failure to act**:

- which (in TPR's opinion) was **materially detrimental** to the likelihood of members' benefits being paid, regardless of whether or not this was its intended purpose (although a statutory defence will be available if the party can show that he gave reasonable consideration to any potential detrimental impact and acted appropriately before the detrimental act or failure to act); or

- one of the **main purposes** of which was (in TPR's opinion) to prevent the recovery of all or part of the deficit or to prevent such a debt becoming due, to compromise or otherwise settle such a debt, or to reduce the amount of a debt which would otherwise have become due.

(TPR has published a Code of Practice setting out the circumstances in which it would consider issuing a contribution notice under the 'material detriment' test).

TPR is entitled to look back at acts or failures which occurred at any time in the **six-year period** prior to TPR issuing the warning notice that it proposed to issue a contribution notice. As well as looking at individual acts or failures, it is entitled to look at the cumulative effect of a series of acts or failures provided that each of these occurred during this period.

TPR's power to issue a contribution notice will apply even where the pension liabilities have been transferred to another pension scheme and the persons to be made liable are associated or connected only with the employers sponsoring the original scheme and not the new scheme.

Finally, a contribution notice may also be issued where a person has failed to comply with a financial support direction (s 47 Pensions Act 2004).

10.8.2.3   When is it reasonable for TPR to act in this way?

There are certain matters which TPR must consider when deciding whether it would be reasonable to issue an FSD or contribution notice.

In the case of an FSD, these include the person's **financial resources**, any connection or involvement they had or have with the **pension scheme**, the relationship they have or had with the employer, including whether they have '**control**' and the **value of any benefits** received directly or indirectly by the other person from the employer (ss 43(5)(b) and 43(7) of the Pensions Act 2004).

In the case of a contribution notice, TPR must have regard both to the extent to which, in all the circumstances of the case, it was reasonable for the person to act, or fail to act, in the way they did **and** such other matters as TPR considers relevant, but including (where relevant):

- the matters already listed above for an FSD; and
- that other person's **degree of involvement** and the **purposes** of the act or failure to act (including whether the purpose was to prevent or limit loss of employment), whether the act or failure to act involved a notifiable event (see Table 10.7) that was not notified and the likelihood of other creditors being paid.

(Sections 38(3)(d) and 38(7) Pensions Act 2004.)

10.8.2.4   When have FSDs and contribution notices been used in practice?

In 2008, TPR issued its first ever FSD to Sea Containers Limited ('SCL'), the Bermudan parent of an English service company. The latter was the principal employer of two final salary pension schemes with significant deficits. In assessing the benefits received by SCL here, it was noted that not only had SCL received services from the employer for which it did not have to pay within normal commercial timescales, but it could also maintain a European trading presence through the employer while itself enjoying a favourable tax regime in Bermuda. The fact that SCL had just entered into formal insolvency in the USA did not prevent the FSD being made.

In 2010, TPR issued its first ever contribution notice to Michel Van De Wiele N.V., the Belgian parent company of the Bonas textile machinery business. The group had been restructured via a pre-packaged insolvency process, leaving the group's liabilities to its UK pension scheme behind. The parent was ordered to pay £5 million to restore the scheme to solvency. On appeal, however, it was held that this order was excessive and that the amount sought through the contribution notice should simply seek to compensate the pension scheme for the detriment caused by the parent's actions. The loss to the pension scheme from the pre-pack was limited to any undervalue in the price paid. The court left this to be determined, but in June 2011 TPR reached a compromise with the parent and re-issued it with a contribution notice for £60,000.

In 2010, TPR also issued FSDs against a number of companies in the Lehman Brothers group, and separately against a number of companies in the Nortel group. Various of these companies were already in administration in England at the time the notice was issued. As noted in Section 2.4.3.2, the Court of Appeal concluded that the liability under the FSDs was an administration expense (*Re: Nortel GmbH (in administration)* (heard together with *Re: Lehman Brothers International (Europe) (in administration)* [2011] EWCA Civ 1124). The fact that TPR could, if it so chose, delay the issue of an FSD and thus improve its ranking in the insolvency process has caused no little debate. TPR issued a statement entitled 'Financial support directions and insolvency' (Ref PN12–25) on 26 July 2012 which was designed to provide reassurance, although the statement does also make it clear that it is not to be read as limiting TPR's discretion in any particular case to take such action as is appropriate.

10.8.3   The clearance procedure

10.8.3.1   What is 'clearance'?

Clearly, there will be various associated or connected persons who are at least potentially at risk of receiving an FSD or a contribution notice. These might include other group companies or shareholders (including potentially lenders who have converted their debt to voting shares in a debt to equity swap). To limit uncertainty, there is a formal procedure whereby parties involved in a restructuring can apply to TPR for confirmation that it will not impose a liability on them in this way. This confirmation is known as a clearance statement and made pursuant to ss 42 and 46 Pensions Act 2004.

TPR encourages groups to apply whenever a transaction is detrimental to the pension scheme either because it will reduce the employer's ability to fund the scheme or because it will reduce the pension scheme's recoveries on insolvency. TPR expects applicants to 'mitigate' any detriment as a condition of any clearance statement.

TPR's expectation is that the group and the trustees will negotiate terms between them, and the application for clearance will present the jointly agreed terms to TPR. In this process, TPR expects the trustees to behave as would any other unsecured creditor in their position. Because of the requirements for 'mitigation' and for agreement with the trustees, the application may become time-consuming and costly, and this will be a factor in deciding whether to make an application in some cases.

The group should make full disclosure to TPR of all relevant matters. A clearance can later be set aside if the circumstances described in the application are not the same as those which actually occur and the difference is material to TPR's ability to exercise its powers.

10.8.3.2   When should clearance be sought?

TPR has issued guidance indicating when it would expect a clearance application to be made (see http://www.thepensionsregulator.gov.uk/guidance/clearance/introduction.aspx). Essentially, the employer and persons associated or connected with it need to apply where they consider that an event will occur which would be materially detrimental to the pension scheme's ability to provide members' benefits (known as 'Type-A events'). The guidance divides such events into employer-related and scheme-related events.

Employer-related events are events which occur in relation to the employer or the group generally which could weaken the employer's ability to meet its obligations to the scheme. Events which TPR has identified as falling into this category include:

• granting or extending of new security over group assets;

• paying dividends or returning capital to shareholders;

• a change in group structure, including a change of control; or

• a 'phoenix event', ie an event resulting in the employer re-emerging as substantially the same entity following an insolvency event.

Scheme-related events are events which affect the scheme directly, such as a compromise of the employer's debt to the scheme. Whilst employer-related events normally only require clearance when the scheme is in deficit on one of a number of bases, scheme-related events always require clearance.

10.8.4   Compromising a pension scheme deficit as part of a restructuring

10.8.4.1   Who will be involved in any discussions?

The trustees have the ability to compromise the section 75 debt with the employer prior to any formal insolvency. However, they would not normally agree to any arrangement which places the scheme members in a worse position than they would be in on a formal insolvency. Any such compromise must now follow one of the statutory processes set out in the Occupational Pension Schemes (Employer Debt) Regulations 2005 (the 'Employer Debt Regulations'). The trustees will also be conscious that, if not entered into at the right time or in accordance with the relevant statutory processes, any compromise they reach could render the scheme ineligible for the PPF should the employer later enter into formal insolvency.

The PPF however is concerned to ensure that it receives fair treatment in any insolvency process and that schemes are not transferred to the PPF with less than the expected dividend in respect of the section 75 debt. The PPF has called upon

TPR to use its moral hazard powers to ensure there is no abuse. Therefore, where a section 75 debt is to be compromised as part of a restructuring, each of the trustees, the PPF and TPR will be involved in any negotiation process. The group will need to demonstrate that the employer could no longer survive if it had to continue to meet its existing pension liabilities and that the compromise will lead to a better recovery for the PPF than the likely alternative, bearing in mind, among other things, that in granting clearance TPR will be giving up the opportunity to recover monies for the PPF from third parties by issuing an FSD or contribution notice in relation to the compromise.

The PPF will aim to ensure that it gains an appropriate share in any upside from the restructured business. Its standard practice is to seek a non-voting shareholding in the amount of one-third if the existing stakeholders are to remain owners following the restructuring, or one-tenth if the business is transferred to an unconnected party. To support the PPF, TPR will generally not give clearance on a restructuring that results in the pension scheme transferring to the PPF unless the PPF is satisfied with the arrangement.

10.8.4.2   Which entity will enter into formal insolvency?

One option is for the employer's business to be sold to a new company through a pre-packaged administration. This will involve a planned formal insolvency of the scheme's principal employer to transfer the pension scheme to the PPF. The PPF would then take its non-voting shareholding in the new company and would receive a dividend in respect of the section 75 debt from the formal insolvency of the employer.

Where the existing employer is a trading company, a sale of its business through pre-packaged insolvency may still prove disruptive. However, a route to avoid this was approved by the court in *L v M Ltd* [2006] EWHC 3395 (Ch). A new company was formed to convert the pension scheme in question into a multi-employer scheme, and took on a couple of employees for this purpose. The scheme rules were amended to provide that, on a winding-up of the scheme, the trading company would bear only £1 of the section 75 debt and the new company the balance. Once the scheme was wound up, the trading company paid the £1 debt and ceased to be an employer for the purposes of the scheme. The new company was unable to pay the balance of the section 75 debt, but on its inevitable insolvency, the pension scheme was able to transfer to the PPF. It is understood that the PPF took a shareholding in the surviving trading company.

The process has since become a recognised structure. However, for the scheme to be eligible for PPF transfer, the modifications required to apportion the trading company's employer debt to the new company would now need to be carried out in accordance with one of the statutory processes set out in the Employer Debt Regulations. (The relevant process here is most likely to be a 'regulated apportionment arrangement' as PPF involvement is likely within the next 12 months, as per reg 7A of the Employer Debt Regulations).

Chapter 11

Cross-border issues

11.1 INTRODUCTION

The chapter deals with the legal considerations which may be relevant in England where there is an international element to the insolvency of a company or a group of companies. This may be because one or more companies in the group are registered in other jurisdictions, or because business is carried on overseas.

Three main legislative provisions are considered in this chapter:

- the EC Insolvency Regulation;
- the Cross-Border Insolvency Regulations 2006; and
- s 426 IA 1986.

None of these provisions seeks to change the rules governing the different insolvency processes already described in this book. Instead, they deal essentially with the use and recognition of English insolvency processes in other jurisdictions, and of foreign insolvency processes in England.

Even where none of these legislative provisions applies, however, the English courts have on occasions held that English common law will apply, allowing them to assist in relation to foreign insolvency proceedings, and this is also therefore considered in this chapter.

Finally, this chapter will specifically consider the circumstances in which the formal processes described in this book might be applicable to foreign companies.

11.2 THE EC INSOLVENCY REGULATION

11.2.1 What is the EC Insolvency Regulation?

The EC Insolvency Regulation is directly applicable in all EU Member States except Denmark. The EC Insolvency Regulation makes no distinction between England and Wales, Scotland and Northern Ireland, notwithstanding that these are different legal jurisdictions. So far as the EC Insolvency Regulation is concerned, it is the UK as a whole which is the relevant Member State.

In addition to its main operative provisions, or 'Articles', the EC Insolvency Regulation starts with a lengthy preamble containing various recitals. The courts may refer to these recitals as a guide to interpretation where the relevant Article is unclear or imprecise.

The EC Insolvency Regulation applies to **collective insolvency proceedings** which involve **the partial or total divestment** of the company and the appointment of a **liquidator** (Art 1(1) of the Regulation). It **does not apply** to insolvency proceedings concerning insurance undertakings, creditor institutions, investment undertakings which provide services involving the holding of funds or securities for third parties, or to 'collective investment undertakings'.

The EC Insolvency Regulation does not seek to harmonise the different insolvency laws of the various Member States. It does, however, set out rules which:

- govern when such proceedings can be opened in any Member State;

- require that proceedings which have properly been opened are recognised by the courts of other Member States; and

- determine which Member State's laws will apply once proceedings have been opened.

11.2.2 What are 'main' insolvency proceedings?

The courts of the Member State in which the company's centre of main interests, or 'COMI' is situated have jurisdiction to open main insolvency proceedings (Art 3 of the EC Insolvency Regulation). Main insolvency proceedings have universal scope and aim at encompassing all the company's assets (recital (12) to the EC Insolvency Regulation). The meaning of COMI is discussed further in Section 11.2.3.

A list of those formal insolvency processes which will qualify as main insolvency proceedings in each Member State are set out in Annex A to the EC Insolvency Regulation. In turn, those persons and bodies who will qualify as liquidators are listed at Annex C. So far as the UK is concerned:

- compulsory liquidation, creditors' voluntary liquidation, administration and CVAs are capable of being main insolvency proceedings; and

- liquidators, provisional liquidators, the Official Receiver, administrators and supervisors of CVAs are all capable of being 'liquidators'.

Any judgment opening main insolvency proceedings handed down by a court of a Member State which has jurisdiction must be recognised in all other Member States from the time that it becomes effective in that first state (Art 16(1) of the EC Insolvency Regulation). This judgment is deemed, without any further formalities, to produce the same effects in any other Member State as it does under the law of that first Member State (Art 17(1) of the EC Insolvency Regulation). The meaning of both 'judgment' and 'court' are construed fairly widely here – a court includes a person or body empowered by national law to open insolvency proceedings (recital (10) to the EC Insolvency Regulation). Thus all of the following may be regarded as judgments opening proceedings:

- The shareholders' resolution commencing a creditors' voluntary liquidation. A liquidator might subsequently apply for a court order confirming his appointment to ensure that the liquidation will be recognised in other Member States (r 7.62 IR 1986). Such an application was granted in *Re TXU Europe German Finance BV* [2005] BCC 90.

- The filing of a notice of appointment in an 'out-of-court' appointment of an administrator. Best practice remains, however, to appoint the administrator by application to the court if it is necessary to ensure that the administration will be recognised in other Member States or when appointing over a foreign registered entity whose COMI is in the United Kingdom. (*Re Kaupthing*

Capital Partners II Master LP Inc [2010] EWHC 836 (Ch) is often cited as an illustration of the disadvantages of making an out of court appointment in the latter situation.)

- The creditors' meeting approving a CVA (see *Re The Salvage Association* [2003] BCC 504).

The phrase 'the time of the opening of proceedings' means the time at which the judgment opening proceedings becomes effective, whether it is a final judgment or not (Art 2(e) and (f) of the EC Insolvency Regulation). Where there is more that one potential candidate as to where a company's COMI may be, the applicant which is able to open proceedings first may still gain a tactical advantage over rival applicants who favour another Member State, as the rival applicant will then need to challenge the opening of proceedings in the courts of the Member State where they were first opened (see *Re Eurofood IFSC Ltd* (C-341/04), discussed in Section 11.2.3.2). This is sometimes referred to as the 'race to the court door'.

Because in England a compulsory liquidation is deemed to commence when the petition is presented, this raises the question of whether proceedings are opened at that point. However, there must be doubt in this regard, as the presentation of a winding-up petition does not in itself divest the company of its assets. In the *Eurofood* case the European Court of Justice left his question open, but held that the appointment of a provisional liquidator did constitute the opening of proceedings, because this was one of the types of 'liquidator' listed in Annex C.

A Member State may, however, refuse to recognise insolvency proceedings opened in another Member State or to enforce a judgment handed down in the context of such proceedings where the effects of such recognition or enforcement would be manifestly contrary to that state's public policy, in particular to its fundamental principles or the constitutional rights and liberties of the individual (the '**public policy exemption**') (Art 26 of the EC Insolvency Regulation, and see the *Eurofood* case).

11.2.3   Where will a company's COMI be?

11.2.3.1   How is COMI ascertained?

The EC Insolvency Regulation does not define a company's COMI. Article 3 of the EC Insolvency Regulation states simply that the place of a company's registered office shall be presumed to be its COMI in the absence of proof to the contrary (the '**registered office presumption**'). Recital (13) to the EC Insolvency Regulation adds, however, that the COMI should correspond to the place where the company conducts the administration of its interests on a regular basis and is therefore ascertainable by third parties. It is possible, therefore, to rebut the registered office presumption if this place is in a different Member State from the registered office.

11.2.3.2   When is it possible to rebut the registered office presumption?

Interested parties may differ as to where they think a subsidiary's COMI is located. For example, the parent might argue that the subsidiary's interests are administered in the parent's Member State if this is where decisions are taken for the group as a whole, but a creditor might argue that it has always understood the subsidiary's COMI to be where its registered office is located.

This was essentially the situation in the *Eurofood* case. The distinction was important because the creditor wished to commence local recovery proceedings whereas the extraordinary administrator of the parent wished to include the subsidiary within a group-wide restructuring procedure. The Irish courts upheld the registered office presumption (as reported at [2004] BCC 383). The case was referred to the European Court of Justice, or 'ECJ' which took a similar view (reported at [2006] Ch 508). The full facts are set out in the box below.

The ECJ made it clear that:

- Where the registered offices of a parent company and its subsidiary are in two different Member States, the registered office presumption could only be rebutted if factors which were both objective and ascertainable by third parties enabled it to be established that the actual situation differed from the presumed position.

- That could be the case where the subsidiary carried out no business in the Member State in which its registered office was situated, ie it was merely a 'letter-box' company.

- However, where the subsidiary did carry on its business in the territory of the Member State of its registered office, the mere fact that its economic choices are, or can be, controlled by a parent company in another Member State was not enough to rebut the presumption.

The ECJ gave no further guidance in *Eurofood* as to what other factors might be relevant in rebutting the presumption.

The ECJ did, however, consider this question further in another case, *Interedil Srl (in liquidation) v Fallimento Interedil Srl* (Case C-396/09) (reported at [2012] Bus. L.R. 1582). Here, it emphasised the need to attach greater importance to the place of the company's central administration. However, this must still be established by objective factors which are ascertainable by third parties. This requirement may be considered to be met where the material factors have been made public, or at the very least, made sufficiently accessible to enable third parties, in particular the company's creditors, to be aware of them.

The ECJ then gave the following additional guidance:

- Factors to be taken into account when analysing whether the registered office presumption has been rebutted include, in particular, all places in which the debtor company pursues economic activities and all those in which it holds assets, insofar as those places are ascertainable by third parties. Such factors must be assessed in a comprehensive manner, taking into account the individual circumstances of each particular case.

- Where a company's place of central administration is in the same jurisdiction as its registered office, the registered office presumption cannot be rebutted.

- Where a company's place of central administration is not in the same place as its registered office, the presence of assets belonging to the debtor and the existence of contracts for financial exploitation of those assets in a Member State other than that in which the registered office is situated cannot be regarded as sufficient factors to rebut the registered office presumption, unless a comprehensive assessment of all the relevant factors makes it possible to establish, in a manner that is ascertainable by third parties, that the company's central administration is located in that other Member State.

In a third case, *Rastelli Davide e C. Snc v Jean-Charles Hidoux, as liquidator of Médiasucre International* (C-191/10), the ECJ held that where two companies have their registered offices in separate Member States, the mere finding that the two companies' property had been intermixed is not enough to rebut the registered office presumption.

The European Commission has made proposals to amend the EC Insolvency Regulation (see Section 11.2.7). These include a formal definition of COMI which would elaborate further on those objective factors which might be taken into account when ascertaining it. It is possible that even before this proposed legislation comes into force the courts will begin to have some regard to these.

11.2.3.3   Companies registered outside the EU

The EC Insolvency Regulation allows main insolvency proceedings to be opened in respect of a company even if its registered office is outside the EU provided its COMI is in a Member State. In *BRAC Rent-a-Car Inc* [2003] 2 All ER 201, the English court made an administration order in respect of a Delaware-registered company which carried out most of its business in the UK under contracts governed by English law and employed most of its employees in the UK.

A court faced with an application to place such a company into an English insolvency procedure would, however, now need to have regard to all of the factors outlined in Section 11.2.3.2 in determining that company's COMI.

11.2.3.4   Groups of companies

The EC Insolvency Regulation was drafted with the intention that it apply on a company-by-company, not on a group basis. Groups of companies with subsidiaries in a number of different Member States therefore pose a potential difficulty here. A series of parallel insolvency procedures governed by the laws of a single jurisdiction is likely to be both legally and administratively more convenient than a series of parallel insolvency procedures governed by the laws of separate jurisdictions. Nonetheless, an applicant wishing to take this approach will need to rebut the registered office presumption in respect of at least some of the companies in the group in order to achieve this result.

In the early days of the EC Insolvency Regulation, the English courts had often taken the view that the registered office presumption was not a particularly strong presumption. They were prepared to accept that it could be rebutted where the head office functions of the group were performed in a Member State other than that in which the registered office was situated, or where the directors of the company lived and took their decisions in a different Member State. However, the Court of Appeal has since emphasised that, in the light of *Eurofood* this test placed too little emphasis on objective factors ascertainable to third parties (*Stanford International Bank Ltd (In Receivership)* [2010] EWCA Civ 137). A court faced with applications to place various members of a multi-jurisdictional group into a series of parallel English insolvency proceedings would now need to have regard to all of the factors outlined in Section 11.2.3.2.

The proposals for reform of the European legislation relating to insolvency proceedings discussed in Section 11.2.6 include proposals relating to groups.

The *Eurofood* case

Eurofood IFSC Ltd ('Eurofood') was an Irish-registered subsidiary of an Italian parent, Parmalat SpA. Eurofood was also tax resident and regulated in Ireland. It had two Italian executive directors and two Irish non-executive directors. It existed primarily to provide financing facilities for other companies in the Parmalat group, and among other things it had entered into a swaps transaction with Bank of America ('BoA').

In December 2003, Parmalat Spa was admitted to extraordinary administration proceedings in Italy and Signor Enrico Bondi was appointed its extraordinary administrator. In January 2004, BoA presented a winding-up petition against Eurofood in Ireland and obtained the appointment of a provisional liquidator. The provisional liquidator duly notified Signor Bondi of his appointment. Notwithstanding this, in February 2004 an Italian court purported to place Eurofood into extraordinary administration in Italy.

The winding-up petition was then duly heard by the Irish High Court. The Irish court was satisfied that Eurofood's COMI was in Ireland as that was where BoA and its other finance creditors had ascertained it to be. It held that main insolvency proceedings had already been opened in Ireland by the time of the Italian judgment, so it did not need to consider the merits of that judgment. It also refused to recognise the Italian judgment on the basis of the public policy exemption, as BoA has been given no opportunity to be heard. Signor Bondi appealed, and the Irish Supreme Court referred various questions to the ECJ.

The ECJ stated that:

- Where the registered offices of a parent company and its subsidiary are in two different Member States, the registered office presumption could only be rebutted if factors which were both objective and ascertainable by third parties enabled it to be established that the actual situation differed from the presumed position. That could be the case where the subsidiary carried out no business in the Member State in which its registered office was situated. However, where the subsidiary did carry on its business in the territory of the Member State of its registered office, the mere fact that its economic choices are or can be controlled by a parent company in another Member State was not enough to rebut the presumption.

- The court of a Member State hearing an application for the opening of main insolvency proceedings should check that it has jurisdiction. However, once main insolvency proceedings have been opened in one Member State, a party which took the view that the company's COMI was situated in a different Member State must challenge the decision to open main insolvency proceedings before the courts of the Member State in which proceedings had been opened.

- Main insolvency proceedings had been opened when the Irish provisional liquidator had been appointed. An Irish provisional liquidator was one of the types of liquidator referred to in Annex C to the EC Insolvency Regulation and when appointing him the Irish court had ordered that the company be divested. In light of this, the ECJ considered that it had no need to determine whether the presentation of the winding-up petition in itself constituted the opening of insolvency proceedings.

- A Member State may refuse to recognise insolvency proceedings opened in another Member State where the decision to open the proceedings was taken in flagrant breach of the fundamental right to be heard which a person concerned by such proceedings enjoys.

11.2.3.5   Can a company's COMI change?

A debtor's COMI may change during its lifetime. The ECJ has held that it is the court of the Member State where the debtor's COMI is situated at the time the debtor lodges the request to open insolvency proceedings which has jurisdiction to open those proceedings, even if the debtor moves its COMI to another Member State after lodging the request but before the proceedings are opened (*Re Staubitz-Schreiber* (C-1/04), reported at [2006] BCC 639).

A company may therefore deliberately move its COMI to a different Member State in order to take advantage of what it perceives to be a more favourable insolvency regime. Thus, for example, during the period from late 2006, a German holding company, Schefenacker AG, effectively migrated its COMI to the UK to take advantage of the CVA procedure in order to cram down a minority of its bondholders. No similar procedure was available in Germany. (The full migration process involved an English-registered company, Schefenacker plc assuming all of Schefenacker AG's assets and liabilities via a German law process known as 'universal succession'.)

In *Re Hellas Telecommunications (Luxembourg) II SCA* [2009] EWHC 3199 (Ch), a financing and holding company wished to migrate its COMI to the UK to take advantage of the administration procedure in order to carry out a pre-pack should restructuring negotiations with creditors fail. In seeking to achieve this:

- its head office and principal operating address were moved to London;

- its creditors were given contemporaneous notice of its change of address and an announcement was made by way of a press release that its activities were shifting to England;

- it opened a bank account in London and all significant payments were then made into and from that bank account, although it retained a bank account in Luxembourg to deal with minor miscellaneous payments;

- it registered under the Companies Act in this country, although its registered office remained in Luxembourg; and

- all negotiations between it and its creditors took place in London.

In making the administration order sought, the court regarded this last step as particularly important, given the need for creditors in particular to know where the company was and where they may deal with the company.

The case of *Hans Brochier Holdings Limited v Exner* [2007] BCC 127, however, provides an example of a migration which was held not to have moved the relevant entity's COMI. The assets and liabilities of a German company had again been transferred to an English company, Hans Brochier Holdings Limited, by universal succession. The English company subsequently encountered difficulties, and its directors appointed English administrators. However, when further information came to light the administrators themselves applied for a declaration that the COMI was in Germany. Applying the *Eurofood* decision, the English court held that this was the only possible conclusion it could reach on the basis of the objective and ascertainable facts. Among other things, the vast majority of the company's employees worked in Germany, its entire business operation was run from Germany, and most of its banking continued to operate through German bank accounts. This suggests that it is more difficult to migrate the COMI of a trading company than it is to migrate the COMI of a holding company.

11.2.4   What are secondary and territorial proceedings?

Recital (12) of the EC Insolvency Regulation recognises that proceedings may need to be opened in another Member State in parallel with main insolvency proceedings in order to protect the 'diversity of interests'. However, the courts of a Member State other than that in which the company's COMI is situated will only have jurisdiction to open such parallel insolvency proceedings if the company possesses an **establishment** within the territory of that other Member State. The effect of these parallel insolvency proceedings will be restricted to the assets of the company situated in the territory of the second Member State (Art 3(2) of the EC Insolvency Regulation).

An establishment means 'a place of operations where the company carries out a non-transitory economic activity with human means and goods'. In the *Interedil* case, the ECJ made it clear that an establishment requires the presence of a structure consisting of a minimum level of organisation and a degree of stability necessary for the purpose of pursuing an economic activity. The presence of goods in isolation or bank accounts would not, in principle, meet the definition. The existence of an establishment must be determined in the same manner as a company's COMI, ie on the basis of objective factors which are ascertainable by third parties.

In *Re Office Metro Limited* [2012] EWHC 1191 (Ch), it was held that a company which had transferred its main headquarters and place of administration to Luxembourg and retained only an English registered office from which another group company continued to deal on its behalf with demands under certain guarantees had no establishment in the United Kingdom. In contrast, in *Re Olympic Airlines SA* [2012] EWHC 1413 (Ch), the court determined that an office from which two contractors were winding down a company's affairs was an establishment. (The reasoning in these two cases is not entirely consistent and at the time of writing the decision in *Olympic* is being appealed.)

Once main insolvency proceedings have been opened, any parallel insolvency proceedings elsewhere are termed **secondary proceedings**, and are limited to **winding-up proceedings** (Art 3(3) of the EC Insolvency Regulation). A list of those formal insolvency proceedings which will qualify as winding-up proceedings in each Member State are set out in Annex B to the EC Insolvency Regulation. So far as the UK is concerned, compulsory liquidation, creditors' voluntary liquidation, and 'winding up through administration' are capable of being winding-up proceedings.

Insolvency proceedings cannot normally be opened elsewhere prior to the opening of main insolvency proceedings. However, an exception will apply if either:

- main insolvency proceedings cannot be opened because of conditions laid down in the Member State where the company's COMI is located; or

- the opening of insolvency proceedings in the second Member State is requested by a creditor who has his domicile, habitual residence or registered office in the second Member State, or whose claim arises from the operation of the company's establishment in that Member State.

Any proceedings opened elsewhere prior to main proceedings will be termed **territorial proceedings**.

Where main insolvency proceedings have been opened in the UK for companies across a group, employees based in other Member States have sometimes sought to open secondary proceedings (or even to attempt to argue that they are entitled to open main proceedings in their own Member State in place of those in the UK) in order to secure themselves more favourable rights. A practice has therefore now emerged in trading English administrations where administrators will seek early orders from the English court to allow them to treat overseas employees in the same way as they would be treated under insolvency proceedings opened in their own jurisdiction (see *Re MG Rover Espana* [2006] BCC 599 and *Re Collins & Aikman Europe SA* [2006] BCC 861, as already discussed in Chapter 4).

11.2.5   What law applies to the insolvency proceedings?

11.2.5.1   The general rule

As a general rule, it will be the law of the Member State where the proceedings are opened which determines the conditions for their opening, their conduct and their effect (Art 4 of the EC Insolvency Regulation). Thus this Member State's law will determine, among other things:

- the powers of the liquidator;

- the effect of insolvency proceedings on contracts to which the company is party;

- the claims which can be lodged against the company and the rules for lodging, verifying and admitting those claims;

- the manner in which proceeds from the distribution of assets are to be distributed and the ranking of claims;

- the conditions for and the effect of the closure of the insolvency proceedings; and

- the rules as to when transactions by the company which are detrimental to creditors are voidable or unenforceable. (However, a party who benefited from such a transaction does have a defence if they can prove that it was subject to the law of a different Member State and that that law does not allow any means of challenging the transaction in question – Art 13 of the Regulation.)

11.2.5.2 Exceptions to the general rule

The EC Insolvency Regulation does, however, make special provision in relation to certain rights of other parties. Thus the opening of insolvency proceedings does not affect:

- creditors' or other third parties' **rights *in rem*** in respect of tangible or intangible, moveable or immovable assets belonging to the company – both specific assets and collections of indefinite assets as a whole which change from time to time. Such rights include, in particular, a creditor's rights under any security it may hold over those assets (Art 5 of the EC Insolvency Regulation);

- a creditor's right to demand the **set off** of his claims against the company's claims where such a set-off is permitted by the law which applies to the insolvent company's claim (Art 6 of the EC Insolvency Regulation); or

- a seller's rights based on a **retention of title** where, at the time of the opening of proceedings, the assets in question are situated within the territory of another Member State (Art 7 of the EC Insolvency Regulation).

None of the above exceptions prevents proceedings being brought to set aside a transaction under the laws of the Member State where proceedings were opened.

In addition, special rules apply to certain types of contract. Thus, among other things:

- the effect of insolvency proceedings on contracts conferring the right to acquire or make use of **immoveable property** will be governed solely by the law of the Member State where that property is situated (Art 8 of the EC Insolvency Regulation); and

- the effect of insolvency proceedings on employment contracts and relationships will be governed solely by the law of the Member State applicable to that contract of employment (Art 10 of the EC Insolvency Regulation).

11.2.6 Where must any civil proceedings be brought?

In addition to considering which law will apply, the courts have on various occasions also had to determine the nature of the proceedings concerned in order to decide which Member State's courts had jurisdiction.

Council Regulation (EC) No 44/2001 of 22 December 2000 (the '**EC Judgments Regulation**') deals with the recognition of civil proceedings and the enforcement of judgments issued in those proceedings. A central principle of the EC Judgments Regulation is that proceedings should be brought against a defendant in his home court.

However, the EC Judgments Regulation does not apply to bankruptcy, proceedings relating to the winding-up of insolvent companies (or other legal persons), judicial arrangements, compositions and analogous proceedings (Art 1(2) of the EC Insolvency Regulation). These are intended to fall within the scope of the EC Insolvency Regulation, and to be dealt with by the court of the Member State where 'main proceedings' were opened.

In *Gourdain v Nadler* (C-133/78) (reported at [1979] ECR 733), the ECJ held that proceedings related to the winding-up of an insolvent company if:

- the proceedings derived directly from the insolvency proceedings; **and**

- there was a close connection between the proceedings and the insolvency proceedings.

Defendants to proceedings will sometimes be able to convince the court that those proceedings do not relate to the winding-up. For example:

- an action by a liquidator to set aside a payment made on the day before the insolvency, could be dealt with by the courts of the Member State where 'main proceedings' had been opened (*Seagon v Deko Marty Belgium NV* (C-339/07) (reported at [2009] 1 WLR 2168)); but

- a claim under a retention of title agreement must be brought in the defendant's home court, as there was no link to the insolvency proceedings other than the fact that the claim had been brought by the liquidator (*German Graphics Graphische Maschinen GmbH v Alice van der Schee* (C-292/08) (reported at [2009] All ER (D) 75)).

11.2.7 Proposals for amendment

On 12 December 2012 the European Commission published the final version of its proposed amendments to the EC Insolvency Regulation. It summarised these into five broad categories:

- Widening the definition of 'insolvency proceedings' to include mechanisms for restructuring the debts of distressed companies which take effect before a company becomes formally insolvent.

- Clarifying the jurisdiction for opening insolvency proceedings by introducing a definition of COMI, including an indication of when the registered office presumption might be rebutted based on the decision in the *Interedil* case, but also granting foreign creditors the right to be informed of and to challenge the proposed opening of proceedings to reduce forum-shopping.

- Enabling courts to refuse the opening of secondary proceedings if this is not necessary to protect the interests of local creditors, but also abolishing the requirement that secondary proceedings must be winding-up proceedings and improving co-operation between main and secondary proceedings.

- Requiring Member States' courts to publish relevant court decisions in cross-border insolvency cases in a publically accessible register and introducing standard forms for lodging claims.

- Co-ordinating insolvency proceedings concerning different members of a group of companies, by maintaining an entity-by-entity approach but obliging the officeholders and courts concerned to co-operate.

At the time of writing, however, it remains difficult to predict when, and to what extent, these proposals might be implemented.

11.3 THE CROSS-BORDER INSOLVENCY REGULATIONS 2006

11.3.1 The UNCITRAL Model Law

The Cross-Border Insolvency Regulations 2006 (the 'CBIR') adopt the UNCITRAL Model Law on Cross-Border Insolvency into British domestic law. 'UNCITRAL' is an abbreviation for the United Nations Commission on International Trade Law.

Like the EC Insolvency Regulation, the Model Law does not attempt to harmonise local insolvency law. Instead, it is designed to assist states to equip their insolvency laws with a 'modern, harmonised and fair' framework to address instances of cross-border insolvency more effectively.

Unlike the EC Insolvency Regulation, however:

● Different states adopting the Model Law are given a degree of discretion as to how they do so. Therefore the fact that the law of one adopting state confers certain rights is no guarantee that the law of another adopting state will confer reciprocal rights.

● Whilst the EC Insolvency Regulation places limitations on the powers of the courts of the various Member States even where main insolvency proceedings have not yet been opened elsewhere, the role of the Model Law is generally to enable the courts of the states which have adopted it to provide assistance where sought rather than to restrict their powers to do otherwise.

● Whilst the European Court of Justice is the ultimate judicial authority in respect of the EC Insolvency Regulation, there is no higher authority than the courts of the individual states in respect of the Model Law.

At the time of writing, the Model Law has been adopted in the following states: Australia, the British Virgin Islands (as an overseas territory of the UK), Colombia, Eritrea, Great Britain, Greece, Japan, Mauritius, Mexico, Montenegro, New Zealand, Poland, Republic of Korea, Romania, Serbia, Slovenia, South Africa, Uganda and the USA. (See http://www.uncitral.org/uncitral/en/uncitral_texts/insolvency/1997Model_status.html.)

The remainder of this section considers the Model Law as it has been adopted in Great Britain, the form of which is set out in Sch 1 to the CBIR.

11.3.2 When will the CBIR apply the Model Law in Great Britain?

Under Art 1 Sch 1 to the CBIR, the Model Law applies where:

● assistance is sought in Great Britain by a foreign court or a foreign representative in connection with a foreign proceeding; or

● assistance is sought in a foreign state in connection with a proceeding under British insolvency law; or

● insolvency proceedings are taking place concurrently in a foreign state and Great Britain in respect of the same company; or

- creditors or other interested persons in a foreign state have an interest in requesting the commencement of, or participating in proceedings under British insolvency law.

It is not essential that the state where the foreign court is located has itself adopted the Model Law. The courts have been prepared to use the CBIR to recognise a Norwegian bankruptcy as foreign main proceedings and the Norwegian trustee as a foreign representative, notwithstanding that Norway has not enacted the Model Law itself (*Re European Insurance Agency AS*, an unreported decision of the Bristol District Registry of the High Court noted by Ian Fletcher in *Insolvency Intelligence* 2007, 20(9), 138–141).

To the extent that the Model Law conflicts with any obligation of the UK under the EC Insolvency Regulation, however, the requirements of the latter prevail (Art 3 Sch 1 of the CBIR).

11.3.3   Recognition of foreign proceedings

A foreign representative can apply to the British courts for recognition of foreign proceedings where the company has a place of business or assets in Great Britain or if, for any other reason, Great Britain is an appropriate forum to consider a question or provide assistance (Art 4 Sch 1).

In a similar manner to that in which the EC Insolvency Regulation distinguishes between main insolvency proceedings and secondary proceedings, the CBIR draws a distinction between two types of insolvency proceedings (see Art 2 Sch 1):

- Foreign main proceedings, ie proceedings taking place in the state in which the debtor has its 'centre of main interests', or COMI. COMI is not defined, but it was confirmed in *Stanford International Bank Ltd (In Receivership)* [2010] EWCA Civ 137 that the English courts will interpret it in the same manner as they would under the EC Insolvency Regulation (see Section 11.2.3).

- Foreign non-main proceedings, ie proceedings taking place in a state in which the debtor has an establishment. Establishment bears a similar definition to that used in the EC Insolvency Regulation.

Foreign proceedings commenced in a state other than that of the company's COMI and in which it has no establishment will not qualify for recognition.

If foreign proceedings are recognised as foreign main proceedings, an automatic stay will apply. This will have the same effect in England as the stay in a compulsory liquidation (see Chapter 3). There will be a moratorium on certain types of creditor action, and on the ability of the company to transfer, encumber or dispose of assets. However, this stay will not affect a creditor's right to enforce security over the company's property or to exercise set-off in the same manner that the creditor could in a liquidation. In addition, it will not stay the commencement of British insolvency proceedings (Art 20 Sch 1). However, if British proceedings are subsequently commenced, their effect will be limited to assets in Britain (Art 28 Sch 1).

For foreign non-main proceedings, no automatic stay will apply.

Upon recognition of a foreign proceeding, whether main or non-main, the court has a discretion to grant various types of relief to protect the assets of the company or the interests of creditors including, as the last listed item, the grant of any additional relief that may be available to a British officeholder under the laws of Great Britain (Art 21 Sch 1). This has been used, for example to allow a foreign officeholder to obtain the disclosure of information from third parties in circumstance similar to those in which an English officeholder could have obtained information in comparable English proceedings (*Re Bernard L Madoff Investment Securities LLC* [2010] EWHC 1299 (Ch)).

There has been some concern that the CBIR could provide foreign representatives with a route to apply foreign law decisions in Britain even where these are inconsistent with relevant British law. However, it presently appears that this concern is unfounded. For example:

• the Supreme Court has confirmed that the CBIR cannot be used to enforce a judgment obtained in a foreign insolvency proceeding where the defendant has not appeared in those proceedings (*Rubin v Eurofinance Sa* [2012] UKSC 46). The facts of this case are set out in the box at the end of Section 11.5; and

• as noted when discussing the *Belmont* case in Section 2.7.3.1, the US bankruptcy court reached a different decision on the same facts. However, the matter has been resolved by co-operation between the US and the British courts without the need to impose the decision of the courts of one jurisdiction in the other.

11.3.4   Rights of access

A foreign representative in main or non-main proceedings is given direct access to the British courts to commence or participate in British insolvency proceedings (Arts 10 and 12 Sch 1). Foreign creditors are also given access to the British courts to commence and/or participate in British insolvency proceedings as creditors in Britain. They must not be given a lower priority than that of general unsecured claims solely because they are foreign (Art 13 Sch 1).

In addition, a foreign representative may apply to the British courts for an order under or in connection with ss 238, 239, 244, 245 and 423 1A 1986 (ie various of the anti-avoidance provisions described in Chapter 5). Provided the transaction or other action which they are seeking to attack occurred after 4 April 2006 (the date the Regulations came into force), the British court may grant such an order even where no British administration and/or liquidation has been opened (Art 23 Sch 1).

11.3.5   Co-operation and co-ordination

The British courts may co-operate to the maximum extent possible with foreign courts and foreign representatives (Art 25 Sch 1). British insolvency officeholders must co-operate to the maximum extent possible, to the extent that this is consistent with their other duties under British law (Art 26 Sch 1). The Model Law also sets out considerations which should be applied by a court when co-ordinating British proceedings with one or more concurrent foreign proceedings – it is relevant to some extent whether the British proceedings were commenced first and whether the foreign proceeding(s) are main or non-main proceedings (Arts 29 and 30 Sch 1).

11.4   SECTION 426 OF THE INSOLVENCY ACT 1986

11.4.1   What does s 426 IA 1986 do?

Section 426 IA 1986 effectively fulfils two functions:

- it enables orders made by courts having insolvency jurisdiction in one part of the UK to be enforced in other parts of the UK (s 426(1) IA 1986). (However, a court is not **required** to enforce an order made in respect of property situated in territory over which it has jurisdiction where this order was made by a court in another part of the UK – s 426(2) IA 1986); and

- it requires the courts having insolvency jurisdiction in one part of the UK to assist the courts having a corresponding jurisdiction in any other part of the UK or in any 'relevant country or territory' (s 426(4) IA 1986).

It is the latter function which will be considered further in this section.

As at the date of this book, the relevant countries and territories are: Anguilla, Australia, the Bahamas, Bermuda, Botswana, Brunei Darussalam, Canada, the Cayman Islands, the Channel Islands, the Falkland Islands, Gibraltar, Hong Kong, Ireland, the Isle of Man, Malaysia, Montserrat, New Zealand, St Helena, South Africa, Turks and Caicos, Tuvalu and the Virgin Islands. (See s 426(11) IA 1986 and SI (1986/2123), SI (1996/253) and SI (1998/2766).)

Whilst s 426 IA 1986 enables the courts of these non-UK countries and territories to send a letter of request to the English courts, it does **not**, however, empower the English courts in turn to request assistance from the courts of those jurisdictions.

11.4.2   What assistance can the English courts provide?

Under s 426(5) IA 1986, an English court receiving a letter of request has the authority to apply:

- the insolvency laws of the referring court's own jurisdiction; or

- English insolvency law.

Case law has confirmed that the courts can also apply their own inherent jurisdiction (see *Hughes v Hannover-Rucksverischerungs AG* [1997] BCC 921, which concerned a request from a Bermudan court to assist it by granting an injunction). The English courts must, however, have regard to the rule of private international law when exercising their discretion.

Section 426 has therefore been used:

- to authorise English provisional liquidators to hand over assets collected in an ancillary English process to Australian liquidators, notwithstanding the fact that Australian and English law differed as to how those assets would be distributed (*McGrath v Riddell* [2008] BCC 349);

- to apply English formal insolvency processes to foreign companies where the referring state has no equivalent legislation. For example, the administration process has been applied to an Australian company (*Re Dallhold Estates (UK) Pty Ltd* [1992] BCC 394) and the CVA process to an Isle of Man company (*Re Television Trade Rentals* [2002] BCC 807). Given the provisions of the EC Insolvency Regulation, this type of assistance now seems likely to be requested only when the foreign company's COMI is outside the EU (and cannot conveniently be migrated to the UK), but there will nevertheless be occasions where this will remain the case; and

• to recognise and enforce an Australian judgment for unfair preferences where it was held that the defendant had submitted to the jurisdiction of the Australian court by filing proofs of debt and participating in creditors' meetings in the Australian insolvency proceedings (*New Cap Reinsurance Corpn Ltd v Grant*, heard together with the *Rubin* case and reported at [2012] UKSC 46).

The Supreme Court confirmed in the *Rubin* case, however, that s 426 could not be used to enforce a judgment obtained in a foreign insolvency proceeding where the defendant has not appeared in those proceedings.

More generally, the English courts do have a limited discretion to refuse a request (see the *Hughes* case). Nonetheless it would be unusual for them to do so.

11.5   ENGLISH COMMON LAW

Whilst it might be thought that common law principles would have become less relevant, given the various provisions described above, the courts have made it clear that they still have a role to play.

A key case here is *Cambridge Gas Transportation Corpn v Official Committee of Unsecured Creditors of Navigator Holdings plc and others* [2006] 3 All ER 829. This case concerned a letter of request from a US court to an Isle of Man court which fell outside of the scope of any of the provisions so far described in this chapter. The court made it clear, however, that there is still an underlying common law principle that bankruptcy proceedings should, ideally, have universal application and that there should be a single bankruptcy in which all creditors are entitled and required to prove.

The court thought it doubtful that common law alone would allow it to apply provisions of foreign insolvency law which form no part of the domestic system. However, it considered that a domestic court must at least be able to provide assistance by doing whatever it could have done in the case of a domestic insolvency. The purpose of recognition is to enable the foreign officeholder or the creditors to avoid having to start parallel insolvency proceedings and to give them the remedies to which they would have been entitled if the equivalent proceedings had taken place in the domestic forum. In *Schmitt v Deichmann* [2012] EWHC 62 (Ch), for example, the court duly applied this principle to allow a German insolvency administrator to bring proceedings in England under s 423 IA in circumstances where again for various reasons, neither the EC Insolvency Regulation nor the CBIR would assist.

The Supreme Court concluded in the *Rubin* case that this principle of universal application would nonetheless not require an English court to enforce a judgment obtained in foreign insolvency proceedings where the defendant had not appeared in those proceedings. (Three of the five judges in *Rubin* suggested that *Cambridge Gas* might have been wrongly decided so far it might suggest otherwise, although they did not dispute the authority of that case more generally.)

Under the common law, the English courts will nevertheless almost always recognise the liquidation of a foreign company carried out under the laws of its place of incorporation (*Baden, Delvaux & Lecuit v Société Générale pour Favorisor le Développement etc.* [1983] BCLC 325). There are also various cases where they have recognised foreign rehabilitation proceedings carried out under the laws of the company's place of incorporation (see, for example, *Felixstowe Dock and Railway Co v United States Line Inc* [1989] QB 360).

However, the case law suggests that they may still refer to English law principles in determining the nature and the degree of the assistance they will give. In the *Felixstowe Dock* case, the English courts were unprepared to grant an order which removed the foreign company's English assets outside of the control of the English courts completely.

Rubin v Eurofinance Sa and New Cap Reinsurance Corpn Ltd v Grant [2012] UKSC 46

The *Rubin* case concerned a trust established by Eurofinance, a BVI registered company. The trustees were resident in England, although many of its beneficiaries and all of its assets were in the USA. The trust was placed into Chapter 11 in the USA. The US liquidators issued proceedings in the US against several parties, including the trustees, in respect of fraudulent conveyances and transfers under US law. The trustees did not participate in these proceedings nor submit to the jurisdiction of the US court. Nonetheless the US court considered that it had jurisdiction and gave judgment against them in default.

The *New Cap* case concerned an Australian insurance company, New Cap. It had reinsured members of a Lloyds syndicate. New Cap entered liquidation in Australia. The liquidator issued proceedings in Australia against the syndicate seeking to recover payments made to them as unfair preferences under Australian law. Again, the syndicate did not participate in the unfair prejudice proceedings nor did they submit to the jurisdiction of the Australian court but the Australian court gave judgment against them. The syndicate did, however, take part in the Australian liquidation more generally, eg by filing proofs of debt.

Both liquidators sought to enforce the judgments in England. This led eventually to the Supreme Court hearing both cases together on appeal and considering the various potential enforcement routes:

- Section 426 IA 1986 was relevant to *New Cap* (but not *Rubin*). The court drew a distinction between those sub-sections which dealt with assistance within the UK and those which dealt with assisting foreign courts. Unlike the former, the latter made no mention of enforcing judgments so could not be used for that purpose.

- The CBIR were relevant to *Rubin* (but not *New Cap*, as the relevant events had taken place prior to their introduction). Again, these contained no express mention of enforcing foreign judgments, so did not give the court the power to do so.

- Recognition under the common law was relevant in both cases. Whilst under normal common law rules a money judgment of a foreign court was enforceable in the UK only where the defendant had been present in the foreign jurisdiction when the proceedings commenced, had made a claim or counterclaim in those proceedings, or had submitted to the foreign jurisdiction either by agreement or choosing to appear in those

---

proceedings, the court recognised that it was necessary to consider the matter broadly.

In *New Cap,* the court held that the syndicate had submitted to the proceedings as a result of its wider participation in liquidation – it took the view that the syndicate should not be allowed to benefit from the insolvency proceedings without complying with orders made in those proceedings.

In *Rubin,* however, this argument did not apply so that question was whether, in the interests of universality of insolvency procedures, the courts should devise a rule for the recognition of judgments in foreign insolvency proceedings which was wider than the traditional common law rule. The majority concluded that it was not appropriate for the courts to do this.

As part of their reasoning, the various judges considered the extent to which the *Cambridge Gas* case might have been wrongly decided, but differed in their conclusions in this respect.

11.6 APPLICATION OF ENGLISH FORMAL PROCESSES TO FOREIGN COMPANIES

11.6.1 Liquidation

A foreign company may be placed into either compulsory or creditors' voluntary liquidation under the EC Insolvency Regulation where the conditions for doing so are satisfied (see Section 11.2).

As discussed in Chapter 1, under s 221 IA 1986, the English courts also have the jurisdiction to wind up any **unregistered company**. An 'unregistered company' means any association and any company other than a company registered in any part of the UK under the Joint Stock Company Acts or under the legislation (past or present) relating to companies in Great Britain (s 220 IA 1986). A foreign company will therefore fall within this definition.

Whilst on its face s 221 IA 1986 gives an English court unlimited jurisdiction, in practice the courts themselves have laid down constraints on when they will assume jurisdiction. In *Re Real Estate Development Company* [1991] BCLC 210, the court laid down three 'core requirements' which an English court will apply in deciding whether to wind up a foreign company:

- there must be a sufficient connection with England and Wales which may, but does not necessarily have to, consist of assets within the jurisdiction;

- there must be a reasonable possibility, if a winding-up order is made, of benefit to those applying for the winding-up order;

- one or more persons interested in the distribution of assets of the company must be persons over whom the court can exercise a jurisdiction.

The EC Insolvency Regulation restricts the court's jurisdiction under s 221 where an insolvent foreign company's COMI is in another EU Member State. It will not be able to wind up such a company in circumstances where secondary or territorial proceedings would not be permitted under the EC Insolvency Regulation.

The EC Judgments Regulation will in turn restrict the court's jurisdiction in relation to a solvent company which is registered in another EU Member State. This is because Article 22(2) of that regulation assigns exclusive jurisdiction for proceedings which have as their object the dissolution of companies to the courts of the EU Member State in which the company has its seat. (See the court's comments in *Re Rodenstock GmbH* [2011] EWHC 1104 (Ch), discussed further in Section 11.6.4).

11.6.2   Administration

For the purposes of Sch B1 IA (ie the part of the IA 1986 which deals with administration), a 'company' includes both a company incorporated in the UK and:

• a company incorporated in an EEA State other than the UK (ie as at the date of publication of this book, the other EU Member States, plus Iceland, Liechtenstein and Norway); or

• a company not incorporated in an EEA State but having its COMI in an EU Member State other than Denmark

(see para 111 Sch B1 IA 1986). This confirms, essentially, the jurisdiction of the courts to place a foreign company into administration under the EC Insolvency Regulation, although it extends that jurisdiction to companies in three non-EU states as well.

Section 426 IA 1986 will also allow an English court to appoint an administrator pursuant to a letter of request from certain foreign courts (see Section 11.4).

However, the EC Insolvency Regulation will still prevent a foreign company from being placed into administration where its COMI is in another EU Member State unless the administration is permitted as a secondary or territorial proceeding under the EC Insolvency Regulation.

11.6.3   CVA

For the purposes of Part 1 IA 1986, ie the part of the IA 1986 which deals with CVAs, a 'company' is defined in the same way as it is for an administration (s 1 IA 1986). Section 426 IA 1986 will also apply as for an administration. However, the EC Insolvency Regulation will prevent a foreign company from being placed into a CVA where its COMI is in another EU Member State.

11.6.4   Schemes of Arrangement

For the purposes of Part 26 of the CA, ie the part of CA 2006 which deals with Schemes of Arrangement, the term 'company' means 'any company liable to be wound up under English law' (s 895 CA 2006). A Scheme can therefore extend to foreign companies, given that the court has the jurisdiction to wind up such companies (see Section 11.6.1). There is a complication here, however, in that the second and third of the 'core requirements' described in Section 11.6.1 will not always be appropriate to a Scheme.

This was considered in *Re Drax Holdings Ltd* [2004] 1 WLR 1049, where the applicants were companies incorporated in the Cayman Islands and Jersey, respectively to raise finance for the acquisition of a power station in England. Various of the financial documents were governed by English law and the security for their liabilities included the power station and shares in English companies. The court made it clear that these core requirements were relevant to the discretion of the court, but not absolute preconditions to be met before the court could have jurisdiction. The court was satisfied that it had jurisdiction because both companies had sufficient connection with England.

In *Re Rodenstock GmbH* [2011] EWHC 1104 (Ch), which concerned a solvent Scheme, the applicant was a company incorporated in Germany and with its COMI in Germany. It had no establishment in the United Kingdom nor any assets in the United Kingdom likely to be affected by the Scheme. However, the creditors who would be affected by the scheme were all senior lenders under a facility agreement which was expressed to be governed by English law and in which they had agreed that any dispute arising out of or in connection with the agreement would be subject to the exclusive jurisdiction of the English courts. The court held that this collective agreement had in itself created sufficient connection with England.

A Scheme is neither an insolvency proceeding nor a winding-up proceeding for the purpose of the **EC Insolvency Regulation**. In *Rodenstock*, however, the court nevertheless needed to consider whether, in the light of the restrictions referred to in Section 11.6.1, a company with its COMI in a different EU Member State and no establishment in the United Kingdom was still '**a company liable to be wound up under English law**'. The court held that it was on the basis that:

- the EC Insolvency Regulation did not appear to be directed at restricting the English court's jurisdiction in relation to solvent Schemes;

- since the CA 2006, which had come into force after the EC Insolvency Regulation was enacted had chosen to retain the words 'liable to be wound up in unaltered form', there had been no intention to narrow the court's jurisdiction following enactment of the Regulation; and

- the phrase 'liable to be wound up' was designed simply to identify the types of company and association which might be made the subject of a Scheme and was thus intended to broaden rather than narrow the court's jurisdiction.

The same argument ought also to apply to insolvent Schemes.

Because a Scheme is outside the scope of the EC Insolvency Regulation, this is turn begs the question of whether the **EC Judgments Regulation** applies to Schemes where the company is registered in a different EU Member State (see Section 11.2.6), The courts have differed in this respect, although for different reasons no court has yet viewed the EC Judgments Regulation as a problem.

- In *Rodenstock* the court held that sanction proceedings for a solvent scheme did fall within the scope of the EC Judgments Regulation but, following the same reasoning as it had applied in relation to the EC Insolvency Regulation, held that it might still treat the company as 'liable to be wound up under English law'. The court noted a separate issue, ie that although Schemes fell within the scope of the Judgments Regulation, this regulation did not expressly provide for jurisdiction in relation to Schemes. However, it was satisfied that it was still able to apply English law to sanction the Scheme on the basis that the majority by value of the Scheme creditors, ie the 'defendants', were domiciled in England.

- In *Primacom Holdings GmbH v Credit Agricole* [2012] EWHC 164 (Ch) none of the Scheme creditors were domiciled in England so the court had to revisit the question of jurisdiction. It resolved this by holding Schemes did not fall with the scope of the EC Judgments Regulation. Scheme creditors were not defendants in the way envisaged by the EC Judgments Regulation, so a test based on the domicile of the creditors was inappropriate. (However, the court added that even if the Scheme did fall within the scope of this regulation, the Scheme creditors had all submitted to the jurisdiction of the English court by appearing before it).

Finally, as part of the sanction process, the courts have had to consider where the Scheme will be effective in the relevant foreign jurisdiction(s). If it is not, the Scheme may be unfair because one creditor could still pursue his claim in a foreign court and thus improve his position compared to that of other creditors. Some courts have found a way around this on the facts of the case (eg in *Rodenstock*). However, it may be necessary in other cases to apply separately for recognition in the foreign jurisdictions concerned.

It remains possible that a foreign court will take a different view on jurisdiction from the English court. For example, the German Federal Court refused to recognise the Scheme of Equitable Life because it did not consider that the English court had jurisdiction under the EC Judgments Regulation to sanction a Scheme for matters relating to insurance (*Equitable Life*, German Federal Court, IV ZR 194/09, 15 February 2012).

11.6.5   Receivership

It is well established that a non-administrative receiver can be appointed over the assets of a foreign company. His powers may be limited to those conferred upon him contractually by the security document, but these may well be sufficiently extensive, particularly if the assets concerned are situated in England where the courts should recognise the receiver's authority.

An administrative receiver can, however, only be appointed over the assets of a company registered under CA 2006 in England and Wales or Scotland (see the definition of 'company' in s 28(1) IA 1986).

Both administrative and non-administrative receivership fall outside the scope of both the EC Insolvency Regulation and the CBIR.

Index

[all references are to paragraph number]

277